Patriots and Bastards

Basque Politics Series No. 26

Patriots and Bastards

Aurora Madaula

Center for Basque Studies
University of Nevada, Reno
2024

This book was published with generous financial support from the Basque Government.

Center for Basque Studies
University of Nevada, Reno
1664 North Virginia St,
Reno, Nevada 89557 usa
http://basque.unr.edu

Copyright © 2024 by the Center for Basque Studies and the University of Nevada, Reno
ISBN-13: 978-1-949805-91-8
All rights reserved.

Library of Congress Cataloging-in-Publication Data

Names: Madaula, Aurora, author.
Title: Patriots and bastards / Aurora Madaula.
Description: Reno : Center for Basque Studies, University of Nevada, 2024. | Series: Basque politics ; 26 | Includes bibliographical references and index. | Summary: "From 1956 to 1970, the history of the Basques in exile is marked by political turmoil and activism. In the late 1950s, thousands of Basque intellectuals and activists were struggling in exile due to ongoing repression of their culture under Franco's dictatorship. The period from 1965 to 1970 witnessed the radicalization of the Basque resistance, with the rise of ETA (Euskadi Ta Askatasuna) and an increased global awareness of the Basque struggle for self-determination. Exiled Basques played a significant role in international solidarity movements, advocating for their cause in various global forums. Overall, this period was characterized by a shift from cultural preservation to active political resistance and growing international support for the Basque cause"-- Provided by publisher.
Identifiers: LCCN 2024033249 (print) | LCCN 2024033250 (ebook) | ISBN 9781949805918 (paperback) | ISBN 9781949805949 (epub)
Subjects: LCSH: Irujo, Manuel de, 1891-1981. | Basques--Politics and government--20th century. | Basque diaspora. | Nationalism--Spain--País Vasco--History--20th century. | País Vasco (Spain)--History--Autonomy and independence movements. | País Vasco (Spain)--Politics and government--20th century. | Spain--Politics and government--1939-1975. | ETA (Organization)
Classification: LCC DP302.B53 M26 2024 (print) | LCC DP302.B53 (ebook) | DDC 305.899/920904--dc23/eng/20240826
LC record available at https://lccn.loc.gov/2024033249
LC ebook record available at https://lccn.loc.gov/2024033250

Printed in the United States of America

Content

Prologue 7

The Basque World Congress (1956)
The harsh reality of exile. Legitimacy and realpolitik 11

Manuel Irujo in Munich.
The IV Conference of the European Movement.
The "*Contubernio de Munich*". Recovering from the loss.
From Aguirre to Leizaola 68

"Patriots and Hooligans" ("Patriotas y Gamberros") 110

We are not alone.
Ideological foundation of the revolutionary Basque nationalism:
From Federico Krutwig to Etxebarrieta's brothers 148

The Burgos trial (1970). The Process to Franco Regime 163

The end of the "eighth province"? Transition to democracy.
The end of the exile and the evolution of the Basque nationalism .197

Abbreviations 217

Bibliography 218

End Notes 231

Index .275

Prologue

After 40 years in exile, on March 24, 1977, Manuel Irujo returned to the Basque Country. He landed at Noain airport, in Iruñea-Pamplona. He was received by a people moved by the enormous strength he exuded, despite his age, and the open manifestation of his ideals, which had been suppressed for forty years due to his explicit fight in defense of human rights. Irujo was remembered for his many actions during four decades of war and exile, but his tenure as Minister of Justice of the Republic was especially remembered. The exact number of lives he saved is unknown, but it is estimated to be more than 10,000. His actions were always supported by the British consul in Bilbao, Ralph Stevenson, and the president of the Red Cross, Marcel Junod. Irujo never believed he had done anything extraordinary. Arantzazu Ametzaga interviewed him numerous times, and each time he would say, almost in a moan, "if only I could have saved them all...". It was said of him that it was preferable to open another war front than to argue with Irujo about the life of a single condemned prisoner during a council of ministers. His first message as minister was "to humanize the war," asserting that "each attack on human life is more pernicious than a defeat: more is lost with a crime than in a battle." He raised his voice against ignominy in a time of war, prohibited executions, and sought to impose the logic of reason over the irrationality of hatred, the legitimacy of law over the brutality of vengeance.

Thousands of people awaited him and the ideals he represented when he arrived at Noain. His story, like that of the more than 150,000 Basques exiled by the Franco dictatorship, began in 1936. After a year of brutal war in the Basque Country (1936-1937), during which the Luftwaffe, serving Franco, bombed Gernika and carried out more than 1,600 bombing operations in an area of just 850 square miles, and another year of war in Barcelona (1937-1938), the capital of Catalonia was taken by the rebel troops of General Franco at the end of January 1939. Irujo, along with the rest of the Basque political representatives, went into exile in Paris. However, following the collapse of the western front in the spring of 1940, the Basque government-in-exile left its headquarters in Paris and established its base first in London and, after the attack on Pearl Harbor, in New York. As repression intensified, the exiled Basques organized support networks and engaged in international activism throughout the Americas and free Europe.

However, unlike the rest of the Axis powers, Francoist Spain did not collapse in 1945. During its 59th meeting on December 12, 1946, the United Nations General Assembly adopted Resolution 39 (I). This resolution declared that the Franco regime was, in origin, nature, structure, and general conduct, a fascist regime modeled after and established largely due to aid received from Hitler's Nazi

Germany and Mussolini's Fascist Italy. The resolution also noted that, during the United Nations' struggle against Hitler and Mussolini, Franco, despite continued Allied protests, provided substantial aid to the enemy powers. For instance, from 1941 to 1945, Spanish troops were sent by Franco to the Eastern Front. Additionally, in the summer of 1940, Spain seized Tangier in violation of international statute, and the presence of a large Spanish army in Spanish Morocco immobilized numerous Allied troops in North Africa. The resolution further stated that incontrovertible documentary evidence established Franco's complicity with Hitler and Mussolini in the conspiracy to wage war against the countries that eventually formed the United Nations. Consequently, the General Assembly recommended that the Franco Government of Spain be barred from membership in international agencies established by or associated with the United Nations and from participating in conferences or other activities arranged by the United Nations or these agencies until a new and acceptable government was formed in Spain. The Assembly also recommended that all United Nations members immediately recall their ambassadors and ministers plenipotentiary from Madrid.

However, after a decade of political pressure on the Spanish dictatorship, Franco's regime did not collapse.

This book begins in 1956, when the Basque Government in exile in Paris faced the acceptance of Franco's regime by the United Nations. This acceptance signified the legitimization of Franco's dictatorship under the dreadful umbrella of the Cold War. A Congress was organized in Paris to champion democracy and human values over the principles of repression, violations of basic human rights, and militarism that characterized the dictatorships of the 1960s. In 1956, the Basque Government in exile understood that with Franco's regime legitimized on the international stage, the Basque exile would extend for two more decades until the dictator's death.

From 1956 to 1970, the history of the Basques in exile is marked by political turmoil and activism. In the late 1950s, thousands of Basque intellectuals and activists were struggling in exile due to ongoing repression of their culture under Franco's dictatorship. The period from 1965 to 1970 witnessed the radicalization of the Basque resistance, with the rise of ETA (Euskadi Ta Askatasuna) and an increased global awareness of the Basque struggle for self-determination. Exiled Basques played a significant role in international solidarity movements, advocating for their cause in various global forums. Overall, this period was characterized by a shift from cultural preservation to active political resistance and growing international support for the Basque cause.

The Basque Government in exile, after having fought the Axis powers from 1936 to 1945, embarked on years of activism and militancy, tirelessly advocating for democracy and human rights within the United Nations and the nascent European Communities. During this period, it generated a new Basque nationalist discourse grounded in the democratic and humanistic ideas of Christian

Democracy, as proposed by influential thinkers such as Jacques Maritain, Luigi Sturzo, and Emmanuel Mounier. These ideas emphasized the inherent dignity of the individual, the importance of community, and the necessity of political and social structures that reflect ethical and moral values. This powerful political movement acted as a catalyst for the modernization and democratization of both Basque society and nationalism. It offered a stark contrast to the authoritarian and repressive principles of Franco's regime, promoting instead a vision of governance based on respect for human rights, participatory democracy, and social justice. The exiled Basque government worked diligently to instill these values within the Basque nationalist movement, fostering a sense of unity and purpose among the Basque diaspora.

Through its advocacy and international activism, the Basque Government in exile built a network of alliances with other democratic movements and organizations, reinforcing its message and gaining broader support for its cause. This period of intellectual and political ferment was crucial in shaping a more progressive and inclusive Basque nationalism, one that was better equipped to address the challenges of the modern world and the aspirations of the Basque people. For decades, this movement served as a beacon of hope and a source of inspiration for those striving for the restoration of democracy in the Basque Country. It provided a coherent and compelling narrative that linked the Basque struggle with broader global movements for human rights and democratic governance. In doing so, the Basque Government in exile helped to sustain the morale and identity of the Basque people during the long years of exile and repression and laid the groundwork for the eventual democratic transition and the reestablishment of Basque institutions.

The role of Manuel Irujo as the ideologue of Basque nationalism in exile was crucial, particularly in the realm of the struggle for independence and social justice. His influence and leadership were indispensable in shaping the direction and strategies of the Basque nationalist movement during a time of intense repression and displacement. Irujo's infinite capacity for work, coupled with his intellectual rigor and unwavering commitment to the Basque cause, set him apart as a key figure in the struggle for Basque autonomy and democracy. One of the most striking aspects of Irujo's contribution was his extensive correspondence with a wide array of agents, including political leaders, diplomats, intellectuals, and activists from around the world. He wrote an average of more than twenty letters, articles and dossiers a day for four decades. Through these communications, he tirelessly advocated for the Basque cause, building a network of support and solidarity that transcended national boundaries. His ability to articulate the aspirations and grievances of the Basque people in a compelling and coherent manner earned him respect and support from diverse quarters.

Irujo's diplomatic efforts were instrumental in keeping the Basque cause on the international agenda. He leveraged his connections to garner support from influential figures and organizations, ensuring that the plight of the Basque people was not forgotten amid the geopolitical upheavals of the mid-20th century. His work helped to frame the Basque struggle within the broader context of human rights and democratic governance, resonating with the global movements of the time.

Irujo's role as an ideologue extended beyond advocacy. He was deeply involved in the intellectual development of Basque nationalism, drawing on his vast knowledge of political theory, history, and philosophy to craft a vision for the future of the Basque Country. His ideas were heavily influenced by the democratic and humanistic principles of Christian Democracy, which emphasized the importance of individual dignity, community, and ethical governance. These principles became central to the Basque nationalist discourse, shaping the movement's goals and strategies. In addition to his theoretical contributions, Irujo's practical efforts in organizing and mobilizing the Basque diaspora were vital. He played a key role in establishing support networks, cultural organizations, and political platforms that kept the Basque identity and cause alive during the long years of exile. His leadership provided a sense of direction and purpose to the exiled Basque community, helping to maintain their unity and morale.

Manuel was my great-uncle. He was a great orator. I remember him at one of the first rallies he gave after the fall of the dictatorship when I was just 12 years old. Daniel Irujo, his father—my great-grandfather—was a close friend of Sabino Arana, the founder of the Basque Nationalist Party. Daniel and Sabino were childhood friends because both families shared political exile after the Second Carlist War (1872-1876), and they maintained a great friendship throughout their lives. Daniel became Sabino's lawyer when Sabino was accused of inciting rebellion after attempting to send a telegram to the President of the United States, Theodore Roosevelt, congratulating him on granting independence to Cuba. Daniel managed to get him out of prison. In those days of protest, Daniel's children played in the gardens of Sabino's house, and it was there that, after being released from prison, Sabino gave a strong hug to the eldest son of the lawyer who had secured his freedom. And this is what Manuel reminded all of us of, flanked by ikurriñas, at a rally in Bilbao in 1977, when he said that he was returning to all of us the hug that Sabino Arana had given him that day. It was the embrace of a man who had dedicated his entire life to fighting for human rights at a time when the Basque nation was beginning to breathe the air of freedom.

Xabier Irujo

The Basque World Congress (1956)

The harsh reality of exile. Legitimacy and realpolitik

After nearly two decades in exile, the notion of returning to the Basque country within a democratic Spain remained alive: "This will be the final Christmas and New Year's Eve statement I make to you from America. May God will it that the next one will be there, where the remains of our dead await the time of justice and freedom."[1] President Aguirre was resolute and confident in altering the circumstances for both the Basque and Spanish exiles.

Those who had been forced into Basque exile had acquired expertise in observing Francoist Spain and how the regime impacted what the Spanish Republic and the Basque Statute of Autonomy had established in the Basque country. Exile granted them a privileged perspective on the political dynamics of the Francoist regime and, more significantly, on the international political relationships that were forming. It also provided them with an opportunity to cultivate their own international connections. The privilege of being removed from the dictatorship was entwined with the sorrow felt for those who remained in the Basque country, making exile a double-edged sword of relief and discomfort.[2]

Nevertheless, the harsh reality of being in exile, distanced from both home and homeland, did not hinder the Basque government from engaging in a form of international politics. Their focus was particularly on establishing ties with democratic forces and reinforcing collaborative bonds with allies who could support the Basques in their endeavors to overthrow the Franco regime.

On the other hand, the connections and relationships fostered by the Basque government not only shaped the direction of its international politics but also depicted the nature of the nation they were envisioning from their exile. In this vision, they were imagining a community, dreaming of the nation, overlooking the political boundaries that had forced them into exile and that did not officially recognize the existence of the Basque nation. The geographical concept and geopolitical borders of the nation on the landscape became a secondary consideration, emerging after the identification of the group as a nation. Consequently, the construction of the symbolic imagery of nationalism, along with the establishment of geographical boundaries for the nation, happened subsequent to a group of people recognizing themselves as a nation, rendering the boundaries variable and less significant.[3]

Given that a nationalist Basque political party led the Basque government, the existence of the nation was unquestioned, although certain aspects of its politics were subject to scrutiny, as we will delve into in this chapter. The Basque government in exile faced the dual challenge of survival and recognition—a formidable undertaking. The Basque Statute of Autonomy of 1936 was gradually fading from the memory of Spanish democrats in exile, particularly within the Spanish republican government, whose political recollections were crumbling along with its very existence.[4]

Recognition was a critical concern not only for the Basque government but also for the Spanish Republican government. In a world divided by the Cold War, where terms like democracy and legitimacy took a back seat to others like capitalism or communism, the legitimacy of democratic elections was no longer a focal point in international political relations.

Approaching the Spanish Republican Government-in-exile

The Basque government initiated a campaign to engage with Spanish democrats in exile, aiming to unite forces and present a well-organized opposition to Franco, as declared in President Aguirre's Christmas message in 1945.[5] With the conclusion of the Second World War, the timing was crucial to garner attention from the Allies, who had recently announced a meeting among the United States, France, and Great Britain to decide their stance on the Franco Regime. Aguirre deemed it strategic to align with the broader Spanish Republican opposition, following the "Pacto de Bayona"[6] signed on March 31, 1945, by Basque political forces and unions. This unity was seen as preparation for the moment when the Allies might assist in toppling the Franco Regime. Strengthened by the trust generated by the agreement with Basque forces and buoyed by his connections in the American administration, President Aguirre spearheaded efforts to join forces with Spanish democratic factions, despite encountering dissent within the PNV.

However, the strategy faced criticism, as it was interpreted as an acknowledgment of the Spanish republic and its legal framework, implying a departure from the aspiration for Basque independence.[7] Participation in the Spanish government sparked controversy within the Basque government and the PNV, particularly among members of the Euskadi Buru Batzar. Even Manuel Irujo, a Basque nationalist involved in Spanish governments on several occasions, expressed reservations about participation. However, his loyalty to President Aguirre and the Basque government led him to join, stating, "I was opposed to our direct participation with political responsibility in the Government of the Republic, marking my opposition with excessive violence, explainable only by singular and painful conditions of all kinds—not only political, but personal—that fell on me at the time. Today I think I was not right in my speech. I accepted the position that was assigned to me and I maintained it with all the tenacity that I am capable of, while I believed that, with my presence in the government, I could serve the cause that had led me there."[8]

Despite the controversies and differing opinions surrounding participation in Spanish institutions, it was evident that Manuel Irujo and President Aguirre harbored a broader agenda that entailed involvement in Spanish Republican bodies. However, this participation in the Spanish government was intended to represent the interests of the Basque people and their government:

> To avoid any misunderstandings, I recalled the New York agreements, wherein the Basque Government urged those holding positions outside its jurisdiction to serve the Government of Euzkadi. I emphasized that Irujo's approach would align with this, representing the entire Basque population in matters beyond the specific interests of their political organization, in accordance with instructions from the Basque government.[9]

Participation in the Spanish government was a component of a more comprehensive plan. President Aguirre's experiences in exile had provided him with a broader perspective on world politics and the significance of active participation. Basque nationalism was not confined to local interests but aimed at more universal goals. Collaborations with Spanish Republicans and efforts towards the Galeuzca[10] agreement did not impede international contacts with Americans, the British, or the French, highlighting the European character of the Basque Government, later fully developed.[11]

The agenda was transparent, with Aguirre, at that moment, emerging as the political leader to bring it to fruition. Confident in his role, the President relied on international support against the Spanish government, particularly from the Americans, the allied force most trusted by the Basque government. This trust was grounded in bilateral relations and rapport, as evidenced in Anton Irala's writings,[12] and was further based on American perceptions of the Franco Regime.[13]

Perhaps it was Aguirre's endeavors and the optimism invested in international politics and allies that left the Basque President somewhat perplexed. He declared the initiation of discussions with France, Great Britain, and the United States to assess the Spanish situation, albeit, as José Félix Azurmendi notes,[14] "maybe with exaggerated optimism" regarding the President's mood. Not only President Aguirre but also all Spanish republicans in exile placed their trust in the newly established United Nations to intervene in the Spanish situation and viewed the progress of the international body with hope. Despite the United Nations condemning the Franco Regime and excluding the Spanish government from its discussions, the Tripartite Note, signed on March 4, 1946, by the United States, Great Britain, and France, extinguished all aspirations for international intervention against the dictatorship. The note stated, "The government of France, the UK and the USA have exchanged views with regard to the present Spanish government and their relations with that regime. It is agreed that so long as General Franco continues in control of Spain, the Spanish people cannot anticipate full cordial relations with those nations of the world, which have by common effort brought defeat to German Nazism and Italian fascism. There is no intention of interfering in the internal affairs of Spain. The Spanish people themselves must in the long run work their own destiny. The three governments are hopeful that the Spanish people will not again be subjected to the horrors and bitterness of civil strife. They hope that Spaniards will soon find the means to bring about a peaceful withdrawal of Franco"[15]

The UN rejected the nature of the Spanish regime, France closed borders and withdrew ambassadors, and the UN's statements in 1946[16] about Spain left no doubt about the decision of non-intervention. However, the Spanish republicans in exile, perhaps caught up in Aguirre's enthusiasm, interpreted the note and UN declarations as a diplomatic step toward reinstating a democratic government in Spain. Despite the disappointing decision of non-intervention, the response to it was the "Manifesto a los españoles"[17] (Manifest to the Spaniards) from Paris, signed by Lehendakari Aguirre, the Spanish president in exile José Giral, and the Catalan president Josep Irla. In the manifesto, they expressed their determination to restore republican democracy to Spain.[18]

The immediate decision included the participation of Basque nationalists in the Spanish government. Manuel Irujo, a key adviser in Aguirre's team and a well-known Basque nationalist among Spanish politicians, was appointed as the Minister of Justice for the Spanish Republican Government in exile from February to August 1947[19] as part of President Llopis' government.[20] Despite efforts to rectify the chaos within the Spanish Republican government in exile and even an offer for Aguirre to become the President of the Spanish government[21] from Spanish politicians, the Basque government declined to join the executive. The 1947 government marked the last time they participated in the Spanish government.

Nonetheless, in this final brief period when the Basque government took part in the Spanish Republican government, President Aguirre played a pivotal role in international relations activities. His inherent optimism, combined with lobbying efforts at the United Nations and the presence of the Basque delegation in New York, bestowed the "Spanish case" with the significance it required. As Ludger Mees notes, "Aguirre encompassed everything. It was him who, more or less behind the scenes, commanded the politics of Spanish exile." Both Aguirre and Irujo impressed Spanish politicians, notably President Diego Martínez Barrio of the Spanish Republic, who had offered the presidency of the Spanish government to President Aguirre multiple times without success.[22]

Participation in the Spanish Government served as a strategic approach to propel the "Spanish case" onto the international stage. Despite potential suspicions among Basque nationalists, President Aguirre emphasized that their collaboration was for a greater cause: "Our struggle has not been confined to the Basque area. We helped, and continue to help, Spanish democracy in its legitimate efforts for liberation. We contributed to re-establish order within the republican camp, restoring the normal exercise of the institutions of the Republic, ensuring with the restoration of the Republican Government the advantages of a coordinated representation that was recognized by several countries and was received by the Security Council of the United Nations."[23]

The pragmatism, "pactism," and gradualism often ascribed to Aguirre's policy[24] had a broader objective, beginning with the recognition of the Spanish Republican government by international institutions and, through it, the automatic recognition of Basque bodies and rights. In this last government when the Basques were directly engaged with Spanish parties, international recognition and the potential to overcome the Franco regime had to be the outcome of a robust Spanish Republican government—with a particular emphasis on the "Republican" aspect, as in 1946, Aguirre was convinced that democracy could not be defended alongside the Monarchists:[25] "Do you conceive that we join the monarchists? Enough jokes, don't you think?"[26]

The circumstances of exile and the Cold War necessitated a more comprehensive political approach, prompting Aguirre to once again deploy his pragmatism and tactics to engage in every possible alliance with the aim of defeating the Franco dictatorship. Speculation arose about the potential emergence of an alternative Spanish government from the Monarchists, endorsed by the British and Americans. In February 1947, José Ignacio de Lizaso, the Basque delegate in London, conveyed his concern to Manuel Irujo regarding the escalating rumors that the Monarchist option was gaining popularity in Great Britain. The British Public Radio, the BBC, relayed information from the Reuters correspondent in Paris, quoting "Señor Martínez Barrio, president of the Spanish Shadow Republican government in exile," who asserted that Spanish exile leaders were increasingly convinced that overthrowing the Franco regime was impossible without the "active cooperation of the still influential monarchists in Spain." President Barrio further emphasized that the anti-Franco movement must heavily rely on Britain and the United States for effectiveness, hinting at the potential restoration of a constitutional monarchy.[27]

The revelation that Martínez Barrio, president of the Spanish Republic in exile, would express support for a Monarchy was indeed shocking, but the motivation behind the letter was the credibility that the BBC bestowed upon the news. From the letter, one could infer the doubts harbored by the Basque nationalists in London, given that the Basque government had been instrumental in developing the reconstruction of the Spanish Republican government in exile. Yet, as previously stated, Aguirre was pursuing something more significant than the mere satisfaction of Basque nationalism. Considering the international implications and endorsement associated with the news and rumors surrounding the Monarchist strategy, President Aguirre could not afford to ignore the proposal.

In reality, the leadership of the Monarchist alternative rested with the socialist Indalecio Prieto,[28] who vehemently opposed the Republican government, and whose popularity grew by capitalizing on the Republican crisis. The Socialist-Monarchist plan also included conservative members from the CEDA,[29] as well as a profound degree of anti-communism that resonated well with the Americans and the British.[30] Although the Basque nationalists had remained loyal to the Republic, and Aguirre and Irujo, in particular, were dedicated to reconstructing a credible anti-Franco opposition, voices within the PNV favoring the Monarchist alternative were on the rise. This was particularly evident in the views of Telesforo Monzón, known for his controversial stance, who argued that the Republican path was flawed and unsuccessful, despite the involvement of high-profile personalities such as Vice-President Jesús María Leizaola or the Minister of Governance, José María Lasarte.[31]

Telesforo Monzón succinctly outlined the goals pursued by the PNV, stating, "The Government of the Republic and everything that revolves around it is over for me. (...) Strengthening our cause and waiting must be our program today. We must throw Franco out with a different mentality and action. We must dissociate ourselves from everything that sounds like a Republican cornet. (...) If it is a question of ousting Franco, today there is only one serious position. Supporting the monarchy. (...) My program is not the monarchy, but if Franco has to be ousted there is no other way, and for me socialism is with the monarchy."[32]

Amidst the crisis of the Spanish institutions in exile, the PNV and the Basque government found themselves divided between declining Republican forces that had previously endorsed the Basque Statute of Autonomy, and the emerging Socialist-Monarchists, Catholics, anti-Communists, as well as some prominent Spanish nationalists and vehement anti-Basque individuals. Monzón remarked, "We all know Prieto, seen from the Basque and Spanish angles, as a generous, Spanish nationalist, demagogue, and proud person."[33]

Despite not being President Aguirre's preferred option, the overarching goal of overthrowing Franco appeared viable, involving the international engagement he had always sought. This shift in strategy began in the second half of 1947, reaching its peak in the October speech mentioned earlier. In this address, Aguirre, while reaffirming the importance of the Republic, left the door open to the formation of a monarchical government following a plebiscite with the involvement of the international institutions mentioned in the Tripartite Note.

President Aguirre, a skilled tactician, clarified that the Monarchist solution did not entail the dissolution of the Republican government but rather the establishment of a Caretaker government, a transitional entity preceding the reinstatement of democracy.[34] Importantly, Prieto's anti-communist stance was seen as favorable in the USA and France, expanding options for anti-Franco democrats.

As evident, President Aguirre took actions in the pursuit of advancing the international recognition of the "Spanish cause" by engaging with Spanish institutions, even if this did not necessarily imply the establishment of a Republic, and perhaps delving too deeply into this approach, leading to tensions with

Basque nationalism. However, despite his efforts, the international intervention he desired most did not materialize.

In his Christmas message of December 1947, President Aguirre began to exhibit signs of mistrust towards the influence and commitment of international bodies concerning democracy. Addressing the Basque people in his annual speech, Aguirre recounted how Basque nationalism had remained loyal to peace and democracy since being displaced from Euskadi during the Spanish Civil War: "Thrown out of the Homeland, we supported the Allied forces since 1939 within our limited means in all parts of the world where Basques existed, while Franco aided German submarines, spread propaganda in South America, occupied Tangiers, dispatched the 'Blue Division' to the camps of the USSR, and brazenly insulted the democratic powers."[35]

Aguirre wanted to maintain belief in the international bodies and allies that the Basque had collaborated with, but the bitter aftertaste left by the Tripartite Note lingered within him, despite his attempts to conceal it. The onset of the Cold War was beginning to divide the world into two spheres, where communism stood in opposition to Western democracies, and totalitarian states like the Franco regime and certain South American regimes were tolerated to impede the advance of communism: "(...) we reject the criminal dilemma of 'Franco or communism' as false and self-serving."[36]

During 1942,[37] the Basque president engaged in travel across South America as part of collaboration with the USA to curb the spread of communism in those regions. He was aware that the UN's lukewarm condemnation of the Franco Regime in 1946 could potentially evolve into an acceptance of the dictatorship for the sake of stability. The global sentiment was one of war-weariness, and the strategy of Western powers aimed at stabilizing societies and governments.

The imperative to present an alternative to Franco's regime as an organized, democratic, and unified movement motivated, in Aguirre's words, the forging of ties with every group within the Spanish democratic resistance in exile. In Aguirre's vision, democracy and the aspirations of a democratic people should determine the return of all democrats to Spain, without exceptions. He stated, "To the pretender himself, Don Juan de Borbón, we recognized in the aforementioned statement, his right to defend the flags of the monarchy and his pretensions to the throne of Spain to submit them to the people, not to impose them."[38]

While Aguirre identified as a Republican, viewing the Republic as a political system,[39] and leaned toward the future lying in the republican path rather than the restoration of the monarchy, his foremost allegiance was to the defense of Basque interests and democracy. The tranquility required to gain trust in the eyes of international bodies and to unite democratic forces could potentially stem from an unusual coalition with the socialist-monarchists. However, this alliance would be nothing more than a political tactic to retain control over the wills of the Basques. Perhaps due to a lack of trust in the Monarchists or the Monarchy itself, or possibly because the "Plan Prieto" was the only plan left since 1946 and the Tripartite Note, Aguirre's natural optimism, as evident in his documents, speeches, and letters, began to waver. Despite this, he never relinquished his enthusiasm for the prospect of a democratic Basque country.

However, the PNV and the Basque government were not the sole actors employing tactics; the candidate Don Juan de Borbón also engaged in negotiations with Franco for a potential return to Spain. In 1947, the Franco regime initiated a referendum to approve the "Law of Succession to the Head of State,"[40] intending to transform the regime into a de jure monarchy. The law's first article stated, "Spain, as a political unit, is a Catholic, social, and representative State which, in accordance with its tradition, declares itself to be constituted as a Kingdom."[41]

However, the execution of this article was contingent on compliance with the second clause: "The Head of State corresponds to the Caudillo of Spain and of the Crusade, Generalissimo of the Armies Mr. Francisco Franco Bahamonde."[42] Franco sought international recognition by presenting the referendum as a democratic feature of the regime while simultaneously designating Franco as a permanent regent legitimized by the referendum and the law.

Despite this, the "Law of Succession" did not prove favorable for candidate Don Juan, who, following a private meeting with Franco on his boat "Azor" in San Sebastian, had signed an agreement with the socialist-monarchists in San Juan de Luz. The exile's return was imminent, both geographically and politically, with speculations about the potential overthrow of Franco. However, the political border and the strength of the Franco regime were still potent enough to keep anti-Franco democrats in exile for several more decades, including Don Juan.

The "Pact of San Juan de Luz" remained unclear regarding the juridical status of the transitional government preceding the establishment of the Monarchy, deliberately ignoring both historical nationalities and the Statutes of Autonomy. Given these conditions, the EBB (Basque Nationalist Executive) could not endorse the agreement, even as the monarchist sector gained significance.[43]

The 1949 Declaration of the Basque Nationalist Party

After internal debates failed to reach a clear decision on the Monarchist option, and with a significant internal rift emerging within the party, the EBB appointed a special commission to formulate an official document to guide the party's political direction and resolve disagreements among its members. The commission included members supportive of Prieto's alternative, such as Leizaola, Lasarte, Julio Jáuregui, and Juan Ajuriaguerra. Joseba Rezola and Ramón de la Sota Aburto[44] joined the commission under Leizaola's decision.

In March 1949, the committee presented the "Political Declaration of the Basque Nationalist Party,"[45] which would serve as the political program of the PNV, particularly during the exile. According to Koldo San Sebastián, this declaration marked a significant postwar statement of Basque nationalism, emphasizing the extraordinary political importance as it affirmed self-determination "as the only juridical source of Basque political status."[46] The document underscored the continued significance of the Basque government despite its exile and the unconventional status of a government-in-exile. Simultaneously, it bestowed a distinct legal status upon the government and the sovereignty of the Basque people: "The Basque Nationalist Party recognizes the Government of Euzkadi as the only legal representation of the Basque people, whatever the current or future de facto situations may be."[47]

Increasingly pressured by exile, Spanish relations, and international politics, Basque nationalism found itself compelled to reinvent and assert its identity definitively.

The 1949 Political Declaration aimed at addressing multiple concerns. Chiefly, it sought to clarify the PNV's stance on Prieto's approach. Simultaneously, the committee aimed to reconcile differences between various factions within the party that had emerged during the Monarchist debate but had deeper roots related to the political strategies employed by the nationalists.[48]

Exile had taken a toll on Basque nationalism, transforming what was once seen as a "blessing in disguise" in the words of Antoon de Baets,[49] had turned into a challenging situation for nationalists on both sides of the political boundary[50] defined by the Pyrenees. The political decisions made by the PNV were especially scrutinized by Basque nationalists within the Basque country, living under the oppression of the Spanish dictatorship. After more than two decades of working for the Basque people and the institutions of the Basque country from a distance, the repression intensified, leading to the imprisonment of numerous Basque resisters.[51] This created a growing divide between those inside and outside, with weakened spirits and heightened differences.[52]

The 1949 Political Declaration reaffirmed the commitment to resist the Franco regime and defend the Basque nation, its institutions, and rights. The party strengthened its Christian-Democratic identity and aligned itself with the European Federalist movement:

> The Basque Nationalist Party supports the initiatives underway for the implementation, on principles of freedom and democracy, of a European organization, whose objectives are world peace and the economic and social well-being of the peoples; it is in favor of federalist conceptions that will allow the creation of European Powers without diminishing the full personality of each of the peoples—including the Basque—that are to be included in the new structure; and it advocates the corresponding world organization based on the principles set out above.[53]

Through this declaration, Basque nationalists reaffirmed their dedication to the international cause, especially to the establishment of a Federal Europe, a political initiative initiated in 1948 at the Hague conference,[54] where the PNV had been actively involved from the outset. This demonstrated the Basque nationalists' desire to assert their presence not only in international politics but also within the broader European context. Basque nationalism sought to transcend local boundaries and embrace a global perspective.

Additionally, the declaration addressed the importance of reinforcing international politics and emphasized the necessity of boycotting the Franco regime to promote democracy: "The Basque Nationalist Party calls attention to the inappropriateness of any international political or economic measure that could be interpreted as aid to that regime and considers it a duty of the democratic countries to combine their action with the anti-Franco forces, which will constitute a guarantee of the peaceful and rapid liquidation of Franco's dictatorship."[55]

In the pursuit of international recognition, Basque nationalism aimed to engage international institutions and involve them in addressing the complex Basque situation. Rather than emphasizing nationalist sentiments, the PNV underscored its commitment to democratic values. In the postwar period, where nationalism had become associated with brutality and totalitarianism, the strategic focus of Basque nationalism in 1949 was to prioritize and showcase its democratic principles, drawing a sharp contrast with the totalitarian regime ruling Spain.

Consistent efforts were made to highlight the Franco regime's connections with German Nazis and Italian fascists, both of whom had been condemned by the international institutions arising from the aftermath of the Second World War: "Twelve years ago today Gernika (Guernica) was destroyed by Hitler's planes in the service of General Franco. The material destruction of the sanctuary of the Basque tradition would be of relative importance if the moral and physical kidnapping of the people subjected to the totalitarian dictatorship of General Franco were not still continuing today."[56]

Despite it being clear that the 1949 Declaration was a reference to the politics of the PNV, it did not solve any of the two main questions.

The socialists contended that the Declaration was ambiguous concerning the defense of the Monarchy, although the document did endorse the Bayonne pact (1945), inherently embodying its Republican aspect. In essence, what the PNV advocated for and championed was the Basque government and its existence, recognizing its close association with Republican institutions. The political strategy of Basque nationalists aimed at safeguarding the Basque government, with the defense of democracy holding even greater significance from the outset. The war had not deterred the democratic objectives of the Basque government or its determination to preserve the institution.

Lehendakari Aguirre staunchly defended democracy and the Basque government as a whole, echoing the sentiments expressed in the "Trucios'

Manifest" of 1937 when he fled from Bilbao to Santoña. In this manifesto, the President stood up for democracy, called on the allies to intervene in Spain against fascism, and declared that the fight had just begun: "The Basque government remains in place, both in the Basque Country and wherever it may be."[57] By 1949, the idea remained consistent: keeping the Basque government alive as a manifestation of Basque sovereignty.

Navigating alliances with both republicans and monarchists was part of the strategy to sustain the Basque government, a tactic sometimes challenged by Spanish politicians and the unique circumstances of the government-in-exile. However, upsetting the socialists could have jeopardized the Basque government and the stability achieved by the Bayonne pact. Soon after the Declaration, a discussion paper titled "Bases for a Basque Transitional Situation"[58] was released, causing controversy. It outlined a plan to restore democracy in Spain, recognizing the Basque country but through an institution named the "General Council," which would diminish the political powers of the Basques. This led to significant disagreements within the PNV, especially between members in inland Spain and those in exile.[59]

The disparities between the internal and external factions were not merely geographical but also political and at times ideological. Despite Juan Ajuriaguerra's participation in the commission responsible for the 1949 Declaration, PNV members in Spain did not feel adequately represented, and the declaration faced resistance from some members in exile. The toll of exile was becoming apparent, and President Aguirre began to worry about a situation initially conceived as transitory, now potentially evolving into an extended transition. Disappointments, such as the repression of the 1947 General Strike and the failure of Prieto's plan, weighed heavily on the generation of Basque nationalists who had fought in the Spanish Civil War. Exhaustion became a familiar companion on the journey of exile, and signs of weariness[60] appeared in President Aguirre and some Basque nationalists, yet their fighting spirit remained resilient.

Despite the Declaration, differing opinions persisted regarding the agreements to be forged with Spanish democrats, whether they were republicans or monarchists. The ongoing debate remained open, yet not entirely unfavorable. Basque nationalism continued to advance, overcoming the challenges of exile and contentious political decisions by the Basque government. The process of sustaining the institution allowed for the potential modification and adaptation of goals.

The acceptance of the document "Bases for a Basque Transitional Situation" could be viewed as a scaling down of objectives within Basque nationalism to secure, at the very least, the Basque Statute of Autonomy.[61] However, as a political strategy, it underscored the significance of other national aspects deserving consideration.

The 1949 Declaration, along with the "Bases for a..." document, raised the issue of Navarre (Nafarroa in Basque) and the prospect of its annexation to the Basque Country. The determination of conditions for the potential voluntary incorporation of Navarre into the Basque regime was a contentious point, intensifying the situation on both sides,[62] as expressed by Manuel Irujo in a letter to Ajuriaguerra following the declaration's publication.

Irujo demonstrated a pragmatic approach, employing realpolitik to navigate the complex political landscape from exile, even in the face of limited resources. His focus remained unwavering on the overarching objective—the preservation of the nation.[63]

Nonetheless, it is equally valid to note that defending the Basque Statute of Autonomy became a focal point that, in turn, required support as an integral part of the Basque government.[64] This emphasis was likely even more pronounced than the advocacy for complete sovereignty through independence. However, this shift should not be perceived as a relinquishment of the idea of Basque independence; rather, it reflects an adjustment to new circumstances, possibilities, and discourse.

"We are an active democracy. We must aspire to deserve more and more this denomination. It is not diminished what our methods have evolved since July 18, 1936. (...) And perhaps there are still today honorable patriots and excellent friends who long for the moment when, once the country has been restored to a functional normality, the Basque Nationalist Party can recede to the positions it occupied on July 18, 1936 or to those that will replace them in the political order that will be in force. To these friends I would like to repeat, as my own criteria, what Van Trich said at the beginning of his conferences: "That is not life, that is a vain illusion,"[65] Manuel Irujo expressed. He continued, stating, "We must find ourselves ready to participate in the management and responsibility of an even broader and more extensive order than that which was necessary to accept in 1936. (...) The elasticity in adaptation has only the marks of decency. Large and powerful peoples sometimes achieve victory by their strength. Small peoples can only deserve triumph by their constancy and fidelity to the principles of morality. We the Basques constitute a democracy. Only democratic means must be accepted in the service of Euzkadi."[66]

Irujo, in his article, underscored the significance of democracy among other attributes but made it explicitly clear that the Basque People were not regressing; they were simply adapting to the new situation. The defense of democracy and the rejection of violence emerged as consistent themes in Irujo's statements, particularly as violence became a growing element within Basque nationalism.

Adapting to the new situation involved conceptualizing the Basque Statute of Autonomy as a means of attaining sovereignty in the post-Second World War era. Manuel Irujo, being a lawyer, extensively studied various political and legal systems applicable to the Basque case, consistently seeking to incorporate new solutions and drawing insights from experiences during his exile. As he said, "Il Popolo publishes a message addressed by Luigi Sturzo to the 'Regional Assembly' of Sardinia.[67] Sturzo[68] has published a book on Regionalism in Italy, which I have not read. But his ideas are contained in the allocution addressed to the Sardinian electors. And it is interesting for the Basques to know them." Irujo was trying to emphasize the importance of learning from diverse perspectives.

The article endorsed the idea of Christian Democracy as an alternative to fascism or totalitarianism and proposed it as a viable solution for addressing national issues within a State, emphasizing the necessity of "regional self-government" for achieving complete decentralization.

Manuel Irujo believed that autonomy within States, particularly in the aftermath of the Second World War, was a pragmatic and effective solution. Drawing on examples like the Aosta Valley in Italy (where on August 19, 1945, two Decrees were approved by the Italian Government, establishing a regime of autonomy that has been in force without interruption), North Ireland, Sudan, and Tunisia,[69] he argued that autonomy, at least in the form of an autonomous government within a democracy, was crucial. Despite his earlier involvement in establishing the Basque National Council in 1940 with a pro-independence [70]aim, in the post-war era (as mentioned in previous chapters), preserving the Basque autonomous government seemed to be the most viable option for the Basques.[71] This was in alignment with their preference for an autonomous region defined by nationality within a federal Europe, as discussed in later chapters.

Nevertheless, Irujo viewed the Statutes of Autonomy not merely as compromises but as opportunities for achieving the full sovereignty of peoples and nations. Citing the example of the Sudanese, he highlighted autonomy as a transitional period leading to the adoption of a definitive national constitution, where choices ranged from absolute independence to union with other entities.[72]

Throughout his articles and speeches, Irujo underscored the intricate possibilities within these constitutional frameworks.[73] The statutes confer certain privileges upon nations like the Basque, and he highlights the way autonomous systems garner assistance in Republics while facing opposition and confrontation in Monarchies:[74] "Our problems are distinct from those of Southern Italy, without a doubt. Our position cannot align precisely with the perspective of the prominent Italian Sturzo. However, the counsel he provides to Sardinia, identifying the adversaries of autonomy and labeling the monarchy as 'the Trojan horse,' holds significance."[75]

The Basque international politics before the Conference. The American friend.

Jose Antonio Aguirre played a crucial role in the relations with the United States, although he wasn't the sole participant. The connections between the American administration and the Basque government were not novel, but the circumstances of exile and the Second World War significantly influenced them.

While exile provided opportunities and a form of refuge for the Basque government, it also brought about a division among the Basques. This division wasn't solely geographical but extended to ideological and tactical differences, as we will delve into more deeply in the upcoming chapters.

Basque society has always been interconnected, with migration and exile being constants throughout its history. Basque communities have historically gone into exile or migrated, especially since the 19th century, towards both South and North America.[76]

The presence of Basque communities, known as the "Basque diaspora," proved instrumental in organizing the Basque exile during and after the Spanish Civil War, particularly after 1939. From the conflict's onset, the Basque government took charge of organizing the exile, collaborating with various organizations, notably the LIAB (International League of Friends of the Basques). Established in Paris in 1938 by the Basque-Philippine Manuel Intxausti and the French Bishop Clement Mathieu, the LIAB had two primary fronts: the Assistance Committee for Basques, led by Mathieu to channel aid to refugees, and the Committee of General Interests of the Basque Country, focused on publicizing the nation's demands and spreading Basque culture.[77]

Existing Basque communities abroad facilitated the evacuation of exiles, especially those fleeing to America. Additionally, Basque delegations established by the Basque government before the war[78] outbreak played a proactive role. During the war, a comprehensive network of Basque delegations was established in various locations, including Paris (1936), Bordeaux (1936), Mexico (1936), Bayonne (1937), London (1937), Brussels (1938), New York (1938), Buenos Aires (1938), and Caracas (1940), among others.

The establishment of Basque delegations was a product of the international relations agenda pursued by the Basque government. While their activities may not be strictly considered "diplomatic" due to their formal dependence on Spanish Republican laws and the Republican government, their political objectives closely aligned with those of any sovereign state. As highlighted by José Luis Castro and Alexander Ugalde in their study on Basque foreign affairs, the main objectives included defending republican legality and the newly achieved Basque autonomy internationally, addressing the population's basic needs, raising awareness of Euskadi as an autonomous region within the Spanish State, articulating Basque foreign projection in various fields, and seeking international recognition for the Basque Government.[79]

While the European network, particularly the Basque delegation in Paris, was crucial—housing the Government for almost the entire exile—the American delegations also played a significant role. They not only assisted exiles relocating to America but also provided essential financial aid to the Basque government from both American delegations and Basque communities in exile.

The timing of the Basque government's exile coincided with the aftermath of the Second World War and the collapse of the Spanish Republic in exile. Initially, the financial burden of the Basque government was borne by Basque communities in exile, followed by personal loans from prominent Basque individuals and companies established by the Basque government. Eventually, Spanish funds obtained by the Spanish Republican government contributed to their financial support, as outlined in a report presented at the Basque world conference in Paris (1956) by José María Lasarte.[80]

Notably, the relationship between the "Basque services" and the United States government served as a substantial source of income, aiding, among other things, in "the conversion of the pre-established Basque delegations into Basque nationalism,"[81] as indicated in the report, even though this aspect was not explicitly mentioned.

The Basque diaspora exhibited a diversity similar to the initial Basque Government, encompassing individuals with varying political affiliations. Not all members identified as Basque nationalists,[82] leading to differing opinions regarding President Aguirre's agenda for exile and the established international relations.

President Aguirre received a cautionary note from Jon Bilbao,[83] emphasizing the distinction between political exiles and emigrants. Bilbao asserted, "The emigrant is not a political person; on the contrary, he flees from all politics."[84] In 1954, during the formulation of an international strategy involving collaboration with British services and the American CIA, certain activities related to South American dictatorships stirred unrest among Basques in America. Bilbao addressed the reactions, explaining, "Already some Cubans who love us and love you… are showing some surprise about your visit to Venezuela, a dictatorial country."[85] While this might appear contradictory to Bilbao's earlier assertion about non-political Basque migrants, his later analysis highlighted a transformation in some Basque delegations in Central and South America, particularly the Cuban Basque center, which he identified as "just a Spanish regional center," controlled by non-nationalist Basques.

President Aguirre had proclaimed the objective of disseminating Basque nationalism among the diaspora to spotlight the Basque issue from the outset of his American endeavors. Upon Aguirre's return to America in 1941, especially after settling in New York, he restructured the Basque government and outlined the international political goal: strengthening and expanding Basque presence and relationships by promoting culture (including the establishment of the Basque press office in 1947 and supporting Basque publications). Additionally, political awareness of delegations was enhanced through participation in international bodies, countering Nazi and fascist influence in South America, and sustaining collaboration with the Spanish Republican government.[86]

For Aguirre, the exile was a challenge, not a setback. Leading the Basque government, he remained focused on ongoing efforts for the Basque people. His defining trait was optimism, capable of transforming challenges into opportunities, even in less-than-ideal international circumstances. The Spanish Civil War wasn't an isolated event; immediately following it, the onset of the Second World War compelled the Basques and Spanish exiles to seek new solutions in a changed wartime scenario.

President Aguirre's presence in the United States resulted in the establishment of the Basque Government's headquarters in New York, elevating the importance of the New York Basque delegation to one of the primary delegations.

Working with the USA. The Basque government in the USA

The course of the Second World War, coupled with the United States' entry into the European theater, brought about a shift in international politics, altering the focus of Basque diplomacy. The American strategy found support, and collaboration was formalized through a cooperation agreement with the Office of Strategic Services (OSS), which later became the CIA, in 1942.

This agreement bore similarities to the one signed by the Basque National Council in London under Manuel Irujo's leadership, though it differed in nature. It wasn't a political accord, but a military collaboration aimed at countering Nazi propaganda in Europe, the Philippines, and notably Latin America. Xabier Irujo notes, "This provoked a heated debate between Irujo and Aguirre." The American agreement was made possible through prior contacts and collaboration agreements with British Services and the efforts of Irujo and the Basque National Council in London. Irujo insisted that the new agreement should encompass the political Basque objective of national independence to justify the undertaking.

However, not all members of the government shared Irujo's perspective. The Lehendakari believed that collaboration should occur without demanding additional concessions, driven solely by the pursuit of democracy and freedom.[87] President Aguirre trusted Manuel Irujo's loyalty, but more importantly, he adopted a strategic mindset. Following his reappearance, Aguirre navigated delicate situations that could impact the Basque government's strategy or tarnish the image of unity.

"I am beginning to study the London conflict in particular. I want to find out well in order to make radical decisions. We cannot give scenes similar to those of the Spaniards, quarreling and provoking scandal everywhere,"[88] expressed Aguirre in his diary entry of November 8th, 1941. Concerned about the events during his absence, he pinpointed issues, particularly those related to the administration of the Continental Transit Shipping Company. His political focus was on maintaining unity within the Basque government and collaboratively working towards creating a conducive environment in international politics. This environment aimed to enhance not only the image of Basque nationalists but also that of Spanish Republican democrats. The latter sought significance to be considered by the Allies for inclusion in their pacification agenda.

Democracy and the fight against fascism were integral aspects of Aguirre and the Basque government's international relations agenda. Christian Democracy in America played a crucial role in achieving these objectives. Embedded in the core principles of the Basque Nationalist Party (PNV), Christian Democracy formed the basic corpus, leading to constant interactions with European supporters and political movement founders, such as Luigi Sturzo. Even in exile, Aguirre and Sturzo collaborated to promote Christian Democracy in America.

While American society, in general, sympathized with the Spanish Republican cause during the Spanish Civil War, opinions among Catholics were divided. Franco's Catholic propaganda framed the conflict as a defense of Catholicism against atheism and communism,[89] complicating the narrative. One of the primary goals of Basque nationalists in exile was to reshape the perception associating Spanish Catholics with Franco's regime. They aimed to demonstrate that Christian Democracy offered an alternative associated with peace and order, aligning with the truly peaceful regime of democracy.

The collaboration agreement with the OSS played a crucial role in fostering the development of Christian Democracy in America, particularly in South America, under the leadership of Basque nationalists. In Latin America, where the influence of the Catholic Church was substantial, the role of Basque nationalists, being Catholics themselves, held significant importance, especially considering that neither Americans nor the British were Catholic. The Basque services utilized the influence of Basque centers, associations, priests, and even bishops (both Basque and non-Basque) to disseminate the ideas of Christian Democracy and counteract Nazi and fascist propaganda.

In Latin America, democracy faced challenges as some countries saw the rise of neo-fascist governments, like the regime of Juan Perón in Argentina, aligned with the Spanish regime. President Aguirre believed that promoting Christian Democracy could be instrumental in resisting and overthrowing these regimes. Despite the marginal presence of Christian Democracy parties in Latin America (except in Chile, Uruguay, and Venezuela), Basque nationalists effectively promoted Christian-Democrats' ideas, notably through the efforts of Pedro Basaldúa with the journal "Orden Cristiano" in Argentina. Strengthening ties with European Christian Democracy through an American union was a goal pursued by Basaldúa, leading to trips and conferences attended by President Aguirre and EBB members like Manuel Irujo, beginning after the collaboration agreement with the OSS in 1942.

The success of these efforts is evident in the creation of new Christian-Democrat parties in South America and the hosting of the First International Conference of Christian Democracy in Santiago de Chile in 1955.[90]

President Aguirre's arrival in New York in 1941 transformed the Basque delegation in the city into the headquarters of the Basque government until 1946. Established in 1938 following José Antonio Aguirre's strategy of spreading Basque national propaganda and promoting Christian Democracy[91] in America, the Basque delegation in New York received support from Manuel Ynchausti,[92] a Basque-Philippine with extensive businesses and relationships in America. He assisted in organizing the delegation, appointing Manuel de la Sota Aburto and Ramon de la Sota McMahon to work there, supervised by Anton Irala, the appointed delegate.[93]

The end of the American dream

After his journey to South America in 1954, José Antonio Aguirre announced a Basque conference to put together the ideas and reflections of nearly twenty years of Basque Government, almost the entire time of the exile. In fact, the exile itself had a special importance at the Conference that would be held in Paris in 1956. The politics followed by the Basque government in Paris were not always accepted by the Basque nationalists inside Spain, and, as we have already seen, the controversy was especially acute among Juan Ajuriaguerra and the members of EBB. The internal exile—which was where the Basque nationalists living in Spain were stuck—was not helping them to agree with some of the decisions taken by those who were living thousands of kilometers away from the Franco dictatorship. Democracy was a blessing for the exiles, despite being forced to live abroad—but the freedom of choosing, comparing, and learning from other experiences in the fight against Francoism sometimes collided with the lack of freedom of those who were suffering and struggling against the Franco regime in the streets of Hegoalde.[94] Political strategies and even national ideas were seen differently from both sides of the political border that the Pyrenees were, and after twenty years of exile, the differences began to grow deeper.

"The work done by the Basque Government is insufficient to a high degree. Moreover, the B.G. does not exist. It does not exist as a collegial force or as a collegial body. The components are completely inactive. The meetings are of zero value. It neither takes directions nor coordinates actions." Such were the tough words addressed to Lehendakari Aguirre in person by Ajuriaguerra at an EBB meeting in October 1950. It was not only the decisions taken by the Government that were questioned, but the Institution in itself. The view of a lack of legitimacy of the Basque (and Catalan) Government in the eyes of the Spanish republicans in exile was now also shared by members of the PNV, in that particular case, from within the Basque country, thus deepening the geographical divide of the exile itself:

> Franco is going to be pushed out from the Inland. If the interior does not work intensely in this sense, there is nothing to do either. (...) We have to get rid of two beliefs: We should not expect the exterior to throw Franco out, nor should we expect it to take any initiative that would bring about his downfall. (...) We have to act on the exterior offensively and not defensively, so that this asphyxiation continues and increases.[95]

Perceptions differed significantly on both sides of the Pyrenees, with the exile evolving into the symbolic eighth province championed by Basque nationalism. The diaspora, including the exile community, gained influence with diverse opinions, fostering alternative perspectives and disagreements on certain stances.

While the international efforts of the Basque government in exile fell short of provoking military intervention, they did succeed in bringing attention to the

Basque conflict in various national chancelleries and even prompting debates on the Spanish question at the United Nations. However, mere declarations and statements proved insufficient.

"The strategy pursued by President Aguirre, collaborating with the American Department of State to garner support against the Franco regime, faced resistance from some Basque nationalists and the Spanish democratic resistance. Despite Aguirre's natural optimism, doubts about the strategy surfaced." Ludger Mess identifies 1951 as the turning point in Aguirre's optimism, particularly following concerns expressed in correspondence with Jesús Galíndez,[96] the delegate in New York between 1946 and 1956.

Collaborative activities with the American Department of State facilitated relationships established by Basque nationalists in the United States. Notably, Lehendakari Aguirre's positive image in the U.S., forged since the English edition of his book "Escape via Berlin," positioned him as a democracy advocate[97] in the late '40s—an era grappling with the aftermath of defeated democracy and the need to redefine freedom. Aguirre's democratic stance gained recognition among Americans, and his Christian-Democracy alternative found a listening audience in cultural and political forums.

In pursuit of international recognition for the Basque cause and the broader Spanish democratic and anti-Franco movement, efforts leveraged newly established international institutions under democratic principles. The emphasis on defending democracy was evident in proposals before the United Nations, such as advocating for a ban on credits to Spain in 1947 and conditioning the application of the Marshall Plan on a future democratic Spain.[98]

Anton Irala and Jaume Miravitlles collaborated on the report-proposal, which Albornoz would present to the President of the United Nations and delegates from different countries. The objective was to forge political alliances rooted in the spirit of democracy, steering away from the less effective strategy of anticommunism.

In the global geopolitical landscape, Aguirre and the Basque nationalists were acutely aware that if the world were to split into two blocs led by the USA and the USSR, Spain's geostrategic position and concerns about potential communist advancements in Southern Europe would present a challenging card for the interests of Spanish democrats in exile. International politics seemed poised to abandon anti-Francoist democrats, opting instead for Cold War alignments. Gradually, "the posture of rejection, criticism, and marginalization towards the former ally of Hitler and Mussolini was eroded by the slow trickle of gestures, statements, and activities that separately lacked political significance but which as a whole constituted a powerful sign of what was going on."[99]

Democracy, initially conceived as an instrument for constructing international institutions with universal aspirations for a better world, ultimately became influenced by local national interests. Even when faced with resolutions against democratic proposals, approved in the UN[100] with American votes, Aguirre clung to hope for American aid, although such hopes would not endure for much longer.

Aguirre's Atlantic strategy centered on promoting democracy, fostering the unity of the Spanish republican resistance, and the later development of anticommunism by the PNV, even though this would lead to conflict within Basque nationalism, as explored in upcoming chapters. While the reliance on international institutions and the pursuit of democracy may appear optimistic given the limited success of this strategy for Spanish democrats, post-World War II analysis reveals an extraordinary political vision on Aguirre's part. He and his government strategically positioned the Basque cause and its democratic aspirations globally, demonstrating that even small nations could play a role in shaping a better world.

Given the atrocities perpetrated by totalitarian governments throughout and after WWII, the democratic cause became a compelling card to play—even in the face of the political interests of nation-states with established governments.

Despite warnings from his contacts in America about the American administration's[101] contradictory stance, Aguirre remained committed to his strategy. He believed that the Americans would not support a dictator if the Spanish resistance could present a united democratic alternative.

The Basque government backed the 1947 strike,[102] emphasizing the need for UN intervention and underscoring their allegiance to democratic causes: "(…) we have helped all over the world to the Allied triumph with efficiency and sacrifice when here it was a crime to support the Allied cause. We recall that Basques and Spaniards died at Narwick, in Africa, in Italy, and in the liberation of France. We now ask for the same freedom for ourselves. Freedom to express our will and to rule our destinies accordingly."[103]

While 1947 held the potential to be a turning point for Basque nationalists in anti-Francoist activities and internal resistance, internal disagreements among participating parties and trade unions, along with the unexpected duration of the strike, revealed challenges within the organization of the resistance.[104]

However, the primary focus of this study lies in the international repercussions of the 1947 strike and the subsequent repression, leading to the detention of between 2000 and 4000 individuals.[105] The strike, jointly organized by political parties—primarily the PNV and the Socialists—and trade unions like ELA-STV, UGT, and CNT, was a response to the mobilization observed during Aberri Eguna (April 6), the Anniversary of the Republic (April 14), and the bombing of Gernika (April 26).[106] While the success of these earlier popular demonstrations prompted the democratic resistance to call for a strike on May 1, the strike's even greater success and its lasting over eight days indicated a lack of adequate preparation for the protest.

The strike's international impact was substantial, with President Aguirre's press conference leaving a significant impression on French, British, and American media. The news also spread through Radio Euzkadi and other international radio channels, fostering optimism about the regime's potential end.[107]

The Franco regime's repression against the strikers matched the massive press coverage of the uprising. This repression prompted the Basque government to launch a fundraising campaign for fired workers and those who remained imprisoned after several months.

The Basque government-in-exile's earlier declaration "To the Basques in America" explicitly urged the delegations in exile to participate in fundraising efforts. Koldo San Sebastián notes that this declaration bestowed political authority upon the Basque delegations in exile, enabling them to engage in activities.[108] The exile's delegations, particularly the American one, organized numerous fundraisers, gathering substantial funds primarily from Argentina, Venezuela, and Mexico. This underscores the growing significance of the delegations in exile, representing the exile as a whole and contributing to the formation of the "eighth province" previously mentioned. This active political engagement aimed at shaping opinions and participating in the envisioning of the Basque country in exile, a role that became even more evident in the World Basque Conference of 1956.

Despite the significant success of the 1947 strike, the Lehendakari still had the "American friend" in mind. This concern led Aguirre and some Basque nationalists to oppose the nature and development of the 1951 strike. They feared that the social unrest might displease the Americans if these popular movements were manipulated by the communists.[109]

Following this decision, Aguirre and the exile found themselves at odds once again with the internal exile and the leadership of the Junta de Resistencia (Resistance Council), controlled by Juan Ajuriaguerra.

In a report signed in Paris on May 31 by the political commission, likely drafted by Manuel Irujo,[110] the impact of the strikes was studied. The document explored the division between the inland and the country in exile, along with the challenges and hopes of reaching an agreement. The report, spanning seventeen pages, emphasized the importance of the exile and praised the activities carried out by exiles, highlighting their connection to the situation within the inland.

"I do not find substantial differences between outland and international activities. (...) I would have written the syllabus in this order: international politics, European politics, peninsular politics, Basque politics," the report stated.

Attached to the document were letters and reports received by Manuel Irujo, addressing relations with Spanish exiles, the impact of the 1951 strikes, and relations with Spanish Federalists within the Federal European Council (CFE). The report also discussed the need to create a Basque council.

Regarding the strikes, the report analyzed their nature and, while not outright rejecting them, emphasized the importance of well-organization. Since the Franco regime[111] labeled the strikes as political, the report argued that they needed to be carefully orchestrated to exploit the damage inflicted on the regime. This would demonstrate the clear unity and solid organization of the anti-Francoists, making their position evident to the exterior and international bodies.

"Insisting that strikes occur seems to me to be a necessity. I am opposed to those who might have a different criterion. I am well aware of the danger of an endemic strike situation. But we have no choice. The international world will esteem us as long as we can prove with facts that Franco is not the ruler of Spain. (...) The idea of giving the strikes a political direction is a necessity. (...) If we do not do it, we expose ourselves to the danger that someone else will do it. And the danger is not only communists or monarchists."

The Basque nationalists in exile were engaged in an international battle, torn between the pursuit of recognition and assistance to bring an end to the Spanish regime or receiving support from fellow Basque exiles. The prolonged exile, as with any, was not the desired outcome, yet the overarching objective of the Basque nationalists remained returning home to establish a sovereign nation. Leveraging their international relations was considered one avenue toward achieving this goal.

However, in the 1950s, the international stage was dominated by the emergence of the Cold War. In this vast geopolitical landscape, the Basque people once again found themselves perceived as inconsequential, particularly by the very American administration they had placed their trust in.

The Pacts of Madrid and the shifting of the helm back to Europe

Following World War II, the focus of the Basque services, which had aided the US in eliminating fascist and neofascist groups, ceased to align with American interests. Anticommunism took precedence as the primary concern for the American administration. Despite President Truman's reservations, the American Congress, in 1950 and 1951, approved various grants and loans to support the Franco regime based on the Economic Cooperation Act of 1948, aimed at combating communism in Europe.[112]

Upon the approval of American loans, President Aguirre still harbored some hope, but his confidence in the "American friend" was waning. In 1952, he erroneously asserted during a meeting with the EBB, "The Francoist position of expecting something from the change of attitude after the elections is absurd because whoever wins, the position will be the same."[113]

With the advent of the Republican administration in the White House in 1953, Spain was formally included in the defense strategy for Western Europe. The signing of the Pact of Madrid in September, an economic and military agreement, and Spain's inclusion in UNESCO paved the way for its admission to the UN on December 15, 1955.[114] Despite efforts by Félix Gordón Ordás, President of the Spanish Republican government-in-exile, to emphasize UN resolutions characterizing the Franco regime as fascist, Spain's admission to the UN was realized without recognizing the legitimacy of the Spanish Republican government. In his letter, Félix Gordón Ordás emphasized, "The Franco regime is a fascist regime, copied from the model of Hitler's Germany and Mussolini's fascist Italy, and instituted largely with their help. It is therefore evident to every sound judgment and to every upright conscience that the usurper government of Spain cannot be granted membership in the United Nations without violating the original meaning of the authentic interpretation of the founding Charter of San Francisco."[115] This appeal had little impact in the United Nations, where the Spanish Republican government, although legitimate, was not recognized.

The end of Spain's "isolation," marked by its absence from international institutions, was sealed with the signing of the Concordat with the Vatican on August 27, 1953. This agreement, following a series of feeble accords, dealt a harsh blow to Basque nationalists who were devout Catholics, as they trusted the Holy See would not formalize relations with a dictatorship, let alone appoint Francisco Franco as a Knight of the Militia of Jesus Christ.

While the Basque government attempted to downplay the significance of these developments in its slow but steady path toward international recognition for Spain, its members were well aware of the importance of these pacts. Following the Pact of Madrid, Ajuriaguerra returned to the inland, and Irujo initiated contacts with the Basque delegate in London, Josu Hickman, in an attempt to resume ties with the British, as the American strategy seemed to have failed.[116]

In addition, Irujo intensified the campaign against the Concordat, which he had initiated in 1952 through articles and speeches on Radio Euzkadi, often using his alias "Javier de Iranzu" when discussing religious topics. This included an anti-American campaign with numerous articles penned by Irujo, criticizing the Franco regime and its manipulation of the Catholic Church in Spain. Examples of these articles include "Franco en UNESCO," "Los hogares cristianos," and "La civilización del trabajo," all written in 1952.

Anticipating American agreements, Irujo wrote articles in 1952, such as "La Miseria de España," responding to information published by London's journal "The Economist" on a potential Spanish-American agreement. Irujo noted, "Spain has become yet another case of the Cold War. U.S. intervention is increasingly tangible in Western politics." Leveraging daily information from Hickman, Irujo, as Javier de Iranzu, initiated a campaign against the USA and in favor of the British during 1953. Articles defending British policies, such as "El Pensamiento Navarro en Kenia," were published, where Irujo advocated for Great Britain and Europe as the cradles of democracy, albeit with a touch of demagoguery in support of British colonialism.

Following the impact of the Pact of Madrid, both Irujo's articles and those under his alias, Javier de Iranzu, were dedicated to defending Great Britain and Europe against the American administration, this time without reservations. In Alderdi, no. 83, February 1954, Irujo defends the European Federal Movement after the London Economic Conference, aiming to create an economic bloc of Europe and the British Community to compete adequately with the United

States. He expresses similar sentiments in the Radio Euzkadi speech titled "La Conferencia económica europea de Londres" as Javier de Iranzu.

In a final attempt to condemn the Pact of Madrid, Irujo, in Alderdi, no. 84, March 1954, boldly states, "El Pardo has received blessings from the Vatican and dollars from North America," vividly expressing the failure of Basque strategies with both the Catholics and the Americans.

However, the Christian-Democrat movement remained closely tied to Basque nationalist ideology, and after the creation of the NEI, the link between Christians and democracy strengthened through the European movement. Irujo's strategy of redirecting Basque interests toward Europe and Great Britain aimed at vindicating democracy, as advocated by Aguirre. Consequently, at every European movement meeting, Basque delegates emphasized the need to treat countries not represented in the European Council equally. This approach sought to liken countries from the Eastern Block to Western authoritarian regimes like Portugal or Spain.[117] Such a strategy aimed to modify the strategic landscape of the United Nations, compelling its admission of several countries to balance the world divided into two blocks.[118]

Following the Pact of Madrid, José Antonio Aguirre's inherent optimism didn't resonate with the members of the Basque government in contact with the President. According to Mees,[119] Aguirre, despite not acknowledging the defeat of the American strategy—since it would be akin to admitting personal failure—was, in reality, shifting towards a European strategy with the persistent goal of internationalizing the Basque cause.

The Basque nationalists connected to the Lehendakari were less optimistic about the American strategy. By 1953, the opposition to this strategy was explicit. Jesús Galíndez, expressing his doubts, emphasized the need for forward-looking programs and a reconstruction of Basque doctrine in alignment with current needs. In a January 1953 article titled "Lo que importa es el futuro"[120] (What Matters is the Future), Galíndez critiqued Basque strategy and nationalism, calling for more than mere patriotism, emphasizing the necessity for social action. In his view, the absence of innovative ideas within Basque nationalism and the call for renewal were apparent: "Those men, although one or two generations ago they were not Basques, today they are; this is another truth that we cannot ignore." He added, "the only way to confront communism is to offer better solutions; we can give them, precisely because we can base them on the tradition of a people that until now, has lived quite well, and among us evolution can avoid revolution. On the basis of freedom."[121]

These statements weren't a direct critique of Sabino Arana, but they implied a demand for renewed ideas and a shift in nationalist Basque policies to enhance their presence among the "new Basques." This term refers to those who migrated from other parts of Spain to settle in the Basque country. The focus should be on addressing social needs to prevent a further decline in popularity.

The example set by Basque nationalism in the 1950s began to wear thin, and Ceferino Jemein[122] reacted vehemently to Galíndez's article in the following issue of Alderdi with the articles "Rojos-separatistas" and "Pasado, presente y futuro de Euzkadi,"[123] under his alias, Bachiller Belandia. Jemein staunchly defended Sabino Arana's ideas and orthodoxy, emphasizing the importance of remembering Basque and patriotic anniversaries to keep the flame of the past alive.[124] This was a direct response to Galíndez's calls for renewal.

However, Galíndez, frustrated with the direction of American politics and disappointed by the decisions of the international bodies they had relied on, expressed his concerns: "The slogan seems to be not to attack the Franco regime, and our persistence cries out without being drowned." Shocked by the international strategy that left Basque democrats to fight against Franco's fascism alone to curb the advance of communism in Europe, Galíndez openly criticized American politics. He began to realize that the spread of anticommunism was limiting the chances of receiving help to overthrow the Franco regime. His strategy was to put Franco on the same level as communism regarding the lack of freedom: "You can't fight communism only with cannons; you can't admit any ally who claims to be 'anti-communist.' Aggression must be met with force, all right. But the problems remain and must be solved. Either we solve them ourselves or we give away their flag to the communists. The biggest difference between the communists and us is that they lack freedom. But with freedom, we have to carry out the necessary work of social justice. And without freedom, it is not possible to do anything."[125]

Gradually, President Aguirre changed his opinion about the American strategy and firmly accepted that the Atlantic option was over. He redirected his focus toward Europe and the European federation. Aguirre had never entirely forgotten Europe; he closely monitored the activities of his associates in Europe, especially Francisco Javier Landáburu[126] and later Manuel Irujo. In June 1947, Aguirre and Landáburu became founding members of the Nouvelles Équipes Internationalles (NEI), the federation of Christian-Democrat parties, where the Basques were the only Spanish representatives until 1965.[127] Their active involvement in the European movement led them to participate in The Hague conference of 1948, the starting signal for the European Federal Movement, and Manuel Irujo would become vice-president of the Consejo Federal Español del Movimiento Europeo (CFE), created in 1949 at the headquarters of the Basque government in Paris.[128]

The shift toward a European orientation was outlined in one of the extensive letters sent by the president to his delegate in New York,[129] titled "Orientaciones sobre el problema de la unidad Europea," ("Orientations on the problem of European unity") penned in October 1953. While not entirely abandoning his faith in the Americans, President Aguirre redirected his democratic aspirations towards the future European Union: "(...) one of the articles of the Political Constitution Draft provides no less than that a State whose democratic or parliamentary institutions are under attack may call upon the supra-national organization to help restore the situation. It is not necessary to think too far ahead to realize how important this provision alone is for all of us."

The concept of the European Union as a substitute for traditional nation-states, formed by nations rather than states, became a key element of the European strategy, as explored in subsequent chapters. Despite the challenging circumstances, Aguirre expressed his optimism, placing his hopes on the future Union as a democratic solution for the Basque people to overcome Francoism:

> The group of these institutions in function will serve us to demonstrate before our people, the Spanish people, and also before Europe our situation of indigence and the right that we have to be Europeans and to belong, therefore, to the continental union and to receive from it the consequent benefits. The obstacle is the dictatorial regime of General Franco. Our democratic program will then have an internal and external raison d'être that will be understood by all reasonable people, since it will not be difficult to oppose arguments based on alleged communist dangers and others of a similar nature, since it is precisely the supranational authority that will constitute the strongest guarantee against any anti-democratic attempt.

With this document, Aguirre solidified his commitment to the European alternative: "We give primary importance here to this political line, which I will insist on in future manifestos and messages."[130]

Paris, September 23 – October 1: Euskal Batzar Orokorra
Governing, what and how? Differences between inland and exile.

Aguirre's inherent optimism and his reliance on the American strategy faced dissent within Basque nationalist circles. As elucidated earlier, certain members expressed reservations about the policies of the Basque government. The prolonged exile, coupled with the passage of time, prompted those opposing Franco's dictatorship to voice their opinions on decisions made by the Government-in-exile, including Aguirre's strategies

Divergent views on the government's decisions grew, coinciding with worsening financial challenges, particularly since the early 1950s. A gradual decline in Basque services for the American Department of State forced the government to seek alternative funding sources, making the Basque diaspora indispensable.[131]

The increasing significance of Basque communities abroad fueled the perception that they played a crucial role in shaping Basque politics from exile. This heightened involvement strengthened their connection to the evolving landscape of Basque nationalism. Aguirre, acknowledging the diverse inputs from the exile, sought to comprehend their needs, aiming to maintain unity within the Basque community:

Today, as yesterday, I intend to unite all Basques around a noble cause, without pretending, moreover, that they all think in the same way about everything. But I intend to do so on the fundamentals, such as the sense of freedom and loyalty to our traditions, without which the way of being of any Basque is inconceivable. (...) Besides, I don't know why many people in our community believe that they want my visit to restore a little of the spirit of the people and the somewhat blurred positions of recent times.[132]

Aguirre expressed himself in this way in a letter to John Bilbao sent in January 1954, as he prepared for a tour to America. The trip would include visits to Venezuela, Cuba, Mexico, and the United States, with Aguirre's intention being to keep his contacts alive and, once again, not without some little hope in his American friend: "In Washington I have from now on interesting interviews to conduct as the situation has not only not changed for us, but I am about to say that the personal political relationship aspect has improved." In the USA, the 1953 election had raised General Dwight D. Eisenhower to the Presidency, giving the Basques a new chance to keep on believing in the American ally. And yet we can make out the new airs in Aguirre's international intentions, which are turning indeed toward Europe:

I wrote to Galíndez telling him to explore the environment so that I could take advantage of my stay in Havana to give some lectures at the university and some other cultural center. The issues I was proposing were those concerning the problem of European unity, which are generally totally unknown in those parts of the world and are currently a vital issue for Europe and for us.[133]

Bilbao had cautioned Aguirre about the necessity of reorganizing certain policies, and Aguirre was open to the idea. However, executing these plans posed more challenges than Aguirre initially anticipated. The exile, though receptive, encountered resistance, particularly among those who did not identify as nationalists, as was the case with the Cuban community. Concerns also arose about Aguirre's political visit to Fulgencio Batista,[134] the US-backed President of Cuba following the 1952 military coup. Some members of the Basque community in America, such as Portés Vilá, García Pons, and Arango, expressed surprise and reservations about Aguirre's visits to dictatorial countries, as highlighted by Bilbao in his response: "Your visit to Batista, even on a private visit, would create a vacuum in the intellectual circles, including journalists."[135]

Aguirre's seeming lack of reservations about visits to Central and South American dictators, despite his staunch defense of democracy throughout his political career, raises questions about their potential impact on his image. In 1954, the Basque community in Cuba was more concerned about local business interests than the development of Basque nationalist politics. As Galíndez and Bilbao had warned Aguirre, the Basques in Cuba were primarily considered emigrants who had settled on the island. While they maintained connections with the Basque Center, which, according to Bilbao, had transformed into a "Spanish Regional Center," most were Basque-born citizens who had raised their families in Cuba and were uninterested in politics or returning to the Basque country.

An illustrative example of their interests can be found in the journal Gordejuela,[136] published in Cuba from 1943 to 1956 by Basque descendants of José Arechabala. This publication, originating from the town of Gordejuela in Bizkaia (Vizcaya), primarily focused on business, maintaining positive relations with the USA, and nurturing the Catholic community. References to politics, the Basque country, or visits by the Lehendakari or other Basque nationalists held little interest for this publication.

The Basque community in Cuba had assimilated so thoroughly into the Cuban society that, by the 1950s, any trace of Basque nationalism or interest in Basque topics had vanished, despite the existence of older publications like Laurac Bat (1886-1896) or Beti Jai[137] (1906) on Basque themes.

Meanwhile, the European strategy was well underway, instilling confidence in the Basque press. In September 1954, Alderdi titled its editorial "Razones de nuestro sentimiento Europeísta," directing attention to the European strategy as a means of championing democracy and isolating the Franco regime:

> Only those who follow totalitarian slogans and the retrograde parties of the old prestige of the national states are still opposed to the constitution of a supranational political authority... What interests the peoples of Europe, and especially peoples like Euzkadi, is a firmly democratic European organization.[138]

During his trip in America, Aguirre underscored the significance of international bodies and, above all, the importance of a democratic global order. He emphasized the need to distinguish the democratic system from often tolerated totalitarian regimes: "But all these institutions or all these purposes of unity, as well as the Atlantic Pact itself, whose purpose of defending democratic freedom is evident... lacked, however, what I call democratic control."[139]

Aguirre redirected his interests and hopes towards a European Union where democracy would be a fundamental aspect, defending the rights of the peoples through the institution:

> The first article of the Treaty to which I have been referring deals with the nature and character of this European Political Community and states that 'it is founded on union among the peoples and States, respect for their personalities and equality of rights and obligations.[140]

Aguirre, having lost hope in the American strategy and intervention in Spain, looks towards the European Union as a potential refuge for his aspirations. He emphasizes the need for unity, recalling past criticisms and divergent opinions within Basque nationalism and alluding to the unity among Spanish Republicans: "We have always stood by the institutions of the Republic. The reason? Among others, the reason we give when we refer to the Community of Europe: because there is no alternative."[141]

Aguirre sees the unity of all democrats who left Spain due to the Civil War as crucial, not only for national goals but also for the international image and the potential for aid. The focus now shifts to democracy and Europe as the new strategy for the recognition of Basque nationalists globally. Despite earlier successes with international bodies like UNESCO or the UN, where Basque voices[142] were heard, the disregard for Basque and Spanish demands by world institutions, influenced by the USA, led them to consider the emerging Europe as a promising alternative.

Basque nationalism's participation in the construction of the new Europe, particularly through the European Federal Movement, offered a supranational structure in which their national aspirations could be realized. Aguirre, a founding member, envisions the European Union as a platform where small nations, legally recognized or not, can find immense opportunities for immediate security and future development: "Europe is of enormous interest to small peoples... In the social, cultural, and economic fields, the European organization opens to these collectivities an immense field of immediate security and of future development."[143]

The idea of the State, and the advocacy for its validation, inherently carries nationalistic undertones.[144] However, in envisioning a new Europe structured as a modern State, the traditional boundaries could dissolve within a supranational framework where the focal point shifts to the people. Aguirre articulates this vision, stating, "For the nationalities that are aware of themselves and that fight for their freedom, any European organization, even if only for the moment of a supra-state character, creates for them a new instance above those States to which they will be able to resort in case of persecution, aggression, genocide of any kind, be it physical, be it spiritual. (...) We Basques and all the European peoples in general have much to hope for from a democratic organization of Europe."[145]

Despite such aspirations, the realization of the "Europe of the peoples" remains intertwined with the existing nature of the States. This realization dawns upon the Basques following their experience with the creation of the European Federal Movement in 1948. Compelled to establish the Consejo Federal Español del Movimiento Europeo (CFE) to secure admission into European meetings, despite being founding members, underscores the complexities involved in striving for a distinct European identity detached from existing State dynamics.

The subordination to the Spanish within this framework becomes a point of contention for Telesforo Monzón, a prominent member of the Basque Nationalist

Party closely aligned with Aguirre. Monzón contends, "My life is not for anti-Francoism. Franco is an incident. Do we have better means to be universal than to be sons of our country? The foundations of Western civilization are the souls of the old peoples of Europe."[146] Monzón, critical of alliances with the Spanish resistance during the exile, believes in the prioritization of Basque nationalism over anti-Franco political strategies. Despite his reservations, Monzón supports the Basque government's decisions until 1951, when he resigns at a Basque government meeting.[147]

While Monzón's resignation is discreetly handled to maintain calm among Basque nationalists, it signals an undercurrent of unrest within Basque nationalism. Aguirre, reflecting on international political developments marked by increasing anticommunism and likely disappointed with American betrayals regarding economic agreements with the Franco Regime, responds by convening a World Basque Congress in Paris in 1956. This decision marks a significant turning point in the trajectory of Basque nationalist aspirations, as Aguirre seeks to address the evolving dynamics within the movement and assert its position on the global stage.

The World Basque Congress, envisioned as a pivotal event for Basque nationalism,[148] emerged against the backdrop of a movement exhibiting signs of fatigue exacerbated by the protracted exile and dwindling optimism. The generation that had actively participated in the Spanish Civil War found themselves enduring almost two decades of displacement, fostering a palpable sense of alienation. The political landscape within Spain remained stagnant, contributing to the erosion of hope among exiles regarding a triumphant return to their homeland. This pervasive pessimism, both within the exile community and among those remaining in Spain, compelled Basque exiles to contemplate a comprehensive reassessment of their circumstances. The proposed remedy for this internal reckoning was the convening of the World Basque Congress, viewed as a strategic platform to take stock of the situation and chart a course forward for Basque aspirations.

Gabon, 1954. Organizing the Basque World Congress.

Upon his return from the United States, José Antonio Aguirre felt compelled to take decisive action. Having gauged the sentiments within the exile community and acknowledging the divergent perspectives among Basque nationalists, he recognized the imperative to initiate a collective dialogue. This would involve a comprehensive discussion of strategies, a confrontation of differing opinions, and a staunch defense of the Basque government and institutions entrusted with safeguarding Basque interests.

In his Christmas message, Aguirre made a momentous announcement, intending to invigorate the Basque nationalist movement—a call for the convening of the World Basque Congress in Paris in the coming year of 1955. This initiative, authorized by the Basque government, sought to bring together Basques from across the globe, uniting them under the common purpose of addressing the challenges faced by their community. The proposed Congress, organized into three major sections—political, cultural, and social-economic—was envisioned as a platform to discuss and guide the future trajectory of Basque endeavors. Aguirre articulated,

> I want this Message to end with an announcement which I hope will please you: I refer to the calling of the World Basque Congress which, in the name of the Government of Euzkadi and duly authorized by it, I will soon convene in Paris to be held, if possible, in the course of the coming year 1955. A White Book of our governmental activities, since our proclamation in Guernica, will summarize our work in the Country, in the war and in exile and will serve as a useful guide to all those who participate in our tasks. The Congress will bring together Basques from all over the world, who will attend it in their diverse representative capacity and the three great sections political, cultural and social-economic, into which, in principle, it will be divided, will be presided over and directed by our Government.[149]

Additionally, Aguirre sought to address the challenges faced by the Basque resistance in Spain, acknowledging the difficulties they encountered, and conveying a message of solidarity and understanding: "I fully understand the difficulties that those of you who live under constant threat and fear will encounter, but I know what your spirit is so that I can tell you things with the clarity and faith of those who know you." He endeavored to inspire not only recognition for the Basque cause but also to uplift the spirits of the entire Basque community—a response to the prevailing pessimism that Aguirre keenly observed. The forthcoming World Basque Congress, as announced, held the promise of being a pivotal forum for strategic discussions and collective introspection, steering the course of Basque nationalism in the years to come.

The undeniable division between the Basque exile and the homeland, between freedom and dictatorship, is succinctly articulated by Aguirre:

> Wherever the Basques live in freedom, as in the countries of Europe and America, they become united and organized, following our flags and participating in our struggle. To what does this unanimity obey, which is in itself the argument of more weight for any judicious observer who wants to know how the Basques think? The answer is that these compatriots keep your spirit, think like you, suffer and rejoice with you; and since you cannot express yourselves freely, they do it for you.

Aguirre asserts the significance of the work undertaken by the Basque community in exile, aligning it with the efforts of the Basque government. In this portrayal, the exile transcends its geographical confines[150], transforming into a realm where the Basque nation flourishes and defends its rights, irrespective of physical boundaries.

The selection of the Basque Congress date was deliberate; Leizaola, Irujo, and José María Lasarte proposed the idea,[151] each independently, considering the 20th Anniversary of the constitution of the Basque Government. Lasarte, a former member of the Basque government who resigned in 1952, played a pivotal role as the founder of the OPE (Oficina de Prensa Vasca) and overseer of information services in America, particularly in New York, Argentina, Chile, and Uruguay. It's noteworthy that the concept of organizing the Basque Congress originated from Lasarte, deeply connected with exile communities and responsible for fostering Basque culture in America, organizing significant cultural events such as the Semana Vasca de Montevideo.[152]

While the announcement of the World Basque Congress garnered warm reception among Basque nationalists, particularly those in Basque-American communities, it was not exclusively intended for them. Instead, the Congress was extended to all Basques. Analyzing the Gabon message and the General Instruction sent to Basque delegations, groups, organizations, etc., reveals two primary objectives: a call for the unity of all Basques and a staunch defense of the Basque government.

The call for the union of all Basques underscored the imperative for Basques to unite, regardless of their ideologies. This encompassed not only critical Basque nationalists but also Basques of diverse ideologies: "(…) we try to gather in its representations of Basques of all shades of opinion, of all ideologies, of all classes and professions, whether they currently reside in the homeland or in any country in the world where political emigration has taken them, either for different and perhaps earlier economic or private reasons."[153]

This inclusive approach, extending beyond just nationalists, sheds light on the ambitions of the World Congress, with President Aguirre's characteristic objective being the unity of all Basques.

By referring to all Basques, Aguirre acknowledged not only political and geographical differences but also emphasized the need for union, which included fostering a good understanding between the exile and the inland:

> On the other hand, the dispersion that has produced the exile, the inactivity forcibly imposed to our compatriots who live in Euzkadi and the physical separation of these with those abroad, urgently advises the celebration of the Congress, where the experiences of those who live inside the country are compiled with those who reside abroad, in order to obtain useful conclusions that allow continuing in the most perfect intelligence the common way.

It became evident that disparities existed, and perspectives differed on both sides of the Pyrenees. The Basque government, the entity calling for the Congress, was fully aware of this and sought to rectify differences, finding a joint solution for the overarching objective of all Basques: defeating Francoism and returning home. The General Instruction, by emphasizing the differences between the exile and inland, acknowledged these concerns while expressing determination regarding the attendance of Basque representatives from within Spain: "The opinions of our brothers from Euzkadi who, because they live there, will tell us what exists, what is missing and what needs to be replaced or restored," also highlighting the experience of the exiles: "the experience of those who have lived abroad will then be much more useful because the confrontation of ideas and purposes will be carried out on realities lived in the country itself."

The distinctions between the Consejo Delegado (CD) and the EBB resurfaced once again, underscoring the imperative to vindicate the experience and efforts of the exiles. This vindication marked the second primary objective behind convening the World Basque Congress: the defense of the Basque government.

Defending a government-in-exile proved challenging, especially when its institution and legitimacy were rooted in a legality that no longer held sway. Despite President Aguirre's tireless efforts, the Republican Government in exile had been discredited, and international institutions were recognizing the Franco regime as the legitimate authority. To sustain the nation and uphold the imagined community, as articulated by Benedict Anderson, the Basque government, representing the Basque nation, had to be staunchly defended. Operating from exile and lacking a well-defined geographical vision of the nation still under construction (Navarre, Iparralde (Northern Basque Country), Laurak Bat), the Basque government bore the responsibility for defending and, significantly, contributing to the nation's ongoing construction process.

When the Basque government summoned the World Basque Congress, it delineated three distinct lines of action: past, present, and future.

Two decades after the establishment of the Basque government, facing the need to counter criticism denouncing its activities and strategies as inefficient, the Basque government, under the leadership of the Lehendakari and through the General Instruction, disclosed its preparation of a White Book. This comprehensive document would detail the Basque government's activities since the Gernika oath of 1936, encompassing the past and the government's endeavors, with the expectation of receiving due recognition. In the absence of a Parliament or elections, the World Congress would serve as a forum for debate, allowing a balanced assessment of the government's activities. Lacking a defined territory for Basque politics, the White Book would account for the Civil War-era activities, including "all the work carried out in the delegations of Barcelona, Madrid, Bayonne, Paris, London, etc. in many matters referred to and later in the many delegations in exile, concerning our organization of assistance in shelters and hospitals, school institutions, in colonies of children welcomed abroad (...)."[154] Furthermore, it would cover civil health, assistance to the population, labor, civil industry, agriculture, transport, the Merchant Navy, the fishing fleet, and culture, encapsulating the entire spectrum, including the Basque University. The activities of Basque delegations worldwide would also find detailed documentation, encompassing various matters and the significant contributions made in exile. The White Book aimed to provide a comprehensive balance of the government's two decades and substantiate its multifaceted activities.

In terms of the present, concerns emerged regarding the lack of freedom, particularly highlighting the challenges faced by the new generation of Basques growing up under a dictatorship: "(...) the harm that the present situation brings to the country, translated into a lack of freedom that uneducates the people and mainly the young generations submerged in a pernicious spiritual atony, lacking the moral stimulus that dialogue facilitates and the noble competition of ideas makes manifest by instructing the popular masses."[155]

Viewed as a blessing in disguise,[156] exile was seen as an opportunity for freedom and cooperation that the young generation was deprived of. It provided an excellent occasion to mobilize all Basques worldwide to collaborate in addressing the problems within the Basque country, particularly focusing on "the unbasquization of the country," a task in which Basques from America were expected to contribute prominently.

The young generation living under the Spanish dictatorship received serious consideration during the Basque Congress and for subsequent years. Interestingly, those who had fought in the war and were forced into exile perceived that the new generation was distancing themselves from Basque politics. Understanding their motives proved challenging for the older generation, who, instead of enduring war, were grappling with the challenges of peace.

The discussion on the future of Euzkadi is arguably the most intriguing part of the Congress (and also the most relevant for my study), as outlining a future is an exercise in nation-building—and, naturally, this exercise would be conducted from outside "the geographical nation." The General Instruction describes the exploration of the future as "(...) the opinion of all by means of well-considered works on the many issues and problems that must be addressed by a people that wants to restore freedom and, with it, its own government."[157] It underscores the significance of the legality of the Statute of Autonomy as the starting point, emphasizing that Basque sovereignty is derived from the agreement embodied in the Statute.

The Congress, as per the General Instruction, was structured into three distinct sections (with an additional section added later called "Basques around the world")[158] to accurately present the debates and papers. These sections included the Political section, the Socio-economic section, and the Cultural section. Given the investigative focus, emphasis will be placed on the political section, designed to propose new forms of nationalist political strategy and introduce new ideological constraints within Basque nationalism. It implies an evolution of national policies: "The political section will not only deal with the modalities of our democratic struggle for the restoration of freedom but will also study, with a view to the future, the internal organization of the country and its relationship with the higher state or supra-state entities whose regulation is included both in the statutory articles and in other projects that expand on the subject."[159]

In accordance with the Congress bylaws, the event aimed to achieve three primary objectives: presenting the work accomplished by the Basque government since its constitution, addressing the criteria and opinions expressed by the congressmen regarding the present situation and the general lines for the future organization of Euzkadi, and adopting recommendations, including initiatives and guidelines, concerning the present and future of the country, to be transmitted to the Euzkadi government.[160]

The Basque government, in response to the President's directive, initiated the organization of the Congress by sending a questionnaire along with the invitations to the event. The Congress was not open to everyone but only to those personally invited by the Basque government, reflecting a commitment to the delicate situation of the Basques from inside Spain who would attend the Congress.

The full members of the Congress included the President of the Basque government and his ministers, the president of the Delegated Council and the Basque Resistance Committee, the president and members of the Basque Consultative Council, former counselors of the Basque government, representatives of the Basque Country in the Spanish Parliament (the Republican Parliament) and those who had served previously, former deputies of Araba, Gipuzkoa, Navarra, Bizkaia, elected mayors, representatives of Basque political parties and labor unions, delegates of the government of Euzkadi abroad, delegates of the International League of Friends of the Basques, and representatives from Basque communities and associations worldwide. Additionally, all Basque citizens who had individually registered for the Congress (possessing personal accreditation)[161] were in attendance.

As the Congress wasn't considered an organic institution according to Basque government laws, its nature was designated as consultative. Nevertheless, an executive committee was formed, consisting of representative members from various political parties, trade unions, Basque associations, and organizations. The composition of the committee included Jesús Solaun (PNV), Gabriel Goitia (ANV), De Pablo (Socialist Central Committee of Euzkadi in France), Herrán (ELA-STV), José Campos (Central Committee of the UGT of Euzkadi), Aransaez (CNT), Alberto Buj (UR), J. López Angulo (IR), Pedro Basaldúa (representative of the Federación de Entidades Vasco Argentinas – Eusko Argentinar Bazkun Alkartasuna—FEVA-EABA), Pedro Aretxabala, Santiago Zarranz (representatives of the Basque organizations in Chile), Juan Bautista Lasarte (representative of the

Basque center Euskal Erria of Montevideo), and the Basque delegation in Uruguay.[162] The selection aimed to cover a broad spectrum of political tendencies, trade unions, associations, and organizations of Basques worldwide, with special attention to those from South America. Priority was given to representatives from within, whose opinions on the current situation of the Basque country were considered crucial, despite the challenges they might face in attending the Congress.[163]

To encourage debate, the sent questionnaire was also published in various Basque newspapers, including Euzko Deya in Buenos Aires in May 1956.[164] The questions were divided into the three previously mentioned future sections of the conferences (Political, Socio-economic, and Cultural). Additionally, a new area was introduced, which would become a new section of the Congress: the special section "Basques around the world."

In analyzing the political section (of utmost importance for this study), the questions were further categorized to focus on the present situation of the Basque country, examining the problems and exploring potential future solutions.

Regarding the contemporary situation of the Basque country under the Franco dictatorship, the Congress organizers showed a particular interest in the perspectives of young Basques—those who had not participated in the war and were born without freedom. The questionnaire addressed inquiries such as:

> Referring to young people: what is their reaction to the past? Do they know it? Do they comment on it? What is their reaction to the future? Do they feel the lack of freedom? What are their aspirations? (...) Do they know that the Basque Government elected 20 years ago under the Tree of Gernica is still standing, uniting the struggle of the Basques for freedom? Do they know that the Basque political parties keep their political cadres acting firmly? Do they know the work of the Basque Government and of the Basque exiles? (...) Do the youth know our history of freedom? Do they know our ancient law or our laws?[165] Do they know our recent history?[166]

The opinion of the new generation was a constant concern in the questionnaire, stemming from the fear that the youth, having never had direct contact with the Basque government, might lack an attachment to Basque institutions. However, behind this concern about the young generation, the Basque government's true apprehension lay in the potential erosion of legitimacy. Twenty years after the first and only elections to choose the Basque government, there was a possibility of the institution being questioned. This concern manifested when the Socialist representative, Indalecio Prieto, declined the invitation to the Congress, arguing that the Basque government should not organize events beyond the control of the Government of the Republic—a perceived clash of political competences between the autonomous and central government. However, other voices within the same political party, such as Paulino Gómez Beltrán, supported holding elections and participating in them. In the end, the CCSE (Comité Central Socialista de Euzkadi) did participate in the Congress.[167]

Emigration and immigration to the Basque country were additional concerns in the questionnaire, and these issues would surface in the communication, as explored later on: "Emigration has produced a variant by displacing many Basques to lands of different physiognomy and even language. What is the effect produced by the forced dispersion of the Basques? How do they maintain their spirit in the country where they live? Is the union among Basques kept alive there?"[168]

The Basque diaspora and the influx of migrants into the industrialized areas of the Basque country, mainly from Spain, became a topic of heated discussion among Basque nationalists. These migrations prompted intense debates on the evolution of Basque nationalism as a political theory.[169]

Concerning future solutions to Basque political problems, the questionnaire delved into another major preoccupation of the Basque government and nationalists, particularly regarding political agreements with other Basque forces, especially those outside the nationalist spectrum. There was a specific focus on the union with Spanish Republican forces, reflecting an ongoing worry about the legitimacy of the Basque government:

> What are the urgent political measures that, even before a situation different from the present one can occur, should be adopted in our people? On what level should these measures be adopted, in the Basque, Spanish, and international spheres? (...) The Basque Government represents the last free will of Euzkadi. It has constantly reiterated that it will not waste any means to ensure that the political freedom contained in the Statute of Autonomy is restored in full force and effect. It is also the program of the Basque democratic forces, which ratified this position in 1945, adding the commitment to abide by and uphold the will freely expressed by the Basque people in its day. (...) Can the Basque Government serve not only as a flag of vindication but also as a platform of Basque democratic majority union? Having established the need for the union of the Basque democratic forces, how should the currently existing relationship be enhanced? What extension should the democratic coalition that replaces the dictatorship in the Basque Country have? What forces should deserve the democratic qualification? What are the relations to be established with the Spanish democratic forces and under what conditions and in what form?

Another longstanding nationalist debate on the political form the future Basque country should take, whether it be a Monarchy or a Republic, was also present in the questionnaire: "Consideration of the monarchical problem. The Monarchy imposed by the dictatorial power. The plebiscite as a way of determination of the form of government of the State. The type of government of the State and the Autonomy of Euzkadi. If it is convenient, what should be the Basque participation in the transition governments if these are constituted?"

The Basque government, as the organizer of the Congress, grounded its legitimacy in the Government born within the Spanish Republic. Consequently, its primary legal framework was the Statute of Autonomy, making it the cornerstone of each and every one of its political and national claims. It's noteworthy that the envisioned future Basque country, as explored in the questionnaire, was deeply rooted in the same Statute of Autonomy in many aspects, albeit without limiting its scope:

> Does the survival of the current Basque Government facilitate the fulfillment of these dispositions or of those that circumstances impose in compliance with those that are the basis of the same? Should it maintain itself firmly until it yields its mandate to the legitimate popular representation? When the time comes, should it widen its representative base to achieve the maximum popular support? (...) Special consideration of the situation of Navarre in relation to the transitional period. Measures to be followed, in agreement with Navarre, so that unity and political freedom may be extended to the whole country by means of its voluntary incorporation.

The question of Navarre underlines the significant influence of Manuel Irujo on the formulation of the questionnaire. As the president of the political section and a tireless Basque nationalist, Irujo played a pivotal role in organizing the Congress from the outset. Beyond his role as the president of the political section, he actively assisted the Basque government in various capacities, contributing to invitations, bookings, and even inspecting the meeting rooms where the Congress would be held. Irujo dedicated long hours to enhancing, modifying, and debating the communications received by the Basque government.

The Communists' Reconciliación Nacional, Landaburu's La causa del pueblo vasco and the Americans: A Cold War mess.

The questionnaire for the Congress included inquiries about the suitability of seeking unity with Spanish political forces, considering that 20 years had passed since the beginning of the Spanish Civil War. One of the questions asked: "Do you feel as a basis of moral, civil, political, and social character the need for a broad national reconciliation that will liquidate the era of strife, rancor, and crime that has characterized the dictatorial era?"

The term "Reconciliación Nacional" (National Reconciliation) served as both a slogan and a political strategy for the Spanish Communist Party (PCE). The PCE declared this strategy in June 1956, acknowledging the necessity for a shift in policies to defend the unity of Spanish democrats who had been divided since the Spanish Civil War.[170]

Interestingly, it appears that Basque nationalists also embraced the concept of "national reconciliation" during the same year. A quote cited in reports from a book purportedly published in Paris by ex-deputy Javier de Landáburu under the title "La Causa del pueblo Vasco" (The Basque People's Cause) was vaguely reminiscent of the "national reconciliation" theme expounded by the Communist Party of Spain. This reflection, enclosed in the Confidential Report no. 29 written by the American Consulate in Bilbao on October 2, 1956, is based on a brief analysis of the Basque World Congress[171] just one day after its closing ceremony. Despite severed relations with the Basque services, the American Department of State closely monitored developments in Basque and Spanish politics. The report, driven by an anticommunist focus, might have drawn some mistaken conclusions due to a mix of information.

The dedication of the book by Javier de Landáburu reads: "In memory of all the Basques who died during the fratricidal war caused by the uprising of 1936: those who fell on any of the fronts under the Basque flags or under the flags of the two Spains, those who were killed in their rearguards, those who died in bed, at home, or in exile, grieving the pain of the evils of the homeland and without understanding that cruel and unnecessary catastrophe. Rest in peace."[172]

The American's conscientious effort to acknowledge the victims on both sides of the Spanish Civil War served as the catalyst for contemplating a comparison between Basque nationalism and the communists. The narrative unfolds with revelations from a "British Vice consul who lives in Bilbao," who, in June, intercepted Communist propaganda from Paris. This material, an enumeration of proposals by the Communist Party of Spain for "national reconciliation" against the Franco Regime, is elucidated in the aforementioned "Reconciliación nacional" document issued by the PCE.

The comprehensive report delves into the transformation of strategy by the Spanish communists, deeming it "fairly widespread popular (...) in view of the emphasis on a 'peaceful' revolution in Spain." The PCE, having staked out positions, now sought innovative approaches to engage the emerging generation of Spaniards within the broader democratic resistance—a shift extending beyond the confines of Basque nationalism. Notably, in a letter dated January 19, 1955, Josu Hickman, the Basque delegate in London, appended Communist propaganda to a missive to Manuel Irujo. He described it as a leaflet from those "who fight for peace, to be the masters of the world." Irujo's response on March 2, 1955, provided a detailed account of the communists' movements, underscoring their inclination to maintain subsidies for the cult and clergy and advocate for Monarchist restoration.[173]

In parallel, the evolving landscape witnessed the Spanish monarchists positioning themselves strategically. Faced with mounting rumors hinting at Franco's contemplation of a monarchy, the monarchists were compelled to take decisive stances. Notably, Mr. Stuart W. Rockwell,[174] the First Secretary-Consul in Madrid, extended an invitation to Mr. Vicente Pinies, a member of the Monarchist party Unión Española, for a luncheon discussion. The focal point was the possibility of a monarchy being tolerated by Franco. In this context, Pinies disclosed a daring maneuver by Franco to lower the age for candidates for the Spanish throne, envisioning Juan Carlos as the prospective king. However, the Council of State, adhering to the referendum procedure, rebuffed this attempt, thwarting Franco's bold move.[175]

Amidst growing rumors that Franco might entertain the notion of reintroducing the Monarchy in Spain, the potentiality stirred unease within the Falange, prompting various political forces to adopt distinct positions. According to a report by Pinies, the Socialist party, denoted as PSOE-UGT in the American memorandum, "recognized that it had been a mistake to support the Republic" and expressed a willingness to lend support to a constitutional monarchy.[176]

As the monarchists prepared for the potential restoration of the Monarchy, considerations turned towards the prospect of Don Juan de Borbón assuming the role of King in a Constitutional and Democratic Spain. This vision materialized when Vicente Pinies, Jaume Miralles, and Joaquín Satrústegui (initially) coalesced to form the Unión Española in 1957, a political movement actively participating in pro-democracy movements against the Franco Regime, notwithstanding their past support for Franco during the Spanish Civil War.[177]

Anticipation loomed among the Americans regarding potential shifts in Spain. With an eye on curbing the advance of Communism, the possibility of a Monarchy emerged as a viable solution should the Franco regime conclude. The Americans sought to avert the establishment of a communist system after Franco's fall, viewing a transition to a Monarchy as a preferable alternative. Pinies conveyed insights suggesting that Franco's maneuvers concerning the Monarchy were not motivated by a sincere desire to shape the Spanish future ideologically. Instead, speculation arose that Franco's health or concerns for his descendants might be the driving force behind the potential pact with the Monarchy, securing an easy future for his family.[178]

The diplomatic landscape between the Franco Regime and the American Administration was marked by cordiality, exemplified by an audience granted to Mr. Fulton Lewis, Jr., a prominent American journalist, at the Palace of El Pardo. This was highlighted by ABC,[179] affirming positive relations during the arrival of the new American Ambassador, Mr. John Davis Lodge, in Madrid in March 1955. However, the American administration remained vigilant, anticipating potential changes in El Pardo.

Mr. Rockwell continued his engagement with Mr. Pinies, inviting him to lunch on June 20, 1955, to glean insights into the developments on the Monarchist front. With the confirmation of the Royal family's presence in Spain and the organization of lectures by the Monarchists, tensions within La Falange appeared to escalate steadily. Amidst speculation, a Confidential Memorandum from R.D. Mc. Clelland to Mr. Rockwell on March 18, 1955, suggested that Franco's rumored interview with Prince Juan Carlos might be intended for publication in Arriba, Falange's official newspaper, despite half of its members being staunchly anti-Monarchy.

Indeed, the Monarchists were actively arranging various events, including a lecture by Mr. Roberto Cantalupo, an Italian Monarchist deputy, as part of a series on "Tendencies in European thought," sponsored by the Minister of Information, Mr. Pérez Embid. During this lecture, Mr. Cantalupo advocated the concept of a "Fascist Monarchy," proposing a federation of monarchies or a return to the Holy Roman Empire.[180]

Confirming information already in possession of Mr. Rockwell, Mr. Pinies disclosed a clear division among Monarchists,[181] categorized as non-collaborationist and collaborationist. The Americans foresaw the potential for a tumultuous transition, highlighting the challenge faced by Monarchists in finding trustworthy individuals to maintain order in the provinces during the takeover, recognizing the delicate nature of such a moment.[182]

The prospect of monarchy and succession became a tangible consideration, with even the Falange positioning itself regarding the issue of continuity in relation to General Franco's successor. Raimundo Fernández-Cuesta,[183] Minister-Secretary General of the Movement ("F.E.T. y de las J.O.N.S."), expressed concerns and advocated for measures to fortify the Falange. These measures included obtaining the enthusiastic adherence of Spain's youth, clarifying the Movement's principles and goals, undertaking organizational reforms, seeking legal and political guarantees for the Movement's future, and persisting in efforts to perfect unity within the Movement.

Once again, the youth of Spain emerged as a focal point for political movements, embodying the hope for change in various forms. The Communists also directed their attention to the youth, as revealed in a letter from Manuel Irujo to Josu Hickman on September 14, 1955, which included Communist propaganda targeting Catholic student youth in San Sebastián.[184]

The PCE, operating clandestinely, exerted significant efforts to organize the anti-Franco movement within Spain, posing a challenge for Basque nationalists, as explored in subsequent chapters. By the close of 1955 and into 1956, as the Basque World Congress convened, Communism was perceived as a threat by American authorities. Their reports indicated a belief that a controlled Monarchy was among the best options in the event of the Franco regime's downfall. While acknowledging potential perils in a transition to the Monarchy, the Americans suggested that with Franco's prudence, bloodshed could be limited, estimating a small number of casualties if he maintained control.[185]

Javier Landaburu's book, the very one referenced in Report no. 29 by the Department of State, serves as a direct letter to the youth. For a Basque nationalism wearied by exile and the passage of years, the new generation born under the

Dictatorship embodies hope and the promise of the future. The strikes of 1947 and 1951 had underscored that, even in the inland, the interior exile, under which opposition to the dictatorship thrives, could potentially catalyze the dismantling of the Franco Regime, paving the way for the return of Basque nationalism.

"La causa del pueblo vasco"(The Cause of the Basque People) contains an entire first part that directly addresses the young Basque generation. Under the heading "Un requerimiento de los jóvenes vascos" (A request from the young Basques), Landáburu elucidates the history of the Basques and the political situation of Basque nationalism in exile. This is a response to a specific demand:

> This book that wants to prove the justice and honesty of our cause is addressed very especially to the youth of Euzkadi. It is a book commissioned by those same young people, children in 1936, who, in their visits to Paris or in their interviews in Continental Euzkadi, or in their letters, urge my fellow exiles and me to explain to them the reasons for our attitude, which they intuitively share, and the possibilities that the future offers to the Basque cause.[186]

The youth's significance and the dichotomy between the inside and the exile for Basque nationalism are recurring themes in this book. The Basque World Congress sought to bridge the gap between the exile and the inside, a topic that will be explored later on. While differing viewpoints had emerged between the inside and the exile, the new generation of Basques also had distinct perspectives on the strategic politics employed by Basque nationalism. Hence, Landaburu's address to them was eagerly anticipated at the Basque World Congress.

Many of the ideas articulated in Landaburu's book resurfaced during the Paris Congress, shaping the new facets of Basque nationalism post-Congress. Although Landaburu asserts in his book that he isn't thinking in terms of a collective entity like a government or political party,[187] the ideas presented align with and would subsequently be endorsed and promoted by Basque nationalism. Therefore, a brief examination of the book becomes essential to grasp the uncertainties and the trajectory of Basque nationalism.

The book, edited by Alderdi after the initial edition, is structured into three parts: "Reasons for an Attitude. Possibilities of Action," "The Real Nation and the Evolving Concept of the State," and "National Self-Determination and the Conditions for a Habitable State."

While not outright opposing the American strategy, Landaburu, alongside Irujo, actively supported the European Federal movement, contributing to a shift from the American to the European strategy. In 1951, following a meeting of the European federal movement in Berlin, he corresponded with Manuel Irujo, noting, "I was in Germany with the Lehendakari. Three days of congress and tourism. (...) They let themselves be loved and will go with whoever will give them the most. Of course, Yankee insight will save us from these and other anxieties. I read your letter to the boss, supporting that 'Fuc.... the gringos!'. And he liked it. I think he had done it several times. (...) However, in all honesty, we do not see that the new American stage has given Franco more than good words yet. Europe still weighs heavily and even our friend Schuman conceals his Francoist fervors."[188]

The American strategy was waning, and despite President Aguirre maintaining positive relations with the Americans, Basque nationalism sought a new approach centered on Europe and the European federation.

In Landaburu's book, following a theoretical section aimed at modernizing the concept of nation, the future strategy is formulated around the unity of the "Iberian peoples," achieved through the free will of self-determination within a federation or confederation. This confederation of peoples is perceived as the optimal solution post-Franco dictatorship: "What is the State that emerges from this Constituent period to be like? Democratic. Confederal. Internationalist."[189]

The notion of renewing the relationship with the State is tied to the perceived differences among the various peoples of Spain:

> Today the criteria for the reconstruction of the State can no longer be that of the standardization of citizens and peoples. Today the State is, in addition to the individuals, Catalonia, Galicia, Euzkadi, perhaps Portugal—if this question is posed without prejudices, without cravings or resentments—and all the other peninsular peoples. Whoever misses the opportunity to unite them, not to unify them, may lose the opportunity that will not happen again.[190]

Democracy and confederation emerged as the foundational principles for a new State in Spain. Alongside these, Landaburu, possibly contrary to American interests, expressed support for the republic over a looming Monarchy threat:

> If the Monarchy is to fulfill the conditions mentioned above, there is no inconvenience in having a king presiding over the peninsular confederation. Would there be a king of Spanish tradition willing to do so? Given the antecedents, we know of, we sincerely believe not. Without disregarding the advantages that a democratic monarchy assures in a certain order; we sincerely prefer a republic that is also democratic.[191]

The concept of a confederation of peoples aligns with the Basque stance on the European federation. However, Landaburu introduced an intriguing new idea in his book. Acknowledging the Cold War's division into blocks, he defended the European Federation as a mediator that would mitigate the clash between the two blocks. This, he argued, would endow Europe with a distinct identity, preventing it from becoming either a Slavic or an American colony: "Europe has an independent personality and must have enough strength to be the moderating element that the world needs today, and will need perhaps for centuries to come, to avoid the clash between these two blocks that will never reach true coexistence if the weight of the European spirit and the strength of an organized Europe are lacking in the world."[192]

The European federation suited the needs of Basque nationalism, as Landaburu advocated for a federation of peoples where the State-Nation took precedence over the Nation-State. In his vision, when the sovereignty of a people must be transferred to a supranational body, a federation like the European one can ensure the democratic protection of small nations. In his redefined conception of the Basque nation and its relationship with the Federation, Landaburu embraced Schelling's idea of the organic nation—a living being. This perspective brought Basque nationalism closer to Catalan nationalism, as defended by Prat de la Riba in the early 20th century.[193] Acknowledging the nature of Catalan nationalism, Landaburu believed that the Basques and the Catalans, as the only European peoples within Spain, exhibited a clear tendency towards the European continent.[194]

A democratic Europe would serve as a safeguard for small nations like the Basque, and not just for them but also for Spain as a whole. Landaburu envisioned the democratization of Spain taking place under the protective umbrella of the European federation, which would also act as a check against State abuses: "Federalism is the democratic protection of the nation in the World and it is of federalist thesis that federalism is integral, that there is not one for outside and another for inside, as many current States practice, there is not an internal and an external federalism, but only one federalism. Federalism has no other enemy than the State-nation, which is the opposite of the nation-State."[195]

The Franco Regime appeared to be in a state of crisis, and even though Franco's health was not as dire as initially believed—"Franco has a prostatic condition but is not acute," as determined by a memorandum[196] on November 8, 1955—the Monarchic option, as a means to renew or somehow alter the regime, presented itself as a viable and secure alternative.

The imagining/making up of the nation from the exile. Differences between Telesforo Monzón and Manuel Irujo, with the spirit of Galindez still hovering about.

The Basque World Congress in Paris commenced on September 24, 1956, with Lehendakari Aguirre delivering a five-hour speech at the Hotel Palais d'Orsay.

Despite concerted efforts,[197] the completion of the White Book remained elusive, and Congress participants were provided only a partial edition, accompanied by President Aguirre's commitment to its eventual completion.

In his comprehensive address, Aguirre took a retrospective look at the 20 years of Basque Government, detailing the wartime endeavors during the Spanish Civil War, including the establishment of the Basque army, logistical challenges in procuring food, harbor management, and aid to refugees. The portion dedicated to exile featured prominently, with the President recounting his own flight and expressing gratitude for the Basque National Council created by Manuel Irujo in his absence. Their legitimacy as government leaders during a period without territory allowed them to establish the Consultative Council and solicit input from various organizations and political parties.

While a significant part of Aguirre's speech chronicled the work of the Basque Government, he also voiced complaints about international aid. He recalled the Basque government's involvement in European politics, highlighting the creation of the Nouvelles Équipes Internationales and the Spanish Federal Council. However, he lamented the lack of support received in combating the Franco Regime. Aguirre expressed dissatisfaction with international bodies, including UNESCO and the UN, characterizing the relationship with them as a failure.

Noteworthy was Aguirre's response to growing rumors about negotiations between the Franco regime and the Monarchy. In contrast to past political maneuvering with Monarchists, Aguirre's stance in 1956 was unequivocal: "Ah, if only monarchists had intelligence. If I were a monarchist, I would say to Don Juan: 'Sir, the people who surround you neither know the People, nor understand it, nor love you.' And if I were a monarchist, I would also say to him: 'Sir, there are peoples with their own will... Why do you not make pacts? Why do you not talk to these peoples? Is the monarchy not capable of understanding this?' Not so far."[198]

The attendance at the Basque World Congress in Paris was robust, boasting 366 congressmen. Among them, 45 hailed from within the Basque Country, 217 were individuals, 58 were affiliated with parties and associations, and 5 were observers without voting rights, as per the internal bylaws.

The Basque government extended invitations to a diverse array of participants, including political parties like ANV, IR, UR, PSOE; trade unions such as ELA-STV, UGT, CNT; organizations like Junta de Resistencia, Consejo Consultivo, Organización de Mendigoxales, and others. Congressmen, ministers or former ministers of the Basque Government, mayors or former mayors, and Basque delegates were also invited. All Basque political parties received invitations, except for the Communist party, as the exclusion of totalitarians, both communists and fascists, had been agreed upon by the Basque Government. "It is convenient, to this effect, to take into account to which individuals the cards are delivered, deliveries that have no other limit but the exclusion of totalitarians, whether communists or fascists. This was agreed upon, at the time, by the Basque Government, and this provision is maintained to this day."[199]

Invitations, accompanied by questionnaires, were dispatched to over 2000 individuals across 20 different countries, including Venezuela, Mexico, Argentina, Chile, Uruguay, USA, Cuba, Colombia, Peru, Ecuador, Philippines, Australia,

France, Italy, Belgium, Switzerland, Portugal, Ireland, England, and Germany. Additionally, 500 invitations and questionnaires were distributed to Basques within Spain.[200]

Recipients were encouraged to send back communications addressing or discussing the questions outlined in the questionnaire. Of the 144 communications received in Paris, 66 focused on the social-economic section, 24 on the political section, and 44 on the cultural section.[201]

The political communications assumed particular significance in the context of the development of Basque nationalism, as emphasized by Joseba Rezola during the opening of the political section. He declared, "I believe that today's meeting is of exceptional importance because in my opinion the Political Section is the key to the other two sections. If the political question is not solved, there is no solution to the economic and social problem, nor to the cultural problem, and there is no solution to the economic and social problem."[202]

The communications had undergone prior scrutiny by the Congress commission in the months leading up to the event, resulting in an agreed-upon and elaborated document. Manuel Irujo, serving not only as a member but also as the President of the political section, played a pivotal role. His archive illuminates the evolution of proposals, debates, the final agreed document presented at the Congress, and the necessary amendments.

Beyond the congressional debates, the crux of my research lies in the political draft prepared by Irujo and circulated to Basque government [203]members for modification by the end of 1955. This documentation, along with the subsequent amendments and debates, provides insights into the interests, convergences, and divergences within Basque nationalism.[204]

The political paper draft, spanning 36 pages, delves into the issues faced by the Basque Government. Irujo, displaying his expertise as a lawyer and historian, navigates the historical-legal landscape, recognizing the document's legal nature while emphasizing its necessity. Despite its historical and legal foundation, Irujo acknowledges the challenge of convincing those whose consciences may not be open to history, reinforcing the document's real-world implications.[205]

While intended as recommendations for the Congress,[206] Irujo's meticulous work, along with contributions from government members and political parties, underscores the event's significance and the imperative of reaching a consensus.

The Political Paper places the Basque Statute of Autonomy and the Basque government at its core. Three main aspects emerge: the Basque code of laws, questions of legitimacy, and the unity of the Basques. These themes, extensively developed in the received questionnaires and communications, were central to the debates during the Congress itself.

The draft of the political paper strongly defends the Basque Code of Laws as the bedrock of Basque sovereignty, serving as the foundation for both the Basque Government and the Basque Statute of Autonomy. It underscores the

Foral tradition of freedom, acknowledging the instrument's role in providing a correct and honorable compromise, even if partial. This aspect is presented as independent of the regime under which the Code was granted, reflecting a commitment to the continuity of the Foral spirit and the collective yearning for the reintegration of those freedoms. The Statute is portrayed as a manifestation of Basque organic unity—a sentiment unanimously embraced by the government on October 25, 1936.

Concerning the legitimacy of the Basque Statute of Autonomy, Irujo initially characterizes it as "a law granted by the legitimate powers of the Spanish Republic (..)," but he underscores that its legitimacy is inherently tied to its origin—a characteristic that would endure even if the institutions granting it legal life were to cease to exist. "If it were the case that the institutions within which it was born with legitimate existence were definitively cancelled, such a resolution would not affect the subsistence of the Statute and the Basque Government as far as this first aspect was concerned."[207]

While recalling the Tradición foral (Foral Tradition, so the old Basque Code of Laws), especially citing the 1839 law abolishing the Basque Code of Laws, Irujo is approaching primordialism nationalism but swiftly returns to the Spanish Republican legal system, linking the Basque Statute to Republican legality. "It is the legitimacy—legality—of its origin, a fact which, in itself, gives it a character that will not disappear even if the institutions within which it was born into legal life cease to exist."

Despite this presentation, the Statute's perceived centrality becomes a source of contention. Joseba Rezola expresses dissatisfaction with the emphasis placed on the Statute, viewing it as overly fundamental. "Too much importance is given to the Statute, presenting it as fundamental for us. (...) I think it would be more appropriate that the disadvantages are presented on the same level as the advantages, so that we can see the sacrifices that nationalists and advocates of a broad freedom have had to make in the interest of union and peace."[208]

He suggests presenting both advantages and disadvantages to provide a more balanced perspective, highlighting the sacrifices made by nationalists in the interest of union and peace. This dissent reflects the divergence of viewpoints within Basque nationalism, with some arguing that the Statute's vindication is overly entwined with Spanish institutions and does not adequately represent a negotiation of equals between the Basque and Spanish governments. "(...) I was extremely disappointed to see that there is not a word about Resistance, nor Resistance Board, nor what it has done, nor what it has to do, nor anything else."[209]

The distinctions between the exile and the inland were clearly observable. The draft failed to acknowledge the resistance efforts and actions carried out by Basque nationalists within Spain, omitting any mention or specification of those who organized the 1947, 1951, or 1956 strikes. Additionally, the draft overlooked the intricacies of relations with the Spanish government in exile, resulting in divergent opinions on Basque legitimacy and sovereignty compared to those held by the resistance within Spain.

A pivotal aspect covered in the draft was the issue of Basque unity, extensively deliberated both before and during the Congress. Irujo, in the section titled "Nuestra actitud ante el futuro" (Our attitude towards the future) (pages 26-34 of the draft), emphasized the imperative nature of Basque unity for political success and resistance against Francoism. He contended that Basque unity had its roots in the challenging circumstances of the Civil War, flourished in exile, and shone during the strikes against Francoism. This unity was deemed essential for achieving national goals and was seen as a manifestation of mature national responsibility in alignment with the Basque government.

Another perspective on unity emerged—unity with Spanish democratic political forces. While President Aguirre and Manuel Irujo fervently advocated for agreements with Spanish republican forces and unity in the Republican resistance in exile, not all Basque nationalists shared this view. Disagreements over these alliances, present in the past, resurfaced during the Basque World Congress, illustrating internal divisions within Basque nationalism.[210]

Irujo's emphasis on unity with the democratic resistance in Spain led to the concept of national reconciliation, a theme that gained prominence in subsequent years. The idea of national reconciliation stemmed from the need to combat Franco and his regime, which aimed to divide the democrats. Despite underlining the importance of unity with Spanish democrats, Irujo insisted that the foremost condition for success was the national vindication of the Basques. He asserted that the continuity of the Basque government was crucial for maintaining unity, cautioning against the influence of particular interests that could jeopardize the hard-won unity: "How could we, then, consent that, invoking the union of Spanish democrats, the union that the Basques have been maintaining without interruption, be destroyed?"[211]

The draft's conclusion comprised 11 enumerated points, subject to multiple revisions, deletions, and reordering in response to input from Rezola, Gonzalo Nárdiz, and Lehendakari Aguirre. Irujo, in collaboration with the members of the Basque government, particularly Gonzalo Nárdiz, engaged in several rounds of modification and reorientation following discussions on the amendments and clarification of ideas. However, due to the controversy surrounding the document, it was ultimately excluded from the negotiation meetings.[212]

On August 28, 1956, the Political Commission of the Basque World Congress convened at the Basque Delegation in Bayonne to review received communications and formulate a political paper for presentation at the Congress alongside papers from political parties. Attendees included members from various political parties within the Basque government—Republicans, Socialists, ANV and PNV members, and the President of the political section, Manuel Irujo. Over two days, participants deliberated on received communications and reached an agreement on the document to be presented and defended at the Congress. Irujo's archives reveal additional amendments, particularly addressing Rezola's considerations on resistance and the socialists' references to the "Spanish people."[213]

Despite being a diligent Basque nationalist, Irujo expressed frustration over the amendments and the ultimate rejection of the draft. In a letter to Lehendakari Aguirre immediately after the Bayonne meeting, he shed light on the tense political atmosphere within the Basque government. Irujo explained the withdrawal of their paper, emphasizing the socialists' erroneous stance and the calculated aggression displayed by some members. He acknowledged a crisis within the Basque government, prioritizing its needs and political strategy over the goals of Basque nationalism. Unity emerged as a primary objective, emphasizing the importance of projecting a united front, even if it did not entirely reflect the internal reality.[214]

On September 25, Manuel Irujo's 65th birthday, a summary of received communications and the complete texts of communications from the four members of the political parties within the Basque government were publicly presented during the regular session of the political section.

In the context of my research focus on the demands of Basque nationalists and the transformative features within Basque nationalism, one recurring theme stands out, shaping the movement's trajectory: language.

While the advocacy for the Basque language had been inherent in Basque nationalism from its inception, a notable evolution occurred as the importance of the language surpassed other traditional elements, such as ethnic origin, marking a significant facet in the evolution of Basque nationalism.

Federico Krutwig, a young philologist residing in Germany, conveyed a radical perspective on the pivotal role of the Basque language in the creation of the Basque nationality. His communication asserted, "Without Basque language, there can be no Basque Country. Violence is necessary to make the Basque national fact come true."[215] Although Krutwig emphasized a preference for non-violence, he argued that historical instances had shown the need for force to garner attention. Irujo, known for advocating peace, commented on Krutwig's stance, underscoring the importance of promoting non-destructive means.

What distinguishes Krutwig's contribution[216] is the direct correlation he drew between the existence of the Basque nation and the Basque language. Notably, his communication, addressed to the political section rather than the cultural one, elevated the Basque language beyond its cultural significance. Krutwig's assertion that "Without Basque language, there are no Basques. Basque language is more important than the rh factor of the blood groups"[217] underscored the language as a foundational element of the nation, surpassing considerations of ethnic origin.

Given the challenges faced by the Basque community, dispersed in exile and under the oppressive regime eroding Basque culture,[218] language evolved to represent the geographical boundaries of the nation, supplanting ethnic origin, particularly in the government in exile. Despite the cultural section's predominant focus on defending the Basque language from Spanish nationalism, its inclusion as a distinct feature within Basque nationalism underscores its significance. The protection of the language was recognized as part of the responsibilities of the Basque government, signifying a pivotal shift in the movement's priorities.

The geographical aspect of the nation is another focal point explored in the communications, emphasizing the inclusion of Navarre within the envisioned Basque community. Establishing the geographical boundaries of the nation follows the initial recognition by the people, and the defense of Laurak bat, zazpiak bat, or even zortziak bat (the incorporation of the exile as part of the Basque country) would be subsequently developed and championed by Basque nationalism.

Federico Krutwig and Izquierda Republicana contended that the limits of the "historical Navarre" were integral to the Basque country, not through forced annexations, but rather through a confederation model similar to Switzerland. The defense of Navarre's inclusion in the Basque country is also echoed in communications from Mexico by Mr. Villanueva and Mr. Esnaola, who invoked the Basque Statute of Autonomy to advocate for Navarre's incorporation, while suggesting the possibility of it forming part of a confederation.[219]

In a communication presented by ANV, which echoed the political draft written by Irujo and ultimately rejected, the legitimacy of the Basque government was defended. This communication reproduced the notion of genocide against the Basque people, as expressed in the conclusions, and emphasized the defense of Basque unity: "United on the fronts as in the rearguard, in prisons as in exile, and always in intimate communication with the Government, that the Basque collectivity can present itself before all and sundry, as a national entity of mature responsibility and firmness of will, from whose consideration no one can escape."[220]

Concerning the PNV, their communication served as an endorsement of the 1949 declaration, which, as previously discussed, entailed a robust defense of both Basque unity and collaboration with Spanish Republican institutions. It also included an anti-communist declaration and outlined the principles of Christian-Democracy, reaffirming the party's political strategy of European federation.[221]

Following the comprehensive presentation of communications from various Basque parties, Mr. Julio Jáuregui, who had served as the Basque delegate in Mexico from 1942 to 1946, proceeded to articulate the meticulously considered political conclusions that garnered approval at the Basque World Congress.

Beginning with a profound acknowledgment, the Congress solemnly reiterated the gratitude of the Basque People towards the nations and governments that, for a span of two decades, had graciously welcomed and facilitated the settlement of Basque refugees. Special recognition was extended to the nations that played crucial roles in this humanitarian endeavor, including France, Belgium, Great Britain, Venezuela, Mexico, Argentina, Chile, and Uruguay. The Congress expressed its hopeful anticipation that a grand tribute would soon be offered under the symbolic Tree of Gernika, a profound representation of Basque freedoms.

Venturing into a broader international perspective, the Congress, in alignment with the enduring traditions of peace, justice, and freedom, issued a compelling appeal in favor of peace—a universal ideal for all peoples. The Congress delineated the pillars that would fortify the foundations of lasting peace, emphasizing the imperative recognition of the right of all peoples to self-governance. Furthermore, it underscored the significance of upholding fundamental human rights and dignity by all states, the unwavering adherence to international conventions and treaties, the harmonious integration of nations and states into overarching bodies like Europe or American confederations, the commitment to enhancing global working conditions, and the provision of substantial, disinterested aid to nations experiencing cultural and economic insufficiencies. In the context of the pressing challenges posed by the Franco-Falangist totalitarian dictatorship, the Congress issued an urgent appeal to the global Basque community, recognizing the grave dangers that threatened the very existence of the ancient human group of Euzkadi under this regime. The call was resounding, seeking vigorous action and support to empower the Basque people to reclaim their freedom and secure their distinct way of life. The Congress explicitly declared its recognition of the government led by Mr. Aguirre as the legitimate authority of the Basque People. It proclaimed this government as the apt instrument to continue directing endeavors aimed at liberating the Country. The Statute of Autonomy was elevated as a symbol of Basque unity, struggle, and inevitable vindication, while the Pact of Bayonne was acknowledged as a safeguard for the agreed Basque union and cordial solidarity, crucial in the collective effort to reestablish freedom and democracy on solid foundations. Expressing solidarity with the burgeoning movements of dissent against the Franco regime within Spain, the Congress recommended robust support and collaboration with the Governments of the Republic and Catalonia, democratic parties, and discerning sectors within the country. This collaborative approach aimed to accelerate the downfall of the Franco regime and pave the way for the establishment of a democratic order, allowing the peoples of Spain to freely express their political will under the assurance of due guarantees. In the spirit of fostering a constructive and reconciliatory atmosphere, the Congress advocated restraint against exacerbating passions that could potentially tarnish the bonds of friendship among democratic Basques. Emphasizing a commitment to total and absolute reconciliation, the Congress underscored the paramount importance of this endeavor. Turning attention to the territorial considerations, the Congress addressed the matter of Navarre, suggesting that should it decide to join the autonomous Basque Country, adherence to the stipulations in the additional provision of the plebiscite Statute would be the appropriate course of action. Concluding on a historical note, the Congress affirmed that the proposed autonomous regime did not imply the extinguishment of the historical rights of the Country. Instead, it recognized that the full realization of these rights, when circumstances allowed, rested in the complete restoration of its Foral Regime[222]—a nuanced stance that conveyed the depth of the Congress's commitment to the enduring historical identity and rights of the Basque people.

The conclusions of the Congress underscored the imperative recognition of both the resistance within Spain and the plight of the exile, advocating for international involvement to ensure that the Basque cause remains in global consciousness. A key objective achieved by the Congress was the reaffirmation of Basque unity and the legitimacy of the Basque Government and President. This endorsement was rooted in the defense of the Basque Statute of Autonomy, while leaving room for consideration of the restoration of the old Basque code of laws and acknowledging the right of self-determination for peoples.

While the theme of national reconciliation was explicitly addressed, it included a notable exclusion of the communists, aligning them with totalitarian ideologies. This decision harked back to the expulsion of the PCE from the Basque government in 1948, emphasizing a particular stance on political affiliations within the Basque nationalist framework.

Following the reading of the conclusions, a debate ensued with active participation from attendees. Some proposed amendments found acceptance, such as the suggestion to expand the Consultative Council for greater engagement between the Basque Government and the people. Additionally, there was explicit recognition of the role played by the Basque resistance in organizing the strikes of 1947, 1951, and 1956—both proposals championed by Joseba Rezola. However, the most controversial and impassioned moment in the debate unfolded during the intervention of Telesforo Monzón.

Telesforo Monzón, who had resigned from the Basque Government in 1951, voiced his long-standing concerns during the debate. His resignation, largely unnoticed, stemmed from his belief that Basque nationalism had become too entwined with Spanish institutions. Monzón expressed his discontent, asserting that the life and resolution of the Basque problem should not be indefinitely tethered to a specific case or a particular solution within the broader Spanish political context, as exemplified by what he referred to as the "Republic of the Institutions."[223]

In his impassioned address, Monzón directed attention to the weariness of the Basque people, particularly the youth, who were growing increasingly impatient for a resolution to the challenges posed by the Franco regime—a solution that, in Monzón's view, the Basque Government seemed incapable of providing. By highlighting this demand, Monzón brought to light the difficulties faced by Basque nationalism in resonating with the emerging generation, both within Spain and in exile. A new wave of individuals was coming of age, and traditional political approaches employed by the Basque government appeared insufficient to meet their aspirations.

Monzón found the defense of Spanish institutions, a key conclusion of the political section, unacceptable. He saw it as a roadblock in solving the Basque problem, expressing skepticism about the viability of persisting with a strategy that lacked the international strength to impose change through diplomatic channels. Monzón questioned whether, after two decades of pursuing new initiatives and witnessing the emergence of youth with novel ideas, it was wise to persist with an approach that seemed stagnant, especially given the dynamic shifts in the political landscape.[224]

His speech triggered a vigorous response from Mr. Irujo, who staunchly defended the conclusions, asserting that they were grounded in the 24 communications received from Basque communities worldwide. In response, Irujo accused Monzón of engaging in demagoguery.

Despite the contentious exchange between Monzón and Irujo, it revealed a deeper issue: a perceived stagnation in the policies pursued by the Basque government and traditional Basque nationalism in achieving the freedom of the Basque people. This sentiment was further reinforced by the submission of a re-edition of the 1949 declaration by the PNV for the Basque World Congress. Communications from figures like Federico Krutwig and the debate led by Telesforo Monzón exemplify the brewing discontent within traditional Basque nationalism.

Drawing inspiration from examples such as Cyprus, Morocco, or Tunis, Monzón contended that there were alternative paths to national freedom beyond the conventional channels followed by Basque nationalism. These alternatives, as he highlighted, diverged from the reliance on international institutions that, in Monzón's perception, were overlooking the strength of Spanish Republican legitimacy.

International repercussions with the spirit of Jesús de Galíndez still hovering around.

If President Aguirre aimed to utilize the Basque World Congress as a platform for promoting the Basque cause,[225] the tragic disappearance of Jesús Galíndez played a significant role in that narrative. Serving as the Basque delegate in New York from 1949 to 1956, Galíndez mysteriously vanished on March 12, 1956, after teaching a class at Columbia University. Abducted upon returning to his apartment at 30 Fifth Avenue, he was transported to Santo Domingo in the Dominican Republic, where he underwent torture at the hands of dictator Leónidas Trujillo before being killed and thrown into the sea.[226]

Extensively investigated, the Galíndez case profoundly impacted[227] the Basque community in America and garnered widespread media attention from publications such as *The New York Times, Diario de Nueva York, New York Post, Herald Tribune, Ibérica, España Libre, Life, Time,* and *The Daily Spectator* at New York, as reported by Manuel Irujo in Alderdi in August 1956.[228] Five months after Galíndez's disappearance, the case remained unsolved. Despite Galíndez's collaboration with American intelligence services (OSS, CIA, and FBI), the matter only gained significant attention in December 1956 when Gerald L. Murphy, the pilot allegedly involved in flying Galíndez to the Dominican Republic, was murdered by Trujillo's men.[229]

Galíndez's abduction occurred shortly after submitting his Ph.D. dissertation on Trujillo's regime, titled "Trujillo's Dominican Republic," a comprehensive study spanning 25 years of the regime. The dissertation denounced Trujillo's atrocities and highlighted the absence of freedom and democratic features in the regime. While many theories converge on Galíndez's criticism of Trujillo as the motive for his murder, it's crucial to note that his academic inquiry wasn't his initial engagement with the Dominican Republic. Galíndez had previously resided on the island from 1941 to 1946, working for the Department of Labour and Economy as well as the Secretariat of Foreign Affairs, developing an early interest in the country's politics. Upon returning to New York, Galíndez maintained connections with members of the Dominican community, expressing concerns to Irujo in November 1952 about potential threats: "Around here we are in the middle of mysteries. A month ago, a friend of mine, a Dominican anti-Trujullist, was assassinated...". Aware of the dangers, Galíndez and others who had spoken against the regime found themselves constantly vigilant. And, he added, he was already aware that he was in danger: "All of us who have allowed ourselves to say something to the Benecifato[230] have to walk around making sure that no one is following us..."[231]

Galíndez, akin to Irujo, harbored a fervent passion for writing and demonstrated exceptional diligence by engaging in various literary pursuits, including crafting books such as "Historia de la civilización hispanoamericana, política y cultural," novels, and articles. Despite his commitments to organizing floral games, fulfilling responsibilities at the Basque delegation, and teaching at Columbia University, Galíndez maintained a prolific output. Irujo acknowledged Galíndez's literary accomplishments, expressing admiration in a letter from February 1955 and encouraging him to contribute to the Basque World Congress.[232]

The correspondence between Irujo and Galíndez reveals a relationship that evolved from considerate and professional to increasingly personal. While their extensive letters delved into political discussions, Galíndez also shared his moods, personal fears, and hopes with Irujo. The letters not only shed light on the personal aspects of their bond but also feature engaging political debates, providing valuable insights into the developmental nuances of Basque nationalism.

Galíndez, a close associate of Lehendakari Aguirre, had early reservations about placing trust in the American administration and international institutions. Having served in the American secret services and engaged with the UN and UNESCO to advocate for Basque interests,[233] he possessed a unique perspective. By 1955, Galíndez, an expert in international politics, embraced a Christian Democratic stance and adopted a growing anti-communist outlook, though he camouflaged these convictions under a democratic veneer.[234] In a world increasingly divided into two ideological blocs, Galíndez considered Christian

Democracy the viable option for Basque nationalists. Moreover, he believed that democracy had secured national recognition for the Basque Country, contrasting starkly with the potential erasure under a totalitarian regime.

Galíndez championed the right to self-determination for Puerto Ricans and praised their new Constitution (1952), drawing parallels with the Basque Statute of Autonomy. He noted similarities, emphasizing the division of legislative and administrative responsibilities between the American State and the island Congress and Government, akin to the dynamic between the central government and the autonomous governments[235] of the Basque Country and Catalonia during the Second Spanish Republic.

In this article, Galíndez asserts that, in the 1950s, the Commonwealth of Puerto Rico emerged as the most viable option concerning independence. He contends that traditional notions of sovereignty and independence were becoming obsolete in the mid-20th century, giving way to the rise of continental federations. Galíndez's perspective aligns with Irujo's article, "El Estatuto de Autonomía de Túnez,"[236] featured in the same Alderdi issue, emphasizing the significance of Statutes of Autonomy as a foundation for complete self-determination—a theme that would later be further explored in the Basque World Congress.

Amid the post-World War II landscape, characterized by shifting borders and the destructive force of extreme nationalism, a political strategy for national vindication that avoided a political fracture of established borders appeared more plausible. The concept of a continental federation, as developed by Basque nationalism through support for the European Federal Movement, resonated with Galíndez's ideas. Irujo, leveraging Galíndez's posthumous contribution, urged the promotion of a Basque International Organization, referencing an article in Alderdi number 107 titled "We need a Basque International Organization." Irujo suggested proposing to the FEVA (Argentinian Federation) to subscribe to a communication to the Basque World Congress, aligning with Galíndez's initiative.[237]

The referenced article outlined a proposal for an "International Federation" of Basque centers, modeled after the Argentinian Federation (FEVA) but embracing the broader spirit of the LIAB.[238] The proposal was intriguing for two distinct reasons: it advocated for Basque unity within a Federation and proposed the establishment of a non-governmental organization (NGO) representative of the Basque people at the United Nations—a strategy reminiscent of the Jewish people's successful initiative in 1947. Galíndez, well-versed in the functioning of the United Nations, sought recognition for the Basque people as a distinct entity and cause, distinct from being a sovereign state, particularly in the aftermath of Spain's admission to the international organization.

In Jesús Galíndez's strategic vision, he advocated for the defense of the Basque national cause through the establishment of an international organization working in parallel with the Basque Government, drawing insightful parallels with successful examples from other nations. His proposed model resembled a permanent World Basque Congress, inspired by the organizational prowess of the Jewish community, and a Federation of Basque Societies characterized by its international reach, mirroring the Irish approach to collective representation. The successful trajectory of Israel, established in 1948, emerged as a compelling model for national movements[239] navigating the complexities of statelessness, significantly influencing the trajectory of Basque nationalism during its exile and eventual return to the Basque country.

Galíndez's conceptualization of a "continental Federation" found a harmonious echo in the political strategy of the Partido Nacionalista Vasco (PNV), particularly gaining traction post the World Basque Congress. This strategic alignment showcased the PNV's inclination towards the principles of European Federalism, mirroring Galíndez's visionary approach to international collaboration and representation.

The influence of Ireland on Basque nationalism, serving as another source of inspiration, gained particular prominence in radical factions such as Jagi-Jagi, Comunión Nacionalista Vasca, and ETA.[240] Galíndez's ideas, while unable to be fully realized or discussed with his colleagues, continued to resonate within the Congress. His mysterious disappearance, a pivotal incident, compelled the Congress to send a petition to the American government, urging a comprehensive investigation into the circumstances surrounding Galíndez's tragic vanishing. Despite potential uncertainties in the trust placed in the "American Friend,"[241] the Basque Government persisted in its unwavering commitment[242] to unravel the truth about Galíndez's disappearance. As of June, however, his absence cast a somber and seemingly irreversible shadow over these efforts.

The Basque Government had done everything to find out what had happened to its delegate: "Beitia is doing everything he can",[243] informed Hickman to Irujo on April 11, 1956, but in June his disappearance seemed all but permanent and fatal.

In June, Columbia University formally acknowledged Jesús Galíndez's absence during the Doctoral ceremony, marking a poignant moment in the lingering mystery surrounding his disappearance.[244] By August, Manuel Irujo, in an extensive article in Alderdi, expressed a sense of resignation, acknowledging the grim reality that hopes for Galíndez's reappearance had waned. *The New York Times* and other media outlets covered the case, criticizing the Federal Bureau of Investigation (FBI) for perceived inaction and generating widespread hemispheric concern and indignation, unprecedented for a case of its kind.[245] The press interest heightened when a note, written by Galíndez in 1952 and addressed to the police, was discovered in his apartment, explicitly pointing to the Dominican Republic in the event of any harm befalling him.

Despite the earnest appeals from the Basque Government and even the Spanish Republican Government, urging the American authorities to investigate Galíndez's disappearance, responses from the U.S. government were notably vague. The National Archives and Records Administration (NARA) contains a folder named "Galíndez" within the Department of State's[246] collection, featuring newspaper clippings and correspondence related to Galíndez. This archival material reflects both the case's significance for the American administration and the lack of a proactive stance toward resolution.[247]

A revealing letter from Jacob D. Beam, Deputy Assistant Secretary of State for European Affairs, and Fisher Howe, Director of the Executive Secretariat, underscored the U.S. administration's position. Despite acknowledging the Basque World Congress's petition on Galíndez's disappearance, the response suggested avoiding any reply to the communication "in order to avoid embarrassment in our relations with Spain." This stance highlighted the geopolitical complexities surrounding the Spanish conflict, with Galíndez becoming an unfortunate casualty. Even without solicitation, the Spanish regime asserted its disinterest in the matter. Ángel Sagaz Zubelzu, the First Secretary of the Spanish Embassy, communicated to the American administration in May 1957 that despite Galíndez's Spanish nationality, the embassy had no interest in the widely discussed case of his disappearance.[248]

The unresolved mystery surrounding Jesús Galíndez's[249] disappearance became a focal point, drawing attention to the Basque World Congress even before its convening. The case captured the interest of both Americans and Dominicans,[250] resulting in international tabloids covering the Congress. *The New York Herald*, as highlighted by the Euzkadi Press Office (OPE), noted Aguirre's enduring presidency since 1936.

The OPE and Alderdi played a pivotal role in disseminating information about the Congress, publishing its conclusions along with articles by prominent figures like Irujo, Landáburu, and Leizaola. Reflections from Basque nationalists, both in exile and within the Basque Country,[251] added depth to the coverage. The overall sentiment toward the Basque World Congress was positive, with Basque nationalists perceiving it as a reinforcement of the Basque Government, a demonstration of unity against dictatorship in favor of democracy, and a staunch defense of Basque cultural distinctiveness, particularly the Basque language.[252]

For the Basque Government, the Congress provided the much-needed legitimacy after two decades in exile, establishing this credibility without the conventional power of democratic elections. Lehendakari Aguirre saw his leadership strengthened, and the Congress contributed to the realization of his personal vision for Basque unity. The event marked a significant milestone, shaping the narrative and objectives of Basque nationalism in its ongoing struggle against the Franco regime.

Despite the PNV missing the opportunity to update its 1949 declaration during the Basque World Congress, the Christian Basque nationalists assigned Manuel Irujo and Xabier de Landáburu the task of advocating for a renewal of Basque nationalism in Europe and strengthening the campaign internally. Lehendakari Aguirre, in his letters to Manuel Irujo, expressed optimism for the upcoming year of 1957 and outlined strategies not only for the Basque government but also for the broader nationalist movement. Aguirre highlighted a major campaign to prevent Europe from resembling just another version of the UN.

In his messages, Aguirre emphasized the need for a well-received publication of the Congress's proceedings, anticipating its distribution among the Basque people, particularly in Euzkadi. Aguirre also mentioned plans to inundate Navarre with a reduced-format book authored by Xabier, prepared by Ricardo de Leizaola. This distribution strategy aimed to reach various sectors, including apothecaries, secretaries, priests, and influential figures, ensuring widespread access to the content.[253]

The political decisions made since October 1956 received endorsement from the Basque World Congress. Aguirre incorporated references to the Congress in his 1956 Gabon message, and throughout 1957, his speeches and interventions continually recalled the Paris Congress, the anniversary of the Basque government, and the unfortunate disappearance of Jesús Galíndez. Amidst these reflections, Aguirre injected a new sense of activism and hope, focusing on the ongoing struggle within the Basque Country and in the broader European context.[254]

Manuel Irujo in Munich. The IV Conference of the European Movement. The "*Contubernio de Munich*". Recovering from the loss. From Aguirre to Leizaola

"All Basques mourn the loss of our President. I, too, have lost a friend, someone with whom I navigated the ultimate test of Friendship, wherein our views may align or diverge. We conformed or engaged in spirited arguments, all the while maintaining our friendship,"[255] wrote Manuel Irujo in an article for Alderdi following the passing of the inaugural Lehendakari, José Antonio Aguirre, on March 22, 1960.

The sudden demise of Lehendakari Aguirre not only deeply affected Basque nationalists due to his symbolic significance but also posed a challenge for the Basque government and Spanish politics at large. Aguirre's unparalleled charisma and global respect for his leadership were evident. He had the ability to forge connections with nearly everyone he encountered, and his diplomacy and unwavering determination were well-known traits.

The funeral service took place at the Basque Government's headquarters in Paris on March 25, following a private viewing of Aguirre's body with close friends and family at his home. The manner in which a person receives their final respects often reflects their importance in life, and in Aguirre's case, he received a farewell befitting his role as the Head of State.

Throughout the night, members of the Basque, Spanish, and Catalan governments took turns standing vigil, with numerous wreaths arriving from Basque delegations, unions (CNT, UGT, ELA-STVA), Spanish political parties (PSE, Movimiento Republicano Popular), Nouvelles Equipes Internationales (French section), Basque language promoters (Euskal Etxea Paris, Eskualzaleen Biltzarra

Paris, Euskalduna Paris), and numerous Basque nationalists' families (Hickman, Maruri, Jauregibeitia, Garate, Arriola, etc.).

Aguirre's funeral underscored the spirit of unity he championed among members of the Spanish Democratic resistance. Attendees included Mr. Gordón Ordás (from the Spanish Republican Government-in-exile), Republican Ministers like Mr. Just, Mr. Valera, or General Herrera; Mr. Joan Sauret (Catalan Parliamentary, member of ERC), Mr. Josep Tarradellas (President of the Catalan Government-in-exile), along with former Spanish Republican MPs and Ministers.

The extensive international diplomacy Aguirre pursued during his 24-year presidency was evident in the diverse international representatives paying respects. The list of funeral attendees highlighted Aguirre's policies and strategies, especially those during his time in exile: Mr. François Mauriac (LIAB's Honorary President), Ernest Pezet (LIAB), M. George Bidault, Maurice Schumann, Edouard Depreux, Léi Hamon, M.Robert Buron (French Minister of Public Affairs), M. Joseph Dumas, Alain Poher (President of the Christian-Democratic group at the European Council), Alfred Coste-Floret (Secretary-General of the NEI), Ambassador Zerega Fombona (Permanent Delegate of Venezuela at UNESCO), Gaston Tesier (Honorary President of CISC), etc.

In addition to this, the Basque government received numerous expressions of sympathy and condolences from the international community, conveyed through condolence notes from prominent figures. These included American Senator Charles O. Porter, Vice-President of the French Council of State Mr. René Cassin, director of the Musée d'Art Moderne in Paris Mr. Jean Cassou, Nobel Literature Prize winner François Mauriac (who wrote a condolence note in the journal L'Express), and writer Pierre Dumas, who sent a piece to Euzko Deya.

The news of the death garnered media coverage, with Basque nationalists' publications dedicating extensive articles and editorials in newspapers such as Herria, Tierra Vasca, and Euzko Deya. International media outlets like *Peuple* (Brussels), *France Observateur, El Nacional* (Caracas), *La Prensa* (Buenos Aires), *El Tiempo* (Bogotá), *Momento* (Caracas), *L'Avenir* (Bretagne), *Le Monde* (France), *The New York Times*, and the *BBC* also reported on the event. Spanish Republican media covered the news in *El socialista español, El Boletín de Acción Socialista, Política*, or *Tribuna*.[256]

The official funeral service took place on March 26 at the church of Saint Pierre du Gros Caillou in Paris, presided over by Basque canon Alberto Onaindia and the priest Larre, who read the epistle and the Gospel in the Basque language. The service emphasized Basque nationalist symbols, featuring a Basque choir and the singing of the Basque Euzko Gudariak (an unofficial Basque government anthem originally used by the Basque army during the Civil War) and the Euzko Abendaren ereserkia (the official anthem of the Basque government), among other Basque songs.

The President's body was transported to Iparralde in a funeral procession, with dozens of cars carrying the Ikurrina, especially notable after passing through Adur. In Donibane Lohitzune (Saint-Jean-de-Luz), a reception organized by a committee led by Telesforo Monzón—a close friend of Lehendakari Aguirre despite their political disagreements—featured the presence of members of the Emakume Abertzale Batza.[257] They led the funeral procession to his house, transformed into a funeral home, where President Aguirre's coffin was draped with the ensign of the Sasaeta Basque battalion.[258]

Amidst heavy rain, Jesús Maria de Leizaola was sworn in as Lehendakari of the Basque Government on March 28, 1956.

"Before you, José Antonio Aguirre y Lekube, Lehendakari elected by the Basque people when the government of Euzkadi was established. In accordance with the agreements of the same Government and the democratic political and trade union organizations of the country that supported this cause in war, post-war, in the homeland, and in exile. To dedicate myself to the tasks of liberation until the free Basque people can elect their legitimate authorities. I assume the functions entrusted to you as President, which I will fulfill unreservedly with my will and effort, following your teachings and your example, as long as God gives me life. And I swear, as you did in Gernika, to be faithful to them and to the Basque people as you have fulfilled them until death, with such exemplarity and zeal."[259]

The wood of Gernika's tree had been transformed into the material for the Lehendakari's coffin, before which the new Basque President was sworn in. The suddenness of the death forced the Basque government to decide on a successor, now that the legitimacy of the Basque government had been affirmed by the Basque World Congress. The prospect of a prolonged exile, with a government under scrutiny and without a President, led them to choose Leizaola as the President. In fact, Leizaola had been serving as the vice-president of the Basque government—a position not even outlined in the Statute of Autonomy. The circumstances of exile had conferred legitimacy to this position, which Leizaola had effectively filled by working alongside the President.

On March 24, 1960, in an emergency meeting in Paris, the EBB, along with Juan Ajuriaguerra, decided to continue the work of the Basque Government: "We have suffered an enormous loss; we must all redouble our patriotic efforts to fill this emptiness. The homeland demands it." A few days later, the new Basque government was formed with the following members: Lehendakari Jesús Maria de Leizaola, Vice-President Francisco Javier Landáburu (PNV), Paulino Gómez Beltran (PSOE), Gonzalo Nárdiz (ANV), Ambrosio Garbisu (IR).[260]

The PNV Declaration of 1960 and the Basques.
A new Lehendakari for a "new" Euzkadi.

The sudden death of Lehendakari Aguirre also forced the PNV to write and publish a Declaration stating the direction that Basque nationalism would take.

The declaration of 1960[261] harkened back to the traditional "Jaungoikoa eta Lege Zarra," reasserting its Christian essence, perhaps in response to the prevailing secular trend permeating the political landscape throughout the Basque Country, particularly among the youth. Simultaneously, the advocacy for the "Lege Zarra," the ancient Basque code of laws, invoked the historical rights of the Basque nation and urged a reclaiming of Basque territories within the Spanish State.

While referencing the traditional motto of the PNV, the 1960 declaration also sought a connection with the future, stating, "We are a movement formed by men of the present with aspirations for tomorrow. We work on the Basque opinion to make the future Euzkadi an avant-garde nation in all fields," defending its European spirit and the right to self-determination. This was a nod to ongoing independence processes at that time: "As we were present from the beginning and continue to be present in the works for the organization of Europe and in all efforts for world peace. As we were present with full sympathy for the emancipation of the young nations."[262]

In an effort to bridge with a discontented younger generation in the Basque Country, the 1960 PNV declaration left the door open to advancing the self-determination process based on the Basque Statute of Autonomy, emphasizing, "The Basque Nationalist Party, without renouncing any of the essential rights of the Basque nation," and addressing the internal need to promote the Basque language against "de-basquization."[263]

It's crucial to note the evolving nature of the PNV, as gradually, the Basque language and culture took precedence over ethnic origin, shifting from traditional Basque nationalism rooted in ethnicity to a more civic nationalism.

The declaration called for the unity of all Basques to honor Lehendakari Aguirre's memory and counter the adversary. However, it also stressed the importance of discipline regarding decisions made by authorities, with special attention to the youth. Recognizing its own shortcomings, the PNV aimed to address weaknesses and renovate traditional Basque nationalism, acknowledging the generational gap that needed bridging. While the youth remained interested in politics and Basque nationalism, there was a growing ideological divide from the traditional PNV, prompting a search for unity as the solution to both geographical and ideological gaps.

Jesús María de Leizaola, one of President Aguirre's closest associates, stood by him from the very beginning until his passing. Accepting the role of Lehendakari after the man forever known as the "First Lehendakari" was not a simple task. Coping with Aguirre's charismatic leadership legacy posed a significant challenge, especially given the less-than-ideal situation of Basque nationalism. While the World Basque Conference of 1956 provided a respite of unity and legitimacy for the Basque government, issues persisted with the younger Basque population. The internal exile demanded a new strategy, and in some instances, a greater role for those on the mainland. Tensions rose within the Franco regime, with strikes, protests, and boycott activities leading to arrests and torture. Detainees and new exiles became commonplace in the realm of Basque nationalism.

Young nationalists believed that the strategies employed by Basque nationalism were ineffective, and they sought more autonomy in their actions. The youth branch of the PNV, EGI (Euzko Gaztedi Indarra), began criticizing the Services and the GBB from 1954 onward. They organized protests and engaged in violent activities, such as burning flags or displaying ikurrinas, without the Party's control. Despite efforts by President Aguirre and some other jelkides[264] to emphasize the importance of unity, life in the inland areas was challenging, and the generational gap exacerbated the divide between those inside and in exile.

The process of industrialization, affecting the entire Basque Country territory, which includes the four provinces within Spain (Navarre, Araba, Gipuzkoa, and Bizkaia), brought about not only economic but also social changes. In the late 1950s, the Basque Country witnessed a significant influx of immigrants from other regions of Spain, altering population density and shifting the Basque economic system from the primary sector (agriculture, with the Baserri[265] carrying weight in the socioeconomic imagination) to the secondary sector. By the 1970s, the total population of the Basque Country had grown by almost 50%, marking the conclusion of this transformative process.[266]

The arrival of immigrants also brought changes to Basque society, sparking a renewed interest in Basque culture during the 1960s. Despite the restrictions imposed by the Franco dictatorship, the promotion of Basque culture and language became more vital than ever. In defiance of these constraints, the Euskaltzaindia (the Basque language academy) and some ikastolas (Basque schools) were established, setting the stage for the emergence of Ez dok amairu,[267] a cultural movement created in 1965.

In July 1959, members of EGI-Ekin (a faction of EGI formed in 1958) introduced a new organization aimed at preventing internal tensions within Basque nationalism: Euzkadi Ta Azkatasuna, ETA.[268] This organization did not outright oppose the PNV or traditional principles but rather sought to modernize the aspirations of nationalists, especially among the younger generation who, unlike their predecessors, had not experienced the war but were facing repression under the Franco Dictatorship. ETA, as outlined in its founding document, declared itself as "non-political and non-religious," a departure from traditional Basque nationalism, particularly in terms of its secular stance.

The second axis, centered on freedom, portrayed ETA as a collective of democrats and workers fighting for the freedom of the Basque country.[269] Initially, ETA did not stand against the Basque Government, the Lehendakari, or the government's efforts, particularly in exile. In fact, a group of exiles in Venezuela, forming ETA's first cell in exile, began publishing "Zutik en tierras americanas" in 1960—an exiles' version of ETA's official publication, Zutik—dedicating its first issue to the figure of José Antonio Aguirre.[270]

Although the relationship with the Basque government and the PNV would evolve over the years, in its early stages, ETA unequivocally supported the Basque government. In the third issue of Zutik en Tierras americanas, it became explicitly clear that the organization's post-Aguirre agenda aimed to persist in the fight to reestablish the Statute of Autonomy. The editorial asserted that the Statute of Autonomy was just the initial step, a starting point for the Basque people. It emphasized that after the reestablishment of the Statute of Autonomy, the next goal would be "National unification," acknowledging that the starting point was too limited: "Navarre was not included in the Statute of Autonomy of the Republic. But there can be no other: We will start from there. We will start from autonomy."[271]

It was clear that the Basque youth needed something else and—as can be inferred from its founding document—politics was not the only way to achieve freedom for the Basque Country; but during those days ETA tried to maintain good relations with the Basque government and Basque nationalists. On May 15, ETA wrote to the new Lehendakari offering its support:

> The National Coordination Committee of Euzkadi ta Azkatasun (ETA), convening on this date, unanimously extends its respectful greetings, informs you of the organization's unwavering support for the Government of Euzkadi under your leadership as President, and reaffirms our offer of collaboration for the resilient efforts that the Government may undertake.[272]

While ETA demonstrated devotion to the Basque government and acknowledged its authority as the custodian of the Basque people's will, its emergence highlighted irreconcilable positions within Basque nationalism.

Attempts to maintain unity proved futile, and not only were the youth a source of discontent, but critical opinions within Basque nationalism also gained prominence. However, the differences between the ideas of the EBB and the policies developed by the Basque government from exile were typical and logical internal disputes. The toll of internal and external exile weighed heavily on a generation weary of living under pressure and sometimes in adverse conditions. The unexpected loss of their leader was the tipping point. Economic struggles, repression from the Spanish regime, the rebellion of young Basque nationalists, and the absence of a leader accentuated differences and contradictions within traditionalist Basque nationalism.

Although some voices were louder than others, and Leizaola faced criticism in Bayonne meetings regarding the political management of the Basque Government, these critiques did not alter political strategies or modify the ideology within Basque nationalism. The only dissent that significantly impacted Basque nationalism was that expressed by the youth who formed ETA, which is the focus of this research rather than internal conflicts within traditional Basque nationalism.[273]

Certainly, the exile influenced changes within the Basque government. Aguirre had garnered legitimacy through democratic elections, but Leizaola did not enjoy the same. While Leizaola was generally accepted, reservations were voiced by some Basque delegations, particularly those from South America, and certain politicians regarding the new President.

"Examining the case from the legal point of view, the substitution seems impossible because only José Antonio, without being able to delegate to anyone, had been granted, albeit with defects imposed by a circumstantial abnormality, the representation of the Country." These words, originally penned by Indalecio Prieto, a member of the Spanish parliament, in an article honoring Lehendakari Aguirre after his death, were reiterated to Lehendakari Leizaola in a letter from June 1960.[274]

He spent a significant portion of his life in politics, but during exile, as Prieto argued, "(...) there should be no government, neither national nor regional, but much more flexible Boards, without constitutional encumbrances, presided over by the most representative personalities."[275] As previously discussed, exile served as a backdrop where the legitimacy of the Spanish government waned, leading to internal struggles among its members and parties for control.

Criticism of Leizaola's election as Lehendakari didn't solely originate from Spanish politicians; it also prompted scrutiny and reservations among Basque nationalists. Exile played a pivotal role in this, as the precarious financial situation—largely supported by the Basques in exile—allowed for greater creative thinking and the formation of individual opinions, sometimes employing different political strategies in the debates. Nevertheless, Leizaola garnered enough support to assume the responsibility of being the "vice-president acting as President," a term initially agreed upon to describe the decision of appointing a new President despite the Basque Statute of Autonomy not foreseeing such a possibility.

"At this time more than ever, we must all unite around the government to decisively and faithfully support our Vice-President acting as President."[276] In his letter, Garmendia also mentions the crowded funeral service held in memory of Lehendakari Aguirre. Among the attendees, which included members of the Mexican government and the Spanish and Catalan Republican Governments-in-exile, Garmendia observed the absence of Indalecio Prieto. "(...) Prieto was personally invited, and despite his tenderness and occasional tears, in a significant political misstep for him, and to our advantage, he did not attend."[277]

Prieto harbored resentment towards the Basque Government following the failure of his Monarchy plan. Despite maintaining some ties until his demise in 1962, Manuel Irujo never forgave this perceived disrespect. As mentioned earlier, the exile was evolving distinctive characteristics, and the specter of what's termed "Tropicalization"[278]—the erosion of Basque nationalism supplanted by a localized identity—began troubling traditional nationalist Basques. They attributed the crisis as the primary cause of the untimely death of the President.

Following the aforementioned letter and upon learning of the decision to appoint Leizaola as President, adopting the title, Garmendia corresponded with Irujo again: "(...) As I know that after the intense moment of grief for the loss of José Antonio (r.i.p.d.) has passed, discussions will begin, etc., I would like you to give me legal and political arguments to defend the position adopted by you, a position that, rightly or wrongly, we are ready to defend unconditionally."[279] Given the Basque government's strategy centered on upholding the Basque Statute of Autonomy, lacking any legal basis for such a decision, Garmendia proposed consulting the Delegates in exile to legitimize Leizaola's election. The same letter reflects on the transformative impact of exile on Basque nationalists. "With exile, a new mentality is cultivated among patriots, and the eagerness to act can lead to disturbances. Individuals of merit, preparation, and patriotism, who could be organizational pillars, might generate specific antipathies due to nervousness, perhaps 'futurism,' or an irrepressible desire to prove superior patriotism, risking serious prejudice (sic.) to our ideology at a certain point."[280]

The exile played a vital role in Basque nationalism, emerging as an entity with its own opinions and occasional intentions to influence decisions of Basque nationalists. Organized mainly into extraterritorial councils in Venezuela, Argentina, Chile, and Mexico by the PNV, the pivotal hub of the exile during that period was the Basque Center in Caracas. Despite Jesús María de Leizaola lacking Aguirre's leadership prowess, he adeptly crafted a political strategy that sought equilibrium between the exile's activities and those within the homeland.[281]

In September 1960, Leizaola embarked on a journey to America. However, unlike Aguirre, he didn't make a stop in Washington to engage with the American Administration. Despite the resurgence of hope in America, the anticipation that the Democratic Party might triumph in the November elections buoyed Spanish and Basque democrats. This raised expectations that Americans would intervene in Spain to overthrow the Franco Regime.

During a dinner in Biarritz in August 1960, Ajuriaguerra conveyed his optimism to Irujo, stating, "(...) the democrats have in their program the need to change U.S. foreign policy, making it democratic not only domestically but also internationally, putting an end to dictators and tyrants, whether they are called Trujillo, Franco, Somoza, or whatever."[282]

By the end of the Eisenhower administration, certain American senators exhibited a favorable stance towards the Spanish democratic resistance. Senators J. William Fulbright and Frank Moss, along with earlier critics like Porter and Church, expressed reservations about the Franco regime. However, the projected change in international relations by the Kennedy administration was more of a formality than a shift in political practice.[283]

Despite heightened expectations, the responses from the American embassy to the Basque government's petitions, conveyed through delegates Beitia and Juan Oñatibia or pro-Basque senators, remained consistent. Spain was deemed a "strategic corner in Europe," and the U.S. strategy aligned with its interests, without constituting an approval or endorsement of the Spanish governments or their handling of internal political affairs.[284]

While Leizaola deviated from Aguirre's practice of stopping in Washington and missed a meeting with Porter in Paris due to his departure for Bayonne, as explained in a letter to Irujo after the latter urged him to focus on international relations,[285] Leizaola sought to establish a dialogue with the new American Administration in anticipation of a potential crisis within the Franco Government. On May 22nd, 1961, Leizaola sent a letter to the American State Department, following the strategy initiated by Lehendakari Aguirre. The Basque government proposed an alternative and stable government in Spain in collaboration with other Spanish democratic forces: "The Government of Euzkadi, which maintains relations with the Spanish Republic-in-exile and with the Spanish and Catalan democratic and free trade union groups, is already today, and will be more so, an effective and irreplaceable instrument in any section toward the re-establishment of democratic normalcy in Spain."[286]

The international political landscape in 1961 was evolving into a more intricate world each day. Europe stood out as a focal point of the Cold War, but Latin America also held its own significance. In his letter, Leizaola alludes to the expansive network of Basques in exile, spanning from Cuba to Spain (referred to as the Iberian Peninsula). He extends his connections within the Basque exile, offering support to topple dictatorships and transform them into democracies. This proposition aligns with Kennedy's campaign pledge to unequivocally support democracies over dictatorships.

Leizaola highlights the complexities arising from the North African decolonization, spurred by the ongoing Algerian War at the time of writing. He presents this decolonization as a genuine threat to the Franco Regime. The Lehendakari goes further, offering the services of the Basque Government to assist in controlling and facilitating a secure transfer of power in the Basque Country in case of an emergency. This commitment is framed within the principles of the Western world, signaling their intention to contribute to thwarting the Communist bloc.[287]

A note attached to the envelope containing the letter sent to the State Department stated: "Attached letters from the Basque and Republican Governments in Exile are being filed without reply in line with standing policy."[288] It became evident that the Kennedy Administration had no intentions of altering its established policy.

The European Movement and the Basques

"The independence of the past has transformed into interdependence and federation. Hence, the Europe envisioned is termed the 'European Federal Union' or the 'United States of Europe,' among other similar designations," stated Manuel Irujo in 1965. This shift in strategy, particularly in the European approach of Basque nationalism, prompted Irujo to write an article on President Aguirre and his connection with the European Movement for publication in Alderdi.

In the article, Irujo elucidated how the period of exile facilitated a closer association with Europe and the conception of a united Europe. This connection originated through the "Cultural Union of Western European Countries," founded in London in 1942.[289] This cultural union, established by the Basque and French national councils in exile, ratified its constitution on October 8, 1942, at the French Institute, with Denis Saurat serving as the president. Originating after the failure of political alliances, particularly the Western Confederation policy[290] and the Franco-Basque agreement, the union aimed to promote the culture of Occidental Europe rooted in Greek Civilization and Christianity.

Irujo underscored the significance of this cultural union as the precursor to the European Federal movement, exemplifying how Europe had perpetually presented an opportunity for the Basques and other stateless peoples. The foundational Statute of the Cultural Union expressed, "Europe must be constituted as an organic whole, composed of cultural units collaborating for the collective good and the world." It elaborated on the nature of European states, emphasizing the collaboration between regions such as Bretagne, Alsace, Flanders, and renaissance national groups like Catalonia and Euzkadi.

The collaboration between Basques and Catalans within the cultural union[291] set a precedent for their participation in the European Federal Movement, specifically within the CFEME (Spanish Federal Council of the European Movement), established in 1949 after the Hague Conference. Disagreements emerged during meetings at the "Casal Català" in London, where representatives such as Carles Pi i Sunyer, Josep Maria Batista i Roca, Mr. Ordeig, and Mr. Perera for the Catalans, and José Ignacio Lisazo, Ángel Gondra, and Manuel Irujo for the Basques engaged in extensive and impassioned discussions on Basque and Catalan nationalism and the importance of preserving specific cultural identities:

> Mr. Madariaga invites us to be candid and loyal. I intend to be both. Basques educated in national theses don't harbor Spanish patriotism. Our homeland is not Spain, but Euzkadi. Our culture doesn't align with that of Castile or Spain; it's the Basque culture. Our history isn't the one binding us to Castile but what unites and distinguishes us from it. Our national will transcends historical incidents. We aspire to Euzkadi's national life with or without history, and even against it. The Castilian language isn't ours. We aim to restore Euzkera to its lost dominion and establish our culture on the genius of our race, Euzkera, and Basque historical institutions.[292]

These succinct lines encapsulate the essence of the discussions. The national issue and the Christian nature of Spanish democracy, as denied by Madariaga,[293] were both challenged. Differences between the Basque and Catalan nationalities led to Madariaga's withdrawal from the project. Ultimately, the agreement was signed without the presence of the Spanish Republican Democrats. The Basques were granted their own group within the union, commencing upon its approval on October 25, 1942. All Basques, regardless of political affiliation, were invited, emphasizing the cultural and spiritual nature of the union.[294]

A letter, endorsed by all Basque participants, was dispatched to Basque refugees in London (with a specific eye on Basque communities in America) to disseminate and foster Basque culture. Notably, this Cultural Union adhered to the principles of unity championed by José Antonio Aguirre throughout the exile, alongside the nationalist and Christian assertions of Basque nationalists that eventually propelled their involvement in creating the European Movement, rooted in the same principles.

Basque nationalists in exile navigated European relations through two distinct but sometimes overlapping channels: the Christian democrat movement, channeled through NEI (Nouvelles Equipes Internationalles), and the European Federal Movement. Their objective in European relations was based on what is now known as Aguirre's doctrine—a plea for a free Basque country within a Federal Europe comprising sovereign nations.[295]

While not within our chronological sequence, it is crucial to underscore that the Europeanism of Basque nationalism did not emerge solely with or because of the exile. Instead, it was a characteristic already present in early 20th-century Basque nationalism as a solution for peoples without a state or facing opposition from an existing state, as articulated by Luis Eleizalde in[296] 1914: "We have to reach the point that the Basque Nation can present itself (...) in the assembly of peoples"[297] (of Europe). The evolution of Basque nationalism in the 1920s transcended the confines of initial Biscayan nationalism, seeking to position Basque nationalism as one among many in the global landscape. Eleizalde based these ideas on the principle of nationalities, envisioning Basque nationalism fitting into a world composed of nations aspiring to control their destinies.[298]

The internationalization of Basque nationalism found fruition through Basque participation in the III Congress of the Union of Nationalities held in Lausanne in 1916. Woodrow Wilson's discourse on national self-determination provided Basque nationalists with the theoretical foundation to recognize their cause alongside similar movements.[299] During the Spanish Republican period (1931-1936), Basque nationalists further developed their Europeanism and presented their nationalism as universal through a "formula of federal interdependence," as articulated by Landaburu. The adoption of the motto "Euzkadi-Europa" for the 1933 Aberri Eguna officially signaled Basque nationalism's interest in federalism and Europe as a means for the Basques to find a place within an international structure acknowledging their distinctiveness.[300]

This interest in Europe was articulated by Irujo in an article for Euzkadi on April 22nd, 1933, where he reformulated the 1919 Versailles Peace Treaty, incorporating Wilson's doctrine and intertwining it with Gandhi's ideas to advocate for self-determination as a natural right of nations, seeking an international space for not only the Basques but all of Galeuzka.[301] However, despite these efforts, the

PNV did not send a representative to the IX Congress of European Nationalities in Bern in 1933. The focus at that time was on defending the yet-to-be-achieved Basque Statute of Autonomy, with all efforts directed towards this goal, while international relations and Europe were temporarily set aside as the European movement could wait.[302]

The PNV, being a confessional party with a predominantly Catholic orientation, naturally engaged in contacts with other Christian Democratic parties during World War II. One notable connection was established with the French Christian Democrats through Ernest Pezet, the representative of the Parti Democrate Populaire (PDP). Additionally, the PNV fostered ties with Italian Christian Democracy through contacts with Democrazia Cristiana (DC), particularly through figures like Sturzo, as previously mentioned in a different section. Among the significant accomplishments of Christian Democracy's international policies was the establishment of Nouvelles Equipes Internationales (NEI). The PNV actively participated in the foundation of NEI, highlighting the party's commitment to engaging with international Christian Democratic movements during this period.[303]

The founding congress of Nouvelles Equipes Internationales (NEI) took place in Chaudfontaine, near Liege, in 1947. Lehendakari Aguirre was appointed a member of the Honor Committee, signifying the Basque Nationalist Party's (PNV) involvement in this international initiative. Additionally, Francisco de Landaburu represented Euzkadi[304] as a member of the Steering Committee. These links with Christian Democrats went beyond mere political association; they served as a means to bring attention to the Basque question, potentially influencing Francisco Franco's perspective through Spanish Catholic organizations aligned with the regime. Although the NEI meetings were considered crucial, the Cold War and economic constraints diminished its effectiveness over time.

The Basque nationalists strategically secured their own nationalist group within the NEI. Representatives directly affiliated with the Basque Nationalist Party, such as Francisco Javier de Landáburu and José María Lasarte, alongside Iñaki Errenteria and Iñaki Aguirre representing Euzko Gaztedi, had a voice in the organization. This independent representation allowed Basque nationalism to directly intervene in European spheres, emphasizing the vision of a Europe built on the diversity of peoples rather than states.

NEI's organization involved conferences and meetings that held substantial importance and had repercussions both in Europe and within the broader European movement, particularly until 1950. Congresses were held annually or biennially, covering a range of topics, including politics, social issues, religion, economics, national minorities, autonomies, human rights, and freedom of expression. The Basques actively contributed to shaping a post-war Europe, utilizing the opportunity to promote the Basque cause on the international stage. Lehendakari Aguirre and Landaburu, driven by a European vocation, served as regular Basque representatives at NEI meetings, often accompanied by figures like Lasarte, Leizaola, or Irujo, from 1947 to 1966.[305]

During the 2nd Congress of the NEI, held in Luxembourg from January 30 to February 1, 1948, Lehendakari Aguirre and Francisco de Landáburu engaged in discussions on European policies. The focus of these discussions centered on analyzing the German situation, studying economic development, and assessing progress towards peace with the assistance of American aid.[306]

Beyond the official and annual congresses, the NEI organized additional meetings, including one held at the Basque Government Headquarters in Paris on March 21, 1948. During this meeting, the final statutes of the NEI were established. The Basque delegation successfully gained approval for its proposal to advocate for a veto against granting the Spanish dictatorship access to the Marshall Plan and to contribute to the development of European reorganization.[307]

Despite limited achievements, the Basques continued their support for the NEI and participated in its transformation in the 1960s when the organization changed its name to the European Union of Christian Democrats. However, after 1950, the relevance of the NEI began to decline due to changing international politics in the context of the Cold War. The rise of anti-communism in Europe and the implementation of the Marshall Plan led to a diminished focus on the NEI's objectives. The fear of communism resulted in the tolerance of totalitarian regimes, including Franco's, viewed as a lesser evil. Consequently, the PNV shifted its focus to maintaining a smear campaign against the Franco regime, capitalizing on its status as a founding member.[308]

In the late 1950s and early 1960s, the reorganization of Spanish Christian Democracy posed a challenge within the PNV. Manuel Irujo, along with José Mª Lasarte and Julio Jáuregui, advocated for convergence into a single Spanish Christian Party to form a strong pro-democratic front. However, others, such as Joseba Rezola or Juan Ajuriaguerra, opposed the idea, expressing concerns that the creation of such an entity might blur Basque identity and potentially lead to a loss of autonomy within the NEI.[309]

Ultimately, the PNV decided to join the Spanish Christian Democrats, although they maintained a separate team until 1963. In that year, an agreement was reached to form a joint team with IDC, DSC, and UDC, known as the "Spanish Team," which gained acceptance from the European Christian Democrats in 1972. According to Arrieta, this cooperative strategy within the Christian-Democratic sphere aligned with the long-term strategy implemented by the PNV from the 1960s onward,[310] anticipating a future period of democratic transition.

However, the decision to align with Spanish forces for the presentation of a Spanish democratic front caused a crisis within the PNV. The divergence in strategies, as seen in the discussion between Monzón and Irujo during the Basque World Congress, reflected differing views on whether to continue with Aguirre's spirit of unity or pursue Basque freedom without interference from Spanish forces. The core of the problem, though, was the intensification of the anti-communist campaign embraced by many European countries. For them, the Franco regime represented a means to halt the advance of communism and establish a Europe based on states rather than nations and peoples.

In 1949, the PNV declared its support for ongoing initiatives implementing principles of freedom and democracy within a European organization[311] striving for world peace and the economic and social welfare of populations. The party endorsed federalist concepts that would enable the creation of European powers without diminishing the full personality of each included people, including the Basques. Lehendakari Aguirre, a declared pro-European, continued to champion European policies in exile after Aguirre, alongside figures like Manuel Irujo, Javier de Landáburu, Joseba Rezola, and Jesús de Solaun.

The concept of the "Europe of the peoples," fully developed by Javier de Landáburu during the 1960s,[312] envisioned a Europe where the Basque country could find its place. Basque nationalists recognized that the freedom of Euzkadi as a nation was not feasible within the confines of a conventional nation-state, especially in the aftermath of World War II, which exposed the dangers of extreme nationalisms. The Basques, like other nations without a state, were compelled to reimagine and construct a new concept of freedom and sovereignty.

While the Basque Government had initially based its legitimacy on the defense of the Basque Statute of Autonomy within Spain, the Federal concept of Europe became the idea that Basque nationalism chose to champion when envisioning a new Europe. The Federal Movement and the idea of a Europe built on federal principles were essential components of this vision. Manuel Irujo, a staunch promoter of the European Union and the Federal Movement, articulated his views in an article titled "Federación occidental Europea" for Alderdi in 1949.[313] Drawing on the work of Bernard Delesalle, Irujo argued that a Federal Europe was necessary to uphold peace and national values in a Christian and Occidental Europe. Concepts like "Regions," "Confederation," and "Subfederation" were employed, echoing the strategies previously embraced by Basques and Catalans in the Cultural Union and the Comité pro Comunidad Ibérica de Naciones (established in 1944).

The European Federation was viewed by Irujo as the best option for the Basque country to safeguard its laws and sovereignty. This concept later evolved into a fervent defense of the Basque language as the essence of the Basque country and the idea of a Federal European Union as a guarantee of equidistance between the two Cold War blocs.

The development of the Pan-European sentiment or the Federal Movement post-World War II found expression through private movements, including the Cultural Union of Occidental Europe and the Movimiento Federalista Vasco. The latter, established in 1947 and affiliated with the European Union of Federalists, garnered support not only from Basque nationalists but also from the Basque Government. While fully developed in exile,[314] the growing influence of the Federal Movement transcended borders, and European sentiments began to permeate Francoist Spain.[315]

The Basques actively engaged in European federal movements, demonstrated commitment to European Christian Democrat associations like the NEI, and participated in various international meetings on law, peace, and trade unions. These efforts formed part of the Basque Government's[316] strategy for international recognition, establishing a political alignment that traditional Basque nationalism (PNV and ANV) would steadfastly uphold.

From May 7 to May 10, 1948, the Movimiento Federalista Vasco, with Aguirre as Honorary President and Irujo effectively chairing the movement,[317] participated in the Conference of The Hague. Over 800 personalities[318] with diverse political affiliations attended, united by a common objective: "The urgent duty of the nations of Europe to create an economic and political union to ensure security and social progress." Resolutions from the congress emphasized the establishment of a democratic social system and the necessity for the Union or Federation to be open to all European nations democratically governed and committed to respecting a Charter of Human Rights.[319] Importantly, Spain was excluded from the movement and any potential future European Union until it embraced democracy—a goal consistently pursued by Basque nationalism in international forums.

Despite being founding members of the Nouvelles Equipes Internationales, a component of the organizing "International Committee of the Movement for European Unity," the European Federal movement that was emerging did not align with the Federation concept the Basques had envisioned. A report, likely authored by Landáburu, titled "Razones de nuestra presencia en el Congreso," highlighted the challenges faced by the Basques in the Congress and the European Union of Federalists' reluctance to accept the Movimiento Federalista Vasco.[320]

According to Irujo's statements in the previously mentioned Alderdi article, the Conference of The Hague played a pivotal role in the projection of the new European formation, starting from the juridical basis of the States. During this event, Mr. Aguirre and Mr. Madariaga, along with others, agreed to establish the Spanish Federal Council of the European Movement (CFEME), allowing Catalan and Basque groups to form part of it while maintaining their distinct identity.[321]

Irujo strongly supported the democratic federal movement, viewing it as the most effective means to combat Franco's dictatorship. He advocated collaboration with other Spanish pro-democratic forces, following the precedent set by President Aguirre. The objective was to present a united block of Spanish democrats against the Franco regime within the Federal Movement.

Despite the initial setback of being refused the opportunity to be their own representatives and being forced to join the Spanish group, the Basques persevered.

They even offered the headquarters of the Basque government in Rue Marceau to establish a base for the Consejo Federal Español del Movimiento Europeo in 1949.

The efforts of Basque federalists were recognized with the inclusion of Manuel Irujo and José Maria Lasarte in the first Executive Committee, with Salvador de Madariaga serving as President. The Executive Committee included four vice-presidents, each representing a founding group. Among them were Rodolfo Llopis (PSOE), Julio Just (Liberals), Carles Pi i Sunyer (Catalans), and Manuel Irujo (Basques). José María Lasarte was appointed Secretary General.

Initially, the CFEME comprised four distinct branches representing different founding groups: Grupo Español del Movimiento Socialista por los Estados Unidos de Europa (MSEUE), Grupo Español de la Unión Liberal Europea, Consejo Catalán, and Consejo Vasco.[322] Collaboration with Spanish pro-democratic forces remained a complex issue for the PNV, given the varying opinions among its representatives; however, individuals like Lehendakari Aguirre and Irujo believed it was essential to unite with all Spanish democratic parties and associations to achieve Basque goals.

Disagreements emerged regarding the decision to join the Spanish Federal Movement, and some critics believed that the Basque movement should have attempted to gain acceptance by the European movement as a distinct country or nationality, rather than aligning with the Spanish Federal Movement. Criticism also arose regarding a perceived lack of communication between the Basque National Executive (EBB) and the Lehendakari's group. Juan Ajuriaguerra and others were concerned that without their own group, Basque representation would be subject to Spanish interests,[323] potentially blurring the distinctiveness of Basque nationalism.

An unsigned document titled "Al pueblo Patriota Vasco," written in 1950 and sent to the PNV in Paris, voiced strong opposition to the decision to collaborate with the CFEME. The document criticized the move, stating that playing politics with the dominator and seeking effective conquests through collaboration would harm the national cause. The author questioned where Euzkadi and Basque national representation appeared in these activities, expressing concerns about the legitimacy of the Basque position within the CFEME.[324]

The study sessions of the CFEME in May 1950[325] further fueled discontent within Basque nationalism. Some members believed that the activities associated with the Federal movement and the collaboration with the Spanish CFEME were linked to Spanish interests, leading to accusations of "strongly Spanishist" tendencies. Félix Irizar, the president of the Paris council, and Ceferino Jemein, a self-appointed protector of Sabino Arana's essences,[326] were among those who criticized the participation in events perceived as compromising Basque nationalism.

In response to the criticism, Manuel Irujo took charge of writing a report that described the resolutions and highlighted the advantages for Basque nationalism in participating in the CFEME sessions. The report emphasized the impact on the international community and the recognition of peninsular nationalities, and it helped organize a meeting at the Basque government's headquarters in Paris. The subsequent report prepared by the PNV in June 1950, based on Irujo's words, defended participation with the CFEME under the condition that it would be a federal body, allowing the Basque group to develop its own personality.

Following these principles, the Consejo Vasco por la Federación Europea (CVFE) was officially constituted on February 1, 1951, and it was included within the CFEME, even though the Basques had been informally acting as a separate group since 1949.[327] The Basque Council represented various international bodies in which the Basques participated.

Reservations continued to be expressed by some Basque nationalists, particularly from Julio Jáuregui (PNV) and certain members of ELA-STV and ANV. They pressured the Basque representatives in the Federal Movement to include the concept of "Nation" rather than the more indeterminate concepts of "Regions" or "Minorities."

The PNV was able to participate independently only in the "Small Europeans Nations Conference," held in Bern in April 1962.[328]

The 60's: A new Era of Hope?

During the period of Nikita Khrushchev's denunciation of Stalin's crimes at the XX Party Congress in 1956,[329] the Eisenhower administration in the United States, from 1953 to 1961, continued its anticommunist policies. The House Un-American Activities Committee, operating from 1939 to 1975, played a role in these policies. The Korean War (1950-1953) also contributed to maintaining an anticommunist climate.

In this context, Europe, especially the Western part, was strategically significant, serving as a buffer between the USSR and the "free world" represented by the United States. The Basque nationalism of the PNV sought to participate in the international scene in support of democracy and freedom. It condemned totalitarian systems, including fascism and communism, without explicitly adopting an anticommunist stance.[330]

In the Cold War world, Basque nationalism aligned itself with democracy and freedom, condemning all forms of totalitarianism. The PNV consistently characterized the Franco regime as a totalitarian regime, similar in nature to those in the USSR. Basque democrats, along with other Spanish democrats, were seen as ready to assume government responsibility once Franco fell. The idea of international, particularly American, intervention to help Spanish democrats overthrow Franco had been dismissed earlier. However, the military presence of American troops in Europe, with bases in West Germany and the Mediterranean, ensured that the Spanish issue was still a matter of international concern.

As national awakening movements gained momentum, leading to the disintegration of remaining imperial pockets in Africa, Basque nationalists emphasized the national-oppressor nature of the dictatorship in Spain since 1939. They denounced the imposition of a totalitarian regime with foreign support, drawing parallels with events such as the Hungarian Revolt of November 1956.[331]

Manuel Irujo and the Basque nationalists, along with the entire Basque government and Spanish democrats in exile, faced the challenge of changing the situation of thousands of exiles who had been expelled from their homeland due to a fascist regime. Amid the Cold War, where Europe became a geostrategic field to counter the advance of communist USSR, the interventions and movements on both sides of the Cold War were unsettling to Irujo.

Expressing his discontent, Irujo invoked Machiavelli, highlighting a political-moral crisis. He noted the irony of figures like Trujillo and Somoza, who, despite their questionable records, claimed to be friends of America, while Somoza supported Franco. For Irujo, the Cold War strategies were causing distortions in alliances and principles.[332]

Despite not advocating for communism, Irujo couldn't wholeheartedly support the American strategy either. The Basques, particularly, found themselves in the crossfire of the Cold War conflict. In this scenario, European unity under the Federal movement emerged as the strategy for Basque nationalism. The belief was that a strong Europe could counteract the interferences of both the Russians and Americans.

Irujo expressed his pro-European stance, emphasizing the importance of sacrificing for universal peace. However, he cautioned against the dangers faced by those caught in the middle of the two opposing blocs. The Basque nationalists, understanding this peril,[333] saw European unity as a means to navigate through the challenges posed by the Cold War.

Javier de Landáburu, describing the situation of Basque nationalists amidst the international political landscape, emphasized the importance of unity among democrats to counter the triumph of totalitarianism. Citing Jacques Maritain's pre-World War II assertion that the weakness and lack of union among democrats contributed to the victory of totalitarianism, Landáburu underscored the need for greater cohesion among democratic forces.[334]

The European movement and Federalism, integral parts of the international strategy of Basque nationalism, gained strength after the death of Aguirre. They were combined with Christian democracy and a firm defense of democracy, particularly as the repression by the Franco regime intensified. In 1960, after 339 Basque priests protested and denounced the regime, and in 1962, two priests faced trial for accusing the police of torture against Basque protesters.[335] These events marked shifts in social dynamics, and Manuel Irujo elaborated on these changes in articles like "En España empieza a amanecer,"[336] describing the evolving situation in Spain from 1939 to 1962.

Irujo highlighted the changing stance of the clergy, noting that during the Spanish Civil War, the majority had supported Franco, except for Basque and Catalan clergymen who stood with the Republican democracy. By 1962, he claimed that there was not a single priest under 45 who supported Franco; instead, they sided with striking workers and supported their protests.

The 1960s witnessed a more repressive policy against Basque nationalism and the opposition to Franco. Many were imprisoned, tortured, and faced death sentences. The exile, reminiscent of the exodus of Basque nationalists in 1939, became a reality once again, as a new generation of Basques sought refuge abroad due to the increasingly harsh conditions imposed by the Franco regime.[337] Despite the appearance of the regime being on its last legs, facing protests from various quarters, it resorted to its harshest tactics, reminiscent of the early postwar era.

The "Contubernio de Múnich"

In June 1960, the idea of arranging a meeting between Spanish pro-democracy exiles and members of the anti-Francoist resistance from inside Spain was first proposed by Enric Adroher, known as "Gironella."[338] In a meeting with Lehendakari Leizaola, Xabier Landáburu, and Manuel Irujo, Gironella explained Salvador Madariaga's plan. The proposal was to organize an assembly within eight months, bringing together around 200 Spanish citizens from both the interior and exile. The apparent objective of the assembly was to jointly study the relationship between Spain and the evolving Europe.[339]

During this period, the CFEME (Consejo Federal Español del Movimiento Europeo) had been inactive for months, despite the ongoing progress in the construction of a Federal Europe. The Franco regime also showed some interest in the European movement, especially as long as it received open tolerance from Western democracies, as evident from President Eisenhower's visit to Spain in 1959.[340]

According to Jordi Amat's book "La primavera de Múnich,"[341] the democratic opposition to Franco had been organizing and meeting secretly on both sides of the Pyrenees since 1956. Encouraged by the strikes and protests against the regime in Spain, representatives like Julián Gorkin[342] (a communist, Trotskyist, and anti-Stalinist) and Dionisio Ridruejo[343] (an old-guard Falangist who had abandoned Francoist postulates in 1942) joined forces with Salvador de Madariaga to advocate for the fight against the Franco regime and the unity of democrats in establishing a new government in Spain.

Despite the regime's efforts to suppress activities organized by the democrats, there was a growing movement for an alternative to the dictatorial system. This alternative was being articulated through the collaboration of exiles and the democratic opposition within Spain, even in the face of persecution by the Franco regime. The proposal for an assembly became a symbol of these efforts towards democratization and the establishment of a new government.[344]

On January 3, 1957, Fernando Baeza, a member of Acción Democrática, presented a project for a Democratic Spain to the Basque delegation in Paris, led by Lehendakari Aguirre. This project closely followed the points that would define the transition to democracy in Spain about 20 years later.[345] However, despite efforts, negotiations to establish a roadmap for democracy encountered challenges. Political differences between politicians who had been on opposite sides during the Spanish Civil War, as well as differences between exiles and those inside Spain, emerged during the preliminary discussions. National differences, often overlooked by Spanish democrats and the narrative of "National reconciliation," also posed a significant obstacle.

The European Federal movement held importance for Basque nationalists. While they were willing to accept unity with Spanish democrats, there were limits. These limits involved the recognition of Basque national identity and respect for Basque laws and institutions. This became evident in discussions about the Transition to democracy. Gonzalo Nárdiz, in a letter to Javier Landáburu regarding meetings with socialists to discuss the transition, expressed hesitancy about the socialist plan: "In the case I consider, our national personality and the objective of our aspirations should be clearly outlined."[346]

Although the Basque nationalists were not advocating full sovereignty at this point, merely seeking respect for the situation of 1936 and the organization of a referendum to allow the Basque people to decide on certain matters during the transition, Spanish democrats perceived these demands as impossible to meet. The Basques proposed asking if independence was on the table as a fundamental condition for further negotiations, a stance that left a negative impression on the Spanish democrats.

The report by Izquierda Demócrata Cristiana highlights the issue of views regarding autonomies in their dealings with the Socialists. The Socialists expressed that they "do not consider it appropriate to grant statutes now either."[347] The report implies that Basque nationalism and its demands were not something that could be easily overlooked. While Aguirre and Landáburu were more open to negotiation and displayed better manners than some Basque members of "The Resistance" in Beyris, the Basque statute of autonomy and national recognition were non-negotiable.

A meeting in Paris in 1958 between Manuel Irujo and Romualdo Rodríguez Vera from PSOE shed light on the firm stance of Basque nationalism. In this meeting, Romualdo Martínez Vera suggested that, during the initial transition period, the Basques might consider moderating their character and aspirations for their own government. However, Irujo was clear in his response, asserting that they would not be swayed by goodwill and should not let themselves be taken for a ride. He emphasized that people understand each other through dialogue but going towards normality should not mean some individuals being satisfied at the expense of others who are left in a state of ashes.

In the report's conclusion, titled "Impresión general," Irujo reflects on the meeting with Martínez Vera and a previous one with José Maria Gil-Robles. He ends by stating, "Pour commencer: no little statue. After that... we'll see. That is all Gil Robles is going to offer us. And since that is all, it is only natural that he does not want to meet with the guardian of the Statute."[348] This reinforces the insistence on Basque autonomy and national recognition without compromising on their core aspirations.

The geopolitical landscape during the Franco regime prompted both the exiled Spanish opposition and those within Spain to engage with Europeanism as a means of challenging the isolated Francoist government. Spain's bid to join the European Economic Community (EEC) in 1962 and its economic reforms were seen as efforts to open up to Europe. However, critics, including the anti-Francoist resistance at the Munich Conference,[349] argued that these changes didn't significantly impact society or improve the rights and freedoms of the Spanish people.

For the Spanish anti-Francoist resistance, Europeanism was a tool to oppose the regime, particularly by emphasizing Spain's integration into European structures as contingent on democratic reforms. The rejection of Spain's entry into the EEC was considered more a decision related to the political nature of the future European Union than to the lack of freedom and democratic structures in Spain. The fear was that admitting Spain without democratic reforms would dismantle an important aspect of anti-Francoist opposition and potentially integrate a non-democratic Spain into the European Union.

Within this context, Basque nationalists, particularly figures like Manuel Irujo and Javier Landáburu, saw the European Federalist Movement as a strategic tool to promote democratic principles and oppose the Franco regime. They advocated for the development of a European federation based on democracy, recognition of distinct peoples, and the exclusion of any form of totalitarianism, including the Spanish regime. This approach aimed to ensure that Spain's inclusion in European structures would be conditional on democratic transformations and the protection of individual freedoms for Spanish citizens.

The proposed meeting between Spanish democrats in exile and those within Spain, initially intended to take place at the Council of Europe in Strasbourg in 1961, faced obstacles, particularly due to pressures from Francoist diplomacy.[350] Salvador Madariaga's vision for the assembly was that it would have significant international resonance, and its practical conclusions would emphasize that Spain could not enter Europe without undergoing democratization. The financing of the meeting was to be achieved through a fund constituted by donations from major international pro-European organizations and possibly contributions from American trade unions.[351]

The connection between the "Contubernio de Múnich" and the Congress for Cultural Freedom is explained by the involvement of individuals like Julián Gorkin and Salvador de Madariaga. The Congress for Cultural Freedom, founded in West Berlin in 1950, is known as a covert operation of the CIA during the Cold War, aiming to counter the influence of Communist ideas by promoting cultural activities, conferences, publications, and support for intellectuals.[352]

Julián Gorkin and Salvador de Madariaga were associated with the "Centro de Estudios y Documentación," an anti-Francoist think tank in Paris that represented Spanish interests within the Congress for Cultural Freedom. This work was financially supported by various American organizations and foundations, including the Ford Foundation.[353]

In a CFEME meeting in Paris on April 18, 1961, Gorkin announced their plan to promote a meeting with the European movement, emphasizing its broader scope. The plan aimed to unite liberal, Christian Democrat, and socialist tendencies within the European Movement, bringing together Spanish personalities from both inside Spain and the emigrant community. This initiative was presented in accordance with the basis of agreement subscribed to by Madariaga and Gorkin in Oxford.[354]

While the direct involvement of the United States in organizing the Munich meeting is not confirmed, the American embassy in Madrid closely monitored the developments and had concerns about any perception of foreign-aided conspiracy or alignment with old-time political elements, especially the exiles.[355] The US embassy's confidential report on the Munich meeting, spanning thirteen pages with additional attached documents, highlighted the significant interest and repercussions the event had in international spheres.

The report suggests that the United States became more interested in the future of Spain after the Congress. Although not directly involved, the US seemed to indirectly contribute in some way to assisting Spaniards who remained in exile: "In agreement with Ridruejo, it has been decided here, in view of the fact that there is no other organization that does it, to help 14 of our friends who are still at large, and the same thing will be done with Cembrero."[356]

Regarding the funding of the Congress, it appears that, while not entirely from the Congress for Cultural Freedom, some funds were obtained through the efforts of Julián Gorkin. Studies by Olga Glondys suggest that Gorkin secured at least five thousand dollars from the CLC (Congress for Cultural Freedom) and another five thousand from the AFL (American Federation of Labor) at Lovestone's direction. Additional funds came from the AFL and David Dubinsky, along with contributions from the Consejo Ibérico in New York. The European Movement also subsidized the meeting with 1.350.000 francs.[357]

The Munich Congress, organized by the European Movement, had the primary objective of studying the democratization of European institutions and ways to create a political community that could progress towards the construction of the United States of Europe.[358] For Spanish democrats, this provided an international platform to discuss various proposals and tendencies within the anti-Franco resistance, all while being shielded from Francoist repression under the European frame.

The Treaty of Rome in 1957, which formed the basis for the European Federal Union, did not explicitly outline the political conditions for states to join the European Union. However, pressure from Spanish pro-democratic forces led to the approval of the Birkelbach Report in January 1962, establishing that democracy was a necessary criterion for a country to become a candidate member. This decision complicated Spain's interests in accessing the common market.[359]

Invitations for the Munich Congress were sent by Robert Van Schendel, Secretary General of the European Movement, to the Spanish representatives on May 18. The invitations specified that a debate on the future of Spain would take place during the congress.[360] Julián Gorkin and Manuel Irujo provided lists of proposed names from both the exile and inside Spain to attend the Munich Congress. Manuel Irujo and the participants in the CFEME meetings were confident about the freedom of movement for those invited from inside Spain in the days leading up to the Munich meeting.

It appears that the news coming from Spain had given a misleading impression, as the Franco regime did not facilitate the participation of the Spanish representatives in the Munich Congress as anticipated. Despite the social situation inside Spain and the pressure from pro-democracy forces in exile, some delegates were arrested, and others had their passports retained.[361]

Ultimately, 118 Spaniards (eighty from inside Spain and thirty eight from exile[362])[363] managed to participate in the pre-conference meeting in Munich on June 4 and 5, focusing on the possible entry of Spain into the Common Market. Initially, there was a plan for a debate led by a group presided over by Madariaga, featuring a table of ten members. However, due to an atmosphere of distrust between inside members and exile representatives, two separate commissions[364] were established to deliberate and formulate a joint statement. This decision was influenced by the reluctance of Gil Robles to engage in discussions with the Spanish representatives.[365]

There were concerns about Gil Robles's intentions, with suspicions that he aimed to align the Europeanist Movement with Cedist (Falangist) principles, a proposition that the members of the CFEME found unacceptable.[366] Despite over two decades having passed since Gil Robles's association with the Falangist movement, the unease with his presence at the meeting was evident.

The suspicions regarding Gil Robles' intentions were seemingly justified, as he expressed a desire for the moderate opposition to collaborate with Franco in guiding Spain toward a post-Franco transition. His proposed collaboration was intended to be constructive, without violence or attempts to overthrow Franco. Gil Robles also indicated that, if accepted, he would not obstruct Spain's admission to the Common Market while Franco remained in power.[367] This information was documented in a Confidential Report by the American embassy in Madrid.

In pursuit of his objective, Gil Robles corresponded with Carrero Blanco, Minister Under-Secretary of the Spanish Government, and other moderate leaders attending the Munich Congress, seeking some form of advance approval.[368]

Upon confirmation of the federal meeting in Munich with the presence of Spanish democrats from both sides of the Pyrenees, the Basque Nationalist Party (PNV), the Basque government, and Basque representatives in the European Federal Movement (CFEME) worked together to determine the participants from the Basque side.

Recognizing the significance of the European Federal Movement for Basque nationalists, it was crucial for them to be present in Munich. The Basque representatives had a dual agenda: to bring attention to the Basque cause and demands among the Spanish participants and to showcase themselves as a noteworthy group within the European Movement.[369] To achieve these objectives, participants were selected from both the Basque exile and the mainland Basque country, representing diverse backgrounds, including industrialists, priests, trade unionists, and young members from organizations like EGI (Eusko Gaztedi Indarra) and ELA-STV. The delegation included members of the Basque government from nationalist parties such as PNV (Basque Nationalist Party) and ANV (Basque Nationalist Action), as well as representatives from ELA-STV (Basque Workers' Solidarity) and EGI (Basque Youth).

Due to the prevailing circumstances of secrecy and the challenges faced by representatives from inside Spain in crossing the border to attend the Munich meeting, the list of attendees is inherently inaccurate. Nonetheless, after cross-referencing existing attendee lists that vary by no more than two or three details, it is confirmed that the Basque representation comprised thirty four individuals: fourteen from exile and twenty from within the Basque country.[370]

The fourteen Basque individuals from exile included Agustín Alberro Picavea, Iñaki Aspiazu, José María Aspiazu, Jon Bilbao (Basque-American), Manuel Irujo, Francisco Javier Landáburu, José Ignacio Lizaso, Gonzalo Nárdiz, Alberto Onaindia, Manuel Robles Aránguiz, Gregorio Ruiz de Ercilla, Jesús Solaun, Iñaki Unzueta, and Julio Jáuregui. The twenty attendees from inside the Basque country were Iñaki Aguinaga Beristain, Kepa Anabitarte, Mertze Arribas Cortajarena, Eugenio Arzubialde, José María Busca Isusi, Juan Celaya Letamanedia, José Luis Echegaray Pagola, Xabier Echeverría Arrue, Andoni Esparza Gallastegui, Isidro Infante Olarte, Ibon Navascués Ugarte, José Salegui, Juan Ugarte Guridi, Martín Zubizarreta Pildain, Javier Alonso Ezcain, Santiago Alonso Esquían, Antonio Anoz G. de Anzuola, Luis Benito del Valle, and Andoni Elorza.

According to the American embassy report's list, an additional name, Jesús Aguirre, brother of the First Lehendakari, is mentioned. This name also appears in the provisional list stored in the Irujo fund in Eusko Ikaskuntza, along with other proposed names like Josu Hickman and Ramon de la Sota, who were not included in the final list published by the Federal movement, despite being prominent Basque nationalists.[371]

On June 5, the two commissions, one from exile and the other from inside, convened separately to discuss pre-prepared documents—one by Madariaga and the other by Gil Robles and his European association. The objective was to advocate for democracy in Spain and compel the European Movement to spearhead the necessary democratic changes before accepting Spain's integration into the European space.

"The adopted agreement will more or less explicitly state that Spain has its place in the Federal Council and in Europe, excluding Franco," elucidated Irujo in a letter to PNV, ANV, and ELA-STV on March 13, 1962.[372]

Handling the mistrust and differences between the exile and internal factions proved to be a challenging task. Gil Robles, in a letter to Carrero Blanco, emphasized his reluctance to be seen alongside the exiles, asserting, "The position I will advocate in Munich is not influenced by external pressures, which I would never accept, or the result of agreements with political forces or social organizations."[373]

Conversely, the exiles were equally uneasy about Gil Robles' presence. Manuel Irujo conveyed the apprehensions of socialist colleagues, expressing concerns about hidden agendas and the infiltration of enemies into Munich. Overcoming this atmosphere of fear and distrust was a significant challenge. In a letter to Salvador de Madariaga in March 1962,[374] Irujo wrote, "Yesterday I had a hard time overcoming this position based on fear and mistrust. In Munich, there will be no possibility of being a Francoist."

Following disagreements and a heated discussion between Gil Robles and Irujo, where Gil Robles accused Irujo of organizing a "pressure group,"[375] on June 8, the Spanish representatives and the chairmen of both commissions (Gil Robles from the internal group and Salvador de Madariaga from the exile) presented the Iberian Resolution. This resolution was approved by the representatives of Italy, Belgium, Great Britain, and France, despite efforts by the Franco representative to thwart the agreement.[376]

The Iberian Resolution, endorsed by the IV Congress of the European Movement, conveyed the unanimous stance of 118 Spanish delegates. It was approved, in spirit, by acclamation. The Congress, held in Munich on June 7 and 8, 1962, asserted that the integration of any country into Europe, whether through membership or association, necessitates democratic institutions. For Spain, in accordance with the European Convention on Human Rights and the European Social Charter, this implies the establishment of democratic foundations.

- Ensuring the establishment of genuinely representative and democratic institutions that derive their authority from the consent of the people.

- Effectively guaranteeing all human rights, particularly individual freedom and opinion, and abolishing government censorship.

- Acknowledging the distinctive personality of various natural communities.

- Promoting the exercise of trade union freedoms on a democratic basis, with workers safeguarding their fundamental rights, notably through the use of strikes.

- Enabling the organization of currents of opinion and political parties, while respecting the rights of the opposition.

The Congress expresses a profound hope that the implementation of the aforementioned principles will pave the way for Spain's integration into Europe, recognizing it as an indispensable element. It notes the conviction expressed by all Spanish delegates at the Congress, emphasizing that the vast majority of the Spanish people desire this evolution[377] to unfold with political prudence and expeditiously, and commits to renouncing any active or passive violence before, during, or after the evolution process.

This resolution is presented as a collaborative effort of democratic forces both within and outside Spain, facilitating a discourse of unity and condemnation against the Franco regime in anticipation of its potential inclusion in the European movement.

Each of the five points of the resolution underwent extensive debate and negotiation since the versions and perspectives of representatives from the exile and the internal factions significantly diverged. For instance, the first point underwent modifications when the exiles rejected Gil Robles' proposal for the automatic establishment of a monarchy after the end of the Franco regime. In response, the concept of "consent" was introduced, with a potential reference to a future referendum. Don Juan promptly disapproved of the actions taken by the Monarchists in Munich and expelled Gil Robles from his private council.[378]

Although the Franco regime and the absent forces attempted to downplay the significance of the Conference, the aftermath must be analyzed in light of the disproportionate repercussions that ensued. Such a reaction is only understandable if the agreement caused a substantial shock.

Nothing without Euzkadi, nothing against Euzkadi.
Internal differences within Basque nationalism on the Munich agreement.

At the Munich meeting, the Basques, particularly Manuel Irujo, a member of both the CFEME and a key figure in organizing the gathering, expressed their contentment with the conference's outcome. The Spanish democrats, notably the exiles closely following the Munich meeting through reports in OPE and articles in Alderdi,[379] found the agreement to be satisfactory.

One supporter conveyed his joy in a message, stating, "My distinguished Friend: With the emotion that you can imagine, we listened yesterday to the radio cables of the happy result of your meeting in Munich, and today the press devotes great headlines and space to this meeting, featuring extensive excerpts from the speeches of Madariaga and Gil Robles, names of many attendants, etc. ... After the strikes, with perfect programming, and now this agreement and naturally joint action programs, it is to be hoped that the Dictatorship will not be able to resist long and will give way to another situation that will allow the establishment of freedom and democracy for all."

From Caracas, Julián Larrea expressed contentment, and Gudari, the publication of EGI (the youth members of the PNV), described the Munich agreement as follows: "The agreement of the anti-Francoist opposition in Munich is based on a humanist affirmation against the Spanish regime, oppressor of the human person and genocidal for attacking natural communities."

The term "natural communities"[380] in the agreement's final resolution was intentionally chosen. Article no. 3, titled "Recognition of the different natural communities," addressed the demands of nationalities within Spain, specifically the Basque, Catalan, and Galician. The minutes of the CFEME meeting on May 25, 1962, highlighted that the addition of "natural communities" to the proposal, as presented by Landaburu, was accepted without any discussion.[381]

The statement proved too ambiguous or overly naive for certain Basque nationalists who, perceiving themselves as a distinctive people within Spain, anticipated a more decisive stance. They sought an assertion that included the defense of "immediate Autonomy" in the event of overcoming the Franco Regime. While the divergences were not insurmountable, they indicated a new discord within Basque nationalism, signifying a crisis in the formulation of a future strategy.

It wasn't solely a matter of generational conflict, although that was a factor. The younger generation of EGI expressed satisfaction with the national definition in the resolution, stating,

> We are against Franco because we are democrats. But our anti-Francoism has another sign: that of the Basque, that of national freedom. We would not accept any solution that did not imply the recognition of our right to self-determination. That is why in Munich, we have worked to achieve and have achieved full recognition of our Basque personality [...] Nothing can be done on the peninsula after the fall of Franco without respect for our national prerogatives. No regime will be able to enter the European concert under other conditions than those that the IV Congress of the European Movement has adopted in Munich [...] Without the condition of respect for our personality as a people, we would not have participated in any agreement [...] Our motto has been: Nothing without Euzkadi, nothing against Euzkadi.

However, not all young nationalists, including some EGI members, shared the same enthusiasm as conveyed in the Gudari report. Certain young representatives of EGI and ELA-STV, who were invited to participate in Munich, believed that the resolution was too vague in its defense of the Basque nation. They held a different conception of what the future should entail after Franco.

According to José Antonio Ayestarán,[382] they expressed dissatisfaction with the Basque representative at the Federal movement because the agreed-upon resolution lacked "Immediate autonomy for the Basque Country and Catalonia as an indispensable condition to speak of democracy and a break with the Franco regime." Ayestarán drew parallels between the Munich Pact and the San Sebastian agreement and the circumstances leading up to April 14, 1931. He pointed out that Catalans, upon the proclamation of the Republic, swiftly achieved autonomy and declared the Estat Català. Some believed that, given the Basque opposition was the only serious and organized one in the Spanish State, the resolution should have demanded more than what was ultimately signed.[383]

ELA-STV welcomed the invitation to the Munich meeting, and the active young members within the Franco regime eagerly anticipated participating in a European gathering. However, the realpolitik approach of the "old guard" of exiled Basques clashed with the energy and impatience of the young trade unionists. In 1964, after two years, they decided to create a new organization, ELA-Berri, to unite the youth against the "elders." Idoia Estornés[384] describes this period as a time when young Basques sought answers to the Franco regime, amid the emergence of various political parties, trade unions, and associations in Spain during the 1960s. ELA-Berri originated from the dissatisfaction with the Munich meeting. "El Bonzo" Aguinaga, "Eladio" Kepa Anabitarte, and "Baroja" José Antonio Ayestarán were the architects of the new ELA, where immediate autonomy was deemed non-negotiable for social and national liberation. It was inseparable, "as in Mao's China," from the struggle to break away from the bourgeois nationalism of the PNV.[385]

The emergence of different perspectives within Basque politics, influenced by the widening breach initiated by ETA, also found expression within the PNV, where opinions downplaying the significance of the Munich agreements were present. Solaun, a member of the Bizkai-Buru Batzar, stated that the Iberian Resolution, particularly its reference to "Natural Communities," fell short of meeting Basque political objectives. According to Solaun, the Munich resolution couldn't be considered a binding pact for nationalists, as it did not outline autonomy or the exercise of the right of self-determination.[386]

In response to criticism and internal divisions within traditional Basque nationalism, Irujo wrote an article in Alderdi to fortify the foundation of the PNV's longstanding nationalism. This move was likely a response to the backlash received after the Munich agreement, especially regarding the controversy surrounding the concept of "natural communities."

In the article published in Alderdi no.183 in July 1962, Irujo made a clear distinction between Basque nationalism and the Basque government. Despite the frequent intertwining of activities between Basque nationalism and the Basque government, Irujo sought to differentiate the two concepts:

One thing is nationalism, or if you will, the Basque Nationalist Party, and quite another the Government of Euzkadi. Basque nationalism is a philosophical, social, and political movement, which aspires to realize the Basque nation in all areas of thought, culture, sociology, economics, spirituality, civil genius, ethnicity, and politics. Basque nationalism is a civilization. This is what we mean when we affirm that Euzkadi is the homeland of the Basques. (…) The Government of Euzkadi is the representative Institution of an autonomous regime achieved by the application of the doctrine of the Statutes affirmed by the Constitution of the Spanish Republic.

Irujo's explanation emphasizes that the policies pursued by the Basque government to fulfill the aspirations of Basque nationalists were intricately connected to the development of sovereignty. He underscores the significance of the European federation, within which the new State order must evolve. Implicit in the article is the defense of the European movement by the Basque nationalism of the PNV as a means to preserve the singularity of the Basque people. "We do not want to place borders on the Ebro. We aim to remove those from the Pyrenees," thus defining the future European Union as a necessary framework.

The staunch support for the European movement is evident in various articles of the same Alderdi issue, such as in one of the editorials titled "El Congreso Europeísta de Munich" or in "El Movimiento Europeo. Las Conversaciones de Munich," which delineate the PNV's interests. During the 1960s and 1970s, Europe and the European Movement became the political strategy adopted by traditional Basque nationalism of the PNV. Their international presence was limited to participating in European federal meetings and some conferences of the Christian Democracy. The idea of promoting the European framework as the battleground for the recognition of the rights of the Basque people was their only viable hope. Although not aligning precisely with the Europe envisioned by Lehendakari Aguirre and distant from the concept of the "Europe of peoples," Europe was in the process of being constructed. It seemed inevitable that, sooner or later, the Franco Regime would be accepted.

"Having realized that this was not the Europe in whose construction it had placed so many hopes, and of course, having relinquished any aspiration to access it autonomously, the PNV chose to advance within the framework of a pragmatic policy of cooperation, albeit limited, with state democratic forces, both at the peninsular and European levels."[387]

The strategy of forming alliances with Spanish forces was a painful compromise for Basque nationalism. Despite being one of the founding members of the European Movement, the condition of State nationalism prevailed. Irujo sought to clarify that agreements with Spanish democrats were the only means to gain recognition in Europe. He defended the Unión de Fuerzas Democráticas (UFD), a 1961 agreement that aligned closely with Lehendakari Aguirre's idea of a unity among all democrats.[388]

The agreements made with Spanish democratic forces became a major point of contention with young Basque nationalists, surpassing even the importance of European Federalism, as discussed earlier. These divergences were public and evident, leading to a decline in followers of Basque nationalism. Manuel Irujo addressed this in his article "Gobierno de Euzkadi y nacionalismo Vasco," stating, "The world is in a constituent period. It is typical of human nature and especially of all constituent periods that men change ideas and oppose attitudes. We the Basques neither can nor want to be an exception to this human condition. Nevertheless, we must be allowed to affectionately call the attention of our friends of the diverse groups detached from the maternal trunk of the Basque Nationalist Party such as Jagi-Jagi, ETA, in whose tribunes we find very often concepts that, perhaps without looking for it and we must suppose that in good faith, give rise to the confusions that motivate the writing of these lines."

Irujo emphasized commonalities with Basque nationalist critics: "We have the same program, the same doctrine, identical aspirations, similar feelings of homeland and nation. For all of us, Euskadi is the homeland of the Basques. Why should there be separate brothers in Basque nationalism?"

Shifting away from the Spanish focus since 1960, the world was no longer strictly bipolar due to changes in global politics. The emergence of countries gaining independence from colonial empires led to the creation of a third way, aligning with the UN under the "non-alignment movement." The blocks of the Cold War were thawing, despite the USSR's attempt to maintain them by constructing the Berlin Wall on August 13, 1961. The ice of the Cold War was melting into water, escaping through the cracks in the wall.

The "non-alignment movement" also signified the rise of popular consciousness and the emergence of European regionalisms or nationalisms looking to the self-determination movements in the third world as an example. This was the strategy adopted by ETA in approaching the "third world movement," which also involved aligning with revolutionary and socialist movements. By the end of the 1960s, Europe experienced political and social turmoil after years of relative economic and social calm. The European middle class was rejecting liberal democracies as a solution to their frustrations.

It's worth noting that the European concept found acceptance among various types of Basque nationalists, not only within the traditional nationalism of the PNV but also among emerging revolutionary nationalisms, especially those of ETA,[389] despite originating from different perspectives.

Simultaneously, it is crucial not to overlook the growing frequency of articles addressing repression within the continental Basque country. Discussions on strikes, the arrest of Basque nationalists, instances of torture, and the rising number of Basque prisoners were bound to alter the dynamics of Basque nationalism, redirecting attention from the exile to the internal struggles. As explored in the next chapter, the acknowledgment that Basque nationalism had not secured from the European movement would eventually be granted due to the repression within the Franco regime.

Actions and Reactions to the Munich Agreement

The success of the Munich agreement was celebrated by the democratic Spanish representatives, viewing it as the conclusive end to the war.[390] Salvador de Madariaga expressed that the agreement symbolized a united front of pro-democracy forces aimed at defeating the Franco Regime and establishing or reinstating democracy in Spain.

Among Basque nationalists, the Munich agreement was hailed as a triumph of democracy represented by exiles, the "inside exile," and the casualties of the Spanish Civil War. Ibon, a member of EGI in 1962, highlighted that Basque nationalists were also affiliated with the European movement,[391] underscoring the significance of the democratic ideals they stood for.

Examining the consequences of the Munich agreement requires considering the swift reaction of the Franco regime. The contemporary understanding of the meeting, even conceptualizing it as the beginning of the transition (a term coined later), emerged as a result of the Spanish dictatorship's disproportionate response.

Franco's regime reacted promptly by suspending article 14 of the Fuero de los Trabajadores (Spain's Bill of Rights) the day after the conference, which allowed the free change of residence. The regime justified this action as a response to an external campaign against them, implicating collaboration from individuals within Spain.

In the aftermath, participants at the Munich meeting faced a choice between remaining in exile or being confined to the Canary Islands, previously utilized for a similar purpose during Primo de Rivera's dictatorship.[392] Notably, individuals like Satrústegui, Álvarez de Miranda, and Jesús Barrios Lis were confined to the Canary Islands, while others like José Mª Gil Robles, Dionisio Ridruejo, Isidro Infante, and Vicente Ventura were forced into exile, with many never returning.

Spanish newspapers, despite not having any journalists at the conference, were compelled to publish two chronicles, relying on an article from the French newspaper France-soir. Unfortunately, this resulted in reports based on a highly inaccurate account of the meeting, as none of the correspondents were present.[393]

One of the published chronicles characterized the meeting between Spaniards from the inside and in exile as a "treasonous conspiracy against Spain" and a "New Munich Pact," explicitly alluding to the infamous Munich Pact of 1938.

In response to the perceived threat, the Franco regime organized demonstrations and launched an intense anti-Europe campaign. Additionally, the publication of the Iberian Resolution was banned as part of these measures.

Internationally, the Franco Regime faced condemnation from various quarters. Entities such as the committee Amitiés Méditerranéennes, *Le Figaro*, *Le*

Monde, L'Express, the Swedish radio, and *The New York Times,* among others,[394] denounced the repression against the democrats who had participated in the Munich meeting. The European Movement even dispatched a delegation to protest against the sanctions imposed on the Spaniards who attended Munich.

On June 12th, 1962, the EEC Commission's spokesman issued a communication condemning the measures taken by the Franco regime against the Munich participants. Despite the supportive statements from the European Federal Movement and some political figures from different European governments, the condemnations remained as statements without concrete actions.

Evidence suggesting that what was being constructed in Europe was a Union of States willing to disregard the rights of peoples and engage in politics with dictators emerged in a telegram available at the NARA archives in Washington. This report, sent on June 20th, 1962, likely in response to a Secretary of State's request, explained the EEC statement and explored its potential consequences.

It is beyond any doubt that the US government, specifically through the Department of State, expressed keen interest in the future of Spain. This interest is evident in the report titled "Speculation on form and nature of a Post-Franco Government,"[395] authored by the American embassy in Madrid on September 11th, 1961. The report clearly outlined the objective:

> Despite the speculative nature of the exercise, it seems worth going into, now and from time to time, if only to seek to avoid being suddenly confronted with a political surprise in this strategic corner of Europe." Additionally, it emphasized the need "to see if there is anything the US can or should do, that is not now doing, to try to influence the course of political events in Spain for the sake of US interests in this part of the world.

In the subsequent year, a telegram was dispatched to ascertain whether the European Coal and Steel Community (ECSC) was contemplating vetoing Spain's entry into the Economic Union. This concern arose from the ECC statement indicating disapproval of the Spanish government's actions against European militants who participated in the European Congress at Munich. The ECC expressed that such measures were incompatible with considering the Spanish request for association with the CM (Community of Members).[396]

US agents stationed in Brussels sought clarification on whether the ECC was earnest about taking measures against the Franco Regime, recognizing the significance of "this strategic corner of Europe" and its relations with the European Union. However, the EEC commissioner reassured the Americans, stating, "Has told me (the person writing the report) that he does not think Spanish Government's sanctions against Munich participants will have an immediate practical effect on the Spanish application, which already was at the bottom of a long list and, in his opinion, might not be acted on 'before many years.'"

Publicly condemning the Spanish repression, the European Community made a declaration. However, despite this public stance, there was a noticeable absence of tangible assistance provided to the Spanish democrats by the European Community.

Irujo and the Congress for Cultural Freedom

> Give me a hundred million dollars and a thousand dedicated people, and I will guarantee to generate such a wave of democratic unrest among the masses— yes, even among the soldiers—of Stalin's own empire, that all his problems for a long period of time, to come will be internal. I can find the people.
>
> Sidney Hook, 1949

If Manuel Irujo gained fame for anything, despite his affiliation with Basque nationalism, it was his reputation as a hard-working and open-minded individual. His extensive archive, encompassing articles, notes, letters, reports, meeting records, reflections, sessions, conferences, and more, serves as a testament to these defining characteristics.

Quoting Joseba Sarrionandia's words, "Exile is paper on which we write,"[397] Manuel Irujo exemplified this idea during his lengthy exile. He dedicated himself tirelessly to writing, aiming to keep the Basque nation alive, champion the Basque cause, uphold Basque institutions and laws, defend democracy, denounce totalitarianism, and ensure that he and his ideals were not forgotten but remembered.

As previously explored, Basque nationalism strategically engaged with the European movement, predominantly led by the PNV, and utilized by the Basque government as a means for international recognition. However, recognizing the potential of international recognition through cultural avenues, particularly given Irujo's cultivated nature, became another avenue worth exploring.

The involvement of Basque nationalists in the "Unión Cultural de los países de Europa Occidental" and prior actions within international cultural bodies, such as UNESCO, especially through Basque delegates in America, has been previously discussed. Exile, with its unique dynamics, facilitated encounters with unconventional companions, leading to diverse connections made by Manuel Irujo.

One such intriguing connection was established with Julián Gómez García, better known as Julián Gorkín, a Spanish communist and member of the POUM. Gorkín, who fought in the Spanish Civil War with the Popular Front and sought refuge in exile in 1937,[398] maintained contact with Irujo not only through the European Movement but also, as this chapter will delve into, through the Congress for Cultural Freedom.

Founded in the last week of June 1950 in Berlin, just one day after North Korea invaded the South,[399] the Congress for Cultural Freedom emerged from a gathering of 118 writers, artists, and intellectuals from 21 countries. Their primary focus was to deliberate on freedom, particularly the freedom of thought, as they were resolute in their commitment to safeguarding creative and critical thinking. This intellectual assembly, held in the midst of the Cold War, aimed to address the lack of cultural freedom, especially prevalent in countries under Soviet influence.

The chosen location for this foundational meeting was not coincidental; it symbolized a landmark moment in the Cold War. During the sessions, the participants pledged to collaborate in preserving the most threatened of freedoms—creative and critical thinking. In a response to attacks on cultural freedom, particularly in regions influenced by the Soviet Union, the attendees decided to establish a permanent organization. This initiative gave rise to the Congress for Cultural Freedom, which subsequently published materials across Africa, Europe, America, and Asia.

To uphold the principles outlined in the "Manifiesto a los hombres libres" (Manifesto to Free Men) approved during the sessions, the Congress for Cultural Freedom was created with the mission of defending freedom of culture. The organization drew together intellectuals of diverse nationalities, all devoted to the ideals of freedom and democracy. Among the notable attendees at the foundational meeting were Julian Amery (UK), Germán Arciniegas (Colombia), Ralph Bunche (USA), R.H.S. Crossman (UK), André Malraux (France), Eleanor Roosevelt (USA), and Tennessee Williams (USA).[400]

A noteworthy aspect of the Congress for Cultural Freedom is its dual role—while it operated as a congress with the mission of advancing cultural freedom and endorsing the work of Western writers and intellectuals, it was simultaneously integrated into the broader American cultural and ideological strategy to counter the Soviet offensive. Michael Warner characterized the Congress as "one of the CIA's more daring and effective Cold War covert operations," challenging the notion that it functioned as an independent intellectual movement.[401]

From 1950 to 1967, the Congress carried out its activities until the revelation of CIA funding led to a scandal. Subsequently, it transformed into the International Association for Cultural Freedom, predominantly funded by private donors, notably the Ford Foundation.[402]

Over nearly two decades, the Congress published various cultural journals, organized numerous conferences, and brought together prominent Western thinkers. Its objectives extended beyond countering the world behind the Iron Curtain; it sought to denounce the lack of freedom, advocate liberal values and freedom of thought, and combat indifference and political neutrality. Manuel Irujo's interest in participating in such a cultural movement was unsurprising.

Irujo contributed to the cause through his writings in the Spanish-language journal *Cuadernos*. His extensive archive and correspondence with Julian Gorkin revealed his keen interest in the issues and articles sent for editing by Gorkin and Madariaga.

The Congress initiated its publications with Preuves, a monthly journal directed by François Bondy in Paris. Subsequent journals included Encounter in London, Forum in Vienna, Tempo Presente in Italy, Soviet Survey directed by Walter Laqueur, and Quest in India. By 1960, the Congress published twelve different journals, including *Cuadernos*, which gained recognition in South America. As the Congress expanded its influence beyond the West, it reached areas like Tokyo with Jiyu and Australia with Quadrant. Headquartered in Paris, the organization's activities, beyond conferences and journals, were carried out through national committees responsible for organizing the publications.[403]

Beginning in 1952, there was a growing interest in establishing national committees in Latin America, and Julián Gorkin was chosen to spearhead this expansion.[404] The approach employed by American services in South America, previously utilized with the assistance of Basque services in the 1940s against Nazis, was now directed against a new form of totalitarianism. This strategy, as Joseph Nye would later characterize it, relied on soft power.[405]

Denis de Rougemont, President of the executive committee and founder of the European Cultural Center in 1949, articulated the multifaceted challenges to freedom in his work "En defensa de la libertad."[406] He highlighted that freedom faced threats not only from totalitarian doctrines but also from the evolution of material progress, which, originally emancipatory, could become compromised by national, ideological, or private ambitions that disregarded living traditions and lacked regulatory criteria. The extension of the parliamentary system and democratic practices, according to Rougemont, presented serious and complex challenges.

While the primary focus of the Congress for Cultural Freedom was countering totalitarianism, especially that emanating from the Soviet Union, its objectives expanded with the growing influence of the conference. It became more than just a creation of the CIA; it evolved from a well-established tradition of spontaneous self-organization within the Anti-Stalinist left, as noted by Hugh Wildford.[407] This spontaneous characteristic allowed the Congress to adapt to the European context and seek a "third way" that could position Europe amid the bipolar world of the Cold War.

Each journal published or edited by the Congress operated independently, expressing the opinions of the respective journal's editorial board rather than those of the Congress itself. This diversity allowed for a range of perspectives, with some journals being technical, others aimed at the general public, and variations in focus from literature to specific political-cultural trends, socialism, liberalism, and even conservatism.[408]

However, the majority of Congress participants consisted of ex-communists, members of the non-communist resistance against Nazism, European federalists, some intellectual refugees from the Soviet Bloc, and a small representation of Spanish exiles. The inclusion of European federalists, Spanish refugees, and even ex-communists provided the Congress with a distinctive feature that the U.S. government occasionally seemed to overlook in its perception of the Spanish resistance. Basque nationalists, in particular, were advocating for a third way in Europe, distinct from both Christian Democracy and European federalism.

A notable expression of this stance came in the editorial of *Alderdi* in November 1962, titled "Comunismo no, Franquismo tampoco" ("Neither Communism nor Francoism"). This editorial denounced both leftist and rightist totalitarian regimes, asserting, "There are two types of totalitarian regimes, leftist and rightist, which have in common the divinization of the State and the minimization of the rights of the human being." In the bipolar world of the Cold War, the fear of a potential communist regime after Franco served as a pretext for non-intervention, despite the efforts of the Spanish democrats' resistance in rejecting that idea. The editorial concluded with a rejection of the false dilemma presented as "Communism or anticommunism," asserting, "Our slogan is therefore, neither communism nor Francoism, but democracy."

At the foundational meeting in Berlin in June 1950, two Spanish representatives were present: the socialist Carmen de Gurtubay and the Basque clergyman Alberto Onaindía. Manuel Irujo and the Basque nationalists were well aware of their participation, and in a letter to Jesús Leizaola, Irujo expressed his irreverence, stating, "I have sent them (the notes) to Carmen Gurtubay. This woman, who is quite foolish, has managed to get Don Alberto Onaindia invited to the Berlin Conferences and, in addition, to have his travel and accommodation paid for. In principle, he has agreed. I guess he will go. What a couple!"[409]

Carmen Gurtubay, Marchioness of Yurreta and Gamboa in Biscay, attended the Congress in Berlin representing Salvador de Madariaga, who couldn't be present, likely due to his visit to India according to Irujo's sources. Alberto Onaindia delivered two speeches in Berlin: "Report on Intellectual Life in present Spain" and "Culture, Freedom, Christianity,"[410] demonstrating that the Spanish representation intended to contribute to the Congress with a strong anti-Franco stance, which was further emphasized through the journal *Cuadernos* and its news bulletin, *Boletín de prensa*.

Francesc Farreras, a former Falangist turned democrat against the Franco Regime, recounted that the Congress of Cultural Freedom, at a meeting in Paris, expressed interest in the situation in Spain and decided to take action on two fronts: a cultural front and a political front led by Julián Gorkin.[411]

For Gorkin, leading the cultural front involved touring Latin America, directing the journal *Cuadernos*, and establishing similar journals like *Cadernos Brasileiros* since 1955. He also played a role in founding the Asociación Argentina por la Libertad de la Cultura in Argentina.

Cuadernos, where Irujo collaborated, was fundamentally anti-totalitarian, featuring articles from other Congress journals such as *Preuves* or *Encounter*. It expressed a staunch anti-Soviet stance and supported the American plan for promoting European federalism. One such article, "La unidad Europea y la coexistencia," written by Gorkin in February 1955, exemplified this perspective.[412]

In its inaugural editorial in March 1953, *Cuadernos* outlined its objectives, stating, "(...) Our notebooks aspire to collect and translate the universal into our language, but also and above all to collect and channel the rich and varied expressions of the Latin American spirit towards the universal (...) A tribune open to the creative thought of the Americas and a means of communication with the spirituality of other peoples and continents."[413]

The journal *Cuadernos* started as a quarterly publication until 1954 when it transitioned to a bimonthly schedule. By 1961, due to the growing importance of Latin America in the Cold War, social changes, the awakening of the masses, and the necessity of engaging new generations, it became a monthly publication.

The deepening relationship between Irujo and Gorkin, particularly through the European Federal Movement and the organization of the Munich meeting, had roots that extended back further in time. In a 1957 article, Irujo recounted a story that highlighted their connection, dating back to the days of 1938. At that time, Irujo had resigned from his position as Basque Minister in the Government of the Republic due to incompatibility with political methods and in solidarity with Catalonia. Meanwhile, in Barcelona, a significant event was unfolding involving the imprisonment of dozens of left-wing socialist intellectuals who were disenchanted with the Soviet dictatorship during the May 1937 "putsch."

Behind the accusations of the Public Prosecutor's Office was the Communist Party's interest, seeking to brand the defendants as traitors and secure guilty verdicts, potentially leading to execution by firing squad for the anti-Stalinists. Despite being a conservative Catholic and Basque nationalist, Irujo, above all, considered himself a democrat who opposed the death penalty and the abuse of violence. In a demonstration of his principles, he traveled from Paris to declare in favor of the accused communists:

> My statement lasted three hours. At the end, the Prosecutor modified his conclusions. Instead of accusing the defendants of treason and asking for the death penalty, he accused them of sedition and asked for various penalties, none of them capital. The conspiracy was dismissed. The communist party had lost the lawsuit and the defendants saved their heads by facing the ruling of Justice. One of those defendants was Julián Gorkin.[414]

This article once again highlights Irujo's ability to establish connections with individuals regardless of ideological differences, as long as they could contribute to his cause. While *Cuadernos* primarily focused on spreading anti-communist sentiments in a Latin America influenced by "Stalinist, Peronist, and pro-Franco propaganda," according to a 1952 report by Gorkin,[415] Irujo recognized the journal as a platform to also promote Basque nationalism.

Exile provided opportunities for cultural endeavors and international visibility for Basque nationalism, and beyond political channels, culture and the intellectual field presented additional avenues for leveraging. Irujo was adept at capitalizing on these possibilities. On June 25, 1953, Irujo wrote a letter to clergyman Alberto Onaindia, attaching an article on Sabino Arana on the fiftieth anniversary of his death. The intention was to publish it in an international medium, specifically outside the fundamentalist circle reached by the magazine ALDERDI, in which Irujo and others were involved.[416]

The chosen international medium turned out to be *Cuadernos*, and Gorkin played a key role in making this happen. After briefly introducing Sabino Arana to Gorkin, Irujo suggested, with his characteristic courtesy, that "the fact and the leading figure deserve a place in *Cuadernos*." He proposed dedicating an article to Arana's memory on the occasion of his fiftieth anniversary, noting that several articles had already been published, including one by Cassou. Irujo expressed anticipation, stating, "I look forward to hearing from you."[417]

While we don't have records of earlier letters between Irujo and Gorkin, it's evident that Irujo was not only aware of the existence of the journal *Cuadernos* but was also keen on collaborating and receiving its issues. The regular contributors to *Cuadernos* were distinguished intellectuals such as Raymond Aron, Germán Arciniegas, Herbert Luthi, Czeslaw Mlosz, Andre Malraux, Denis de Rougemont, Salvador de Madariaga, Claudio Sánchez Albornoz, and Americo Castro.

The article on Sabino Arana, titled "Sabino de Arana, propulsor del renacimiento vasco," was eventually published in issue number five of March-April 1954. Gorkin informed Irujo in a letter dated February 22, 1954,[418] that he would receive 14,000 French francs for the contribution.

While there aren't more articles by Irujo in the journal, his continued interest is evident in the letters exchanged with Gorkin, where he repeatedly requested issues of *Cuadernos*.

In Irujo's archive, along with issues that can be found in specialized archives, there are some copies of *Cuadernos*. These issues provide insight into the journal's efforts to promote culture. *Cuadernos* featured a blend of articles on Latin culture, such as "La agonía de don Miguel de Unamuno" by Benjamín Carrión, "Aproximación a la obra de Jorge Luis Borges" by A.L. Revol, and "Orígenes de la novela en el Brasil" by J. Lins do Rego. The journal also included political articles like "Aspectos de la sociedad post-stalinista" by Franz Borkenau, "¿A dónde va Rusia?" by Alex Weissberg, and "Comunismo y asalariados en Francia."

The anti-communist stance of the journal *Cuadernos* is evident, and the collaboration of Basque nationalism in this regard aligns with the political strategy employed in the Cold War and the ideological trend of traditional Basque nationalism. This alignment is notable, especially considering that Basque revolutionary nationalism had initially embraced socialist ideas.

It's essential to note that the anti-communism promoted by *Cuadernos* was specifically focused on anti-Stalinism. This focus led the Congress for Cultural Freedom to establish a new organization in the 1960s, where Basque nationalists also collaborated, as will be discussed later in this section.

However, *Cuadernos* was not exclusively oriented toward the Spanish case, despite operating under a totalitarian regime. Until 1958, the publication had only dedicated a few articles to the Spanish situation. It is from 1958 onwards that a shift in orientation is observed, with an increasing number of contributions from authors inside Spain,[419] likely coinciding with the adoption of the "independent feature" that Congress publications embraced.

Even before the explicit turn toward Spain in 1958, certain articles published in *Cuadernos* attracted the interest of Manuel Irujo, prompting him to underline them. Examples include "El problema de las nacionalidades hispánicas" by Antoni Rovira i Virgili and "Las autonomías en España" by Salvador Madariaga.[420]

As mentioned earlier, *Cuadernos* was not the sole activity undertaken to promote freedom of culture. Specialized journals like *Science* and *Freedom* also played a role, founded after a congress in Hamburg in 1953. The congress received funding from the Rockefeller Foundation and the Fairfield Foundation. Directed by Michael Polanyi, a Hungarian-British intellectual, Science and Freedom addressed similar objectives as the Congress, delving into challenging issues such as racial segregation in the U.S. or apartheid in South Africa.[421]

In August 1956, Manuel Irujo successfully published an article titled "The disappearance of Professor Galíndez," denouncing the tragic vanishing of Jesús Galíndez, a figure cherished by Basque nationalism. The article served as a final effort to raise awareness about Galíndez's fate, emphasizing his tireless advocacy for freedom. Irujo highlighted Galíndez's dedication to the cause of the Dominican Republic's liberation from tyranny, drawing parallels between the lack of freedom in the Basque country and Galíndez's academic pursuits at Columbia University.

The article underscored Galíndez's significant doctoral thesis, a 700-page documentary study approved by Columbia University. This thesis systematically assessed the origins, development, and current characteristics of dictatorship. Irujo skillfully connected the absence of freedom in the Basque country with the tragic fate of the well-known academic at Columbia University, who was pursued and killed due to the information contained in his research. The issue containing Irujo's article also featured discussions on academic freedom in the USA and the state of cultural freedom in the Soviet Union.[422]

The collaboration between Gorkin and Irujo continued, encompassing cultural and political activities related to the Congress of Cultural Freedom. This collaboration solidified Irujo's favorable standing with Gorkin. From their joint activities, it can be inferred that the orientation of the Cultural Congress gradually shifted from general anti-totalitarianism to a more specific focus on anti-Stalinism, a cause for which Gorkin was well-known. The events and meetings attended by Irujo in connection with the Congress were seen not only as opportunities to promote Basque nationalism in intellectual circles but also as part of an ideological framework aligned with anti-communism.

An illustrative example of the shift from anti-totalitarianism to anti-Stalinism can be observed in a meeting organized by the association "Amigos de la libertad," a branch of the Congress of Cultural Freedom. In 1953, Irujo was invited to speak about forced migrations from totalitarian countries, but subsequent discussions centered on participation in the "Spanish Truth Commission on Stalin's Crimes."[423]

While there is no explicit evidence that Manuel Irujo participated in these meetings on behalf of the Basque government or as a representative of Basque nationalism, his letters and comments, as found in his correspondence, suggest that the PNV and the Basque Government were well aware of his activities. Given Irujo's loyalty to the PNV and the Basque Government, it can be asserted that Basque nationalism did not feel discomfort with Irujo's involvement in activities related to the Congress for Cultural Freedom. On the contrary, they actively sought international spaces for intervention on behalf of the Basque country.[424]

The Commission for the Truth of Stalin's Crimes, established on December 21, 1961, organized national and international commissions with the objective of researching, studying, and exposing crimes committed during the Stalinist era worldwide. The commission's establishment can be linked to the XXII Congress of the PCUS held in Moscow between October 17 and October 31, 1961. Khrushchev, who had faced criticism for his "Secret Speech" of 1956, stirred controversy again by attacking the Stalinist regime of Enver Hoxha in Albania during that congress. Given Gorkin's role as the director of *Cuadernos* and his strong advocacy against Stalin, it becomes evident why such a commission emerged in response to the developments at the XXII Congress of the PCUS.[425]

Gorkin played a pivotal role as the initiator and organizer of a Spanish commission to participate in the Commission for the Truth on Stalin's Crimes. In a communication to the executive committee of the PSOE on February 12, 1962, Gorkin detailed his involvement and the support received from 25 French personalities, as well as political parties such as the S.F.I.O., the P.S.U., the Radical and Radical Socialist parties, and the National Union of Teachers. Gorkin emphasized that multiple national commissions were being established, including a Spanish one.[426]

The Commission for the Truth on Stalin's Crimes sought to investigate and expose the crimes committed during the Stalinist era, particularly focusing on acts of revenge for the actions of the Spanish Communist Party during the Spanish Civil War. The commission aimed to probe the crimes against individuals such as Andreu Nin, Camilo Bernieri, and Marc Rein-Abranovitch, who were arrested and killed in 1937 by Stalin supporters on charges of treason.[427]

The Commission's objectives reflected a form of soft power, as evidenced by the channels it intended to use for disseminating its findings: "By all possible means of publication, newspapers, magazines, newsletters, which the Commission shall ensure the publication."[428]

Manuel Irujo was invited to participate in this commission due to his expertise as a legal professional, his experience as Minister of Justice during the Spanish Republic, and his significant contributions to educating the new generations about the communist intervention during the Spanish Civil War.[429]

While the Spanish commission did not ultimately succeed, Gorkin continued working within the International Commission. In a letter to Irujo dated April 4, 1962, Gorkin reported on communist activities, sent reports on Stalin's crimes to the Soviet Union representative in Paris, and wrote articles on the Spanish investigations for the Bulletin.

The experience with the Spanish commission and his connection with Gorkin provided Manuel Irujo with the opportunity to be invited to participate in the International Commission in 1963. In this role, he would engage with prominent intellectuals such as Victoria Ocampo (Argentina), Wolfgang Leonhard (Germany), Joseph Berger (Israel), Ignazio Silone (Italy), and Alexandre Solzhenitsyn (Soviet Union). The International Committee operated under the French commission, with figures like François Bondy, Jean Cassou, and André Ferrat coordinating the office alongside Gorkin and other French socialists and anti-Stalinists.[430]

While it is unclear whether Irujo ultimately accepted the invitation, their relationship continued until the end of the exile. In the 1960s, especially during the preparation and execution of the Congress of Munich, Irujo and Gorkin exchanged various letters in which the Congress for Cultural Freedom, the Centro de Documentación y Estudios, and the CFEME (Spanish acronym for the Center for Studies and Documentation on the Freedom Movement in Spain) were often conflated as if they were the same entity.

The Centro de Documentación y Estudios, established toward the end of 1959, operated as an anti-Franco think tank based in Paris. Directed by Gorkin and presided over by Madariaga, it played a role in the Spanish operation developed by the Congress for Cultural Freedom. The founding meeting included the participation of intellectuals such as Michel Josselson, Raymond Aron, and Denis de Rougemont.[431] The Centro published a bulletin called *Boletín Informativo del Centro de Documentación y de Estudios,* serving more as a newsletter to inform on events in Spain than as an intellectual platform like *Cuadernos.*

The Boletín, published quarterly between 1960 and 1964, played a role in anti-Franco activism by featuring articles and reports denouncing the situation in Spain. The last issue of 1961 (number 8) focused on the repression of Basque nationalism. Additionally, the bulletin presented a democratic and European alternative through articles on European Federalism.[432]

While Manuel Irujo and the Basque nationalists collaborated with the activities proposed by Gorkin and the Centro, their priority was always their national cause and its vindications. On March 15, 1962, Gorkin proposed a project to be sent to the CFEME titled "Por las libertades culturales, civiles y penales en España y Portugal" (For Cultural, Civil, and Penal Freedoms in Spain and Portugal) and asked Irujo to study it and suggest any needed amendments. Irujo sent the project to the PNV, ANV, and STV for consideration. Afterward, it was sent back to Gorkin with a proposal for some amendments related to the use of languages:

> Freedom for the use of languages other than Spanish spoken in the different territories of the Spanish State and which must be able to be used, both in the life and expression of citizens and in their application to the different media, printing, radio and television, as well as in the official centers and activities within the respective country.[433]

In this case, Basque nationalism utilized international bodies and their potential influence to advocate for the Basque cause, focusing on the Basque language, along with other national languages of the State, such as Catalan.

However, despite the ongoing relationship between Irujo and Gorkin, Manuel Irujo continued to surprise with his independent views. On December 6, 1962, in a speech for Radio Euzkadi, he criticized the American attitude towards the anti-communist campaign in South America, stating:

> The said anti-communist policy, applied from Washington to the Ibero-American countries, is supported, more often than not, by people who were once communists, still adhere to the communist ideology, but because they are anti-Stalinists, they joined the ranks of democracy."

Manuel Irujo's criticism in his December 6, 1962 speech for Radio Euzkadi was a direct attack on Julián Gorkin and most members of the Congress for Cultural Freedom, but there's no indication from their letters that Gorkin was informed of this speech. Despite the critical stance, the mood of their letters did not change.

In his speech, Irujo was questioning the direct link with American funds, expressing concern that democratic politics should not be solely based on elements that were dispensers of economic and other aid from the U.S.A. He was cautious about relying exclusively on these elements, and his words reflected his awareness of the funding sources behind Gorkin's activities.[434]

Once again, the Basque national cause was a central focus in Irujo's statements. He emphasized the Basque minority in Ibero-America, portraying them as a democratic and cohesive group that could serve as a base for permanent action. Irujo saw the Basque community in Latin America as an alternative, highlighting its positive characteristics, such as cohesion, good relations with the host community, and democratic values. These features were deemed essential to attract the interest of those in America, presenting the Basque community as a viable and appealing group in the context of exile.

"Patriots and Hooligans" ("Patriotas y Gamberros")

Manuel Irujo's response to the young patriots and his criticism of their attitudes came in the form of an article titled "Patriotas y Gamberros,"[435] published in May 1962 in Alderdi. In this article, Irujo expressed his disapproval of the behavior and views of the young nationalists who had participated in a conference in Paris during the fall of 1961. He referred to them as part of the "Bloisons noirs," an alternative French cultural movement, and aimed to discredit their stance, particularly their advocacy for violence and their criticism of the Statute of Autonomy and the political work of the PNV.

The delay in Irujo's response, waiting almost eight months after the conferences took place, can be attributed to the increasing differences between traditional Basque nationalists and the revolutionary faction. The rift between the two groups became more apparent, and their positions seemed irreconcilable. The speeches of the new generation at the PNV's headquarters in Paris stirred strong emotions among Basque nationalists, leading to a series of editorials and articles that reflected the significant ideological distance between the two factions.

In March 1962, Tximistak, the National Front's publication in Argentina, took a bold step by publishing the conference of the young Basques in Paris along with an editorial directly addressing Manuel Irujo. The editorial challenged Irujo's ideas and methods, portraying them as outdated compared to the fresh and courageous manifestations of the new generation. The young nationalists rejected Irujo's emphasis on autonomy, calling for a more radical approach akin to the Irish Republican Army's actions in Ireland.

This exchange of editorials and articles marked a period of heightened tension within Basque nationalism, with the revolutionary faction advocating for a more radical, independence-focused agenda, while Irujo and the traditional nationalists sought a more moderate path emphasizing autonomy.[436]

This editorial, coupled with several preceding ones, served as the driving force behind the creation of "Patriotas y Gamberros" eight months following the conferences—and also triggered the conflict between Irujo and Gallastegi.

The conferences had garnered anticipation from both young and old Basque nationalists. However, the radical stances of the youth immediately sparked controversy among traditional Basque nationalists. Nevertheless, voices such as Xabier Landaburu and Telesforo Monzón sympathized with the new generation, though not without raising eyebrows among some

Telesforo Monzón's stance towards ETA members wasn't peculiar; he simply adhered to the strategy employed by old Basque nationalists to confront the Basque Government and the PNV, as outlined in the Basque World Conference of 1956, discussed in previous chapters.

Regarding Xabier Landaburu, his interest in young Basques is evident in his book "La causa del pueblo vasco," written to persuade the new generation, born under dictatorship, to align with Basque nationalism and democracy and shun violent reactions. The book, well-received and highly regarded by the youth, became a reference, according to Iñaki Anasagasti.[437]

Landaburu maintained a close relationship with young Basque nationalists in exile, as evidenced in a letter he exchanged with Elías Gallastegi on November 30, 1962. In it, he details his interactions with Gallastegi's son, one of the participants at the Paris conferences: "I have seen Iker quite often this season. As he has had the attention to consult me about some things, I always try to help him with my advice and I have put all my official and private means at his disposal."[438]

Following the conferences, Irujo penned an article, published in Alderdi, titled "Fueros sí, estatuto no,"[439] in which he criticized the attacks by the youth Basque nationalists on the Statute of Autonomy.

The new generation of Basque nationalists promptly embraced the cause of independence without hesitation. To them, achieving the Statute of Autonomy appeared as futile as the Basque government 25 years after the outbreak of the Civil War, encapsulated in Irujo's assertion:

With more noble intentions than those pursued by traditionalists in 1933, the Basque patriots in 1961 echoed a similar sentiment. They challenged the Basque Nationalist Party and the Government of Euzkadi, stating that these entities had fulfilled their mission before 1939 but had since aged, become obsolete, and were now useless. The new generation aimed not for a Statute of Autonomy but for the Basque Code of laws and, ultimately, for independence.

The young Basque nationalists were challenging everything Irujo had fervently defended since the inception of the Basque Government and throughout his prolonged exile. While they maintained respect for the Basque government, they no longer acknowledged its legitimacy based on the Statute of Autonomy, a document they categorically rejected.

However, Irujo did not stand alone in his dismay over the youth and the positions articulated at the Paris conferences; he shared his doubts and disillusionment with certain other traditional Basque nationalists. The novel ideas of the new generation were not only challenging the Basque government but also the unity of the Basque people—a cause these traditionalists had fought for since their expulsion from the homeland. In their correspondence about articles to be published in Alderdi, Irujo and Iñaki Unzueta reflected on the youth's attitude:

"The conferences you have organized there are beneficial for me and allow young people to let off a little steam," and "I can see from Etxebarrieta's conference that these young people are disoriented (...)," according to Unzueta.[440]

This disorientation transformed into pessimism, possibly stemming from their upbringing under the dictatorship. Yet, according to Irujo, "Pessimism is a disease or a temperamental modality," and someone aspiring to govern a country couldn't afford pessimism, especially considering Basque history's successful trajectory, attributed to the Basque government, the Basque Statute of Autonomy, and the Basque Nationalist Party.[441] Irujo remained unwavering in his dedication to defending these principles.

Assessing the conferences in Paris and the varied political strategies proposed, it became apparent that the new generation of Basque nationalists, despite their disagreements with the Basque government, faced pursuit and imprisonment by the Franco regime to an extent comparable to, if not exceeding, that of the previous generation. By 1961, some of them had already sought refuge in exile during the Conferences, and in 1962, several dozen more joined the ranks of Basque nationalists in exile.

The introduction of these young and innovative ideas also sparked debates within the exile community, spanning not only Europe but also America. While their initial choice of exile was Iparralde, where they found refuge among established Basque nationalists like Telesforo Monzón or Elías Gasllastegi, they swiftly expanded their influence and began migrating to America, particularly Venezuela.

From Rebellion to revolution. "El amargo Cubalibre del exilio"[442]

ETA produced and published its own journal, Zutik (meaning "standing" in Basque), primarily from Bayonne. However, shortly after the initial issues, Zutik Berriak (Zutik News) emerged, featuring news, documents, and directives from ETA. Additionally, an American version, Zutik en Tierras Americanas, was established to amplify their message in America. Despite its initial intention to present alternative viewpoints, the American journal often lacked the regularity of the original and predominantly reproduced articles from the Bayonne publication.[443]

Beyond ETA's official outlet, the ideas of the new generation garnered support from various Basque communities and publications. This situation raised concerns among Basque delegates in America, leading to worries about potential divisions. Lucio de Aretxabaleta, the Basque delegate in Venezuela, conveyed this apprehension to the Lehendakari on October 3, 1961,[444] anticipating a period of disagreeable disagreements. However, his analysis regarding the limited following and impact of these ideas in Venezuela proved incorrect. Revolutionary notions from the new Basque nationalism had found fertile ground, inspiring and energizing many Basque nationalists in Venezuela.

The exile and the American setting provided an opportunity to reside in free communities where alternative ideologies and emerging trends could be openly debated, discussed, and experienced. Iñaki Anasagasti vividly describes the freedom of life in Venezuela and the engaging debates that took place:

> We used to talk about the bitter cubalibre of exile. We used to argue about whether the armed struggle was good or not, about whether Marxism-Leninism was good or not, about whether Fidel was good or not…

These discussions occurred against the backdrop of influences from Cuba and Algeria. According to Anasagasti, Venezuela was notably influenced by Cuba, and the new Basque revolutionaries drew inspiration from the "barbudos" (the bearded), a clear reference to the Cuban Revolutionaries. They used this example to advocate for political resistance against the Franco dictatorship in the Basque Country.[445]

Violence emerged as one of the responses offered by the new revolutionary Basque nationalism to advance the Basque cause. It served as an example drawn from the exile but was also defined as a product of the realities faced by the new generation. In this context, violence was attributed to the oppressive nature of living under the Franco dictatorship. Combined with external influences, it began to be perceived as a viable solution to achieve the aspirations of the Basque nation.

As previously mentioned, the momentum of the new generation garnered increased support from certain Basque communities in exile. They viewed this as a fresh opportunity for the youth to advocate more radical options for the Basque cause. This helps elucidate the radical positions taken by the Euzko Mendigoizale Batza in Argentina against the Basque Statute of Autonomy and in favor of independence, as expressed in a letter addressed to the Lehendakari on November 9, 1960:

> We, the Basque nationalists who are part of the Euzko mendigoizale batza de la Argentina (sic.), driven by our unwavering loyalty to the Basque cause which, by logical and inexorable consequence of Basque nationalism, is translated into the National independence of Euzkadi, formulate to you the following statements because we understand that you should be interested in knowing the postulates that support each and every one of the organizations in Euzkadi and abroad.[446]

The Euzko Mendigoizale Batza, named after the original entity founded in 1934 by Elías Gallastegi and others in the Basque Country, held a special significance in Biscay as a pro-independence, anti-capitalist organization preserving Sabino Arana's nationalism.[447] One of its primary objectives was the establishment of a pro-independence National Front, an idea that never fully materialized but found organization within the exile under the name "Frente Nacional Vasco." This entity managed to gather various Basque nationalist organizations and publications, including Frente Nacional Vasco (Delegación extraterritorial de Venezuela) or Tximistak (Frente nacional Vasco).[448]

In the letter addressed to Lehendakari Leizaola, the Mendigoizales, representing themselves as members of the Basque National Front, launched a critique against the Basque Statute of Autonomy. They argued that the statute merely represented three out of the seven Basque provinces and censured the Basque Government's policy of aligning with Spanish political forces to combat the Franco regime. The Mendigoizales advocated for "rebellion and struggle" as the sole effective means to achieve the goal of "full national sovereignty." These words resonate with the sentiments expressed by young nationalists at the Paris conference a year later.

While ETA initially placed trust in the Basque government and exhibited respect for Lehendakari Aguirre, as well as for Lehendakari Leizaola when he assumed office, their stance shifted after the first assembly. With new members like Etxebarrieta's brothers, ETA began to emphasize Sabino Arana and his early nationalism, attempting to surpass the Basque government and positioning themselves as his true heirs. According to Beltza, "In a certain way, ETA appears as the continuation of the political intransigence of the Aberrianos."[449]

The connection with Elias Gallastegi in exile mirrored the link with the old Aranism of Jagi-Jagi. However, the exile, perceived as an eighth province, promoted this idea and exploited disagreements with the Basque government to forge a new strand of Basque nationalism. The proposals of the young Basque nationalists found acceptance and support not only among the youth in exile but also among older Basque nationalists dissatisfied with the Basque government, willing to endorse an alternative vision.

Among the Basque community in Venezuela, one of the exile locations where the ideas of the new generation found fertile ground was particularly noteworthy. ETA had established a kind of branch in Venezuela, gaining special significance during the 1960s, as a substantial portion of the economic resources supporting the Basque Government in exile originated from this South American country. The initial encounters between ETA and the Basque government delegation arose in connection with the collection of financial resources. What initially began as a challenge to the legitimacy of the Basque Government or skepticism about the policies of traditional Basque nationalism evolved into questioning the authority and effectiveness of the Basque government in fundraising for the Basque cause.

Since the commencement of ETA's "active resistance" against the Franco regime, the focus of the Basque Government's resources and the activity of Basque nationalists in exile had been directed toward assisting Basque prisoners and new exiles. This emphasis raised concerns about the management of resources.

In a letter addressed to Lehendakari Leizaola, signed as "ETA of Venezuela," the issue of resource management and divisions within Basque resistance played a central role in their demands. ETA identified itself with three different groups within the Basque resistance in Euskadi, treating them equally: "Eusko Gaztedi, a group controlled and directed by the PNV; ANV resistance; ETA; non-partisan."[450] While the letter is undated, its apolitical self-definition suggests that it likely predates the first assembly, placing it around 1960 or early 1961.

According to the letter, the diversity among Basque resistance groups is impeding the smooth development of actions, which could be more effectively executed under a unified front. The document specifically reflects on the situation in Venezuela, where challenges, distinct from the "active resistance" observed in the streets of Euskadi, are linked to confusion among the Basque patriots residing there. There is a "confusion and scandal in the minds of many Basques who cannot understand how it is possible for us to be divided on a matter of such vital importance." Due to this confusion, Basques in Venezuela are refraining from contributing to the Basque cause. In response, ETA suggests a potential solution by creating a common front for fundraising. To address the issue in the Basque Country, the organization proposes establishing a General Staff responsible for managing resistance and coordinating resistance organizations, albeit within a common committee.[451]

From the letters exchanged between the Basque Government and Caracas, as well as those between the Basque delegation in Bayonne and the Basque government in Paris, it can be inferred that ETA members in Venezuela, along with members of the National Front, have adopted a more radical stance against the Basque Government and its policies. However, relations with ETA in Iparralde, especially with the organization's founders (Madariaga, Benito del Valle, and Txillardegi), have become warmer despite existing differences.

The funding issue raised in Venezuela is resolved when members of ETA deliver over 38,000 French francs to the Basque delegation in Bayonne. This closure marks the episode as a misunderstanding and acknowledges the legitimacy of the Basque Government's authority, as conveyed by Dorronsoro when he hands the money to Gonzalo Nárdiz.[452]

While ETA does resolve the issue by recognizing the Basque government's role as the intermediary managing resources for the prisoners, the dispute showcases the influence ETA wields in exile and the capabilities of the new generation to assert their independence.

In 1961, the noticeable presence of ETA supporters in Venezuela becomes another subject of discussion within the Basque community in the South American country, as described by Lucio de Aretxabaleta[453] in his correspondence with Lehendakari Leizaola in 1961:

> Setting aside the issue of ETA, which has been satisfactorily resolved, I must emphasize that these incidents have provided us with the opportunity to further strengthen the unity of those who 'are with the Government,' and I hope this strengthening will yield satisfactory results for the monthly collections. (....).[454]

In this statement, Aretxabaleta was alluding to the escalating conflicts with ETA supporters in Venezuela and the management of donations crucial for the Basque Government's activities, with the Venezuelan community being one of its primary contributors. In the weeks preceding this letter, discussions at the Basque center in Caracas centered around the fund management, with some opinions suggesting that the Basque government should not exclusively handle all the money—a manifestation of total distrust and a perceived lack of legitimacy for Basque institutions. The increasing number of prisoners generated new needs and expenses that would accentuate the differences between the two nationalisms represented by the Basque Government and the emerging forces of ETA.

Despite ETA's initial defense and respect for the Basque Government, their strategies diverged from the outset, as noted by Aretxabaleta:

"(...) they want the money to be sent to a committee formed in Continental Euzkadi by E.G., ETA, and the Front. I argued with those from ETA, making them understand that this was not accepted by the representatives here of E.G. of the interior, of E.G. of Caracas, of the PNV, STV, and ANV, nor by myself as Delegate."

It became evident that the PNV and the Basque Government had lost control over the mainland Basque Country, and ETA sought to manage funds on an equal footing with the Basque Government. The implications were dire for the unity of the Basques and, especially, for the Delegate Council:

From the meeting with them, I drew the conclusion that ETA acts with instructions from the Interior. They aim to capitalize on the fundraising circumstance to create an organization within the interior outside the Delegate Council or to exert pressure for their interference in that Council with their own personality.[455]

Despite the resolution of the money issue, the publications in America, situated between ETA and the National Front, persisted in their campaign against traditional Basque nationalism. They questioned policies and even leadership, as mentioned earlier, with articles directly opposing Manuel Irujo. While the authority of the Basque government itself was not directly challenged or formally attacked, the ideological gap became more than evident, leading to a divergence in the development of Basque nationalism in exile.

The split Jagi-Jagi of the 30s found renewed vigor in exile and, since the inception of ETA, transformed into a new Aranism that opposed the Basque Government and wholeheartedly supported the new generation of Basque nationalists, now adding "revolutionary" to their list of definitions.

The Venezuelan base became the most active group of Basques, giving rise to a new nationalist current that demanded more from the Basque Government-in-exile, advocating for new policies, new political strategies, and even new actors.

According to Iñaki Anasagasti, if there was any place in exile with the power to independently generate a new trend in Basque nationalism, it was Venezuela: "More than a few professional Basque journalists are in exile in Venezuela: Genaro Egileor 'Atxerre,' Luis Ibarra Enciondo 'Itarko,' Bernabé Orbegozo 'Otarbe,' Andoni de Astigarraga, Manuel Fernández Etxebarria 'Matxari,' José de Abásolo Mendibil."[456]

The presence of numerous journalists and writers, along with the publication of various journals and newspapers, facilitated debates, discussions, and controversies within Basque nationalism.[457] One of the most controversial journals supporting the new generation of Basque nationalists, linked to the Jagi-Jagi movement and the National Front's defense, was Irintzi. This journal was published and directed by Manuel Fernández Etxebarria from 1957 until 1962.[458]

In Irintzi, subtitled "Erri aske batean- Euzkadi'ko azkatasunaren alde" ("In a free country, until the freedom of Euskadi"), Matxari and fellow Basque nationalists aligned with Jagi-Jagi's ideals staunchly advocated for the independence of the Basque Country. They directly criticized the political strategies of the Basque Government, as evident in Matxari's letters to Manuel Irujo in 1961:

"Yes, sir, Mr. Manuel, you may not realize how much I value you, and yet, I have you by the neck (sic.). I appreciate Landaburu; I appreciate 'your friend' Axuriaguerra and Artetxe. However, if I could confine them with a stroke of the pen to a room in Sabin Etxia, they would remain there for a long time. Between them, Basque nationalism is reduced to nothing more than 'Spanish federalism.' They have transitioned from Sabin to Pi (3-14-16) and Margall."[459]

Despite the apparent familiarity and cordiality in their correspondence, Matxari's criticisms were severe, constituting a direct assault on the legitimacy and efforts of the Basque Government. The constant calls to revive the spirit of Sabino Arana, embodying the essence of original Basque nationalism, were entwined with ideas embraced by the new generation of Basque nationalists—embracing violence and categorically rejecting the Basque Statute of Autonomy.

Matxari, aligned with the Jagi-Jagi movement, the National Front, and ETA supporters, adopted a critical stance against the traditional Basque nationalism emanating from exile, particularly from South America, notably Venezuela (with Argentina also playing a role in the opposition movement).

Within the editorials of Irintzi, Matxari and his fellow Basque nationalists opposed the "official" Basque nationalism represented by the PNV. Instead, they propagated an anti-Statute-of-Autonomy Basque nationalism dedicated to the complete independence of the Basque Country. Consequently, they vehemently opposed any alliances with Spanish democratic forces in exile—a strategy championed by the PNV, particularly by Manuel Irujo.

This form of nationalism represented a return to the primal ideals of Sabino Arana. It involved a reinterpretation of Arana's writings and thoughts, such as his 1897 dispute with Eustaquio de Echave-Susaeta[460] on the Fueros. In 1961, those defending the Statute of Autonomy were equated to the defenders of Spanish hegemony, as the Statute was perceived as a "political ploy to stifle us and keep us under Spanish control."[461] The refusal to recognize the Basque Statute of Autonomy extended to the non-recognition of the Lehendakari and, consequently, the Basque Government, showcasing a more radical stance than even the youthful members of ETA.

The document titled "Manifiesto de Caracas," released in 1962,[462] articulated the necessity for a national front to supplant the Basque Government, citing its provisional status and dependence on Spanish institutions. The manifesto argued:

Considering that the present Provisional Basque Autonomous Government is unable to lead the Basque people to freedom due to its lack of legal authority, relying solely on the authority derived from the Spanish Republican Government. It functions as a legal appendix only for a portion of the Basque territory, excluding Nabarra (Navarra), Lapurdi (Labourd), and Zuberoa (Sole).

The proponents of this manifesto, identified by Gaizka Fernández Soldevilla as PNV dissidents José Estornés Lada and Augusto Miangolarra, alongside Francisco Miangolarra,[463] proposed the replacement of the Basque Government with a National Government. This proposed government would comprise organizations, sectors, and entities with a clear pro-independence agenda from both exile and within the Basque Country. The envisioned national Basque Government would promptly address various issues, including the defense of Zazpiak Bat—with Iruñea-Pamplona as the capital of the Basque Confederation—the official status of the Basque language in the national government and its institutions, and economic and social measures to address the challenging situation.[464]

The emphasis on the Basque language as a crucial element of Basque nationalism was coupled with criticism of PNV Basque nationalists for allegedly abandoning their original language. Throughout the 1960s, the advocacy for the Basque language became a prevalent theme in the evolution of Basque nationalism, gradually replacing ethnic origin. In a Basque nationalism that was emerging after more than two decades of exile, the significance of ethnicity tied to place of birth diminished. Instead, it gave way to a more civic feature, connected to culture, and, in this context, the language.

It's noteworthy that the increasing interest in the Basque language was not exclusive to publications associated with the opposition against the traditional Basque nationalism of the PNV. Even in Alderdi, the official journal of the PNV, there was a monthly section in Basque language, titled "Iletik Ilera" (hair to hair), along with other monthly articles in Basque. However, in the publications of Basque nationalists during the 1960s, it became more prevalent to find sections in Basque language and articles advocating for the preservation of the Basque language. The Basque language took center stage in the national Basque assertion, gradually displacing the emphasis on ethnic origin.[465]

The most evident manifestation of this heightened interest in the Basque language and the subsequent shift away from the ethnic component is reflected in the PNV declaration of January 26, 1966. This declaration, penned and presented at the conclusion of events commemorating Sabino Arana's centenary, respected and upheld the previous declarations of 1949 and 1960. However, the 1966 declaration integrated the Basque language as an integral part of the national definition of the Basque nation:

The Basque nationalist party proclaims the reality of Euzkadi, the Basque nation, a natural community created in history; expressed in its language, customs, and way of being; affirmed by the will of the Basque People, in its civil manifestations, in persecutions and prisons, and with the spilling of its blood.

Furthermore, the first item in their proposal for the reestablishment of the Basque Country added: "In the Basque national: The national characteristics and especially the Basque language, live and develop; and the conscience of our collective being is authentically affirmed in all Basques."[466] As the days passed in a prolonged exile, it became increasingly incomprehensible to anchor the essence of being Basque solely on one's place of birth, especially with an entirely new generation born in exile.

In addition to this, the National Front's opposition found expression in the publications of Frente Nacional Vasco (Delegación Extraterritorial de Venezuela) (1960-1968) and Tximistak (1961-1967) from Argentina, serving as their most significant publications. Much like the Jagi-Jagi followers, the supporters of the National Front advocated for a more active and direct form of Basque nationalism, including the use of violence. They envisioned the organization of a national front of Basque nationalist organizations—regardless of political party affiliation—that would, in some way, replace the Basque Government. Notably, the National Front did not expressly aim to join or replace the Basque Government but rather stood as a substantial focal point of opposition.[467]

The leaflet Tximistak, published in Argentina, emerged as one of the most contentious and explicitly anti-Basque-Government publications. Nevertheless, its primary objectives, much like other publications, revolved around advocating for the independence of the Basque Country, endorsing the use of violence, and supporting the National Front.

In 1962, following the Paris Conference at the headquarters of the PNV and the Basque government, the most critical and abrasive articles against the Basque government surfaced, with a particular focus on Manuel Irujo and the strategies employed by traditional Basque nationalists, as previously mentioned. The introduction of a new generation of youth, especially those representative of ETA, intensified the criticism against traditional Basque nationalists and led to unwavering support for the youth movement.

The exile, particularly from America (at least a significant part), not only rebelled against traditional Basque nationalism but also sought to bolster the revolution that would propel the development of ETA's movement. Additionally, Venezuela, aside from being the epicenter of opposition to the PNV's orthodoxy, served as a fertile ground for the incubation of new ideas, as previously discussed. It also stood out as the primary source of economic resources for the Basque Government. Perhaps owing to the imperative of acknowledging the contributions of the Venezuelan Basque community and the necessity of elucidating and preserving the sentiments of the new generation raised in exile, traditional Basque nationalism began to undergo a transformation, shifting from an ethnic conception to a more inclusive and civic meaning.

In 1962, the Basque Government initiated the promotion of a "Carta de Condición Vasca," aligning with the trajectory of modernizing Basque nationalism to reflect the evolving features of Basque society, particularly taking into account the circumstances of the exile. Life in exile not only influenced the decision to modify the ethnic nature of Sabino Arana's Basque nationalism but, in fact, demanded such a modification. The issuance of this Basque identification document was in response to the demands put forth by Basque organizations in Europe and America:

"The Basque status card, approved by a recent decree of the Government of Euzkadi, has been put into service. This document, accrediting the holder's Basque status determined by origin, birth, or residence, will also serve as proof of contribution to the Basque Government's taxes."[468]

With the issuance of the "Carta de Condición Vasca" and the establishment of new criteria for "being Basque," there is a noticeable shift where place of birth ceases to be an essential requirement. Instead, residence or origin takes precedence, shaping an inclusive nationalism not determined by ethnos but by a shared willingness to be Basque.

Nevertheless, it's essential to acknowledge that this change and the introduction of the new "Basque condition" were largely driven by the critical financial situation facing the Basque government. The revised criteria for Basque recognition extended to individuals who contributed to the cause, irrespective of their place of origin. In a ceremony held in Venezuela on October 19, 1962, the Basque Government expressed its recognition for those who had supported the Basque cause:

> Being born Venezuelan, Japanese, or Basque does not confer any spiritual quality that identifies one with the soul of a people. What gives a person the true merit of nationality is his work (...) To be a Basque identified with the aspirations of his people requires today more than ever that will and that responsibility (...).[469]

Recognition as part of the Basque nation was granted to those who demonstrated a sense of responsibility towards the Basque cause. While the change had been necessitated by economic circumstances, it is crucial to highlight the evolution of the concept of Basque nationality and underscore the significant role played by the exile in shaping this transformation.

Getting to know each other. Paris, October 1961

In October 1961, the PNV in Paris, under the presidency of Manuel Irujo, and its Local Council organized a series of conferences aimed at providing a platform for various expressions of Basque nationalism, whether conforming to the orthodox perspective or deviating from it. According to Irujo, as stated in his article "Patriotas y gamberros,"[470] the objective was to "open its tribunes to all current expressions of Basque nationalism, whether orthodox or heterodox, whether they agree with the doctrine and policy maintained by the E.B.B. or disagree with them, assuring those who occupy the stand full academic freedom."

The idea of renewal was clearly present in the minds of some traditional Basque nationalists who recognized the growing gap between their views and those of the new generation. This distancing was not solely a matter of age; the exile experience was also contributing to the ideological divisions.

Irujo, recognizing the need to bridge the gap with the youth, actively engaged in efforts to connect with the new Basque generation, evident in his continuous exchange of letters, articles, meetings, and conferences. Given Irujo's character and his close ties with both the PNV and ETA members during that period, as detailed in previous chapters, his approach to the youth aligns with his personality.

Recognizing the widening generational gap, the meetings organized in Paris, termed as an "Ecumenical therapy" by José Antonio Rodríguez Ranz,[471] aimed not so much to influence the youth but rather to prevent extremism. The meetings saw the participation of "radicals" such as José Luis Álvarez Enparantza "Txillardegi," Iker Gallastegi, and José Antonio Etxebarrieta, among other traditional nationalists familiar with these gatherings in Paris.

Txillardegi, presenting himself as a member of ETA, delivered the opening conference titled[472] "The Basque Youth on October 7, 1961," directly criticizing the Basque government and traditional Basque nationalism in exile after 25 years.

In Zutik Caracas, the conference titled "The Basque Youth on October 7, 1961" is published alongside the leading editorial "A quarter of a century has gone by," where ETA reflects on the 25 years of existence of the Basque Government, calling for a renewal and an opportunity for young nationalists.

ETA expresses that the hope for the future lies in the Basque youth, as the Basque institutions have ceased their activities and lost the trust of the Basque people. The editorial asserts, "The Basque people have not stopped in 1936; OUR INSTITUTIONS HAVE (sic.) (...) There are institutions that do not exist and that have an audience in our highest authorities. There are parties that neither believe in Euzkadi nor feel the Basque problem, and that have a voice and a vote in the highest bodies of the country."

A conflict between the internal and external factions is also highlighted. ETA praises the Basque resistance within the region but links the work done to age, emphasizing the actions of ETA and EG members, connecting the Basque youth with the Basque nationalist Party. Similar to the challenges faced by the exile, age becomes a dividing line among Basque nationalists. The youth demand their role in the Basque resistance, expressing fatigue with waiting and now calling for active participation.[473]

Txillardegi's conference, with a preface in Basque language, explicitly refers to the 25th anniversary of the Basque Government. As an ETA member, Txillardegi defends the active Basque youth nationalists and their strategy, along with highlighting the Basque language as a crucial element of Basque nationalism.[474]

In his address, Txillardegi discusses the new Basque generation raised under the Franco dictatorship, unaware of the creation of the Basque Government and the Statute of Autonomy, awaiting action from the Basque national structure. According to him, both the new generation and Basque nationalism necessitate a new strategy, as the previous approach of "conserving" and "waiting," along with "counting on the people," has progressively lost its meaning.[475]

The new generation of Basque nationalists is eager for action, rejecting a passive approach, and Txillardegi proposes an "Estrategia abertzale" (Strategy of Basque nationalism) that relies on the "Patriotic Front" to update the national Basque strategy. While the Basque government is respected, there is a strong perception of the need for a shift in strategy, including abandoning political agreements with Spanish forces.

Txillardegi's new strategy centers on the "Patriotic Front," an idea previously promoted by members of Jagi-Jagi and the Basque National Front. This front consists of patriotic organizations, deliberately avoiding the term "national," particularly ETA and EG. However, it remains open to any other Abertzale forces. Importantly, the concept of a National Front or Patriotic Front does not necessarily entail the establishment of a new Basque Government. It primarily involves the commitment of Basque nationalist organizations to actively advocate for Euskadi.

Although Txillardegi's conference might have contained elements that could upset traditional Basque nationalists like Irujo, it was likely the October 29 conference titled "El sentimiento de nacionalidad" (The sense of nationality) that stirred controversy and led to the article "Patriotas y Gamberros."

As mentioned earlier, Irujo's displeasure was not solely due to the content of the conference. Still, it was exacerbated by the fact that it was published in Frente Nacional Vasco in April 1962, accompanied by a strong preface attacking the Basque Government. This publication heightened tensions and contributed to the growing ideological divide among Basque nationalists.

While Irujo refrained from explicitly naming the author "for reasons of discretion," it is revealed through the correspondence of Eli Gallastegi that the author in question was none other than his son, Iker Gallastegi.[476] Iker, according to his father, had crossed the border on multiple occasions, returning from exile to Euzkadi to actively participate in the struggle for freedom within the region.

Described by Eli Gallastegi as someone who not only engaged in resistance activities but also played a significant role in national restoration, Iker became a Basque speaker and directed a group involved in theater and choirs in the Basque language. As a member of Euzko Gaztedi, Iker was well-acquainted with the Basque resistance within the region, likely contributing to his critical stance toward the work carried out by the Basque Government in exile.

Aligned with other youths who participated in the conferences, Iker was committed to the idea of Basque Country's independence and rejected any form of political compromise regarding the issue of autonomy. He expressed, "We seek a free Euzkadi, and for us, freedom has more than one definition. It does not mean limited freedom, a freedom conditioned to the interests of another nation, but an absolute freedom, the sovereign control of all the destinies of the Basque Country."[477]

While acknowledging the historical contributions of the Basque Government and the nationalists before them, Iker (speaking on behalf of the youth) believed that Basque nationalism had misunderstood the concept of nationalism. He asserted that nationality is something spiritual, not material, and cannot be determined by statutes, agreements, or interests. Consequently, he emphasized their desire for a clear and unambiguous expression of their goals:

> We want the complete separation of Euzkadi and Spain. Not to go back to 1839, but to act in accordance with 1961; not to restore the so-called Fueros or the old Law, but to found a new nation; to create a people that is free, and strong as well as free, and self-confident as well as strong.

Their demands directly challenged the strategy pursued by the Basque Government, accusing it of abandoning the independence project in favor of the Statute project through agreements with Spanish democratic forces, perceived as "Statutes, conferences, and alliances with exiled Spanish politicians."

The criticisms leveled by the new nationalist Basque generation against traditional Basque nationalists were indeed a stern rebuke, expressing the protest and desire to actively participate in the fight for the freedom of Euzkadi from their distinct perspectives. However, these critiques did not significantly perturb Manuel Irujo, who had become accustomed to dissenting voices during those times.

What truly disturbed Manuel Irujo was the realization that violence had taken root in the minds of these young individuals, and their acceptance of its use as a given in the struggle for the Basque cause. Iker Gallastegi, shaped by his experiences under the Franco dictatorship, held the belief that passive resistance would be futile against an armed state suppressing the Basque people. The severe repression, detentions, tortures, and even assassinations perpetrated by the Franco regime against Basque nationalists inside the region, especially during the last quarter of 1961, led Iker to make striking statements.

He asserted, "And there are times when only guns satisfy the need. Policemen and soldiers are impregnable arguments against reasoning, but not against bullets. We will reason with whoever wants to reason; but only the patriotic arm that wields a weapon can prevail against armed despotism. Unarmed Euzkadi will obtain exactly the freedom that Spain wishes to grant it. Armed Euzkadi will obtain in the long run, all the freedom that it desires."

The violent actions carried out by young Basque nationalists, particularly those associated with ETA, and the resistance within the Basque Country were not impulsive actions but rather a deliberate decision to respond in kind. Violence became an unfortunate companion for the Spanish people on the streets during those days, with attacks on Spanish nationalist monuments, the burning of Spanish flags, and the escalating nationalist Basque propaganda.

The Franco regime, disturbed by these actions, decided to quash the insurgency by directly targeting ETA's founders. This led to a tragic incident in March 1961, where police opened fire on a car in Vitoria, mistakenly believing that ETA leaders were inside. In reality, the occupants were not the intended targets, resulting in the killing of Javier Batarrita, who was not engaged in any political activity.[478]

In Iker's words, one can discern the influence of his father, who fled to Dublin during the Spanish Civil War and even changed his nationality to Irish. Iker quoted Mayor of Cork and Irish martyr Mac Swiney, stating, "It will not be those who can offend the most, but those who can suffer the most who will triumph. It will not be us who will shed innocent blood, but us who will offer it."

The reference is unmistakable and straightforward: the new generation of Basque nationalists was resolute in resisting the violence imposed by the Franco regime. One of the critical distinctions lay in the approach toward violence. ETA was established in 1959, and there were also factions within the PNV, such as EGI, advocating for the use of violence and drawing inspiration from Irish violence.

While the use of violence was not entirely new to traditional Basque nationalism, Jagi-Jagi, a radical breakaway faction formed in 1934, represented one of the most extreme versions of Basque nationalism. Advocating for Basque self-determination, the ideas of Sabino Arana in his most anticapitalistic moments, and the formation of Basque battalions during the Spanish Civil War, Jagi-Jagi was led by Elias Gallastegi, known as "Gudari."[479]

Initially, ETA was perceived as a youth section of the PNV, not causing much concern, as reflected in their correspondence in 1960.[480] Traditional Basque nationalists, including Irujo, regarded these "radicals" as part of the nationalist family, with some being actual family members—the next generation after the first Basque Government-in-exile. However, the key difference lay in the fact that these radicals had been born under the Franco dictatorship.

This distinction sheds light on the differences between the exile and the internal development of Basque nationalism. Despite the notion of an "internal exile" experienced by the democratic resistance during the dictatorship, the evolution of Basque nationalism, particularly since the emergence of the new generation, underwent gradual changes.

As previously discussed, the interest of Basque nationalists in exile intensified when the new generation became politically active. While this interest could be interpreted as an attempt to attract and control them in a strategy to regain control over the internal movement, it also aimed to prevent them from aligning with the PCE, the political force dominating anti-Francoism within Spain.

Conversely, the new generation did not feel drawn to the traditional PNV, expressing disappointment with the references they had among the Basque leaders. Iker reproached traditional Basque nationalism for distancing itself from the new generation and their struggles within the region. He criticized leaders who continued to discuss irrelevant issues and attempt to solve problems that no longer existed in Euzkadi. The disconnect between the old generation and the new was perceived as a challenge to restoring trust in the leadership: "It can still be achieved that the people trust their leaders. But it will not be easy because the myth is fading and with it their authority."

Iker was articulating two distinct strategies and conceptualizations of fighting for the Basque cause, and violence was just one facet of the divergence. The fragmentation within Basque nationalism was influenced by factors such as age, violence, ideology, and strategy, which will be further explored in the subsequent section.

From Gallastegi's conference, it becomes evident that the young nationalist Basque generation felt abandoned by both the Basque government and traditional Basque nationalism, primarily represented by the PNV. The solutions proposed by traditional Basque nationalists did not address the immediate challenges faced by the younger generation, especially those related to living under the dictatorship. Different concepts and speeches were emerging from both sides of the border, reflecting diverse origins of their demands.

Iker's strategy, as outlined in his speech, was designed for use in the internal struggle, incorporating not only the use of violence but also an insurrectional approach involving the Basque population against the institutions of the Franco regime within the Basque country. The perceived enemies were identified as those actively participating in Spanishizing the population, including teachers, bishops, police, Guardia Civil, and other forces of repression operating within Euzkadi. Iker's emphasis was on confronting these entities directly rather than relying on political agreements with Spanish democratic forces or seeking international assistance. This direct and active campaign was influenced by other international experiences and stood in contrast to the influences that the Basque Government had received, as will be explored in the following section.

Who are the "Patriotas y Gamberros"?

Following the conferences, traditional Basque nationalists, like Manuel Irujo and Francisco de Belausteguigoitia,[481] expressed concerns about the evolving tactics of the youth. The increasing divergence of the younger generation, particularly their embrace of violence, caused unease among the traditionalists, centered around the PNV and the Basque Government. While efforts were made to attract the youth, certain practices, notably violence, were deemed unacceptable by the older generation.[482]

Manuel Irujo, in his correspondence, acknowledged his aversion to violence, attributing it partly to his age. He recognized the sacrifices made by the youth but questioned the effectiveness of their methods in the face of the power wielded by those in control. The reflections hinted at the shifting dynamics within the Basque Country, where the activities of the young nationalists, often marked by violence, began to overshadow the traditional Basque nationalist party's strategy.[483]

Despite disagreements with ETA members, the Basque Government continued to support Basque prisoners, adhering to a diplomatic strategy and engaging international bodies, consistent with their approach throughout the exile. The Basque cause gained recognition, partly due to the violence employed by the young nationalists, a departure from the traditionalists' strategy. Yet, from the outset, the government and the PNV had supported the prisoners, or "gudaris."

When ETA disrupted a train carrying Falangists celebrating the 25th anniversary of the Coup d'état, resulting in the imprisonment of some ETA members, including Julen Madariaga, the Basque Government continued its support for the prisoners. Madariaga's arrest, as reported by the American consulate in Bilbao, involved severe beatings and accusations related to the train derailment attempt near San Sebastian on July 18, 1961.[484]

After the train derailment attempt[485] involving Falangists, attention turned towards the Basque revolutionary nationalists. Initially, even Basque nationalists within Spain were skeptical that ETA could have orchestrated such an event. Ángel Zarraga, a Basque nationalist providing information to the American Consulate in Bilbao, stated that the arrested group, including Julen Madariaga, had no involvement in the attempted derailment.

Manuel Irujo, while critical of the derailment, suggested a strategic approach in a letter to Solaun and Landáburu in September 1961. He proposed addressing the U.N. Commission on Human Rights or involving the Liga, believing it would be beneficial for propaganda against Franco.[486]

Despite the challenges posed by the violent actions of the revolutionary Basque nationalists, some of whom were in jail and subjected to torture, the Basque government in exile had to manage the situation. Aretxabaleta and other Basques visited the Cardinal to seek humanitarian aid for Basque prisoners in Spain. Additionally, the Basque delegation in Biarritz engaged in diplomatic efforts with Anglo-Saxon countries.

While not universally pleasing, this strategy aimed to obtain support from Anglo-Saxon countries, their institutions, and public opinion, as well as religious institutions in European countries, Rome, and the hinterland. The Basque government's efforts, especially from its Biarritz delegation, focused on influencing the English Parliament and using publicity to prevent irreparable condemnations.[487]

The strategy employed by the Basque government focused on diplomatic efforts to garner public and political support against torture and the death penalty, emphasizing the defense of human rights. The defense of Basque detainees and their safety became a primary concern for the Basque Government in exile, recognizing its inability to control events within Spain but seeking to act on behalf of the Basque people suffering under Franco's repression.

While diplomacy was used to address the issue of torture and detainee conditions, it also served the broader political cause of Euskadi. Solaun highlighted this dual focus by quoting from a document sent to Basque delegations, stating that the chosen attitude was ultimately the most useful in the service of Euskadi and its freedom.

In addressing the torture of detainees, the Basque government employed diplomatic channels with states and international bodies, coupled with mediation through ecclesiastical institutions, unions, and humanitarian organizations. Contacts with the Christian Democracy movement, particularly in Rome, facilitated the dissemination of information about the Basque cause and the suffering of the Basque people under Franco's dictatorship.

The challenging situation in exile and the treatment of Basque prisoners posed difficulties for traditional Basque nationalists, especially concerning the leadership of Leizaola. The unity of the traditional Basque nationalists faced strains, and the differences in opinions among the older generation became apparent. Managing such a situation was complex, and the loss of hegemony in the Basque nationalist world revealed divergent views within the old guard.

In 1961, young ETA members on trial for their involvement in a train derailment faced court-martials and substantial prison sentences.[488] The PNV and the Basque government offered their support to the ETA members and prepared a report detailing the conditions of the detainees, exploring ways to assist them.

In a letter expressing his disagreement with certain procedures taken to aid the detainees,[489] Irujo provides insights into the Basque Government's actions in response to torture and imprisonment. The Basque Government, or the PNV, sought assistance from the International Law Commission in Geneva through the English group. In response, a detailed report on the tortures suffered by the detainees was requested. Juan Jauriaguerra, their contact inside Spain, delivered a comprehensive list of detainees and the police-inflicted tortures. However, Leizaola disapproved of the International Law Commission's proposal to publicize the tortures. Consequently, the documents were sent to the Secretary of State of the Vatican.

Correspondence between Solaun and Irujo sheds light on the difficulties faced by traditional Basque nationalists in managing a situation involving torture and potential death penalties. While Irujo favored publicizing the issue, Leizaola and Solaun believed that doing so might worsen the sentences.[490] The divergent opinions reflect the challenges in dealing with an extreme situation, and the debate over methods persisted.

The strategy employed by the Basque Government regarding imprisoned and tortured Basques mirrored their approach during the Burgos trial, as detailed in the subsequent chapter. When conferences took place in Paris, young Basque nationalists, including ETA and EG members, were experiencing forced exile due to Franco's repression. The derailment in Donostia-San Sebastián had led to numerous arrests, prompting some nationalists to go into exile. ETA, having lost members and facing repression, planned its first assembly in Iparralde during the summer of 1961. The assembly aimed to restructure the organization and establish a cohesive ideology, culminating in May 1962.[491]

Despite Manuel Irujo's loyalty to the government and international efforts to address torture and imprisonment issues, he struggled with witnessing the violent nationalism of the Basque youth directed against Spain.

In 1962, Manuel Irujo wrote two consecutive articles in Alderdi, titled "Juventud pesimista" ("Pessimistic Youth") and "La violencia inútil"[492] ("Useless Violence"), before penning "Patriotas y gamberros," which led to the conflict with Elias Gallastegi.

In "La violencia inútil," drawing on his historical expertise, Irujo argued that violence was an ineffective strategy, referencing Eamon De Valera, the President of the Irish Republic, and the IRA's decision to abandon armed struggle on February 26, 1962. He compared the Home Rule movement in Ireland in 1913 with the Statute of Autonomy in Spain in 1931, asserting that politics always prevails over violence. Irujo questioned whether the fifty years of violence in Ulster were necessary for the eventual resolution, emphasizing the futility of such struggles.[493]

While acknowledging the legitimacy of violence to overthrow a tyrant when all other options are exhausted, Irujo opposed "useless and unnecessary violence."[494] He criticized the youth, particularly those advocating for revolution against Spain, stating that no sensible person could believe Euzkadi could free itself from Francoism without simultaneously freeing itself from Spain.[495]

In a relatively rare expression of tolerance toward violence, Irujo argued for organized violence if necessary, opposing "useless and sectarian violence" carried out by individuals lacking the authority and skills to command and implement orders. Despite his reservations about violence, Irujo recognized the potential need for it under specific circumstances.[496]

In Alderdi no. 183, corresponding to the months of May and June 1962, Manuel Irujo published the controversial article "Patriotas y gamberros." The ongoing criticism directed at the PNV and Irujo himself by Basque youth nationalists and their supporters in America likely prompted him to write the article. This piece marked a significant point of contention and disagreement between Irujo and Elias Gallastegi, reflecting the broader ideological conflicts within the Basque nationalist movement during that period.

Correspondence between Manuel Irujo and Elías Gallastegi.

On July 19th, 1962, Elías Gallastegi penned a letter to Irujo in response to his article "Patriotas y Gamberros"[497] (Patriots and Hooligans). The letter, spanning

45 typewritten pages, included an eight-page attachment titled "Hacia la solidaridad nacional" (Towards National Solidarity). While initially intended as a defense of his son, the expansive nature of the letter allowed for a comprehensive examination of the attitudes, opinions, thoughts, and actions of the young Basque nationalists, categorized as "patriots and hooligans." Although Gallastegi strategically avoided explicit mention or reference to ETA throughout the letter, it becomes evident that he was alluding to the organization.

Gallastegi's son, Iker, affiliated with EG, and despite the challenges of discerning casual encounters from organized groups in clandestine conditions, there is no conclusive evidence that he formally joined ETA. Nevertheless, Elías Gallastegi did host ETA members, including José Antonio Etxebarrieta, an influential ideologue of the group. Etxebarrieta likely imparted some of his ideologies to these young Basque patriots, as will be explored further.

Manuel Irujo and Elías Gallastegi shared a history as old acquaintances, having met in Dublin where Gallastegi resided during Irujo's visit for the Interparliamentary Union. Their friendship developed, with Irujo describing Gallastegi in a 1953 letter to Jon Bilbao.[498] Irujo acknowledged Gallastegi as an aged Basque nationalist who, like himself—albeit not explicitly admitting it—did not always align with the official stance of the PNV. Gallastegi was characterized as a theorist of nationalism, an inspiration for the Jagi-Jagi, a separatist wing, and a co-founder of the Eusko Mendigoizale Bazkuna. Despite ideological discrepancies, Irujo maintained his association with Gallastegi until the rupture caused by the "Patriotas y Gamberros" incident.

In 1962, when Gallastegi composed the previously mentioned letter, he resided in San Juan de Luz in Iparralde, the northern Basque Country. There, he provided shelter to young Basque nationalists who had fled the Franco regime, including Etxebarrieta, as mentioned earlier, with whom Irujo attempted to establish connections. Despite their divergent perspectives on Basque nationalism, their differing outlooks did not impede the continuation of their relationship. Gallastegi, just before the publication of the article that would irreversibly strain their ties, shared with Irujo his dream of a more humane vision that leaned towards coexistence, harmony, and national solidarity.

In a letter accompanying the aforementioned correspondence sent to Irujo, Gallastegi introduced the concept of "National Solidarity"[499] as an alternative explanation for the National or Patriotic Front. This term, frequently referred to by authors such as Robert P. Clark,[500] held significance in revolutionary Basque nationalism. Although it echoed the ideas developed since the Bayonne pact of 1945 and aligned with the Basque Government's early calls for the defense of Basque unity, the revolutionary nationalists advocated for a unity exclusive to Basque nationalists. This notion was met with resistance from traditional Basque nationalists, especially Irujo, who consistently championed unity with Spanish democrats.

Furthermore, the proponents of the National Front identified Irujo as a major obstacle hindering their objectives. In a detailed letter to Antonio Ruiz de Azúa Zabalbeaskoa in October 1962, Irujo disclosed the activities of the National Front and its association with Gallastegi: "Those of the 'Basque National Front' are unleashed. I know about four pamphlets directed against me." Irujo attributed the leadership of the National Front to Gallastegi, the founder, intellectual force, and director of the organization, as per Irujo's account.

In subsequent letters to Ogoñope, Irujo accused Gallastegi of leading the National Front, although it appears that Ogoñope disputed this claim in his response. Following the submission of his extensive response to "Patriotas y Gamberros" to Irujo, Gallastegi, seemingly perturbed by Irujo's silence, opted to have the letter published in Euzko Deya México. Ogoñope sought Irujo's counsel on whether or not to proceed with the publication.

When Irujo visited Gallastegi in August, they were on friendly terms: "In August, I visited Eli Gallastegi at his home. I spent an hour and a half with him. He spent all his time defending his son Iker against the attacks I had directed at him. You can't argue with a father melted by his son's affection. I just listened to him." The longstanding friendship between the two nationalists allowed them to engage in conversation, but it appears that the visit did not soothe Gallastegi, as he later wrote and sent the aforementioned letter following Irujo's visit.

Irujo, a man who acknowledged to Ogoñope that he tended to write extensively—"I write to you more than to a girlfriend"—received the letter and, struck by the volume and aggressiveness of Gallastegi's words, paused to consider possible courses of action: "The tenor of the letters is of such a nature that there are only three possible positions: One, to return them, because that is not acceptable; another, to visit his house and hit him twice; another, do not answer. The latter is what I have done."[501]

Their relationship deteriorated after the incident of "Patriotas y Gamberros," and while it's possible they may have exchanged a few spare letters, they did not resume their cordial rapport. In 1974, when Irujo learned of Gallastegi's illness, he sent a letter seeking forgiveness: "An unpleasant incident drove us apart. Let me ask you to forgive me for what I failed to do, and I beg you to be generous with me and let us return to the friendly relations we had before."

Unfortunately, according to Gallastegi's siblings, the letter arrived after Gallastegi had passed away. Irujo received an unpleasant response: "Dad did not owe you any forgiveness. In any case, it would be you who should forgive yourself if your conscience is not clear. The only thing that dad demanded of you was that you repair the harm done to the good name of one of his sons in your article 'Patriots or Hooligans' (...). As your letter does not show any such purpose, we return it to you."[502]

The awakening of young Basque nationalists led to a fatal dispute between old Basque nationalists, ending a long relationship. Although Irujo and some traditional

Basque nationalists maintained relations with the "new generation" of Basque patriots, a formidable obstacle divided and distanced them. The lengthy letter sent by Elías Gallastegi to Manuel Irujo serves as a valuable reference for analyzing these young Basque nationalists and the evolution of ETA's ideology in exile.

Developing *"Patriotas y Gamberros"*

By the time Irujo published his article "Patriotas y Gamberros," ETA had already held its inaugural Assembly in Urt, Lapurdi, at the Benedictine Monastery of Belloch. Despite the organization's earlier dissemination of its ideology through various editions of *Cuadernos* ETA and the Libro Blanco (1960), it was at this point that ETA's presence became more pronounced.

In his article, Irujo expressed respect for the alternative proposed by the new generation, stating, "I have the utmost respect for the ways of conceiving our political action, even when they are opposed to those applied by the Basques in the course of history and to those currently followed by their rectors."[503] However, he was disheartened by what he deemed the bad manners of those he labeled as "hooligans of patriotism."

In response, Gallastegi argued that this treatment of the younger generation, whose views deviated from the orthodox, resembled the PNV's past treatment of those like him who dared to challenge the PNV's ideas. While acknowledging that these young Basque patriots had deficiencies in their patriotic formation and historical judgment of nationalism, Gallastegi vehemently disagreed with the notion that the young insurgents were a product of the Franco Regime, as asserted by Irujo.[504]

This idea was a recurring theme among traditional Basque nationalists, attempting to comprehend the insurgency of the youth, particularly concerning the use of violence and the conferences in Paris in 1961. Unzueta, for instance, expressed his opinion about the youth: "(...) who unfortunately have not been breathing fascist propaganda their whole lives with impunity. The methods of fascism have penetrated some of them."[505]

Whether or not influenced by fascism from Spain, Basque nationalist youths had developed their own ideology in exile, akin to what traditional Basque nationalists had done. The construction of ETA's ideology from the outset was characterized by the diversity of international sources, reflecting a keen interest in internationalizing the conflict and the considerable academic training of its founding members.

ETA's ideology was shaped by various influences, initially documented in the Libro Blanco (1960). This comprehensive work served an instructional and informative purpose, summarizing parameters that underscored the Basque people's clear inclination towards nationalism and the defense of the Basque language as a foundational element of citizenship.

While ETA and the new Basque generation analyzed and reinterpreted the primitive Basque nationalism of Sabino Arana, they diverged from Aranism on two fundamental pillars: Religion and Race.[506]

In *Cuadernos*, a section titled "Iglesia y Estado" (Church and State) delved into the relationship between Church and State within the framework of Basque nationalist training. Examples from Pakistan, Israel, or Tibet were analyzed as models to compare with the Basque case. The section aimed to move beyond philosophical discussions and linked the demand for Basque nationalism with the confessional nature of the PNV. It posited that the challenges to achieving Basque autonomy during the Spanish Republic were connected to the PNV's clear secularity, contrasting with the concepts held by Spanish Republicans.[507] Additionally, the section examined the religiousness of Basque society, with a focus on the working class, suggesting that the working class in Gipuzkoa and Bizkaya, constituting over 60%, had distanced itself from religion.

The analysis also delved into the relationship between the Catholic Church and the Franco regime, asserting that the Church's increasing unpopularity was a consequence of this association.

After numerous issues of *Cuadernos*, debates, meetings, and discussions on ETA's principles, the document generated after the First Assembly, considered ETA's first official statement on its ideological principles, was titled "Euzkadi ta Askatasuna. Principios." In this document, ETA declared its secular, non-religious nature, explicitly distancing itself from the religious characteristic that had previously defined versions of Basque nationalism: "ETA declares its non-confessionalism and advocates it for the Constitution of Euzkadi."[508] This marked a significant departure from the religious elements that had been part of earlier Basque nationalist ideologies.

While the non-confessional nature was an unquestioned trait within the PNV during the 1960s, it would become a fascinating topic of debate during the Spanish transition to democracy, a subject we will explore in the next chapter.

ETA deviated from old Aranism, particularly in its treatment of race and its relation to Basque nationalism. Gurutz Jáuregui's analyses have shown that although the idea of Basque superiority persisted, the racial aspect was replaced by an ethnological or, primarily, a cultural-linguistic feature.

Two crucial elements contributed to this shift from race to language: firstly, a significant number of ETA members did not align with the concept of biological origin according to Arana's theories, as they had non-Basque origins (such as Álvarez Enparantza or Krutwig Sagredo); secondly, the approach to Basque nationalism through the language (Basque) allowed some members to focus more on the cultural and linguistic aspects rather than biological origins.[509]

Álvarez Enparantza, known as "Txillardegi," one of the founders and a self-taught linguist, exhibited a strong interest in the Basque language, evident in the initial documents and the conference he delivered in Paris, as previously discussed. Choosing language over race as a key feature of the new Basque nationalism transformed it into an open, civic, voluntary nationalism that could be acquired. Thus, the old ethnic Basque nationalism evolved into a new civic Basque nationalism.[510]

The social and economic changes of the 1960s led to the rapid growth of the working class and an intensive declassification, resulting in a crisis of traditional values. Simultaneously, it fostered a cultural defense against mass anonymity, described by Jean Chesnaux as the "vindication of the right to difference." This cultural defense, characterized as the "emergence of culturalists," prompted changes in Basque nationalism and advocated placing the Basque language at the core of Basque identity.[511]

While ETA and the new nationalist Basque generation were not the sole advocates and promoters of the Basque language, their public denunciation of its neglect and clear support for its promotion compelled other Basque nationalisms, particularly the PNV, to adopt similar stances.

In their *Cuadernos*, the section "Euskera y patriotismo vasco"[512] (Basque language and Basque patriotism) establishes a connection between Basque nationalism, the pro-independence movement, and the defense of the Basque language. While the advocacy for the Basque language could have sufficed to define a new ethnic trend—such as associating the Basque nation exclusively with Basque speakers—ETA avoided this issue. Instead, they attributed the decline of the language to the actions of the Basque Country's leading class:

> There is another setback, which we will call "social." The aundikis, jauntxos, aiton semes,[513] and other leaders of the country have abandoned Basque since time immemorial: and they continue to do so in somewhat fewer absolute terms.

Identifying the three major causes for the decline of the Basque language, they stated that these were: the geographical factor, the diversification of dialectal variants, and the abandonment of the language by the Basque leading classes. Interestingly, the immigration factor, which pertains to the ethnic use of the language, was not mentioned. On the contrary, the message conveyed was positive, emphasizing unity and social progress. According to ETA, the construction of the nation and the sense of being Basque were built through the language:

> Strictly speaking, only the Basque language maintains at an indisputable level the objective unity of Euskadi, throughout its Basque-speaking areas of the Spanish and French states (...) Neither the people of Bearn nor the people of La Rioja feel themselves to be Basque, nor do the Basques consider the people of La Rioja and Bearn to be patriots. The fundamental reason for this split is that six to eight centuries ago, the people of Bearn and La Rioja stopped being Basque speakers.[514]

In their conceptualization of the imagined nation, the Basque language becomes the unifying factor and, consequently, one of the main objectives for a future Basque State and Basque government.

In the early twentieth century, illiteracy rates were high among the Basque-Navarrese population, with 38% of 10-year-old children unable to read or write. However, with the advent of the Second Spanish Republic and the implementation of a compulsory free education system, this percentage dropped to below 10%. The role of the State in relation to language was crucial for the recovery or decline of a language. Spain, especially during the Franco dictatorship, acted like many other states, using the force of the State as a homogenizing power on the cultural level. The national education system promoted a single common language and culture, often ignoring minority languages that existed only within the political institution.[515]

The Basque provinces of Iparralde, integrated into the revolutionary French government since 1789, faced a similar fate. The Republican administration directly ignored the Basque language, recognizing only French as the language of unity in all departments. Fortunately, the absence of industrialization in the three Basque provinces contributed to a slower decline of the Basque language.

Government support is crucial for language development. Statistics show that the growth of education in the Basque language has been closely linked to the development of Basque nationalism.[516] This growth has mainly occurred when the powers were in the hands of Basque nationalists with the support of the administration.

The early Basque-speaking masses in Bizkaia were primarily fishermen and inhabitants of some inland villages and baserris (Basque cottages). However, industrialization in the city, along with the influx of workers, led to the common use of Spanish. Unlike the Catalan bourgeoisie, the Basque bourgeoisie did not initially champion the Basque language as a symbol of Basque nationalism. Instead, they used their ancestral Basque last names to legitimize their nationalism.[517]

According to Xabier Kintana, one of the key figures in the modernization of the Basque language, nationalist Basque political parties initially did not do much to recover and identify the language with the national movement. Kintana, along with Krutwig, Txillardegi, and poet Gabriel Aresti, played a significant role in the Congress of Bayonne (1964) and the Congress of Arantzazu (1968), where the first rules for the language were established.[518]

While the Basque language was not the primary pillar of Basque nationalism for the PNV, several congresses on Basque studies were organized, starting with the one in Oñati in September 1918. These congresses covered topics such as race, language, history, art, education, political and social sciences, and Basque studies. Additionally, the promotion and creation of the Basque University, as well as the establishment of Ikastolas (Basque-medium schools), were activities influenced by traditional Basque nationalism and predated the surge of revolutionary Basque nationalism.[519]

In its endeavor to correlate the utilization of the Basque language with the nation and state's advancement, ETA's principles articulated political goals for the

Basque Country. These objectives included, as expressed in their principles: "The declaration of Basque as the sole national language. It must reclaim its position as the language of all Basques. Its paramountcy and official status within Euskadi will be absolute, alongside the establishment of a provisional trilingual system, acknowledging current linguistic realities."[520]

Promoting the Basque language and envisioning its future development in the Basque country wasn't contradictory with exile; on the contrary, it saw language as a means to transform into the "tangible residue of homeland that the exile can carry, preserving memories and roots."[521] In a foreign land, language became a tool to resist assimilation, yet the real necessity, akin to politics and Basque nationalism at large, was linguistic unity. The varied dialects complicated communication and language study. In *Cuadernos*, Txillardegi and early ETA members emphasized the urgency of selecting a Basque dialect, stating, "We must promptly choose a Basque dialect—one with ample literature for clear definition—and exclusively support it when establishing the Basque school, the Basque press, etc."

The inspiration for this standardized or unified language was sought in exile, mirroring examples like Israel or Finland, while steering clear of unsuitable models in the realm of nationalisms, as recalled by Kintana: "The Irish reference was not a good example on the language issue because they did not control it, but rather based their opposition to the English Empire on religious matters, and that was not a valuable example for us."[522] The Irish case wasn't an ideal reflection, given the loss of their language, Gaelic, in favor of English. However, Ireland served as an example and influence for the Basque movement, particularly in the context of armed conflict. According to Kintana, the defense of the Basque nationality relied heavily on the Basque language, with many believing, "It was not independence that would save the language but that saving the language would lead to independence."

Due to the insufficient comparable elements in the Irish case regarding language, Basque nationalism shifted its focus towards Israel and its national language system by the end of the 1960s and throughout the 1970s. However, unlike the Basque country where the promotion of the national language arose as a response to the dominance of another language, Hebrew in Israel became a national language and a unifying factor independently.

In 1976, Caja Laboral Popular, a Basque bank, organized raffles offering a trip to the Holy Land as a prize, strengthening cultural ties with Israelis. This connection prompted Ariel Shoval, an Israeli linguist from the Ministry of Education, to speak on language in the Basque country. Israel, then seen as a model of social democracy, influenced Basque thinkers. Shoval, a socialist, discussed how the Arabic language served as a model for developing the Hebrew method of language integration in a sociolinguistic context.

Following the meeting with Shoval, Kintana and a group of writers commissioned by the PNV to study the recovery of the Basque language were captivated by Israel's approach. They began traveling to Israel in 1976 to understand the method used to unify a nation of immigrants from various places worldwide, using language as a unifying force.

Israel had chosen Hebrew as the original language for the Jewish people and the State, foregoing options like Yiddish or English to ensure language served as a unifying element. Facing the urgency of creating a learning method for Hebrew, they developed the "Easy Hebrew" method in 1976. This method rapidly and efficiently taught Hebrew through straightforward and common words and sentences, employing all available information channels in the country.

In Israel, they observed specialized newspapers for newcomers with basic vocabulary matching that used in television and radio. Crucially, these outlets were all coordinated and operated with the same teaching method. The similarity between the Semitic languages, Arabic and Hebrew, along with the geographic proximity of Arabic, facilitated Hebrew promoters' attention to Arabic's evolution, allowing for the creation of a modified Hebrew and the birth of a standardized language. Similarly influenced, the Basques resolved the issue of dialects, evolving towards a standardized common language through an easy teaching method for all Basques: Euskara batua.

Race and Coreanos

The Principles originating from the first Assembly unequivocally rejected any racial conception, as stated: "The condemnation of racism and, therefore, of the principles of legal superiority of some peoples or races over others. It does not support, consequently, the segregation or expulsion of foreign elements from the country, as long as they do not oppose or threaten the national interests of Euzkadi."[523]

However, a notable disparity existed between the earlier Aranism and the emerging Basque nationalism, prompting Gallastegi, in his letter, to intervene. In contrast to the principles of the younger generation and diverging from the new understanding of Basque ethnicity, Gallastegi explored the notion that, years earlier, various tendencies within Basque nationalism had competed with each other. Discussing the Basque country's economy, Gallastegi recalled the controversy stirred by Manuel Irujo's 1957 article "Los Coreanos"[524] in Alderdi, addressing the treatment of Spanish immigration in the Basque Country.

In June 1957, Irujo published the article in Alderdi, attempting to update the discourse on Spanish population immigration to the Basque Country and their role in its economy. Irujo referenced Sabino Arana, stating: "(...) That this is not at odds with the fact that, each being master of his own house and without admitting foreign impositions, the foreigner is treated with all kinds of considerations, and with affection born from the heart."

Irujo defended some of Arana's ostensibly racist theories, explaining that the use of pejorative terms like "maketo" or "coreano"[525] was not meant to be offensive. He argued, "We cannot pretend to throw the Koreans out of the Basque Country," emphasizing their role in Basque industry. Irujo advocated for integrating them into Basque society by providing better living conditions, asserting that, through this process, they would become part of the Basque human group.

The article sparked controversy, leading Ceferino Jemein,[526] a traditional Basque nationalist defending Sabino Arana's orthodox nationalism, to respond with articles countering the perceived insult directed at the memory of Aranism by Manuel Irujo.

In his initial article, "No estoy conforme" (I don't agree), published in Alderdi under the pseudonym "Jadarka" in August 1957, Ceferino Jemein launched a vehement attack on Manuel Irujo. Jemein asserted that Spanish immigration in the Basque Country was orchestrated by the Franco regime with the intention of annihilating the Basques and their homeland.[527] He contended that the "premeditated invasion organized by Franco to gouge out the eyes of Euzkadi is not protected by Human Rights," a stance directly opposing Irujo's call for defending the rights of immigrants.

Although Jemein addressed Irujo as "my old friend Manuel Irujo" in his article, their ideological differences had severed any real friendship long ago. Jemein made this clear in a 1950 letter to Irujo, stating, "In my previous correspondence it was very difficult for me to call you my friend, because you have never been my friend. Today less than ever, because you are an enemy of mine."[528] Their earlier dispute in 1950 revolved around Arana's orthodoxy, and a similar theme recurred in Jemein's response to "Los Coreanos" in 1957 when he advocated for controlling immigrants, labeling them as "Invaders," through legal measures and work permits.

The controversy surrounding the "Coreanos" article extended beyond Jemein's response, sparking a debate within Basque nationalism. The evolving societal landscape, coupled with the fact that many debating the issue were living in exile, led to diverse opinions illustrated by examples from life and foreign experiences.

Irujo contributed a new article to Tierra Vasca in August, concurrently with Jemein's response. In "Maquetos y Coreanos," Irujo presented the idea that there were two types of "coreanos." He classified them as those undertaking a Francoist agenda against Basque identity and those who came solely to earn a living.[529] Irujo advocated a positive attitude of integration towards the latter group, considering them part of the Basque community. He believed that the Basque autonomous government, in the future, could resolve the only issue—the Basque language—by reclaiming its use.

The controversy among Basque nationalists expanded to the extent that the August issue of Alderdi featured not just one but two articles on the matter. The first, titled "Al servicio de la verdad" (In the service of truth), chronicled the impact of Spanish immigration, aligning with Irujo's perspectives on the rights of immigrant workers and the necessity of their integration. Departing from ethnic nationalism, the article, focused on Bizkaia, considered all residents, whether by birth or adoption, as Basques who had dedicated their lives to the Basque Nationalist Ideal.

Contrarily, Ceferino Jemein, writing under the pseudonym "Belandia," revisited Sabino Arana's nineteenth-century ideas on immigration and the Basque industrial economy to critique the distorted system. Jemein used Arana's thoughts to attack the industrial system, claiming that "Bilbao used to be an honest town, with clean business and healthy habits (...) commerce has lost its natural honesty (...) All the dirty business is allowed; there is no iron in the Blast Furnaces, but one can buy it in the cafés, through smugglers with no other conscience than making millions (...)."

Jemein's distorted perspective and use of Arana's ideas to justify his racist opinions about immigrants and the Basque industrial system fueled a heated debate in the exile, leading to a clash of ideas among Basque nationalists. The internal-exile element played a significant role in the debate, with some nationalists contributing ideas and positive solutions for the immigration issue, while others viewed immigration and the industrialization of the Basque Country as threats to Basque essence and traditional values.

Using this debate as an example, we can observe how Basque nationalism evolved and changed in the exile, contributing to the creation of an imagined nation, despite not being geographically located within the nation's borders. As Devleena Ghosh notes through her quotation of Richard Eder, "Exile is the only country with no geography."[530]

Recognizing the importance of the debate, and under indirect pressure from Manuel Irujo to involve the Basque Government,[531] the Lehendakari decided to address the question in his annual Christmas Message. He rejected racist solutions and appealed for understanding and compassion: "This problem, therefore, must be placed on a human level, a profoundly human level, which can never be solved—and even less among Christians—with grudges, easy 'slogans,' and even less with hatreds of any class."[532]

In his speech, the president also touched on the controversy surrounding the Coreanos and advocated for their integration. He criticized Basques who neglected their national duties: "Anyone who forgets his national duties belongs to this school, any Basque who forsakes his language and, knowing it, does not pass it on to his children, is a herald of a Koreanism much worse and more serious for the homeland than the one who, coming from a foreign land, wants to assimilate to ours."

The Lehendakari effectively concluded the controversy through his Christmas speech, providing a contemporary solution to the issue of Spanish immigration. He appealed to Human Rights, Christian duties, and the integration of immigrants into Basque society, drawing on their own exile experiences: "Nobody better than the one who lives in exile to understand what is and means the good or bad treatment in a foreign country, and every emigrant has something of exile, the Basque who leaves or the foreigner who comes to Euzkadi."

Ceferino Jemein, deeply involved in the polemic, had been a member of Jagi-Jagi, as previously mentioned. Despite engaging in a heated debate with Elías Gallastegi, the two remained good friends. In 1962, they lived together in exile at Gallastegi's home in Biarritz. The letter sent to Irujo after "Patriotas y Gamberros" suggests that Gallastegi had not forgotten the issue and continued to fall back on the immigration cliché of 1957. He expressed his opinion, stating, "I do not believe that there has been a more serious or prejudicial problem than the one provoked by the genocidal Spanish government, carrying out this massive invasion without any control and without taking into account the moral values of our people or the economic interests of the country's workers, with the deliberate purpose of extinguishing our race."[533]

Gallastegi and the Basque nationalists of the Jagi-Jagi movement were distant from the PNV, the new young Basque nationalism, and ETA. Their adherence to Sabino Arana's theories kept them entrenched in a racist and ethnic version of Basque nationalism that failed to adapt to the political and social trends of Basque society in the 1960s.

Moreover, Gallastegi linked his racist statements against immigration to the economy and the development of the industrial sector in the Basque Country. This provides an opportunity to discuss the economic model that the young Basque nationalists were advocating.

From anti-capitalism to communism

In 1962, when workers' tensions erupted in the streets of the Basque Country, ETA and the young Basque nationalists seized the opportunity to connect the national movement with the workers' movement. This strategic alignment had already begun taking shape in 1961 during a major strike in Beasain (Gipuzkoa), where ETA recognized the significance of the workers' movement in challenging the Franco regime. To articulate their stance, ETA identified three enemies of the Basque cause: capitalism, the Franco regime, and the Castilian dictatorship.[534]

In an extended letter written by Elias Gallastegi, it is challenging to discern whether he was explicating the youth's ideas or expressing his own, as seen earlier in the context of immigration concerns where contradictions with the youth's documents arose. Nevertheless, when addressing the criticism against industrialists and traders that had drawn Irujo's ire,[535] Gallastegi indicated that the Navarrese had misconstrued the speaker's declarations, asserting that the criticism was directed at capitalism rather than individual industrialists. In Gallastegi's words, the young Basque nationalists were concerned about the plight of Basque workers, aligning with ETA's early explanations in their first Zutiks[536] regarding their position on the Basque working class.[537]

Gallastegi's letter includes criticisms of industrialism that echo the positions taken by the Aranists[538] and Jagi-Jagi during the earlier polemic with the "Coreanos." Although Gallastegi frequently refers to Sabino Arana in this part of the letter, it can be challenging to discern whether he is championing his son's thoughts or expressing his own.

Considering that ETA and the young Basque nationalists were still in the process of constructing their ideological framework, with diverse opinions and trends coexisting, it is evident that the national struggle became increasingly intertwined with the social struggle during this period. However, a clearly defined strategy for defending the Basque working class[539] did not emerge until 1964.

In its early years, ETA did not explicitly align itself with Marxist or communist ideologies, which were commonly associated with the working-class movement. However, its initial documents did analyze these political currents. An annex to the Libro Blanco del Exilio (White Book of Exile) examined Leninism and Bolshevism, responding to perceived gaps in explanations of the Revolution and referencing the Revolutionary Marxist Party of the October Revolution.

The section on Marxism published in *Cuadernos* proclaimed, "Marxism is fashionable," and explored key aspects of Marxism and communism through the works of Karl Marx, Frederik Engels, Henry Lefebvre, Jean Baby, and André Piettre.[540] While ETA and the young Basque nationalists, especially Iker Gallastegi, were not overtly Marxist, it was evident that they were exploring ideas that traditional Basque nationalists were unwilling to entertain.

On August 25, 1962, Francisco de Belausteguigoitia expressed his doubts about the ideology of his son-in-law, Julen Madariaga, in a letter to Irujo:

> Upon my arrival in these lands, I have encountered a great uproar, as we usually say here, on account of ETA's activities. Even though I have met my son-in-law several times in Biarritz, I am not in the habit of talking to him about politics because I realize that we are not on the same path.[541]

Belausteguigoitia, affectionately called Patxo by Irujo, believed that rumors of communism spreading among young Basque nationalists were unfounded and likely a product of Francoist anticommunist paranoia. However, he acknowledged that the Franco regime could make such allegations believable due to its hate propaganda being counter-productive.

For Manuel Irujo and traditional Basque nationalists, the potential alliance between nationalism and communism posed a problem, especially in 1962 during the Munich Congress, as previously described. Irujo, in his response to Patxo's impressions, analyzed the increasing influence of communism among young Basque nationalists:

The current situation, the circumstances in which the world lives, the marked reactions in all the peoples of the world—not only in the Basque Country—reveal the birth of nationalist movements, which, due to their extremist radicalism, fall within the sphere of stimulating influence of international extremist movements.[542]

Manuel Irujo frequently emphasized the recurring link between extremists and communism or fascism when discussing the growth of totalitarianism. In his view, a political strategy involving an alliance of democrats could effectively counter the advance of extremists on both the left and right sides, both of which were represented within Basque nationalism, with the PNV at its center.

"Today, Basque nationalism finds itself with two offshoots, one of the extreme right, the F.N., and the other of the extreme left, ETA, which are natural candidates to be stimulated, solicited or engulfed by the great international fascist and communist movements.

While Irujo was initially optimistic about the young Basque nationalists before the Paris conferences of 1961, believing that their radical ideas were a result of youthfulness, by the end of 1962, his optimism had waned: "People are inclined to suppose that all this will not be more than a juvenile hot-headedness. I, unfortunately, am not so optimistic, or luckily, I am not so foolish."

Despite ETA not explicitly identifying as communist, its alignment with the working class movement during the resistance in the Basque Country, particularly in the tumultuous year of 1962 with numerous strikes and demonstrations, fueled rumors of increasing ties with Spanish Communists: "We know that on the occasion of the recent strikes, ETA has signed with several pro-communist organizations and with the union of communist youths a manifesto dated last 8th (...) We have very good reasons to believe that ETA has signed, in addition to this manifesto, a pact with the communist youths."[543] This report by Gonzalo Nárdiz to Lehendakari Leizaola focused on activities coordinated with communist movements but overlooked the fact that in both the Libro Blanco and Principios de ETA, the organization had distanced itself from communism—a stance that would spark a prolonged debate lasting almost ten years.[544]

In Principios de ETA, the organization articulated economic ideas critical of liberalism and industry: "The disappearance of economic liberalism as the basic system for the future Basque economy (...)." However, certain statements within Principios de ETA, such as advocating a profound modification of private property and the socialization of resources and industries, might have raised concerns among traditional Basque nationalists.

The increasing concern about the perceived communist and socialist tendencies of the youth was evident in various articles and editorials on the subject. While ETA and the new generation of Basque nationalists appeared to be taking left-wing positions that could align them with the communists, the PNV and traditional Basque nationalism sought to emphasize their commitment to democracy. They positioned democracy as a middle ground between the blue and red totalitarianisms that, according to them, had devastated Europe.

"There are blue and red totalitarianisms and democracies that in their gradation are so distant from each other that it is difficult to identify them, but this does not prevent establishing essential differences between both regimes," stated an editorial article in Alderdi no. 184 in September 1962. The article specifically referred to the great workers' strikes, accused communists of politicizing the anti-Francoist movement—being "an organization that draws its inspiration from Moscovite imperialism"—and refused to participate in any anti-Francoist front, denying participation to their youth section.

Another example of the PNV's perspective, framing communism and Francoism as opposing totalitarianisms to democracy, is found in the editorial article in Alderdi issue no. 187 of November 1962, titled "Comunismo no, Franquismo tampoco" (Not communism, nor Francoism either).

The suspicions or accusations that ETA had communist ties were not limited to traditional Basque nationalists but were deliberately spread by the Francoist-controlled press, particularly by the Ministry of Information-sponsored weekly, El Español,[545] as reported by the US embassy in Madrid in October 1964.

Representatives claiming to be from ETA visited the US Embassy in Madrid during a visit to the city in connection with ongoing political trials. According to the embassy report, one of the men was German Urbizu. Their purpose was "to acquaint foreign embassies and foreign newspaper correspondents with the aims of ETA."[546] This document offers insights into how ETA presented itself, its goals, and how it defined the organization to external entities such as foreign embassies and journalists during private meetings.

The two young men emphatically asserted that ETA was a nationalistic movement with no Communist influence. Their primary goals were to overthrow the Franco dictatorship and secure complete independence for the Basque people. They made it clear that their objective was not to exchange a right-wing dictatorship for a left-wing one, reinforcing their non-communist stance.

The American perspective on the young nationalist Basque movement is intriguing, as reflected in the report. One notable aspect was that the Americans believed the movement would be content if Spain granted the Basque Country some form of cultural autonomy. Despite ETA's cultural image associated with activities related to the Basque language and cultural vindication, representatives of ETA emphasized that their movement was unequivocally separatist. Their ultimate aim was to unite all Spanish and French Basques in an integrated democratic government within a European Federation.

However, they acknowledged a willingness to consider a federal arrangement within a Spanish Republic, as long as Basque culture and language were preserved. Surprisingly, they admitted that violence must be employed to achieve their objectives. The report concludes with insights from revolutionary Basque nationalists, who stressed that ETA should not be perceived as a youth group or an offshoot of the PNV. They delineated key differences: ETA was an activist group focused on immediate action, non-confessional with some members being young priests opposing the Church hierarchy collaborating with the Franco government, had a social program distinct from the PNV, and aimed for an independent Basque democratic republic without ties between the State and Church.

From the Basque Statute of Autonomy to Independence

Regarding the political strategy and the efforts of the Basque Government, the young Basque nationalists expressed increasing criticism and skepticism. Initially acknowledging the Basque Government, they later grew more skeptical due to its connection to the Republican Spanish legal system. Irujo, reflecting on the Paris conference, expressed dismay at the youth's reaction, particularly during Iker Gallastegi's speech opposing the political agreement strategy pursued by the Basque Government. This strategy aimed for collaboration with all Basque forces while demanding the complete separation of Euzkadi.

The youth's dissent extended to their opposition against the Basque Statute of Autonomy and, according to Irujo, the ancient Fueros (Basque regional code of laws). This contradicted Irujo's lifelong defense and advocacy throughout exile, leading to his visible frustration. Irujo staunchly defended the Basque Government's work, highlighting its efforts to represent the Basque people internationally and defend their rights before the United Nations.[547]

While Iker Gallastegi's conference wasn't as harsh towards the Statute or the Basque Government, the published article in Tierra Vasca used offensive language against the Statute. Despite criticizing the Basque Government and the policies of traditional Basque nationalists, Gallastegi also expressed some affectionate words towards them in his conference. Elias Gallastegi pointed this out in his response to Irujo, quoting from the conference, "In spite of this, I believe that our predecessors were honest, because their intention was good."[548]

In the eyes of the new generation of Basque nationalists, the older individuals who had fought in the Civil War and assumed leadership in the Basque Government during exile were considered honorable and to some extent respectable. However, for the younger generation, mere advocacy for the Basque Statute of Autonomy seemed insufficient. Growing up under the Franco dictatorship, they perceived the Statute as having little importance or feasibility. The legality of the Basque Government and, consequently, the Statute of Autonomy, was an unfamiliar concept to them, rendering the idea of representation seemingly inconsequential.

Instead, their Cuadernos del Rebalaje del Ser (Notebooks of the Rebellion of Being) delved into envisioning the Basque Country based on the political principles of a State. They analyzed concepts such as Parliamentarism, Democracy, and Republic, always emphasizing the importance of respecting Human Rights and suffrage.[549]

The Principles of ETA underscored the importance of Human Rights and democracy as the chosen political system for the Basque Country. They advocated for "the establishment of a democratic and unequivocally representative regime, both in the political and in the socio-economic and cultural sense," and emphasized the "certain and effective guarantee of the Rights of Man," including freedom of expression, assembly, association, and religious practice.

Despite being perceived as aligned with communism, ETA clarified its adherence to Human Rights, provided they were not instrumentalized to undermine the sovereignty of Euzkadi or impose a dictatorial regime, whether fascist or communist. While initially distancing themselves from communism as a possibility for the Basque Country, the organization later adopted strategies and patterns associated with Marxism and communism.

For these young Basque nationalists, the political objective was "absolute freedom," translating to a clear pro-independence stance. This stood in stark contrast to the orthodox PNV and traditional Basque nationalism, which had shifted towards European federalism in previous chapters. The message conveyed at the Paris conference encapsulated their vision: "We want a Free Euskadi, and for us, freedom has only one definition. It does not mean limited freedom, conditioned to the interests of another nation, but absolute freedom, the sovereign control of all the destinies of Euzkadi."[550]

Manuel Irujo expressed his criticism of the youth's goals, describing the proclamation of the "absolute freedom" of the homeland as the use of hollow words that imply greater patriotism. He argued that the concept of "absolute" freedom applied to the homeland was a fascist doctrine and part of totalitarian absolutism.[551]

In earlier articles, Irujo had already disapproved of the pro-independence ideas of the youth, expressing skepticism when they talked about independence and associating the idea of autonomy with the voice of the enemy or a weary compatriot. In his response letter, Gallastegi recalled Irujo's criticism and drew a direct link between the legacy of Sabino Arana, who had advocated independence, and the new generation of young Basque nationalists. Gallastegi pointed out that the pro-independence ideas were not a product of living under the Franco dictatorship but rooted in the words of Sabino Arana, the father of Basque nationalism.[552]

ETA, in the first paragraph of its principles, defined itself as a "Basque Revolutionary Movement for National Liberation" and stated that the freedom of Euzkadi was not its supreme interest but the only realistic means for the development and invigoration of the Basque Nation in all its spheres.

Despite advocating for independence, ETA did not outright dismiss the international policies of the Basque Government, particularly those promoted by Manuel Irujo in favor of European Federalism. ETA acknowledged European Federalism as a viable option for the survival of minorities, emphasizing its qualitative rather than quantitative nature. In the early documents of *Cuadernos*,[553] ETA defended federalism as a system that grants minorities the same rights as the majority, without being solely based on numbers. ETA recognized the importance of the European community and supported efforts to back it, viewing it as the Basque patriot's greatest hope and emphasizing the need to spare no effort in its support.

Furthermore, the principles of ETA in 1962 acknowledged the significance of Basque political administrative entities, such as the municipality and the region. They emphasized the importance of the European Federation but with the condition that it be implemented at the level of nationalities. ETA categorically rejected the Union of the States as a viable option.[554]

Political violence

One notable aspect for which the history of ETA and young Basque nationalism gained notoriety is the use of political violence. Although it took the organization some years to adopt political violence as a strategy to achieve the freedom of the Basque Country, the potential for violent response was always a distinctive feature of the new Basque nationalist organization.

In contrast to the strategy of traditional Basque nationalism represented by the PNV and the Basque Government, which involved making political agreements with Spanish republican forces, this approach fell short for the youth Basque nationalists. They deemed these political agreements ineffective in addressing the plight of the Basque people under the dictatorship and viewed them as closely resembling the Carlists' political strategies.

In Txillardegi's 1962 article "Neo-Carlismo," the voice of the youth resonates, connecting their thoughts once again to those of Sabino Arana. The article suggests that ETA and the Basque generation comprehend the essence of neo-Carlism dominating nationalist politics, labeled as republican legalism.[555] The young generation did not recognize the legitimacy or authority of republican legality, leading them to unequivocally reject Spanish republican institutions, the Statute of Autonomy (deemed an infra-statute), and any trust in other Spanish institutions.

For Irujo, these ideas were intricately linked to the endorsement of violence, as articulated in the conference:

"The text of the conference calls for 'absolute freedom' for Euzkadi, with the 'complete separation of Euzkadi and Spain,' which the Basques must seek by 'all means at their disposal.' He says that today there is no room for pacts with Spanish political forces, and therefore, there is no room for political and legal methods in our country. Today there is only one method, today there is only one path… the road of arms, the only road."[556]

In Irujo's perspective, the only conceivable conditions that could justify war as the sole solution to the Basque problem were if a direct offense was launched against those who had fought in the Spanish Civil War, and if there were a complete negation of the extensive political work undertaken by the Basque Government over nearly 25 years. He believed that such a stance insulted the old nationalists and, in his view, transformed the young men into "hooligans."

Elias Gallastegi attempted to justify his son's words by suggesting that what they truly meant was that violence should be the last resort. However, Irujo's response highlighted the perception that the young Basque nationalists did indeed have violence in mind, though not as a preferred solution. Gallastegi justified their stance by stating, "Let the Spanish state promise not to discuss the issue using barracks, torture, prisons, and executions as arguments, and we will not use force either."

Violence, for the young nationalists, was conceived as a defensive weapon—a response to Francoist violence. The influence of the exile was significant in shaping their views on violence, as it was in the exile where they found some successful answers to the Basque cause. Gallastegi, in his response, portrayed violence as a last resort for the young nationalists, describing them not as inherently violent individuals but as pacifists in the vein of Gandhi or Sabino Arana.[557]

Elías Gallastegi defined the violence of the young Basque nationalists as an exercise in "active resistance," introducing some of the strategies and vocabulary that ETA would later adopt when implementing its armed strategy. The armed struggle was envisioned as a means to awaken Basque society and internationalize the cause. This would involve resorting to guerrilla warfare, active or passive resistance, as well as organizing strikes and boycotts.

Elias explained that the turn to violence as a response was a result of the disappointment the youth felt in the Basque government and traditional nationalism. The seemingly passive strategy summarized by the motto "let do and wait" had failed to satisfy the young people who had endured the violence of the Franco regime. Contrary to Irujo's insinuations of fascist influence, the shift towards violence was attributed to a lack of confidence in Basque organizations and their leaders.

The young Basque nationalists expressed a readiness to fight for the freedom of the Basques, uniting violence, nationalism, and language in defense of the Basque Country. They were determined to resist repression and were willing to resort to peaceful means and moral forces if the Spanish government limited itself to such methods. However, if faced with alternatives, they were prepared to use force.

The concept of National Resistance was employed to analyze the Basque people's clear commitment to nationalism and the defense of the Basque language as a fundamental aspect of their identity. This idea of resistance, embedded in their historical and political symbolic framework, led them to compare the situation of the Basque people with national conflicts in Algeria or Cyprus. It also flirted with the idea of anti-colonialism, which would later become a significant link with various liberation movements, particularly in North Africa and Israel.

ETA, with members educated abroad, saw no internal solution to the Basque conflict and sought inspiration by comparing it with other armed struggles globally. As they decided to militarize their fight, they imported strategies, drawing on the experiences of national liberation movements in Algeria, Vietnam, and Israeli urban commandos.[558]

Concerns about the future of the conflict are reflected in the analysis of national conflicts in Tunis and Ireland presented in the Libro Blanco.[559] The document explicitly cited similar national conflicts that had achieved independence, notably Israel, and emphasized internal resistance.

Up until then, ETA's ideological foundation had been shaped by what they considered analogous national conflicts, emphasizing a pure ideology of class and giving special attention to the conflict itself. After establishing its ideological principles from the First Assembly in 1962, the organization positioned itself as anti-racist, anti-clerical, a defender of socialism, and opposed to economic liberalism.

We are not alone. Ideological foundation of the revolutionary Basque nationalism: From Federico Krutwig to Etxebarrieta's brothers

The ideological evolution of ETA in the 1960s resulted from the influence of exile, not only in the adoption of international and revolutionary ideas but also because its primary ideologists were compelled to seek refuge abroad following the initial significant violent actions, as discussed earlier. As we concentrate on researching the development of Basque nationalism, its international dimensions, recognition, and political constraints, it is crucial for us to scrutinize key documents and their authors. This analysis will enable us to comprehend the impact of exile on the evolution of revolutionary Basque nationalism.

The emergence of a new strategy in exile is evident in Krutwig's "Vasconia."[560] Over time, the ideological framework was constructed, with an increasing emphasis on anti-colonialism, particularly influenced by Federico Krutwig's work. Krutwig, born Federico Krutwig Sagredo in Getxo and of German descent, exhibited an early interest in philosophy and linguistics. He became a member of the Euskaltzaindia (the Basque language academy) in 1943. After residing in Germany and Portugal during the Spanish Civil War, his family returned to the Basque Country post-conflict. Living under the Franco dictatorship, Krutwig developed a keen interest in the Basque language and culture, notably after a chance meeting with Resurrección María de Azkue,[561] a prominent Basque linguist who had presided over Euskaltzaindia since its inception.

Involved in the reorganization of Euskaltzaindia and the Athenaeum of Bilbao, Krutwig faced accusations of incitement to rebellion by the Francoist authorities, leading to his exile to avoid sentencing.[562] His journey took him through various countries, starting with Iparralde, where he encountered members of Jagi-Jagi. He then moved to Paris, exchanging ideas with Basque members of the "Rue Singer," including Manuel Irujo and Landaburu. From there, he traversed Germany, Brussels, Italy, Algeria, and more. Of particular interest to our research, his work "Vasconia"[563] was written and developed in exile, published in 1963 in Biarritz, with the first edition dating back to his Buenos Aires years. This period was characterized by exile and clandestinity.[564]

During his initial exile in Iparralde, Krutwig interacted with various Basque refugees representing different facets of Basque nationalism, such as Agustín Zumalde, Lezo Urreztieta, and Iker Gallastegi from Jagi-Jagi, as well as Jon Bilbao and Francisco Miangolarra, American refugees. According to Krutwig, it was Miangolarra who urged him to write "Vasconia," stating, "Look, Federico, in order to get out of this impasse, we need the formulation of a new type of nationalism, which must be both very nationalist and entirely progressive."[565]

In "Vasconia," Krutwig delves into the concept of "traditional" war based on the experiences recounted by Colonel Trinquier[566] in his efforts to suppress Algerian guerrilla resistance. Krutwig asserts that the so-called Revolutionary War represents a strategic evolution involving the organization of guerrillas to overcome a formidable adversary associated with the metropolis. This draws a clear parallel with the Basque situation and the role of Spain.

Krutwig's work and ideas, particularly those expressed in the "Bellica" section of Vasconia, became a fundamental source of inspiration for ETA, earning the label of the "Bible of ETA." This designation came from voices such as Manuel Fraga Iribarne, the Francoist Minister of Industry and Tourism, who sought to discredit the organization. Fraga Iribarne propagated the belief that Vasconia embodied the soul of ETA, with its spirit superseding even the primitive material cells[567] as new members joined.

Vasconia comprises seven insightful parts—Ethnica, Oeconomica, Dynamica, Historica, Politica, Bellica, and Dialectica. Krutwig analyzes and updates Basque nationalism in accordance with his political, economic, and linguistic perspectives. However, the part that left the most profound impact on young Basque nationalists in ETA was the "Bellica" section, introducing a warlike proposal as a strategy for the national liberation of the Basque Country.

The book explores the intellectual war, emphasizing considerations regarding the idea of the colony. Krutwig applies the successful anti-colonial movement in North Africa[568] to Basque nationalism, equating Spanish domination of the Basque people with the common strategy employed by metropolises in various colonies striving for freedom and dignity.

Krutwig advocates for revolutionary war as the strategy for the "gudaris," presenting it as the evolution of traditional war and providing the necessary ideological foundation for the Basque people. This ideology transforms them into "gudaris," akin to medieval crusaders, garnering support from Basque citizens.

The impact of exile is evident in Krutwig's ideas, extending beyond strategic warfare concepts. As an intellectual, Krutwig placed greater faith in revolution than rebellion, aligning with the sentiments of Marxist author Eugene D. Genovese. Genovese, in 1979, emphasized the importance of ideology in revolution, a sentiment echoed by Krutwig. The influence of Asian philosophers, particularly Mao Tse-tung and Ho-Chi-Minh, is apparent in Krutwig's defense of the necessity for ideological preparation to craft a successful national strategy. He highlights the role of an ideological flame in revolutionary wars, motivating the population to support and assist guerrillas as champions of their aspirations.[569]

The significance of Krutwig's work became particularly apparent in a text that would serve as the cornerstone for ETA during that period: "La Guerra Revolucionaria / Insurrección en Euskadi."[570] Composed in 1963 and published in 1964, this document marked the establishment of ETA's strategy in the pursuit of the national and social liberation of Euskadi. In "La Guerra Revolucionaria," the young members of ETA outlined a novel path hitherto unexplored by Basque nationalism, advocating for direct action to realize their objectives. While the authorship of this influential document remains unknown, several studies attribute it to Julen de Madariaga, one of the founders of ETA, who was at the forefront of the decision to take up arms but would later express criticism of armed struggle and commit to political activities.[571]

Julen Madariaga, along with his wife Osane, sought refuge in exile after the train derailment incident and enduring torture by the Spanish police. Their initial exile was in Iparralde, like many other Basque refugees, until October 1964 when the French Prefecture in Iparralde (Basses Pyrénées) issued an expulsion order due to Madariaga being found illegally in possession of a firearm. Despite efforts by Sven Johannsen,[572] president of the Union Fédéraliste des Communautés Ethniques Européennes (UFCE), to reverse the expulsion by highlighting the constant threats from the Franco Regime, the order was executed. Subsequently, Madariaga, Txillardegi, and Eneko Irigaray relocated to Belgium.

The expulsion stirred confusion and controversy among Basque nationalists in exile in Iparralde. According to ETA members, the expulsion resulted from an accusation by Patrick de la Sota, a member of the PNV. Txillardegi, in a letter to Manuel Irujo, urgently called for action against De la Sota to prevent further deterioration of relations between ETA and the PNV. In the same letter, an agitated Txillardegi implored Irujo to write an article dispelling rumors propagated by traditional Basque nationalists, who were alleging that ETA had communist affiliations. Once again, rumors circulated regarding the perceived association of young Basque nationalists with communist ideas, prompting Txillardegi to address and counter such claims.[573]

Manuel Irujo reached out to Txillardegi expressing solidarity and concern after the expulsion order, but he declined to meet Txillardegi's request regarding De la Sota, citing an attack on him by ETA members. Concerning the communist rumors, Irujo referred to a round table organized by the PNV in Paris, where the perceived communist affiliation of the young Basque nationalists hindered reaching any agreement.

Despite maintaining contact with ETA members, especially Txillardegi, Irujo condemned the increasingly embraced Marxist ideas and the violent methods employed by the new generation of Basque patriots. He questioned the feasibility of engaging in dialogue with individuals he viewed as "robbers" and urged self-reflection on the chosen methods: "Use the current difficulties to examine your conscience. Where are you going with these 'manners'?"[574]

However, Irujo and Lehendakari Aguirre worked actively to prevent the expulsion and imprisonment of the four ETA members affected by the order. In a letter to Solaun on November 30, 1964, Irujo explained their efforts: "I hope that the President will tell you how, upon learning of the confinement of the four ETA members, he approached Labeguerie, and I approached Txillardegi, telling him that the President had been in direct contact with that deputy and asking him what he thought we could do to oppose the government measure of confinement."[575]

Returning to "La Guerra Revolucionaria / Insurrección en Euskadi," it should be noted that, while greatly influenced by Vasconia, its analysis goes beyond, presenting revolutionary war as a just war—a "war of national and social liberation" against an unjust counter-revolutionary war. The latter is seen as oppressive and driven by conquering elements promoted by oppressive states, specifically referencing the Spanish State and the situation in the Basque Country.[576]

The work draws inspiration from constant revolutions and national liberation movements in North Africa (Tunis, Algeria) and Israel, presenting them as modern examples of the biblical battle of David against Goliath. The rising colonies against metropolises and the ensuing national and state victories captivated the attention of progressive Europe. The military strategy of revolutionary war is based on recent experiences, with a notable emphasis on the Israeli case, particularly in relation to Irgun, the Sephardic armed group of national liberation against the British Empire, a reflection ETA saw in itself.

Israeli influence also surfaces in the analysis of the "Asphalt guerrilla"[577] since the Basques, with their high urban population (80% urban population), couldn't replicate strategies from the rural guerrilla in Tunis. Instead, they identified more with the Israeli example, where "Urban guerrilla warfare prevailed over rural guerrilla warfare."[578]

Both Julen Madariaga and Eneko Irigaray confirmed that the young Basque nationalists were indeed drawn to the Israeli experience during that period. Madariaga explicitly expressed this attraction, stating, "We are attracted by the huge conflict they had with the British Empire, the blowing up of the King David Hotel... and other things, there was the Haganah, the Irgun, etc." The successful example of Zionism in the creation of the State of Israel served as a model for other national movements, such as the Basque struggle.

Madariaga's fascination with the Jewish people predated their transformation into Israelis, rooted in the intense battle they fought in the Warsaw Ghetto against the Germans. He recalled the memory of people fighting, facing tremendous odds, and ultimately triumphing. The pivotal year of 1948, marked by Balfour and the direct battles involving the Irgun and the Haganah,[579] left a lasting impression on Madariaga.

Federico Krutwig affirmed that the earliest influences leading ETA toward armed struggle came from Israel's example and Menachem Begin's[580] book, "The Revolt." The group embraced these experiences, evident in the bibliography of their early documents like the "Libro Blanco," where "The Revolt" featured in the section on the Moral of National Resistance, addressing the situation of nationalism and the Basque people. Madariaga nostalgically recalled being deeply moved by Begin's book, which he read in French translation during his confinement in the prison of Carabanchel, a gift from José María Retolaza, later the first Minister of the Interior of the Basque Government.[581]

Jewish influences primarily pertained to the military side, with the action on July 22, 1946, against the King David Hotel in Jerusalem leaving a profound impact on the Basques. This event inspired Madariaga's idea of blowing up the civil government's seat in Bilbao, applying the Jewish strategy of a direct attack against the "enemy" bases stationed in the Basque Country.[582]

Admiration for the Jews' successful strategy, coupled with the Basques' connections with the people of Israel, led ETA leaders to seek a meeting with the heads of the young State of Israel, aiming for technical and military assistance. The meeting was arranged through contacts of the Basque Government-in-exile and the PNV with the Jews and the Israeli government, scheduled to take place in Paris in 1963. Represented by Julen Madariaga and Juan Luis Irusta, ETA scheduled a meeting with Shlomo Stiemberg, a representative of the State of Israel, at a location near the Paris Opera, facilitated through PNV contacts, including Juan de Ajuriaguerra, "El Amirante," a former partner of Madariaga in the early days of EKIN.[583]

ETA's interest in spreading their cause against the Spanish invader extended beyond seeking sympathy and understanding. They also needed materials for carrying out their armed struggle, making the meeting with Israeli representatives crucial for obtaining weapons and access to training camps. ETA members recognized that a successful campaign against Spain required a military arsenal and technical knowledge, needs the Israelis were well aware of, having overcome similar challenges in their own struggle.

During the meeting with the Israeli contact, ETA members presented their cause, hoping for support. However, the Israeli representative, while understanding and respecting their cause, expressed reservations due to a claim that interfered with the French State, making any direct assistance risky. The Israeli contact committed to reporting everything to Menachem Begin, including the ETA members' requests and his personal viewpoint, clarifying his lack of favor for providing aid.[584]

Despite the challenges in obtaining direct assistance from Israel, the influences on ETA stretched across war fronts that would later involve Arabs and Israelis. Algerian influence was particularly notable, especially in the organization of ETA as a national liberation front. The Algerian National Liberation Front (FLN) influenced ETA to the extent that they later referred to themselves as the Basque Socialist Movement for National Liberation. In the early stages, this influence was evident in the organization of resistance and the strategy of placing bombs, inspired by the example of the city of Algiers.

Eneko Irigaray, one of ETA's founders, who had been in exile in Algeria since 1965, highlighted the impact of Algerian influence on the organization. Before the

5th Assembly, Federico Krutwig and Irigaray prepared the green report, which defined ETA as the Basque Socialist Revolutionary Movement for National Liberation.[585]

Irigaray and Julen Madariaga sought refuge and assistance in Algeria, aligning with another successful national movement. With the help of Leopoldo Igarralde, they traveled to Germany, where Madariaga bought a Volkswagen Beetle. They crossed Germany, Switzerland, Austria, and Italy to reach Naples, from where they would be transferred to Algiers. During the ferry journey, they encountered an English settler and a young man, later revealed to be a member of the Algerian secret services, who facilitated their contact with Antonio Cubillo. Cubillo welcomed them into his home, and after spending a few days there, he connected them with the FLN (National Liberation Front).

During ETA's first visit to Algeria, Antonio Cubillo,[586] leader of the Movimiento por la Autodeterminación e Independencia del Archipiélago Canario (MPAIAC), which had been established a year earlier in Algeria, assisted them in making contact with the FLN, although the strategy did not succeed. The revolutionary Basque nationalists sought weaponry, training camps, and a radio station to broadcast their messages, inspired by the MPAIAC, which already had Canarias Libre Radio broadcasting from Radio Algiers. This initial meeting marked the beginning of a long-term relationship with the Algerian government, reaching its climax during the peace talks in Algiers from 1987 to 1989.[587]

However, just as the relations with Jews and later Israelis faced challenges due to the difference in status between a revolutionary group and the diplomacy inherent to a new state, the initial encounter with the Algerians followed a similar pattern. Madariaga and Irigaray quickly realized that, despite receiving humanitarian aid and lodging as refugees, trade relations between Algeria and Spain took precedence over the international solidarity relationship that ETA had hoped for.

In Vasconia, the Algerian example is not just another conflict analyzed; it holds ideological significance, with three appendices dedicated to it. These sections provide a clear comparison with the territorial organization of the urban area of Algiers and a practical application of the Algerian experience in the Basque Country.[588]

During this initial stage, the strategy was just that—a strategy. Armed actions were not as significant or efficient as one might infer from the preparations, likely because ETA had not yet acquired enough capacity to initiate a true revolutionary war. Ibarra noted a "clear mismatch between theory and practice," attributing it to the insufficient training and social conditions of the young ETA members to create structures supporting commandos for a Basque insurgency. However, despite the limited violence, their initial actions did instill some hope and revive national consciousness, which had languished due to the ineffectiveness of the PNV, perceived as "sleeping the sleep of the just."[589]

During this period, ETA's leadership, facing the forced exile of key members and influenced by experiences abroad, was undergoing an evolution toward a form of socialism aligned with the internationalist trend. Patxi Iturrioz, particularly influential among inland members, played a significant role in shaping this socialist orientation and eventually gained control of ETA's leadership after the departure of the founders.

These developments unfolded during the years of the Fourth Assembly, which took place in two different locations: the monastery of Loyola and the mountain refuge of Oñate, both in Gipuzkoa. It was during the second part of this assembly in 1965 that the strategy of revolutionary war was formally approved. Madariaga, who had recently returned from Algeria under the war name "Ahmed," played a pivotal role in endorsing this strategy based on his firsthand experience in that territory.

Simultaneously, this assembly marked ETA's deepening into socialism.[590] The organization modified some of its 1962 principles to align them with a Marxist conception of the future Basque State. This shift towards socialism would later contribute to internal conflicts within ETA.

The influence of Algeria became evident, showcasing the deep admiration ETA had for the FLN. This admiration is clearly reflected in the document "Bases Teóricas de la Guerra Revolucionaria,"[591] presented during a lecture by José Luís Zalbide. In this document, Zalbide emphasized the need for a new strategy that embraced more socialist positions.

The document laid the foundation for the new armed strategy that ETA would predominantly develop after the Fifth Assembly. However, traces of this strategy were already present in the systematic enactment of the action-repression-action spiral. This spiral was closely linked to the Algerian example, as explained by Zalbide. According to him, the goal of the action-repression-action process was to compel recognition of the Basque country by the oppressor, Spain. The strategy aimed for Spain to grant increasing autonomy until achieving political independence, with the belief that repression, when logically pursued by the oppressor, would ultimately grant the oppressed people their charter as a nation. Zalbide drew parallels between this strategy and the experiences of the English and French colonial empires, explicitly citing Algeria as an example where the metropolis lost control over a once-submissive people.

José Luis Zalbide was associated with the Anti-colonialist or Third World movement, profoundly influenced by the national liberation movements emerging in the "third world." His efforts to integrate this particular socialist ideology were not without turmoil among ETA's members. The document "Bases teóricas para la Guerra revolucionaria" outlined ETA's strategy to achieve self-determination and absolute independence, drawing inspiration not only from those peoples who had recently achieved such goals, with Algeria as a primary example but also from other anti-colonial victories.[592]

Zalbide's international experience, especially the Third-World element, was evident in his work, embodying ETA's internal conflict between its working-class and Third-World supporters, eventually leading to the organization's split into two branches.

Another key point in ETA's Third-World ideology was the document titled "Carta a los intelectuales,"[593] first published in 1964 and reedited in June 1965. In this document, ETA sought to reorganize and regenerate its ideology to achieve national freedom. The influence of revolutionary Third-World movements is apparent, and its structure and objectives reflect similarities to the letters of Franz Fanon during the Algerian Revolution. This indicates the impact of external intellectuals on the organization, with Gurutz Jáuregui noting, "The influence of Fanon and other authors directly linked to the Algerian revolution is patent." Proof of this is the fact that both Fanon's Pour "La révolution africaine" and Albert Memmi's "Le portrait du colonisé" were translated into Basque."[594]

The "Carta a los intelectuales" was the last attempt to consolidate the various ideological tendencies within the organization before internal differences led to a split. The document analyzed and combined the two major trends – the Third-World strategy and the labor tendency – in an effort to adapt Third-World revolutions to a modern working-class society like the Basque region.[595]

The divergence from the national and independence movements in the Third World, distinct from the Basque scenario, shocked a segment of the Basque nationalists' community, particularly members of the PNV. They were dismayed by the strategies employed by the young members of ETA. Despite the lack of an in-depth analysis of peculiarities and distinctions, the organization seemed intent on identifying commonalities with successful examples. The aim was to inspire the Basque population to initiate a revolution rather than focusing on aspects that might deviate from the revolutionary path.[596]

Contrary to a comprehensive examination of the Basque and Algerian conflicts, as noted by José Mari Garmendia, the labor faction within ETA, led by Iturrioz, initiated a campaign that increasingly emphasized Spanish and working-class characteristics. Simultaneously, the national element of Basque nationalism was critiqued and questioned, either dismissed or relegated to a secondary level.[597] The emphasis shifted towards the workers' struggle, with the belief that the nationalists' fight belonged to the bourgeoisie.

Advocating for stronger ties with the Spanish labor movement and alignment with the class struggle following the Third International principles, this group criticized the Third-World faction for drawing comparisons between the Basque conflict and unrelated situations like the Algerian struggle. They debated whether nationalisms were inherently conservative or could be redefined from left-wing perspectives.

To counter the advancing labor front in ETA, a publication in Zutik's issue No. 31 from July 1965, governed by the organization's rigorous assemblies, presented an article from the Third-World/Anti-colonialist faction.[598] Once again, the Algerian example was cited as a model for the national liberation movement. The article featured an excerpt from the memoirs of Algerian military soldier Ahmed Ben Cherif, chronicling his evolution within Marxism based on personal and professional experiences. Ben Cherif concluded that unless the social revolution shifted from the hands of the French, there would be no progress for the Algerians. He criticized the reliance on the French Communist Party and its opportunism, linking it with the politicians at the Parliament of Paris, stating that such dependence would hinder any chance of a revolution.[599]

By presenting the example of Ben Cherif, the anti-colonial front, also representing the faction of ETA in exile, aimed to draw parallels between the experiences of Algerian revolutionaries and the emerging dynamics within ETA and the broader Basque revolutionary movement. Specifically, they observed the strengthening Spanish labor front, which inclined towards the realization of an internationalist proletarian Leninism. The tension between working-class interests and national concerns would intensify over time, particularly following the Vth Assembly, a pivotal event in the organization's history.

With Iturrioz at the helm of the organization's political front and exerting influence over Zutik, the development of ideology was primarily shaped by the Spanish labor faction internally. However, the old guard in exile, emphasizing the significance of Basque nationalism, reacted swiftly. This reaction materialized in an alliance between Txillardegi and Krutwig, marked by a series of writings denouncing the perceived deviation of the Spanish Zutik.[600]

The return of Julen Madariaga to Belgium prompted a reaction from the historical founders, mostly congregated in exile in Flanders, against the working-class front within ETA. To address the situation, the organization opted to consolidate forces and appointed Madariaga as Burutzagi (supreme head), contradicting the spirit of the assembly on which the organization was originally founded. This strategic move was orchestrated by ETA in exile to regain control in the face of dissension, arrests, and declining militancy resulting from police activities that were severely impacting the organization.[601]

The exile in Algeria played a crucial role in shaping ETA's ideology and armed struggle. Not only did Algeria become a long-term refuge for ETA members, but it also exposed revolutionary Basque nationalists to various national liberation movements, influencing them significantly. As recalled by Irigaray, the Algerian movement served as inspiration, but it was not the sole influence. The contact with diverse national liberation movements in North Africa and America, such as the Quebec Liberation Front, representatives from Uruguay, Brazil, Vietnam, Cambodia, and encounters with figures like Che Guevara, enriched and shaped ETA's perspective. The Algerian camps became a meeting ground for revolutionary minds from different parts of the world, fostering a broader understanding of global struggles.[602]

Etxebarrieta brothers, political violence & poetry.

In Enrique Krauze's book "Redentores: Ideas y poder en la América Latina,"[603] Ernesto Che Guevara is characterized as embodying an ancient spirit akin to Spanish guerrilla Javier Mina and Lord Byron in his adventures against the Turks.

Krauze links poetry with violence, suggesting that the revolutionary use of violence is considered a superior form of poetry. This connection between violence, poetry, and "el Che" resonates with the special significance that violence, poetry, and the Basque revolutionary poets, the Etxebarrieta brothers, held.

Among the members of ETA who wielded influence through their writings, blending nationalism, Marxism, and violence in shaping the armed struggle and the strategy of action-repression-action, the Etxebarrieta brothers stood out. Txabi, the younger brother, joined ETA in October 1963, following in the footsteps of his older brother and mentor,[604] José Antonio, who had gone into exile in 1960 with the intention of deepening his involvement in the Basque cause.

The Etxebarrieta brothers played pivotal roles in redefining ETA during the notable Vth assembly, held between the end of 1966 and March of 1967. This assembly was crucial for establishing a new ideology to address the diverse tendencies within ETA and also marked a period of crisis for the organization. The crisis was resolved in 1971 by affirming the legitimacy of the Vth assembly, presenting its values and ideology as the true and authentic ETA.

Contributing both theoretical insights and practical strategies to ETA's armed struggle, the Etxebarrieta brothers made it the centerpiece of the new ETA.[605] Simultaneously, they replaced working-class advocacy with the concept of "Pueblo Trabajador Vasco" (PTV) or Basque Working People, introduced by José Antonio in his influential report, "Informe Txatarra." The intertwining of Basque nationalism and violence gained prominence, particularly after the assassination of Melitón Manzanas in 1967, as analyzed by Pedro Ibarra.[606] However, one could argue that the trajectory of violence and the action-repression-action strategy had already begun with the assassination of Txabi Etxebarrieta, considered the "tragic subject," the first martyr of the homeland and a necessary victim of the revolution.[607]

The writings of the intellectually brilliant Etxebarrieta brothers significantly influenced the revolutionary nationalist Basque organization, contributing to an enduring ideological framework that spanned decades. Our focus in this research will be on José Antonio and his experiences in exile, where he engaged with a diverse spectrum of Basque nationalists, from the Gallastegi family to traditional PNV nationalists. During this period, he was introduced to a plethora of philosophers, including Rousseau, Sartre, Kierkegaard, Hegel, Marx, Engels, Lenin, Fanon, Ho Chi Minh, Mao, and Ernesto Che Guevara, all of whom left distinct marks on his intellectual work.

In Iparralde, José Antonio established connections with the EG organization in San Juan de Luz, encountering the Gallastegi family. Iker Gallastegi acknowledged his eagerness to undertake new projects for the benefit of his people. However, lacking a suitable role in Iparralde at that time, it was decided to send him to Paris, where numerous young refugees and Basque students were present, providing an opportunity for meaningful contributions.[608]

Participating in conferences organized by the PNV in Paris, José Antonio played a role in the generational shift within Basque nationalism, as previously discussed. Manuel Irujo, who closely monitored his political and ideological activities, described Etxebarrieta as part of the new generation of Basque nationalists. In a letter to Elias Gallastegi on May 4, 1962—after the Paris conferences—Irujo, acknowledging the Gallastegi family's support, characterized Etxebarrieta as a member of the avant-garde, a dissenter, and the intellectual force behind Euzko-Gaztedi.[609]

The letter also informed Etxebarrieta of *Cuadernos* journal's interest in publishing his article on the Spanish situation. With a touch of humor, Irujo remarked that he preferred not to know the content in case it might be better left unpublished, stating, "It is always good to get rid of bad temptations."

Despite being part of the old guard, Manuel Irujo remained active in his political and intellectual pursuits, maintaining awareness of the activities and involvements of the young Basque nationalists. This vigilance was evident in his early concerns about potential connections between ETA and communism after only a few encounters with them.

In a letter to his friend Francisco Belausteguigoitia, previously discussed in relation to suspicions about the communist aspect of ETA, Manuel Irujo reveals some of the insights and criticisms that José Antonio Etxebarrieta would later expound in his work on Basque history, "Los vientos favorables. Euskal Herria 1839-1959." Following his interactions with the Basque Government, meetings with traditional Basque nationalists in Paris, and the influence of Gallastegi's family, Etxebarrieta's interest in Basque nationalism grew. This interest led him to develop a theory in his book, analyzing the history of Basque nationalism, defending Sabino Arana, and chastising the Basque government for what he perceived as mismanagement.[610]

Irujo recounts the thoughts expressed by Etxebarrieta in a Parisian round table, where he criticized the PNV's role in the evolution of Basque nationalism, categorizing it as "interventionist" or "non-interventionist." The interventionists, represented by political forces like the PNV, engaged in Spanish politics, while the non-interventionists, like ETA, worked with the people towards freedom and independence. These ideas were a reinterpretation of concepts originally used by Arana's brothers, showcasing the strong connection young Basque nationalists maintained with Sabino Arana while bypassing the PNV's legacy.

For José Antonio, the PNV's mistake was accepting and recognizing the "oppressor," Spain, thereby acknowledging its authority. He criticized the PNV's acceptance of the oppressor's legality, freedom of association, and freedom of assembly, considering it a doctrinal inconsistency that undermined realistic politics.[611]

His analysis of Basque nationalism's history is detailed, highlighting perceived mistakes and proposing a new strategy. Drawing on Lenin as a primary source,

Etxebarrieta identifies the lack of a clear objective as the main problem for the PNV. In his view, this objective should be independence and revolution.[612]

Through his intriguing theory of steps, José Antonio Etxebarrieta explains that the PNV's political trajectory advanced up certain steps, exemplified by their defense of the Statute of Autonomy. However, this progression was halted when they shifted from being interventionists to legalists, adhering to the Spanish legal framework, which, in Etxebarrieta's view, limited them to autonomy. The persistent problem for the PNV, according to Etxebarrieta, was the absence of a political project beyond autonomy. Despite describing Manuel Irujo as a "PNV mouthpiece," he acknowledges that Irujo, along with Monzón and Jáuregui, had distinct plans during the war, particularly concerning the Basque National Council in London, representing an "overcoming of the statute adventure and the framing of the Basque problem in its proper national context."[613]

Etxebarrieta's goal, and by extension ETA's national mission, was to achieve the national plan—to ascend to the top of the stairs, reaching the last step of Independence.

The PNV's lack of ideology, as illustrated by the 1956 Basque Congress in Paris, led to political stagnation, marking the fracture between the old guard and the new Basque generation. The young Basque nationalists sought an ideology beyond interventionism.[614] This quest drove José Antonio to study the history of Basque nationalism, make comparisons, and ultimately embrace revolutionary nationalism with a Marxist-Leninist framework. This ideology was not just associated with the communist party but was considered essential for the socialist and revolutionary transformation of society.

In the Basque case, revolutionary patriotism—with independence linked to a socialist society—replaced the Catholic confessionalism of the PNV. Patriotism became a new passion, exemplified in the case of Txabi Etxebarrieta, for whom it became fate and curse.[615] Generally, revolutionary Basque nationalism adopted revolutionary patriotism as a form of desacralization of Christianity and an instrument of a comforting religion capable of giving meaning to existence.[616]

Txabi and José Antonio Etxebarrieta had been contemplating the idea of armed struggle since the Vth assembly, drawing inspiration from classical Marxist texts and the Cuban revolution. However, it was the Irish experience of Iker Gallastegi that provided José Antonio with the opportunity to implement the theory of armed struggle. Federico Krutwig, in his memoirs, details this initial Basque attempt at guerrilla warfare,[617] an experiment that did not succeed. Using the alias "Gatarrieta" for Iker Gallastegi and Etxebarrieta, Krutwig explains that they had organized and prepared groups of young Basque nationalists for action in the Basque Country.

While the founders of ETA were primarily influenced by the national conflicts in Israel and Algeria, the next generation of revolutionary Basque nationalists, informed by the experience of Gallastegi's family, drew inspiration from

Ireland and the tactics employed by the IRA. Gallastegi, in contact with various Basque nationalists, secured funding for the guerrilla from America. With the initial support of Joseba Rezola, he traveled to Ireland, where he connected with IRA members to acquire weapons and military training.

After a failed attempt to obtain training in Ireland and Rezola withdrawing from the armed strategy, Gallastegi returned to Iparralde. There, he contacted Etxebarrieta in Paris to pursue the guerrilla idea. Etxebarrieta had been studying "La guerre revolutionaire" by Claude Delmas and works by Mao Zedong, but the strategy they prepared was also inspired by the Israeli experience, from Gallastegi's farewell to José Antonio— "Abi Gezund!"[618]—to the recruitment strategy of "hirurkos" trained in Iparralde.

Although they successfully took about fifteen young Basques for instruction in Donibane, Gallastegi's expulsion from Iparralde in 1962 and José Antonio's illness forced Etxebarrieta to seek help from Julen Madariaga in ETA.[619] In 1963, after returning to Bilbao, the group of young Basques trained by José Antonio Etxebarrieta in Iparralde joined ETA, and Txabi Etxebarrieta took over from his brother, tasked with continuing the reinterpretation of Basque nationalism—this time from within ETA.

Txabi Etxebarrieta was drawn into ETA during a meeting with Madariaga in Bilbao, representing his convalescing older brother. It was Madariaga who believed in him, the young intellectual from Sarriko's university, to lead the Vth Assembly, where the works of the Etxebarrieta brothers first came to light.

In the initial segment of the Vth Assembly held in December 1966 at a parish house in Gaztelu, the central focus was on the work presented by Txabi but authored by José Antonio, which served as the linchpin of the entire assembly: "Informe Txatarra."[620] This report compiled warnings and criticisms primarily expressed by Txillardegi against the political office, then under the influence of Iturrioz. Txillardegi had been communicating his concerns to ETA's executive, cautioning them about pro-Spanish and communist inclinations within the organization. Collaborating with Krutwig, he conceived "Branka,"[621] an alternative publication within the ethnolinguistic and Third-World tendencies, intending to counter Zutik, which, in Txillardegi's view, had transformed into a journal that was "pseudo-left of imperialism and the political colonialism of the Spanish state."[622]

The "Informe Txatarra" aligned well with the group of exiles who had crossed the border from exile to the inside to counter the Iturrioz campaign. After meeting with them, José Antonio authored the report directly opposing the political office. He accused it of being utopian for failing to analyze the working-class struggle from the Basque perspective; anachronistic for not discerning the phases of the revolution and the necessary alliance with the national bourgeoisie; non-national for disregarding political oppression and viewing national diversity as an obstacle; reformist for addressing the revolution solely through unions, avoiding political struggle; anti-organizational due to its intention of dissolving ETA into a leftist front; and finally, pacifist for renouncing armed struggle.[623] The report displayed a significant influence from the teachings of Lenin and likely Mao, as mentioned earlier.

Due to José Antonio's illness, Txabi received credit during the Vth assembly. After restructuring the organization into four fronts (cultural, political, military, and socio-economic), he played a role in the new executive, formed after the expulsion of the Spanish labor faction led by Iturrioz. The new executive was based on the structure of the "Biltzar Ttipia" (small assembly), controlling the organization. Its members were Txabi Etxebarrieta, Beltza, Eskubi, Etxabe, Balduino, Aguirre, Azurmendi, and Krutwig. These eight individuals then selected two more: Arregi and Madariaga. These ten leaders held the executive power to call an assembly.

The ideological foundation of the Vth Assembly was outlined in the "Informe Verde," written by Krutwig in exile, defining ETA as a "Basque Socialist Movement for National Liberation." This ideological basis, persisting until 1970, underscored the national and social struggle, the use of the Basque language as a cornerstone of Basque identity, collaboration with the Basque national bourgeoisie, and the involvement of the working class in the national revolution.[624]

The role played by the Etxebarrieta brothers in the new ideological development of the organization was bifurcated into two distinct aspects: the advocacy for a working-class connection with the Basque national cause and the maturation of the action-repression-action strategy, with Txabi assuming a central role in the latter.

Following the withdrawal of the labor front from ETA after the Vth assembly, the reconstruction of the working-class front and its integration into the national struggle owed much to the efforts of Txabi Etxebarrieta. In articles penned for Zutik, specifically in issues 44 and 45, Txabi addressed the Basque working class. An article in Zutik no. 44, dated January 1967, titled "Pueblo Trabajador Vasco" (Basque Working People), exemplified Txabi's emphasis on the connection between the new working-class Basque generation and national oppression. He depicted the national and social oppression of the Basque people, asserting, "Yes, there are two dictatorships. And there are two oppressed nations. Because if Euzkadi is oppressed by Spain and France, the workers' 'nation' is oppressed by the bourgeois nation."

Txabi's writings underscored the link between revolution, independence, and the Basque cause. For him, Aberri-Eguna (Homeland Day) and May 1st were inseparable, emphasizing that there could be no working-class liberation without national liberation. Common themes in his work included a critique of reformism, identifying both national and social forms as reactionary. Social reformism, aiming at reforming capitalism while maintaining the capitalist mode of production, was contrasted with national reformism, associated with the defense of the Statute. Txabi criticized those advocating statutism, stating, "Instead of fighting for national independence, those who preach statutism are not reactionary because they have adopted a longer and more peaceful path, but because they have taken another goal concerning the freedom of Euskadi." The attack on traditional Basque nationalism, particularly against the Basque government, was evident.

The revolution, according to the Etxebarrieta brothers, united the national and social struggles. However, achieving that revolution required a fight—and for Txabi, especially, that fight might involve sacrifice if necessary.

Txabi Etxebarrieta, despite his brief life cut short at the age of 23, left behind a poetic legacy through five books, revealing a profound connection with the concept of death.[625] His relationship with death was influenced by Feodor Dostoyevsky, who, for Txabi, symbolized the struggle between Christianity and faithlessness, crime and punishment, freedom and guilt[626]—a theme reflecting the dualities inherent in his worldview, encompassing the national and the social, life and death, action and passivity, and action and reaction. Txabi, in essence, became the catalyst for the action-reaction chain, marking the first victim and the inaugural martyr for ETA.

In January 1968, ETA distributed Zutik no.48 widely, featuring a text penned by José Antonio Etxebarrieta titled "What we do. Why we do it. What we have to do. Why we have to do it." The influence of Mao Zedong is evident in this text, which defends revolution and links the national revolution with social oppression, drawing examples[627] from China and the Japanese occupation. After a period of reflection, it became apparent that ETA was prepared to embark on a new chapter, advancing to the next step of the metaphorical stair, embracing the revolution and, consequently, armed struggle.

By the end of 1967 and the beginning of 1968,[628] repression in the streets had become commonplace in the Basque Country, marked by routine tortures, detentions, explosions, bank robberies, and shootings. The 1968 Aberri Eguna manifesto[629] by Txabi Etxebarrieta encouraged the Basque population to initiate the revolutionary fight against the oppressor. It articulated a radical confrontation with the oppressor across four fronts of struggle, with the ultimate aim of raising awareness among the Basque people and establishing a Basque socialist regime through the seizure of power by the working class. This revolutionary strategy led to activities that triggered a fierce reaction from capitalism.

Txabi, in the manifesto, drew parallels between Lenin and Jesus Christ, emphasizing that the revolutionary process must be grounded in concrete practice. He quoted Lenin's idea that to understand a socialist, one must look at their hands, not their mouth, echoing Christ's statement: "By their works, you will know them." According to Txabi, revolution is not confined to paper; it requires tangible actions. The Aberri Eguna Manifesto acknowledged the action-reaction-action strategy, asserting that while the conditions of Basque society might not be fully mature for success, the time had come to initiate the revolution.

"Sólo queda marcharme, Sólo. Y esperar que la tierra aún nos quiera."

(Txabi Etxebarrieta. Spring, 1968).

The Burgos trial (1970). The Process to Franco Regime

Following the Munich meeting, the focus of Basque nationalism's activities shifted from exile to the domestic front, primarily in response to the escalating violence and repression witnessed on the streets of Spain. Despite this shift, these activities maintained a consistent connection with the exiled community. In the late sixties and seventies, Spain experienced a surge in strikes, demonstrations, and protests against the Franco Regime. A new generation, unburdened by the fears associated with the Spanish Civil War, embraced democratic and revolutionary ideals flowing in from external sources, taking to the streets in protest. However, the dictatorship responded with repression, torture, and imprisonment, prompting Basque nationalism to redirect its strategy towards defending incarcerated individuals, managing new exiles, and seeking international recognition through a heightened state of violence rather than political or national advocacy.

In the public sphere, national consciousness gained prominence, marked by a progressive proliferation of signs and symbols. It signified the public expression of difference, a collective identity staunchly opposed to the existing social structures of the country.[630]

While violence had been commonplace during the Franco Dictatorship, the advent of ETA and its adoption of the action-repression-action strategy intensified street violence, particularly in the Basque country. The Spanish State responded with detentions, torture, imprisonments, and killings.

In response to the escalating political and social unrest, the regime enacted the Ley de Orden Público in July 1959. This legislation defined new parameters for public order, targeting activities such as strikes, illegal business closures, unauthorized gatherings, and the endorsement of violence or subversion. Additionally, the Francoist government regulated the State of Emergency, which it invoked eleven times between 1956 and 1975. These states of exception curtailed fundamental freedoms, including the right to residence, and suspended legal safeguards against arbitrary detentions, resulting in heightened episodes of violence and repression against citizens. Each state of emergency was declared following episodes of violence, riots during demonstrations, or as a preventive measure against potential future disturbances.

In September 1960, the regime further reinforced its stance by promoting the Decreto Ley sobre Rebelión Militar, bandidaje y terrorismo[631] (Decree-Law on military rebellion, banditry, and terrorism). This decree reaffirmed the use of court-martials, summary processes, and death sentences against specific forms of political subversion.

Meanwhile, the establishment of the Tribunal de Orden Público (TOP) in 1963 served as a new tool for the Franco regime. Its objective was "to hear crimes committed throughout the national territory, distinguished by the tendency, to a greater or lesser degree, to subvert the basic principles of the State, to disturb public order, or to sow anxiety in the national conscience."[632] This institution became a potent weapon for repressing the population, particularly those perceived as jeopardizing the political unity of Spain. The TOP, backed by the special police brigade known as "Brigada de investigación social," or popularly as "Brigada politico social" or "La social," played a pivotal role in the detention, interrogation, torture, and killing of numerous victims during that period. [633]

The Basque country, encompassing both the Basque country and Navarre in the Spanish administration, experienced ten states of emergency declared by the Franco authorities. These states of emergency suspended the articles of the "Fuero de los Españoles" (the Spanish jurisdiction during the dictatorship). Reproducing violence emerged as a foundational principle of the Franco order, as highlighted by Ander Gurruchaga: "(…) the states of emergency[634] symbolically reproduce the functional act of the new Francoist State because they imply that violence openly becomes the founding principle of the Francoist order." [635]

The years surrounding Burgos, marking the late 1960s and early 1970s, witnessed the heightened visibility of social nationalism embodied by the ETA movement. However, it's crucial to note that ETA could not have conducted its activities without the support of the Basque people, who actively shaped ETA into a social movement. [636]

ETA and the Revolutionary war

After the 5th assembly of 1966, during which ETA established its ideological foundations, the organization fully developed its strategy of armed struggle aimed at achieving the National Revolution. This strategy involved a fusion of the workers' movement with the Basque national front and guerrilla warfare. Internal secessions and divisions within ETA were exacerbated by the expulsion of historical founders Txillardegi, Irigarai, Del Valle, and Madariaga from France in 1965.

The endorsement of armed struggle occurred at the IVth assembly in 1965, and the document "Guerra revolucionaria- Insurrección en Euskadi"[637] became the guiding framework for its implementation. Another document presented during the assembly, "Bases teóricas de la guerra revolucionaria," was notably inspired by the aforementioned document. Federico Krutwig's influence is particularly evident in ETA's writings during this period. Krutwig's work, especially "Guerra revolucionaria- Insurrección en Euskadi" published in 1964, played a crucial role in defining ETA's strategy for the national and social liberation of the Basque Country.[638] The concept of revolutionary war proposed by ETA suggested a departure from traditional Basque nationalism, emphasizing direct action as a means to achieve their goals.

The document reflects the influence of Krutwig's earlier work, "Vasconia," but goes further by presenting revolutionary war as a just war. It argues that this war is a "war of national and social liberation," opposing the unfair war represented by the counter-revolutionary war of conquest and oppression practiced by oppressive States or empires, specifically referencing Spain and the Basque situation.[639]

Pedro Ibarra chronologically places this stage between 1963 and 1965,[640] although the influences on ETA's ideology extend until 1970. In advocating armed struggle, ETA emphasizes the importance of basing it on the principles of revolutionary war, highlighting that this war is not solely military but also ideological. Recognizing that classical war between States and armies is not feasible in their case, ETA opts directly for guerrilla warfare as part of the revolutionary war strategy, which incorporates a significant ideological component to compensate for the lack of armed troops.

ETA meticulously developed a substantial ideological framework for its defense, recognizing a crucial deficiency within the Spanish army and armed forces. This ideology centered on individuals embracing these beliefs, preparing for a conflict where they could make significant advancements. The emphasis in their work lies in portraying the inferiority of soldiers and policemen, asserting that individuals without a vested interest are less willing to face danger.[641] ETA later tested this theory by engaging in armed actions against army members and border police officers, leading to these officers struggling to avoid confrontation, as disclosed by a Guardia Civil captain to Antoni Batista in subsequent years. The captain's arguments align precisely with the notion that ETA fought for an ideal, while Franco police and Civil Guard officers fought primarily for a salary, resulting in an uneven ability to sacrifice. It is precisely due to this reason that Lieutenant Colonel Troncoso patriotically advocated for a modernization of the Spanish army.[642]

The strategy of revolutionary war claimed its initial casualties early on. Following the IVth assembly, Xabier Zumalde, also known as "el cabra" (the goat), led an autonomous group that adhered to revolutionary war principles. Hiding in the Basque mountains, they prepared as guerrillas until 1968, when their activities were exposed, leading Zumalde to flee into exile.[643]

ETA's armed activities, encompassing bank robberies, bombings in official buildings, attacks on police vehicles, and bombings on Francoist monuments, combined with mass events like the celebration of Aberri Eguna and a surge in workers' struggles, fostered an atmosphere of tension.[644] This situation could be compared to the effects of colonial wars against the metropolis, echoing the anti-colonialism trend present in ETA's theories.

Despite the armed struggle being just one facet among various fronts, the propaganda stemming from these violent activities heightened the perception of strategic success. Criticism of the passivity of traditional Basque nationalism grew. In a declaration authored by Txabi Etxebarriaeta and published in March 1968, coinciding with Aberri Eguna, the organization unequivocally expressed their intentions and staunch support for armed struggle. Etxebarriaeta asserted that the harmonious development of the four fronts was crucial for a Basque revolutionary path, safeguarding against opportunistic positions. The declaration emphasized that mere symbolic gestures or financial contributions were insufficient; genuine Basque nationalists were those actively contributing to the daily pursuit of concrete actions for national liberation.[645]

The incident that triggered the implementation and further definition of the action-repression-action strategy was the death of Txabi Etxebarrieta, ETA's first martyr. Etxebarrieta, a prominent ETA member, gained notoriety, especially after the Vth Assembly.[646] On June 7th, 1968, he shot and killed Civil Guard José Pardines at a police control point, marking the first fatal victim of ETA. After seeking refuge in Tolosa, Etxebarrieta and his accomplice, Iñaki Sarasketa, were intercepted by the Guardia Civil. Etxebarrieta was fatally shot in front of Benta Haundi's bar, where a commemorative plaque remains. Sarasketa managed to escape but was apprehended shortly after.[647]

When ETA emptied the entire magazine of a Czechoslovakian pistol into the head of Melitón Manzanas, the infamous torturer responsible for the Brigada Político-Social in Gipuzkoa, on August 2nd, 1968, they aimed to strike a blow against Franco. However, they did not anticipate that the murder would lead to a summary process two years later. The Burgos Process, the military court tasked with judging the 16 ETA members accused of Manzanas' murder, significantly altered the regime's image.[648]

ETA retaliated using their distinctive cycle of action-repression, declaring that Manzanas would not be the last. They framed the execution as a crucial step in their revolutionary struggle and emphasized its significance within the broader context of their fight. The response was immediate: a new state of emergency was declared exclusively in Gipuzkoa on August 3, 1968, initially for three months but ultimately extended until December. This state of emergency led to the suppression of articles 14, 15, and 18[649] of the Fuero de los Españoles, enabling the regime to detain, torture, and nearly dismantle ETA, leaving it with limited capability.

A trial against the Basque people

The response of the Basque people, and even the Basque Church, which had already signaled disagreement with the Franco regime in 1960 with a document signed by 339 Basque priests,[650] marked a turning point for the dictatorship. It wasn't solely the Basque nationalists who found the Franco Regime uncomfortable; workers from various backgrounds were also participating in demonstrations of social unrest. Even the Church, a pillar of the regime, began raising its voice against it. The regime's evident weakness prompted a fierce reaction to control dissent, presenting an image to the international community that hindered its strategy of gaining acceptance. The Basque nationalists viewed the document as one of the most compelling presentations of the Basque problem in Spain. Consequently, Ajuriaguerra, from within, decided to print a special edition of one hundred thousand copies of the document.[651]

The arrest of Sarasketa and the subsequent court-martial, resulting in the imposition of the death penalty on the ETA member, initiated another facet of the action-repression-action strategy: protests against repression. Basque society refused to accept the repression and vulnerability implied by the state of emergency. During funeral commemorations for Etxebarrieta, some of which were prohibited, mass demonstrations against Sarasketa's detention occurred, leading to repression by security forces. After weeks of mobilizations, protests, detentions, and social unrest, Sarasketa was ultimately pardoned by the Minister's cabinet, with his sentence commuted to 58 years in prison.[652]

The collaboration between ETA and the workers' movement amplified the impact of Basque nationalists' demands but also broadened the scope of repression. Despite the detentions nearly dismantling ETA during the state of emergency, the prolonged repression resulted in the arrest of individuals previously uninvolved in politics.

Determined to provide an exemplary response to the protests, if decrees or court-martials weren't enough, the decision on Manzanas' substitute signaled clear intentions. Antonio Juan Creix, a notorious torturer from the police station in Via Laietana (Barcelona), was called to replace Manzanas in the Basque country. Vicente Cazcarra, responsible for the political committee of the Partit Socialista d'Unificació Marxista (PSUC) in Barcelona, described Creix as a real monster, recounting his personal experience of being detained and tortured by Creix in 1961. Cazcarra portrayed Creix as someone who fiercely hated the democratic opposition, one of the most experienced and feared torturers of that time, acting with real viciousness. Creix's use of drugs during torture sessions was well-known, and his eyes, bulging and abnormally bright, revealed the extent of his brutality. Antonio Creix, head of the political-social Brigade of Barcelona, reportedly died of a heart attack many years after engaging in acts of torture.[653]

The youth section of the PNV, as published in the Venezuelan journal Gudari, penned a letter to the Commissioner in the same issue that detailed the assassination of Melitón Manzanas. The letter decried the subsequent repression, denouncing it as "razzias." Creix's notoriety had transcended borders, and the sense that repression in the Basque country had reached cruel and brutal extremes was gaining momentum. The Basque Country perceived itself as under attack, becoming the target of intensified repression due to nationalist struggles. The youth of EGI described Creix as the one tasked with executing the "final solution" to the Basque problem, accusing him of forming the anti-Euzkadi organization (O.A.E.) with the collaboration of governors.[654]

As the regime faced challenges to its pillars—the army and the police—it reacted with even greater violence than anticipated. The consecutive states of emergency undermined the "Paz social" (Social peace), a slogan developed by the Franco regime to present a favorable international image, ultimately concluding its European campaign.

Although exact figures are elusive, sources on the repression of the Franco Regime indicate its impact on Catalonia, Madrid, and other "subversive" regions of Spain, with particular focus on the Basque Country. The number of detainees and imprisoned individuals reached hundreds since 1968, worsening in 1969. According to Euskadi eta Askatasuna, published in 1994, in 1968, there were 434 detainees, 189 imprisoned, seventy five deported, and thirty eight exiled. In 1969, these figures increased significantly to 1953 detainees, 352 exiled, fifty three judged by a martial court, and ninety three receiving sentences by the TOP. Bizkaia had the highest number of detainees and repressive actions, with over 900 detainees, followed by Gipuzkoa with 589, Navarre with 328, and Araba with 101.[655]

The repression during those months was characterized by its extent and indiscriminate nature, a pattern that the dictatorship's police forces struggled to abandon in the subsequent years. Throughout the year, numerous arrests occurred, but the absence of evidence in many cases prevented criminal prosecution. In Biscay in 1968, of the 312 persons arrested by the regional Brigade of Social Investigation, 108 had to be released "without responsibility." Of the remaining 204, 112 were classified as "separatists," providing an indication of the prominence Basque nationalism had taken concerning "subversion" in the Basque Country, or at least the concern it generated among police authorities.[656]

Basque nationalism emerged as a more significant challenge than initially envisioned, but the indiscriminate nature of the repression expanded the issue to encompass the entire population of the Basque Country. Initially conceived by the Franco regime as a crackdown against "el repugnante y sangriento separatismo vasco" (the repugnant and bloody Basque separatism), as described by the Falangist journal Libertad,[657] the sheer scale of the repression transformed it into an assault on the entirety of the Basque Country.

The repression came to be viewed as an attack on Basque society at large. The use of torture and explicit violence during detentions, marked by car chases, gunshots in the streets, and accidental killings,[658] fostered a defiant spirit in a fearless population. In response, the people engaged in mobilizations, demonstrations, and novel forms of protest, including hunger strikes and church occupations. The regime's attempt to portray the conflict through the lens of terrorism had the opposite effect, with the populace seeing their neighbors and young people being killed for resisting the dictatorship.

Leveraging the state of emergency to carry out detentions without substantial evidence and subject detainees to hours of torture, exemplified by the case of Andoni Arrizabalaga after the assassination of Melitón Manzanas in Ondarroa, triggered a spiral of people's reactions. Arrizabalaga's ordeal, tortured in multiple police stations, became the focus of protest songs, such as Telesforo Monzón's "Itziaren Semea" (Itziar's son), exposing police abuse. This period witnessed the rise of protest song groups like Ez dok Amairu (There is no thirteen) and political songs against the dictatorship, including "Baga, Biga, Higa" and "Zenbat Gera?" (How many are we?), resonating through the streets.[659]

Examining Alderdi, the official bulletin of the PNV, reveals that most issues concentrated on the violence. The focus shifted inward, addressing urgent problems requiring solutions, and traditional Basque nationalism had to share its influence with the emerging revolutionary nationalism.

Gradually, a unanimous consensus emerged that the repression constituted an assault on the Basque people as a whole:

> In recent months, especially since the declaration of the State of Exception in Gipuzkoa, this repression has taken on such proportions that to describe it as brutal and sadistic is by no means an exaggeration. Priests, workers, men of liberal professions, merchants and industrialists, students, churches and convents, notaries' and lawyers' offices, the entire Gipuzkoa in its various sectors and social classes have suffered the bestial onslaught of a police force drunk with hatred that has sought revenge on the haughtiness and dignity of our People, thus trying to dominate it by means of terror.[660]

While the traditional Basque nationalism represented by the PNV had been opposed to violence and the use of political violence by ETA, the repression of the Franco regime surpassed the limits of the conservative party. As Alderdi's pages filled with files, lists of persecuted individuals, reports of torture, repressive acts, and records of resistance activities,[661] Basque nationalism attempted to unite against the Franco Regime. The repression was strongly condemned, and efforts were made to foster solidarity, inspired by the Gabon message sent by Lehendakari Leizaola on December 24, 1968:

> This presidency has emphasized in its documents of previous years and the current one that the unanimity of the Basques in their action for freedom is made up of the concurrence of all the ideologies that defend human freedom, and that its own representation and that of the Government of Euzkadi are based on the plural representation of all of them.[662]

The recurring notion of continuous violence against the Basque country since the Spanish Civil War needed to be denounced before the international community. The international strategy of traditional Basque nationalism focused on defending those who had been tortured, the detainees, and the victims of reprisals, treating them as new "gudaris" on certain occasions.

In an article written on January 17, 1968,[663] Manuel Irujo details the extreme situation of violence in the Basque country caused by the regime's battle against Basque nationalism. He emphasizes the need to solve the Basque problem rather than create martyrs. In "Gudariak" — the name of the article, meaning "Soldiers" or "Warriors" in Basque — Irujo reflects on the use of violence by young Basques. For the first time, he acknowledges the situation and subtly criticizes the strategy followed by the PNV:

> The men and women who come from the Basque Country recognize that we have reached the current situation because a long period of immobility has been brought to an end by the dynamic attitude of ETA. The youth is attracted by those who preach and practice 'action.' And after the youth, intellectuals, men of liberal professions, workers, students, priests, patriots of all ages and conditions.

Drawing on his experience in exile, Irujo proposes the idea of creating an association of war veterans to care for present-day Basque "gudaris" in order to preserve Basque unity and the authority of the Basque government and the PNV. He acknowledges the problem that violence is causing young nationalists to distance themselves: "Going to jail for feeling like a gudari is an honor. Killing a man can be a crime. To allow the climate of violence to spread would be irresponsible. Trying to control patriotic demonstrations and activities by using a popular organ may be a good idea and a solution."

While Manuel Irujo had been critical of violence and rejected it in any form, he received news about the repression in the Basque country while in America during his longest trip in that continent, between February and December 1969. In Venezuela, where revolutionary nationalism had taken root among the Basque community, Irujo delivered a passionate speech in defense of Basque patriots:

"There are dead people, there are wounded, there are tortured. Those who give everything for the homeland are not asked about their ideas. They are not asked their affiliation. They are not asked their political philosophy, with which we will be or will not be satisfied. They are men, they are Basques, they are heroes. For them, our greetings, Agur Jaunak!"[664]

The strategy employed by the defense attorneys during the Burgos trial was embraced by the Basque population several months before the trial itself. What the regime aimed to portray as an attack on the regime by terrorists transformed into an examination of a regime accused of being a terrorist regime, one that utilized torture and violence against its own population.

Making up the trial

The strategy of the Franco regime revolved around judging ETA as an "organización clandestina ETA de tipo separatista-terrorista-comunista" (Clandestine organization ETA, separatist-terrorist-communist type), irrespective of individual actions by the accused. Membership in the organization itself was considered sufficient grounds for guilt, as explicitly stated in the prosecutor's indictment:

"Having carried out through their armed groups of surreptitious existence in urban and rural areas a multitude of illegal meetings, illegal demonstrations, sowing of subversive propaganda, graffiti, theft of weapons and explosives, armed robberies—nine in the last three years—, murders—in number of three—, placement and explosion of devices—in number of forty-six officially registered in the last few years."[665]

The regime, despite being unable to admit its weakness, demonstrated signs of vulnerability by resorting to this strategy, indirectly acknowledging that an armed organization was posing a threat to the strict military regime. The initial lines of the summary proceeding provided a detailed list of attacks suffered by the regime:

"(…) with the aim of disrupting internal order, public safety, social peace, national unity, discrediting the government, institutions and authorities, and to carry out political and social reprisals."

Instead of a trial against the accused specifically for the assassination of Melitón Manzanas, what transpired was a summary proceeding against ETA. The organization was accused of disrupting the "paz social," threatening the unity of Spain, and undermining the prestige of the government. The incarceration of the 16 ETA members accused at the Burgos Trial began in November 1968 with the arrest of Aranzazu Arruti Odriozola in Iruña. She was the first to be detained and tortured, resulting in the loss of the baby she was expecting.

Subsequent detentions included Eduardo Iriarte Romero, José María Dorronsoro Ceberio, Mario Onaindía Nachiondo, Joaquín Gorostidi Artola, Francisco Javier Izco de la Iglesia, Francisco Javier Larena Martínez, Jesús Abrsiqueta Corta, Enrique Gesalaga Larreta, Juan Echave Garitacelaya, Victor Arana Bilbao, Gregorio López Irasuegui, Juana Dorronsoro Ceberio, Itziar Aizpurúa Egaña, José Antonio Carrera Aguirrebarrera, and Julián Calzada Ugalde.

The detentions were accompanied by a press campaign orchestrated by the regime, aiming to rally the population against ETA members. The processes of detention were extensively broadcasted, featuring sensational arrests like that of José Mari Dorronsoro in December 1968, presented as one of ETA's leaders, under headlines such as "Arrest of an E.T.A. chief in San Sebastian."[666] Another dramatic incident involved the arrest of Xabier Izko and Goio López Irasuegi, who were shot in a provisional prison while attempting to free Arantza Arruti. Izko suffered a gunshot wound to the lung and required emergency surgery.

News of the treatment given to the detainees spread rapidly through thousands of leaflets, reports, and statements, proliferating in the streets in 1969. This dissemination extended beyond the Basque country to the rest of Spain and even Europe. The regime had underestimated both the strength of the enemy and the reaction of the people.[667]

In an attempt to rectify their unsuccessful strategy, the regime tried to exploit the fact that two of the accused, Julen Kalzada and Jon Echabe, were priests. They sought to hold the trial behind closed doors, invoking clause XVI of the Concordat signed with the Vatican in 1953. This clause had been used previously to hold martial courts privately, judging both clerics and laypeople together. However, the hierarchy of the Spanish Church opposed the regime in this case and respected the detainees' wishes. Kalzada and Echabe rejected the "on-camera" privilege and asked the Holy See to honor their decision to avoid harming the other accused. In May 1970, the Vatican announced through Monsignor Dadaglio, the nuncio in Spain, that they had renounced the privilege. On November 21, the Bishops of Bilbao-Bilbo and Donostia-San Sebastián demanded a public trial. Although the regime initially decided to maintain the closed-door privilege, in the end, faced with the firm position of the Basque clergy and protests from the detainees' families, it was announced on November 25 that there would be a public hearing for the trial.[668]

The Burgos trial went beyond the Basque mobilization, sparking social unrest throughout Spain. Various social movements, including students and workers, identified with the trial and rejected the repression imposed by the Franco regime, leading to strikes and demonstrations.

Demonstrations, strikes, and repression were particularly pronounced in the cities and industrial towns of Bizkaia and Gipuzkoa. However, the impact extended to Barcelona, where on November 30, around ninety companies called for a strike, and thousands of people occupied the streets in a massive demonstration in the center of the Catalan city.[669]

"Against the court-martial—For freedom On Monday, November 30, the regime wants to hold a court martial in which six death sentences and 754 years in prison are requested against Basque patriots and revolutionaries. The dictatorship that arose from a struggle against the people, that has lasted for 31 years oppressing and exploiting (sic), tries to prevent, by means of a new assassination, the people from achieving freedom. The time has come to say enough! to carry out all kinds of strikes, demonstrations, to carry out a general strike on Monday, to carry out all actions to prevent them from being condemned. The time has come to say no! to the dictatorship, to unite all the forces that are against repression, oppression and want freedom. Against the court-martial."

The protest against the Burgos trial extended beyond the Basque country, reaching Catalonia[670] with various social groups, including workers, unions, students, and Christian associations, rallying against the trial and the repression. The movement gained momentum through assemblies, articles, and leaflets, creating a solidarity movement that was not only class-based but also national in scope.

Catalan intellectuals, including artists, writers, actors, and activists, occupied the Montserrat Abbey on December 12 in a protest against the trial and in solidarity with the accused. Over three days, they discussed the political and social situation and issued a statement denouncing the court-martials, lack of freedom, repression, and media manipulation in Spain. The conclusions of the declaration were political in nature, emphasizing the need for amnesty,[671] the repeal of repressive laws, and the establishment of a popular state guaranteeing democratic freedoms and the rights of peoples and nations within the Spanish state.

The trial, intended to portray Basque ETA members as terrorists, backfired, and the Spanish population became increasingly unsettled by the spectacular arrests, violence against the accused, torture, killings, and consecutive states of emergency. The people transformed the trial into a broader indictment against the Franco regime.[672]

In late summer, the sentences for the accused[673] were announced: six death penalties, 754 years of imprisonment, and other sentences. Eduardo Uriarte Romero, Xabier Izco de la Iglesia, Mario Onaindia Nachiondo, Joaquín Gorostidi Artola, Francisco Javier Larena Martínez, and José María Dorronsoro Ceberio received death sentences. Izco, Uriarte, and Gorostidi each received two death sentences. Arantza Arruti was absolved, though she had been interned in a Madrid prison's psychiatric hospital ward by the time the trial began.

As the growing rumors insisted that the trial would begin in November, the mobilizations, demonstrations, leaflet distribution, and proposals of strikes did nothing but increase, crossing borders to spread the protest against the Franco regime abroad.

The process against the Franco regime. The trial from the exile.
International Reactions

The violence, including the assassination of Melitón Manzanas, the subsequent repression, torture, states of emergency, and protests, brought attention to the Basque conflict abroad. This was particularly significant in the context of the social upheavals of "May 1968" in Europe, especially in France.

During the 1960s, Europe experienced a demographic explosion, with a significant youth population. The younger generation sought radical changes and found inspiration in Marxist theories, which had become a secular religion for many.[674] The distance between the youth and their parents' generation was notable, marked by differences in perspectives on freedom, culture, sex, music, drugs, and politics.

The youth of the time were not content with the peace that Europe was experiencing; they sought to change the political system that seemed to exclude them from participation. The events of May 1968 in Paris and the Prague Spring[675] exemplified the discontent and rebellion against established systems and orders.

News from Spain reached the rest of Europe through outlets like Le Monde, providing coverage of the conflicts in Madrid, Barcelona, and the Basque Country.

The French journal reported on demonstrations and protests against the Burgos trial and death sentences. Clandestine trade unions organized demonstrations in Madrid, drawing thousands of workers to the streets.[676]

November 3, 1970, marked an amnesty day in Spain, with protests and demonstrations in various cities, particularly in Barcelona and Catalonia. Riots erupted in the city center, and work stoppages affected companies like SEAT in Terrassa, Catalonia.

Given the censorship in the Spanish press, foreign media became a crucial source of information about the events in Spain. The Basque and Spanish exiles organized efforts to reach out to correspondents, journalists, and media to defend the Basque cause and garner international support against the trial and death sentences. The strategy involved creating a favorable opinion abroad and raising awareness about the situation in Spain.

Ramon de la Sota, the son of a Basque nationalist who collaborated with the CIA in South America, became actively involved with the nationalist Basque party in 1969. His proficiency in English, gained through academic studies in the English capital, made him a suitable person to work with the media in England. He dedicated substantial efforts to engage with the press in London and Paris, making repeated visits to journalists to support various party campaigns, including Aberri Egunas. His work intensified before and after the Burgos trial on December 3, 1970, particularly focusing on preventing the death sentences and executions of the six ETA members and seeking their pardon.[677]

Basque nationalism, marked by political violence, attracted international media attention. However, Franco's regime's violence, characterized by the death penalty and brutal repression, also drew global scrutiny. On October 19, over 100 people gathered in front of the Spanish embassy in London to protest against the trial and human rights violations in Spain. The protesters, mostly Catalan, Basque, and Galician exiles, received support from English trade unionist Mr. Jack Jones and Sir Harry Nicholas, Secretary General of the Labor Party.[678]

Clandestine leaflets distributed in Spain provided information on the protests and international reactions to the Burgos trial. Reports indicated a sense that the world was challenging the Franco regime. On the 7th, the International Confederation of Labor (WCL) took action, sending letters to the International Commission of Jurists and the International Commission on Human Rights of the United Nations, urging intervention regarding the Spanish Government. The letters highlighted concerns about the closed-door proceedings of Military Courts, aiming to prevent evidence of torture from being presented. The torture served a dual purpose: extracting confessions and names from the tortured individuals and instilling a state of terror.[679]

During November 1970, numerous demonstrations took place in European cities as a response to the Burgos trial. On November 3, a demonstration occurred in Perpignan with over ten thousand attendees, followed by another in Paris on November 10. A five-minute national work stoppage in France was organized on November 16, showing solidarity with the accused in Burgos and involving all workers' unions. Additional demonstrations and acts against the trial took place in various European cities, including Rome, Bern, Basel, Milan, Stockholm, Copenhagen, London, and Berlin. In Münster (Germany), an "ETA's friends committee" was established, and mobilizations against the Burgos Process occurred in America, with protests in New York, Caracas, and Buenos Aires.[680]

The strategy of the Basque nationalists and the Basque government involved highlighting the use of violence, torture, and human rights violations against Basque detainees as part of their resistance to the repression under the Franco regime. In a previous case, the Basque Government had used a human rights strategy to seek clemency and assistance from international bodies, such as the Ligue des Droits de l'Homme.[681]

The issue of torture and the plight of Basque prisoners had been a concern for the Basque government since the early 1960s. In 1961, the presence of ETA supporters in Venezuela became a topic of discussion within the Basque community in the South American country. Lucio de Aretxabaleta,[682] in a correspondence with Lehendakari Leizaola,[683] mentioned the incidents involving ETA supporters and emphasized the opportunity to strengthen unity among those "with the Government." The incidents also highlighted financial management issues and differing opinions on fund handling, revealing tensions between the Basque Government and ETA forces regarding legitimacy and trust in Basque institutions. The increasing number of prisoners further accentuated the differences between the two strands of Basque nationalism.

While ETA had consistently defended and demonstrated respect for the Basque Government since its inception, their approaches diverged early on, as recounted by Aretxabaleta: "(...) they desire funds to be directed to a committee established in Continental Euzkadi by E.G., ETA, and the Front. I engaged in a disagreement with ETA members, making them recognize that this was not acceptable to the representatives here of E.G., the interior, E.G. of Caracas, PNV, STV, ANV, nor to me as the Delegate."

It became evident that the PNV and the Basque Government had relinquished control over the mainland Basque Country, and ETA sought to administer funds at a level equivalent to the Basque Government. The repercussions were dire for Basque unity and, notably, for the Delegate Council: "From the encounter with them, I inferred that ETA operates under instructions from the Interior. It aims to exploit the fundraising circumstance to establish an entity within the interior, independent of the Delegate Council, or to press for interference in that Council with its distinct identity."[684]

Despite disagreements with ETA members, the Basque Government persisted in supporting Basque prisoners, adhering to a diplomatic strategy and involving international bodies, consistent with their approach during the exile. The Basque cause gained recognition due to violence, which was not a part of the traditional Basque strategy. Yet, from the outset, the government and PNV had supported the prisoners, the gudaris.

When ETA disrupted a train carrying Falangists on their way to commemorate the 25th anniversary of the Coup d'état, the subsequent repression resulted in the imprisonment of some ETA members. Julen Madariaga, a co-founder of ETA, was apprehended, and according to a confidential report from the American consulate in Bilbao: "Was apprehended by police officers and taken to a local police station where he endured severe beatings, resulting in three broken ribs. Later, he was transported to Madrid and charged with direct involvement in an attempt to derail a train near San Sebastian on July 18, 1961."[685]

Suspicion fell on Basque revolutionary nationalists, though initially, even those inside the Basque nationalist movement doubted that ETA could have orchestrated such an act. Ángel Zarraga, a Basque nationalist informant to the American Consulate in Bilbao, informed the Consul that the arrested Basque nationalists, including Julen Madariaga, had no connection to the attempted train derailment.[686] Few could believe, or were unwilling to believe, that the young Basques were capable of such actions.

From London, Manuel Irujo was highly critical of the derailment, but he outlined the strategy to follow in September 1961 in a letter to Solaun and Landáburu: "Have you approached the U.N. Commission on Human Rights? Or has the Liga done so in your case? Because that would appear favorable to me, both for the incident itself and the potential propaganda against Franco's government."

Despite the turn to violence by revolutionary Basque nationalists, some found themselves imprisoned and subjected to torture. The Basque diaspora had to navigate this challenging situation. Aretxabaleta and others sought assistance from the Cardinal, informing him about the plight of Basque prisoners in Spain and appealing for humanitarian aid. Simultaneously, the Basque delegation in Biarritz engaged in diplomatic efforts with Anglo-Saxon countries.

While not universally appreciated, especially by Manuel Irujo, the Basque government initiated contacts through its delegations, primarily in Biarritz. Jesús Solaun, in a November 1961 communication to the Lehendakari, highlighted efforts to secure support from Anglo-Saxon countries, institutions, and public opinion, as well as religious institutions in European countries.[687]

The government's strategy emphasized diplomacy to sway public and political opinion against torture and the death penalty, primarily by championing human rights. Safeguarding the well-being of Basque detainees became a paramount cause for the exiled Basque Government. Unable to control events within the country, they focused on advocating for the Basque people suffering under Franco's repression.

Despite the emphasis on humanitarian concerns, the Basque government's diplomacy also worked towards furthering the Basque political cause. Solaun, quoting from a document explaining the strategy, stated, "For the political future, it also seems that this attitude is ultimately the most useful in the service of Euskadi and its freedom."

Regarding the torture of detainees, the Basque government combined diplomacy with states and international bodies with mediations through ecclesiastical institutions, unions, and humanitarian organizations, particularly those associated with the Christian Democracy movement. The PNV's connections with the Christian movement, especially in Rome through Basque delegate Ángel Ojanguren, helped raise awareness of the Basque cause and the suffering of the Basques under Franco's dictatorship.

The situation in exile, coupled with the treatment and torture of Basque prisoners, posed a delicate question for traditional Basque nationalists. Leizaola's leadership faced internal scrutiny from both young Basque revolutionaries and elements within the exile. Managing such a complex situation was challenging, and the diminishing hegemony of traditional Basque nationalists exposed differences of opinion within the old guard.

In 1961, the juvenile individuals undergoing trial for their involvement in the train derailment in July faced court-martials, potentially leading to prison terms of 25, 15, and 12 years—a severity seldom witnessed until then. There was a looming possibility that the verdict could escalate, resulting in even graver consequences such as death penalties.

As per information provided by Solaun from Beirys, the assigned sentences were as follows: Albisu and Laspiur, 25 years; Urrestarazu and Larramendi, 15 years; Balerdi, Arrieta, and Ferrán, 12 years and a day.[688] In response to these legal challenges, both the PNV and the Basque government extended their support to the ETA members. They collaborated on a comprehensive report outlining the detainees' conditions to explore potential courses of action.

In a letter expressing disagreement with certain measures taken to aid the detainees, Irujo detailed how the Basque Government (or the PNV, as he wasn't entirely clear) sought assistance from the International Law Commission in Geneva. In response, the English group requested a detailed report on the tortures suffered by the detainees.[689] The letter further revealed that Juan Jauriaguerra acted as their liaison, furnishing a comprehensive list of detainees and the police-inflicted tortures. Although Leizaola disapproved of the International Law Commission's suggestion to publicize the tortures, the documents were eventually sent to the Vatican's Secretary of State.

The correspondence between Solaun and Irujo illuminates the challenges traditional Basque nationalists faced in navigating a new situation involving tortures and potential death penalties. The primary point of contention lay in the methods employed. While Irujo, typically cautious, concluded that publicizing the issue, as suggested by the International Law Commission, was the optimal solution, Leizaola and Solaun believed it would exacerbate the sentences.

The use of torture and the protection of human rights remained central to the strategy employed by traditional Basque nationalism in the case of the Burgos detainees. In 1968, recognizing the declaration of the year as the official Year of Human Rights, the Basque Government directly approached the UN through their Basque Delegate in New York, Pedro Beitia. They sought to condemn the violation of human rights and the use of torture in Spain. On July 14, the Basque delegate presented a memorandum condemning the situation in Basque country police stations, particularly during states of emergency, wherein torture was prevalent, and detainees were unlawfully held without evidence for more than 72 hours. Unfortunately, this strategy proved unsuccessful.

Manuel Irujo penned an article in Alderdi, recalling the International Year of Human Rights,[690] delineating various human rights violations in Spain. These included restrictions on freedom of speech, labor association, and election, alongside instances of torture and repression by security forces. For traditional Basque nationalists, engaging with international bodies remained crucial in addressing the Basque cause. The PNV and the Basque Government, throughout their exile, sought to amplify the Basque voice within influential organizations. Unfortunately, the attempts of the Basque delegate at the UN proved futile as Euskadi, not being a recognized state, could not be considered independently from Spain in matters of human rights.[691]

Similar challenges were encountered by the Basque Delegate in the USA, despite gaining support from entities like the United Automobile Workers (UAW) and the World Confederation of Labor. Despite these efforts, the American Government maintained a distant stance. A propaganda strategy against the death penalty and torture, crafted by Beitia, found some success as *The New York Times*, *The Washington Post*, and International Amnesty initiated an information campaign on the Burgos process. They highlighted the manipulation in holding the trial on camera, the plight of the detainees, and the broader repression of human rights in the Basque country.

Despite the attention garnered in the media, the efforts of the Basque delegation and American politicians to involve the Department of State yielded vague responses. A letter from Margaret J. Tibbets to Victor Reuther on December 5, 1970,[692] acknowledged shared concerns for human rights but cited the impropriety of intervening in a sovereign nation's domestic matter under Spanish laws. The European landscape provided slightly more attention to Basque nationalism, with the Basque government alerting different chancelleries about the Franco Regime. Lehendakari Leizaola, in a message published in Alderdi, highlighted the rejection of Franco's Spain by the Council of Europe and the Common Market, framing it as a totalitarian dictatorship incompatible with the democratic principles of Europe.[693]

Even with the Burgos Trial exposed, the Basque government deemed it necessary to uphold its European strategy, recognizing the potential admission of the Franco Regime into European institutions. Primary interactions with

European chancelleries were facilitated through connections with the Christian Democracy and the European Federal Movement, with a focus on activities in Italy. Ángel Ojanguren, as previously mentioned, diligently worked to bring attention to the Burgos Trial, as detailed in Joseba Rezola's article "El proceso de Burgos en la prensa italiana":

"Through the newspaper <Il Popolo>, we have followed these intense palpitations of the Italian organs of diffusion starting from November 26, in which there was already talk of the proximity of the War Council and of the interpellation addressed to the Government by the deputies Fracanzini, Rognoni, Padula, Scotti, de Poli, and Marchietti of Christian Democrat affiliation, demanding urgent intervention in favor of the accused. The various groups in the Senate formulated a similar request, with the only exclusion of the Italian Social Movement, which is explained by its Fascist character."

The Italian Christian Union, the Christian Democrats' youth movement, and former Italian president Mariano Rumor, also President of the Christian Democrat European Union, joined the Italian protest against the death penalty and tortures inflicted by the Franco Regime on the accused in Burgos. When the sentences were announced, Mariano Rumor conveyed in a telegram to Franco: "Upon learning of the very serious Burgos sentence, in particular the six capital sentences, on behalf of Christian Democrats from all over the world, I beg you to consider with extreme attention the seriousness of the fact. Please exercise your high responsibility so that the sentences may be modified."[694]

The Basque government's contacts and letters to Italian authorities may have yielded results. In September and October 1969, when ETA members faced arrest and the possibility of a martial court loomed, the Basque government corresponded with European contacts. A letter addressed to Amintore Fanfani, president of the Italian Senate and member of Italian Christian Democracy, sought help to prevent the death penalty for the Burgos detainees. However, it emphasized, "The Basque activists in question in no way belong to our discipline." Similar pleas for assistance were sent to other European governments to exert international pressure on the Franco Regime.

In a letter directed to Prieto Nenni, Italian socialist and Minister of Foreign Affairs until 1969, the petition for help was made in the name of the Basque government, highlighting its heterogeneity, including socialists, republicans, and Basque nationalists. Cognizant of the challenges that public support might pose for the Basque cause, Lehendakari Leizaola clarified:

> Regarding the facts and the possibilities of aid from the Italian Government, obviously not public aid, we have left a report at the Ministry of Foreign Affairs (Directorate of Political Affairs) at the Farnesina. Enclosed is a note excerpted from this report.[695]

In the eyes of Basque nationalists, the young patriots entangled within the Franco regime's clutches were perceived as warriors for the freedom of the Basque Country. Despite the employment of violence, they garnered support from the "old guard" of nationalists. The Trial of Burgos evolved into a struggle for freedom, depicting a legal battle against a dictatorship utilizing torture and repression against the Basque people. In a statement underscoring this sentiment, it was expressed:

"It is imperative that my last words be addressed to all those in Euzkadi who fight for Basque freedom. Whatever their political sign, those who live for their homeland and who are willing to die for it, deserve our applause and, as far as we can give it, our support. (...) The responsibility for the violence, neither then nor now, was ours. Now, as then, the only responsible is the tyrannical regime we suffer, which, besides oppressing, provokes, which is not satisfied with commanding in chief, but has the need to submit the country to the torment of living under the violence of the terror imposed as a system of government."[696]

On December 3, 1970, the trial in Burgos commenced against 16 accused and detained individuals, with an additional 16 tried in absentia,[697] as detailed in the 31/69 Summary, a document exceeding 5000 pages that stirred significant public interest. Xabier Izko was accused of assassinating Melitón Manzanas and Teo Uriarte, while Jokin Gorostodi, Xabier Larena, Unai Dorronsoro, and Mario Onaindia were alleged instigators. All six received death sentences in a summary where the court-martial needed only evidence. According to the Military Code, the defense was allotted a mere four hours to peruse the summary and prepare their case. Ultimately, probably due to the trial's anticipation, lawyers gained access to the summary in early November.

While the trial captured the attention of a considerable portion of the Spanish population, the mobilization of lawyers was equally striking. It was a trial against the Franco regime, and well-known anti-Francoist lawyers were integral to the defense. The accused individuals and the lawyers who defended them are detailed as follows:

Name	Age	Place of Birth	Sentence	Lawyer
Josu Abrisketa Korta	21	Miravalles (Bizkaia)	80 years	Josep Solé Barberà
Bittor Arana Bilbao	27	Bilbao (Bizkaia)	76 years	Gregorio Peces- Barba
Itziar Aizpurua Egaña	27	Deba (Gipuzkoa)	15 years	Francisco Letamendía
Arantza Arruti Oriozola	24	Zarautz (Gipuzkoa)	Absolved	Jesús María Bagués

Jone Dorronsoro Zeberio	31	Ataun (Gipuzkoa)	54 years	Gurutze Galparsoro
Unai Dorronsoro Zeberio	29	Ataun (Gipuzkoa)	Death Penalty, 30 years	Pedro Ruiz Balerdi
Jon Etxabe Garitazelaia	37	Alzola, Elgoibar (Gipuzkoa)	70 years	Ramón Camiña
Enrique Gesalaga Larreta	27	Eibar (Bizkaia)	70 years	Juan Miguel Moreno
Jokin Gorostidi Artola	26	Tolosa (Gipuzkoa)	2 Death Penalties, 50 years	Juan María Bandrés
Xabier Izko de la Iglesia	29	Berango (Bizkaia)	2 Death Penalties, 75 years	José Antonio Etxebarrieta
Julen Kalzada Ugalde	35	Busturia (Bizkaia)	6 years	Pedro Ibarra Güell
Antton Karrera Aguirrebarrena	27	Amezketa (Gipuzkoa)	12 years	Artemio Zarco
Xabier Larena Martínez	25	Sestao (Bizkaia)	Death Penaly, 40 years	Ibon Navascués
Goio López Irasuegi	24	Bilbao (Bizkaia)	30 years	José Luis Castro
Mario Onaindia Natxiondo	29	Lekeitio (Bizkaia)	Death penalty, 60 years	Miguel Castells
Teo Uriarte Romero	25	Sevilla (Sevilla)	2 Death penalties, 90 years	Elías Ruiz Ceberio

Source: Txalaparta (Ed.), 1994, op. cit., vol. 3. pp. 51-56.

The accused individuals, especially those facing death sentences, had become widely known in society by the time the trial commenced. This recognition was a result of mobilization campaigns and the active involvement of working-class members. Their names, faces, and life stories were ubiquitous, featured in leaflets, posters, foreign newspapers, television, and radio broadcasts.

"The Burgos trial began as the trial of 16 ETA members. General Franco's government has turned it into the trial of the Basque People. All Basques are involved in it. We all feel that the sentences that are pronounced are our own," expressed Manuel Irujo in one of the numerous drafts he prepared for his articles.[698]

As the trial approached, a prevailing sentiment emerged that the proceedings were not only unjust but also exaggerated. In Burgos, on a chilly December morning, the city woke up amidst stringent security measures. Journalists, lawyers, relatives, and supporters of the accused gathered around the "Gobierno Militar," engaging in conversations, waiting, and queuing to attend the trial.

At nine o'clock, journalists and lawyers entered the court, presided over by Colonel Manuel Ordovás, Captain General in Madrid, accompanied by four vocals and two acting vocals. The public prosecutor for the Fiscal Ministry, Antonio Troncoso de Castro, also served as a speaker vocal and sat with the Court-Martial in front of the 16 accused, who remained handcuffed throughout the trial.

Simultaneously, in the Basque Country, students and workers were mobilizing at universities and workplaces. Despite official media suppressing information about the mobilizations, the success of the protests was evident through the increasing presence of police agents, army personnel, and even armored vehicles on the streets.

A document circulated from one of the workshops detailed the efforts to mobilize the people, despite limited knowledge of the extent of success: "The women, the housewives of the town, had a great influence on the closing of the stores (...) It is important to point out that the bakers took care to talk to each other, to reach an agreement and to close all together. The same was done by the bars, which undoubtedly played an important role in ensuring that the strike did not relax and continued on its course."

The mobilization reached its peak on the first day of the trial when strikes and protests on the streets were widespread: "At 8:30 a.m., all the students of the E.P.O. silently demonstrated in the streets, and the Civil Guard intervened and dissolved the demonstration. Later, around 10 o'clock, the students regrouped, joined by groups of workers (some had managed to stop and others had not entered the factory), managing to close the only three establishments that were still open (one of them had to be threatened with destroying the establishment for resisting the closure)."[699]

In Donostia - San Sebastián, the city center thronged with people, closely monitored by both police and armed forces, outfitted with weaponry, helmets, and shields in anticipation of potential disturbances. The work stoppage had extended across the primary industrial zones in Gipuzkoa, spanning from the factories in Goierri, including the influential train company CAF, to the coastal shipping hubs and cooperatives in Mondragon. In Greater Bilbao and its significant industrial region, the police maintained control, vigilantly observing the unfolding protests.

Despite the heightened surveillance, the police were unable to thwart the widespread mobilization, particularly in Gipuzkoa, where in places like Tolosa or Urnieta, protesters erected barricades to impede police access. The Basque Country found itself at a standstill, yet the regime's media persisted in asserting that only a mere 15% of workers supported the protests.[700] On December 5, *The New York Times* reported, "Spain puts curbs on Basque area. State of emergency invoked in Province that is center of agitation over trial. The Government decreed a three-month state of emergency tonight (Dec. 4) in the Basque province of Guipuzcoa (Sic.), where a West German consul was abducted Tuesday."[701]

Regarding the widespread mobilizations, protests, and workers' stoppages organized across Spain and certain European cities, another significant development captured attention on the first day of the trial: the kidnapping of the German Honorary Consul in Bilbao. On the night of December 1, an ETA commando seized Eugene Beihl Schaafer from his garage as he returned home. Although the initial claim of responsibility[702] was murky, with ETA disavowing involvement, a subsequent press conference held at Anai Artea[703] (the center for Basque exiles in Donibane Lohitzune, presided over by Telesforo Monzón) affirmed ETA's responsibility for the kidnapping.

Despite traditional Basque nationalism support for the accused in Burgos, perplexity surfaced in the exile community. In a letter to Victoria Kent, editor of the journal Ibérica of New York, where Manuel Irujo collaborated, the Navarrese sought to allay the confusion among those following events from exile. The letter outlined the current state of ETA, revealing the emergence of two factions at the August congress in Bayonne: the Marxist-Leninist group, represented by the 16 defendants from Burgos, led by Eskubi and based in Brussels, and the nationalist group, led by Echabe and headquartered in San Juan de Luz. The missive clarified that the faction retaining control of the Movement apparatus excluded the "activists" from Burgos and the "military" responsible for bank robberies, strikes, and the kidnapping of the German consul in Donostia.[704]

What Irujo conveyed was not entirely accurate, as during those days ETA was divided into three different groups. However, it does highlight the interest from the exile community and the confusion stemming from the kidnapping, later compounded by the trial's progression and statements from the accused.

From the outset, the Basque government in exile sought to resolve the consul's kidnapping. Diverging from ETA's intentions, traditional Basque nationalism and the Basque Government believed the action would not benefit the accused in Burgos. They were concerned about the negative impact on international relations and the global acceptance of the Basque cause. Lehendakari Leizaola took charge of the matter in an attempt to bring closure to the episode.

Julián de Illarramendi, a Basque professor residing in France, expressed his surprise to Manuel Irujo after receiving a hurried call from Lehendakari. Illarramendi recounted, "He called me a few days ago in a bit of a hurry. When he explained the reason for his call, I was shocked. The first thing that came to my mind was to look at the calendar to see if it was already marked December 28… It turns out, at this point, that I am the only person able to save the German consul… and I had to go to Bayonne to convince the ETA members of them."[705]

The press conference held at Anai Artea indicated support, at least tacitly, from Telesforo Monzón and Father Larrazabal for the ETA faction responsible for the consul's kidnapping. Clear links between ETA and the PNV were evident, and historical connections, almost familial, facilitated contacts despite Monzón no longer being a member of the Basque nationalist party.

In parallel, Manuel Irujo contacted Federico Krutwig to exert pressure for the consul's release. Krutwig, with German ancestry and considered an ETA member in 1970,[706] was one of the few individuals who could intervene in the kidnapping. Although he had no involvement in the abduction and learned about it through the press, Krutwig, a member of ETA's Biltzar Ttipia, the highest authority in the organization chart, acted as an intermediary. Krutwig, accompanied by journalist Giulio Cataolfi as a witness, wrote a telegram to Larzábal, proposing negotiations with ETA contingent upon the German government's recognition of the Basque cause.

Despite the earnest efforts of Krutwig and Mrs. Von Bretano, the Chancellor declined the proposed exchange, a decision attributed by Krutwig to the political and economic ties between Germany and Franco's regime. Krutwig expressed his view, stating, "Personally, it is obvious that I would be very sorry if anything were to happen to the life of the Consul. But I must emphasize that the German Government seems to be more interested in the defense of its material assets than in the life of a simple consul."

The schism within ETA became apparent, and according to Krutwig, a member of the "Authentic ETA," those loyal to the Vth Assembly found themselves with limited options. He asserted, "In ETA, power had been divided between those who 'possess' it and those who 'exercise' it, in order to avoid Stalinism. Thus, while it is true that the Biltzar Ttipia is the supreme authority of ETA, the Biltzar Ttipia does not exercise the authority of the organization itself." However, Krutwig refrained from acknowledging the internal divisions within the organization.

Telesforo Monzón and Father Larzábal, on the other hand, established contacts with the German Consul in Bordeaux, Christian Sell, who visited Anai Artea to seek a solution. Anai Artea became the hub for intermediation with ETA, disseminating information to international journalists through press conferences, thus propagating the Basque cause. It not only served as the center for mediation during the kidnapping but also emerged as the focal point for the new Basque exiles.

For Monzón, who had distanced himself from traditional Basque nationalism, ETA represented not only the rebel offspring of the PNV but also a renewal of Basque nationalism. He viewed them as the new Gudaris, connecting the jeltzale tradition with radical nationalism, fighting for the Basque cause. In Monzón's eyes, the young Basque nationalists of ETA were carrying on the legacy of their parents who had fled due to fascist attacks. The Basques tried in Burgos and the bombing of Gernika were, in Monzon's words, "Today's soldiers."[707]

While not everyone in exile shared Monzón's enthusiasm for ETA and their actions, most acknowledged the impact they were having. The Burgos trial marked a pivotal moment for Basque nationalism and recognition, also signaling a turning point for the Franco regime, which was increasingly realizing the diminishing tolerance for its injustices.

ETA not only presented a revolutionary nationalism with an ideology distinct from traditional Basque nationalism but also introduced new methods of opposing the dictatorship. The kidnapping, though not a tactic employed as frequently as direct violence, symbolized a fresh approach in the Basque struggle that resonated with many Basque patriots.

During Beihl's captivity in a small attic in Berorize, Zuberoa, Iparralde, his family received updates on his health, while Monzón and Father Larzábal engaged in discussions with the French authorities, who mobilized a substantial military contingent and air force members to search for the Honorary Consul in Iparralde. Despite Monzón's announcement in a press conference on December 24 that the Consul had been released "somewhere in Europe," Beihl had actually been transported to Germany in the company of the German journalist Albert Gaum. The document presented by Anai Artea and delivered to the Consul General in Bordeaux, Christian Sell, left no doubt about ETA's intentions with the kidnapping, expressing that ETA demanded nothing in return and directing attention to the peril faced by sixteen Basque compatriots in Burgos.[708]

Federico Krutwig, who endeavored to contribute to the liberation cause, also saw significance in the action for internationalizing the Basque movement. The abduction, orchestrated by Etxabe's faction—the group Irujo referred to as the "ETA direct action patriot group"[709]—generated considerable anticipation and drew the attention of international authorities, thereby implicitly acknowledging the legitimacy of the Basque cause. Correspondence between Irujo and Krutwig reveals their shared belief that the kidnapping yielded tangible outcomes, underscoring the diverse perspectives on the employed methods.

Krutwig, residing in Italy at the time, noted a growing interest in the Basque struggle within the Italian press and media, particularly focusing on the kidnapping but with a predominant concern for the fate of the Burgos defendants. Esteemed publications such as "Il Messaggiero," "L'Unità," "La Stampa," "Il Giorno," and "Il Corriere de la Sera" dedicated extensive coverage, articles, and even front-page features to the Basque cause.

In his analysis, Krutwig emphasized a dichotomy between revolutionary Basque nationalism and the traditional stance represented by the PNV, advocating for autonomy—an approach perceived as outdated by the younger Basque generation. His remarks implicitly criticized the PNV's strategy of alliances and the defense of the Basque Statute of Autonomy. Krutwig contended, "Nobody here (except the fascists) has spoken of the Basques fighting for autonomy, but everyone has discussed the struggle of the Basque people for their independence." He further underscored the need for a different approach to presenting the Basque issue, one not constrained by alliances with the PSOE, stating, "It seems evident that it was necessary to frame the Basque problem differently than what the alliances with the PSOE allow."[710]

During that period, the prospect of establishing a National Front resurfaced. The EBB initiated efforts to form an alliance with the young patriots of ETA, sparking an open debate within the Basque political landscape.[711]

Following the release, ETA issued a public statement outlining the objectives of the action and their political aspirations: "We have liberated Consul Beihl. Our aim was to draw global attention to the existence of our People and the unwavering determination to fight for its complete liberation: national independence, reunification of the South and North of Euskadi, and the establishment of a modern, democratic, Basque-speaking, and socialist Basque State."[712]

Gradually, the divide between the two Basque nationalisms widened. While they recognized and showed respect for each other, disparities not only in their methods of struggle but also in their objectives for the Basque Country became evident.[713]

"ETA has undoubtedly stirred the pot; it has compelled everyone to engage in discussion, making the world resonate with Basque concerns. I see certain advantages in their actions in our country—it has awakened consciences, instilled pride in us Basques, and perhaps, given prestige to the nationalist movement. However, regarding the core issue of Francoism and its aftermath, I believe we have regressed significantly... From now on, it seems imperative to delineate the history of nationalism, and even that of Francoism, into two stages: before the trial and after the trial."

Burgos & ETA's Fronts

The Burgos Trial was far from ordinary, and emerging from a dictatorship, it lacked fairness despite the regime's attempts to feign impartiality. The prosecution's dearth of evidence, the use of torture and violence against detainees, and the military court proceedings were manifestations of a judicial system under dictatorship control, operating within a framework of restricted freedoms.

Even from exile, Manuel Irujo, a seasoned lawyer, scrutinized the trial, drawing parallels with the Trial of Leningrad involving the judgment of Jews. It became apparent that the purported trial against ETA members for terrorist acts had been extended to pass judgment on the entire Basque people, particularly Basque nationalism.

The trial's progression, starting on December 3, exacerbated the situation. The defense's strategy aimed to portray the trial as an unjust process, emphasizing the mistreatment of the accused, from the aforementioned tortures to their courtroom appearance in handcuffs and visible bruises. Lawyers consistently demonstrated that the trial was rife with irregularities.

Apart from the issue of torture, the defense's strategy aimed to frame the proceedings as a political trial, acknowledging ETA as a political entity engaged in a political struggle for the Basque cause. While the trial against the Burgos defendants had evolved around the concept of a political fight, it was the focus on torture that captured the attention and advocacy of the defense and supporters of the Basque people.

Throughout the trial, the defense sought to dismantle the accusations of terrorism and violence through its interrogations, portraying the accused as political victims targeted by a regime opposing the interests of the Basque people. This narrative was particularly emphasized in the defense of Xabier Izko de la Iglesia, accused of the murder of Melitón Manzanas and represented by José Antonio Etxebarrieta.

Etxebarrieta, a well-prepared lawyer and influential ideologist within the Basque organization until the Vth assembly, articulated the notion of a political trial against the Basque country and the political cause of Basque nationalism in his defense of Izko. He expressed, "Over and above the legal problem of the summary proceeding before us, there is the political problem that is witnessed. And it should not be said that the Council is only here to solve the legal problem because the way to raise and solve the legal problem is already part of the political problem."[714]

By outlining a political dimension to the struggle of revolutionary Basque nationalism, Etxebarrieta portrayed ETA's actions as responses to a relentless and brutal attack by the Franco regime on the Basque people.

The trial, initially framed as a case against 16 alleged terrorists, disregarded legal procedures, exposing the weakness of the dictatorship, particularly once international attention focused on it. According to Irujo's analysis, "The Burgos trial is tainted with nullity since the Tribunal prevented the lawyers from freely exercising their office, denying them the use of the floor and preventing the testimony of the proposed witnesses, among whom were the bishops of Bilbao and San Sebastian."[715]

In this context, it became evident that exile provided more opportunities for obtaining information about the trial compared to those within the country. The Basque people, increasingly accustomed to receiving information through foreign media, followed the trial's developments via Radio Pirenaica, the French press, and, where possible, French television broadcasts.

On days 5, 6, and 8, during the accused's declarations, moments of heightened tension occurred. Following the defense's strategy, ETA members detailed the tortures they endured and outlined ETA's activities, primarily centered around cultural sessions, the defense of the Basque language, and the promotion of their political aspirations.

As previously noted, despite the regime's strenuous efforts to censor, distort, and suppress the trial's proceedings, the Basque people managed to track the process through various means, some of which were blatantly illegal, such as employing recorders within the courtroom.

The statements of the accused regarding their political convictions sparked surprise, particularly those tied to their adoption of Marxism-Leninism or their emphasis on the organization's internationalist stance, consciously avoiding the use of the term "nationalist." However, the declaration that held the potential to generate the most anticipation, and even bewilderment, came from Mario Onaindia towards the conclusion of his testimony on Wednesday, the 9th:

> "- Miguel Castells (Defense Lawyer): Let's see, Mario Onaindía. Don't tell us what ETA is, in your opinion, but tell us what you understand specifically by ETA. What is its political ideology?
> - Mario Onaindía: Personally, not at the organizational level?
> - M.C.: Personally, not at the organizational level.
> - M.O.: I, personally, am a Marxist-Leninist.
> - M.C.: Mario Onaindia, do you consider yourself a separatist?
> - M.O.: Hey, I am an internationalist.
> - M.C.: You are an internationalist, and how do you see your internationalism?
> - M.O.: Well, the struggle of the Basque people against the Spanish state, greatly favors the struggle of the Spanish people against the oppressor state and our struggle, in this case, favors the struggle."[716]

At this juncture, Mario Onaindia's declaration, though interrupted, elicited not only disapproval from the Court and the public but also outrage among the forces loyal to Franco. When asked if he considered himself a war prisoner and affirmed this status with reference to the Geneva Convention, Onaindia seized the moment to passionately and loudly defend the Basque people's struggle against oppression. He concluded his statement by standing up, raising his closed fists, and shouting, "Gora Euskadi Askatuta!" (Long live free Euskadi!)

In response, public prosecutor Antonio Troncoso and stand-in Julián Fernández García drew their swords amid the uproar created in the courtroom. The 16 defendants raised their voices and sang "Eusko Gudariak." The incident so outraged the Francoist regime that Radio Nacional provided a biased account on the evening of Wednesday, the 9th. However, thanks to a recorder clandestinely introduced into the courtroom, thousands of people almost immediately listened to the recording of Mario Onaindia's declaration, the disturbance, and the singing of "Eusko Gudariak." The recording circulated underground as a "single" and became a popular hit among the anti-Francoist movement.[717]

Rumors about the statements of the prosecuted individuals in Burgos crossed borders and were discussed in exile. The references to Marxism-Leninism, the avoidance of the term Basque nationalism, and solidarity with the revolution in the rest of Spain raised concerns. Manuel Irujo, deeply troubled by what he termed "a youth movement," was particularly upset by the "radicalization driven by the persecutions of General Franco that aspires to obtain recognition of the Basque national identity through violence." The embrace of Marxist or socialist principles added to his distress, and suspicions of a Spanish tendency within ETA nearly overwhelmed him.[718]

These suspicions about divergent tendencies were not baseless. Despite the popular support garnered from the Burgos trial, ETA was facing challenges. After the assassination of Melitón Manzanas, the organization believed the strategy of action-repression-action was effective. However, consecutive detentions began to seriously impact the organization's structure. The popularity gained by the action against Manzanas attracted numerous Basque youths to ETA, enhancing the organization politically and strategically. This led to a false state of euphoria, as expressed in Zutik no.50.[719]

In November 1968, with the detention of Arantza Arruti, a new spiral of detentions unfolded, weakening the organization significantly. The successive detentions and repression by the Spanish police affected the Executive Committee established after the Vth assembly, leaving only Jose Mari Eskubi to continue. The original leadership had been dismantled through resignations and forced desertions, including those of Mikel Azurmendi, Txato Aguirre, Julen Madariaga, Federico Krutwig, and Juan José Etxabe, who fled into exile.

To recover from the extensive detentions, the remaining members within ETA were focused on organizing a new assembly, the VIth, to lead the "Internal Front." This move ignored reservations from the military front and the exile. The new internal authorities included Patxo Unzueta (Political Office), Peru Erroteta (Worker's Front), Jon Fano, and José Vicente Idoyaga.[720]

According to José María Garmendia's analysis, the provocative declarations of the prosecuted individuals in Burgos find their roots in the work of Patxo Unzueta, the actual ideologist of that period within ETA. Unzueta played a crucial role in steering ETA's focus toward a "workerist" tendency, reshaping the nature of their struggle. Garmendia observed a shift in ETA's vocabulary in documents leading up to the Burgos Trial, where terms like "Basque working people" were replaced with "working class." The "Carta a los Makos," addressed to prisoners, similarly overturned the previous strategy, prioritizing the worker's front over the national front. ETA aimed to attract labor movement activists, many of whom were non-nationalists or aligned closely with the PCE and MCE.[721] Gradually, ETA shifted its revolutionary efforts to capture the interest of the working class, sidelining Basque nationalism and removing national demands from its agenda.

Simultaneously, the military front led by Etxabe, primarily based in Iparralde, acted without significant control. Etxabe, known for participating in hunger strikes in Bayonne protesting the French police's repression against Basque refugees, was essentially defined as a nationalist in favor of political violence. His group was responsible for actions such as the kidnapping of the German consul and several bank robberies.

The exile found itself perplexed by the declarations in Burgos and the conflicting actions claimed and denied by ETA, including the consul's kidnapping. Manuel Irujo attempted to explain ETA's divisions in a letter exchange with Victoria Kent but inaccurately identified only two groups. Irujo, despite mixing up details, wasn't entirely off the mark.

The VIth assembly, held in Itxaso, Iparralde, on August 31, 1970, marked a turning point. While the division was already a reality, the assembly was a symbolic enactment by the inside leadership. The VIth assembly represented the culmination of the crisis in ETA, manifesting a division that, as before, would result in the expulsion of members from the organization. Unlike previous divisions focused on strategies and conflict management, this division primarily revolved around Basque nationalism.

During the VIth assembly, the inside executive, led by Patxo Unzueta, advocated for the "Proposiciones generales" document, which replaced independence with the right of self-determination, disregarding national references and strategies approved by the Vth assembly. Meanwhile, the exile split into two distinct groups. One group, representative of the Vth assembly and the Biltzar Ttipia, included members like Krutwig, Edu Arregi, López Adán, and Etxabe. Despite lacking control over Etxabe's military front, they supported political violence and the action-repression-action strategy.

The second group in exile, known as the "Red cells," aligned with Marxist theories and rejected Basque nationalism as bourgeois. They adamantly opposed the National Front idea and supported the proposal by the inside executive to transition towards a Workers Revolutionary Party. Influenced by the May 1968 events and their experiences in Paris and Brussels, they progressively rejected their previous nationalist stance in favor of Marxism. Mikel Azurmendi was a notable theorist, with Eskubi serving as their main reference.[722]

The confusion surrounding these divisions made it challenging to ascertain the true situation regarding the groups and fronts within ETA. Reports on the VIth assembly were no more reliable than rumors, and the statements made by the prosecuted individuals in Burgos only added to the complexity of the situation.

In 1970, exile was not a new experience for ETA members, as they had been compelled to flee the Basque Country since their early actions. However, the situation in 1970 was particularly intricate due to the growing number of exiled members, diverse opinions and political tendencies (primarily Marxist but spanning various factions), and personal disputes and confrontations.

The impact of the Burgos Trial, coupled with its success in terms of popularity and as a challenge to the Franco Dictatorship, led to a situation where different ETA groups sought to claim the prosecuted individuals as part of their own faction. When Manuel Irujo inquired about the potential influence of Spanish elements, especially post-declarations in Burgos, Federico Krutwig, residing in Italy, denied the infiltration of Spanish PCE members in ETA:

"The people condemned in Burgos all belong to the ETA of Biltzar Ttipia (I do not believe that any of them belong to the Spanishist group of those expelled, some of them because I know them personally and the others because of the statements they have made)."[723]

Krutwig defended the legitimacy of Biltzar Ttipia, particularly after the expulsion of their representative during the VIth Assembly. The executive committee organizing the VIth Assembly invited eleven members of the "Red Cells" group and four members of Biltzar Ttipia. However, the latter, in clear disagreement with the assembly's organization, decided to send Madariaga as its sole representative. Madariaga was subsequently expelled from the assembly—a decision presumably the only consensus reached during that turbulent assembly.

Correspondence between Krutwig and Irujo sheds light on the challenging situation within the exile and ETA. Basque nationalists had been ousted from the organization, replaced by what Krutwig characterized as "Spanishist."

As the VIth assembly unfolded and after Madariaga's expulsion, the two remaining groups engaged in a political debate that escalated into personal accusations, ultimately resulting in the departure of Red Cells from both the assembly and the organization. The situation proved challenging to comprehend for both the exile and the internal factions, leaving questions about Eskubi unanswered.

Despite the confusion, the Burgos prisoners and militants participated, opting to support the decisions made in the assembly as a show of solidarity with its legitimacy and the executive committee. In a document released by the prisoners while awaiting the trial's sentence, which would determine if the death sentences were confirmed, they discredited the legitimacy of Biltzar Ttipia, represented by Krutwig's group in exile. Instead, they defined ETA according to the principles of the Vth assembly, moving away from nationalist stances:

"One of the fundamental agreements of the Vth assembly was the affirmation of the Basque working class, the most revolutionary class and the one that must lead, therefore, the Basque revolution."

The document released by the Burgos prisoners marked a significant shift, prioritizing the class front over the national front. It explicitly stated, "ETA is a socialist organization. ETA is not a national front." Basque nationalism was relegated, even condemned, as if it had no place in the new executive or the emerging generation that had assumed power within ETA. The proposed national front emphasized class as the predominant feature, diverging from the national front advocated by Biltzar Ttipia, which, according to the document, would exclude popular political forces.

Rejecting the national front and Basque nationalism, the document outlined a roadmap for the development of the "National Liberation Front." It envisioned the creation of an independent, socialist Basque Country led by the Basque working class, preceding a Basque socialist revolution aimed at eliminating all social classes.[724]

With the emergence of this document, options for Biltzar Ttipia to regain control of the organization dwindled. The strategy adopted by the five members in exile involved launching a "new anti-Spanish crusade," focusing on the disqualification of Eskubi, who was perceived as the one introducing Spanishness into the organization.

This campaign pitted the exile against the internal faction. While they shared commonalities, the schism revolved around Basque nationalism. According to Krutwig, the internal ETA, particularly those aligned with ETA VI, had forsaken Basque national vindication due to Eskubi's influence.

In a critical letter to Irujo in December, Krutwig accused Eskubi of organizing Spanish infiltration into ETA, dating back to the origins in the Vth assembly. This accusation was an attempt to legitimize the defense of Biltzar Ttipia. For Krutwig, the authentic ETA was the group defending the resolution of the Vth assembly, considering the organization of the VIth assembly as illegal. He labeled the internal group behind the VIth assembly as a "Group of infiltrated Spaniards, members of the Spanish Communist Party." What drew even more criticism from Krutwig was the use of Marxism by the internal group. In his view, this group, by denying the Basque nation, was rejecting even Marxist theories on nationalism.

The authentic ETA, as portrayed by Krutwig, was Marxist, but with a distinction. Biltzar Ttipia, representing the authentic ETA, followed Maoism, while the internal ETA embraced Stalinism. Krutwig clarified the comparison by stating, "Those who follow the Maoist strategy, we are the ones who have expelled them precisely for this reason that in order to reach socialism in concrete terms, we have to fight for national liberation, just as Mao Zedong did in China." He further differentiated their stance by comparing it to Ceaucescu or Mao Zedong, while asserting that the internal ETA aligned with positions akin to Husak, Ulbricht, or Kadar within the communist world.

ETA Vth, represented by the Biltzar Ttipia, reflected on the events of the IV Assembly, where Patxi Iturrioz's faction embraced a labor-oriented approach, distancing themselves from Basque nationalism. According to the Biltzar Ttipia, the shift within ETA members towards prioritizing the workers' front over the national front was perceived as an influence from the Spanish Communist party.

Following the Burgos trial, the imperative of regaining control of ETA became even more apparent.

The ETA in exile failed to recognize an ETA on the inside, which, as per Krutwig, had developed features more Spanish and anti-Basque than the Iturrioz group. Post-Burgos Trial, ETA underwent a definitive split. ETA VI took control of the organization, gaining support from members in Spain and receiving recognition from the 16 accused in Burgos, already celebrated as anti-Franco heroes. ETA VI identified as a Socialist revolutionary organization, prioritizing class-based struggle over national identity, with Basque ethnicity and language relegated to secondary interests.[725]

The Biltzar Ttipia in exile defended the legitimacy of the Vth assembly, persisting as ETA V. Despite lacking internal support, ETA V found backing from the intellectual group around Txillardegi and Branka, a cultural journal created by intellectuals, influencing the "milis" group. Krutwig, in a letter to Irujo in early 1971, asserted, "I have not talked about the 'militarist' group in particular because, in fact, it does not exist but is part of the real ETA led by the Biltzar Ttipia democratically elected in the Vth assembly."

ETA V adopted Marxism and staunchly supported political violence, influenced by the resurgence of global armed struggles in the 70s. This belief, as explained by Robert P. Clark, led them to consider themselves part of a globally significant wave. The rise of the Tupamaros in Uruguay during the late 1960s and into 1970 and 1971 provided ETA V with a valuable model emphasizing links between mass revolutionary movements and the leadership of a relatively small but activist armed group.[726] The exile allowed ETA V the opportunity to globally advocate for the Basque cause.

Furthermore, the defense of Basque nationalism, a feature overlooked by ETA VI, garnered support from PNV and EGI. They were uneasy with ETA VI's alignment with positions resembling those of the PCE. The defense of the national front, gaining prominence near the end of 1970 and reaching its zenith after the Burgos trial and during the spring of 1971, provided a robust definition of the Basque struggle and organizations' positions.

In contrast to ETA VI, which relegated the Basque national cause to a secondary level, ETA V staunchly defended the national front. However, due to Marxist ideology and differences in imagined social societies, there were breaches too wide to reconcile fully. The rebuilding of ETA V centered on a national struggle incorporating political violence, inspired by the anti-colonialism strategy outlined in the Vth Assembly, and anti-imperialism directed against both the USA and the Soviet Union.

Despite abstract internationalism, Krutwig emphasized a return to the era of imperialism, framing the struggle as horizontal—the oppressed against the oppressor, rather than a vertical class struggle. ETA VI's identification with the PCE and Spanishness provided ETA V with reasons to combat Spanish infiltrators.

Krutwig, without abandoning Marxism, defended the link between socialism and nationalism, criticizing Marxists who had forsaken the national cause under the influence of Stalin's theories. Krutwig's letter to Manuel Irujo in April 1971 asserted that ETA VI's abandonment of Basque nationalism resulted from a lack of ideology and preparation among members infiltrated by the PCE, who were not accustomed to broad thinking or reading.

Highlighting an anti-Stalinist and anti-Soviet Union sentiment, Krutwig, following Mao's Marxism, advocated for a combination of cultural revolution, anti-imperialism, and national uprising against the oppressor. This marked the gateway to a new trend about to enter ETA: Third-Worldism.

Prisoner and Exiles

On December 30, 1970, Franco granted reprieves for all six death sentences, amidst demonstrations and riots with opposing sentiments filling the Spanish streets. The anti-Franco mobilizations persisted not only during the trial but also while the sentences awaited ratification. The pro-Franco movement, previously indifferent, responded to the constant mobilizations, feeling compelled to defend the Regime.

While some of Franco's supporters viewed the decision as an act of clemency unrelated to Church petitions or international pressure,[727] others perceived it as a concession to liberal democracies and a display of weakness. In retrospect, the Consejo Nacional del Movimiento later acknowledged the significance of international pressure and the consul's kidnapping in the decision to commute the death penalties.[728]

International opinion, including that of the exile community, unanimously agreed that mobilizations in the Basque Country and various European cities, especially during the trial, played a crucial role in prompting clemency. Editorials and articles in publications such as the International Herald Tribune, The Times, and certain French newspapers emphasized that regime repression would likely intensify post-sentencing.[729]

Despite the commutation, Basque nationalism faced exacerbated challenges with increased repression and a growing number of political prisoners and exiles after the Burgos trial. OPE and Alderdi published the complete list of prisoners and detainees, also highlighting internal differences within the Spanish regime among three significant factions: Opus Dei, the Falange, and the army. Dissatisfaction with the aftermath of the Burgos trial led to army demands for more influence and power within the Franco Government, creating a crisis within the Spanish Government.

The army's renewed patriotic demands became evident during the memorial celebration in Madrid for the first three victims of ETA,[730] José Pardines, Melitón Manzanas, and Fermín Monasterio. This event was followed by a massive demonstration in support of Franco and the army. While Le Monde reported a few thousand people protesting against separatism and in favor of the unity of Spain, official media claimed half a million attendees. As Franco observed the army march, some individuals at his side raised their arms in a fascist salute, a gesture abandoned by the regime in the 50s.[731] The saber-rattling grew louder.

Meanwhile, the Basque government continued its strategy of internationalizing the Basque conflict, concurrently aiding the increasing number of Basque prisoners, as previously mentioned. Manuel Irujo and Lehendakari Leizaola reached out to the UN's Human Rights Commission in Geneva, highlighting the Basque cause and human rights violations in Spain, particularly the use of torture and the death penalty against political prisoners.

Despite not endorsing the violent methods employed by the young patriotic Basque members of ETA, the Basque Government, led by the PNV, staunchly defended the prisoners as political detainees, aligning with the adopted strategy to present the Basque cause as inherently political. The Basque Government aimed to prevent the potential blurring of political demands due to violence from Basque nationalists.

In their report to the UN, Irujo and Leizaola, representing their respective political positions in the Spanish Republican Government and the Basque Government, traced the roots of the Basque cause back to the Spanish Civil War and the establishment of Franco's Fascist dictatorship. They framed the defense of human rights as an integral aspect of Basque society, persistently upheld even when it became a crime following the creation of the Public Order Tribunal (TOP) in 1963 and subsequent court-martials introduced by decree since 1968.

The report detailed instances of torture, emphasizing the proliferation of cases, particularly in the Basque Country, affecting students, lawyers, and even clergymen. Alongside seeking a condemnation of the Spanish situation from the Human Rights Committee, the Basque Government requested protection for the rights of Basque exiles facing challenges in European countries where they sought refuge.

The letter concluded with an appeal to the international body to intervene in safeguarding human rights: "(…) We kindly ask you to take note of it and to support it with all the legal, humanitarian, and political reasons, in order to promote a change in the policy of the Spanish State towards the Basques, which should be in accordance with the respect of human rights."[732]

The difficulties faced by refugees in settling down, outlined in the letter to the UN, reflected the ongoing challenges experienced by new arrivals. While the traditional Basque nationalism represented by the PNV and the initial generation of exiles encountered its own struggles, the reception of the new generation of exiles was less welcoming.

The post-Civil War situation, marked by the flight of hundreds of thousands from Spain, posed challenges for both the exiles and the receiving countries, exacerbated by the onset of World War II just months after the Spanish War's conclusion. In France, the primary destination for most Basque exiles, the situation was already challenging, as discussed in previous chapters. By 1970, ETA refugees faced deportation or imprisonment, with new forms of protest such as hunger strikes and occupations, along with the political assertion of the French Basque Country, unsettling the French Government and leading to the initial deportations of ETA members, including Julen Madariaga, Benito del Valle, Txillardegi, and Eneko Irigaray, expelled from "Basses Pyrénées" in 1964.[733]

While Telesforo Monzón was not among the new wave of exiles, his involvement in the kidnapping of the German consul, coupled with his efforts to secure refuge for ETA members, placed him in a challenging position with the French Government. Anai Artea had emerged as the primary reference for Basques in exile, leading to discontent expressed by Alberto Onaindia in a letter to Irujo in February 1971, lamenting the perceived silence of Lehendakari over Monzón's prominent role.[734]

Monzón, a significant figure in Basque resistance and the cause in Iparralde, faced danger when a Francoist propaganda campaign targeted him, culminating in a Molotov cocktail attack on his house in Donibane, likely orchestrated by the Spanish far-right group Guerrilleros de Cristo Rey. On May 5, 1971, Monzón was ordered to leave Iparralde by the French Government, prompting a defiant public statement, "A toutes les Basques" (To all Basques), and a hunger strike organized in Bayonne's cathedral.[735]

The expulsion order affected not only Monzón but also Txillardegi and Arregi, prompting a campaign by Basque nationalists to reverse the French decision. Despite past disagreements between Irujo and Monzón, their friendship endured, and Irujo, aiming to unite Basque nationalists, supported Monzón and secured a political refugee certificate for him. Despite Monzón's growing distance from the PNV and his critical stance towards Leizaola's leadership, his tireless efforts for unity platforms, such as the National Front or National agreements, remained evident.

Upon learning of Monzón's expulsion,[736] Irujo promptly expressed his support, and the Basque Government, without consultation, also extended its support. In July 1971, Monzón received his political refugee certificate, accompanied by a detailed political letter from Irujo outlining the presumed intentions of Anai Artea to replace the influence of the Basque Government, especially in America.[737] Their longstanding friendship prevailed over disputes.

The end of the "eighth province"? Transition to democracy. The end of the exile and the evolution of the Basque nationalism

The era of exile concluded on March 24, 1977, when Manuel Irujo returned to his homeland, the Basque Country, receiving a warm and enthusiastic welcome in Pamplona. While the PNV journal attributed Irujo's return to a party member's persuasion in Leigh-on-Sea (Essex), in an interview with Iñaki Anasagasti,[738] Irujo confirmed that he, his brother, and Pello Irujo were instrumental in urging the former politician to return, while he was in Paris.[739]

Following Franco's death on November 20, 1975, the political landscape started shifting, though the prospects of democracy in Spain were not yet certain. The year 1976 witnessed the active return of Basque exiles, although not without challenges, as highlighted by Alberto Elósegui in a March 1976 letter to Irujo from London. Economic struggles and legal complications,[740] such as the newly discovered criminal offense of "continued subversive activity abroad,"[741] prompted some exiles to seek solutions in Euskadi.

The political climate in Spain was evolving, but it was not entirely prepared to embrace all political exiles and acknowledge their diverse perspectives. The PNV, in its declaration after Franco's death, aligned itself with organizations opposing a political transition, advocating for a clear democratic rupture, including the recognition of political prisoners. The party acknowledged the need for political reorganization, particularly in the face of growing interest among young Basque nationalists for an alternative represented by ETA.[742]

Amidst the changes, Juan Ajuriaguerra maintained a significant role within the Euskadi Buru Batzar, bridging the experience of the older Basque nationalists with the new generation. Irujo, concerned about the impact of ETA violence, hunger strikes in Bayonne,[743] and the expulsion of Monzón from Iparralde linked to the kidnapping of the German consul, shared with his friend Martín García Urtiaga in Mexico the dynamics within the political party and the sentiments of the new generation. He acknowledged a prevailing opinion, especially among the youth, that considered the PNV an outdated 19th-century formation, calling for renewal or substitution.[744]

Irujo is alluding to the young Basque nationalists of ETA, who expressed similar sentiments about the PNV in their documents[745]—something he recognized had to be addressed from within.

"With all the related scenario, the Government and the Party are in their place, tending to their responsibilities, navigating with caution, perhaps with excessive caution (...). But how much I would like to see them attired in a different dynamism!"[746]

The party's renewal involved replacing various bureau representatives (Gipuzkoa, Bizkaia, Euzkadi Buru Batzar) with younger individuals, albeit not without some discomfort: "That cost a certain amount of violence with the old people who remain in Beyris. It has been overcome with difficulty and without elegance." Nevertheless, Irujo acknowledges that "Juanito is the dominant figure in the new EBB (...), and has become an advisor and performer at the service and by order of EBB, an order that the new burukides [members of the executive] consult with him before adopting it."[747]

Irujo aligns himself with the party's renewal, and as revealed later, he and Ajuriaguerra will be among the "elders" who gain the confidence of the young Basque nationalists in shaping the party, building a bridge between the two generations, and unifying the exile and those inside.[748]

Despite efforts to transform the party and the changing situation in the Basque Country, Manuel Irujo was uncertain about returning. Nearly 40 years in exile warranted careful consideration, even as calls for the return of exiles grew louder each day. During a meeting of the Spanish Christian Democracy team for the European Union in February 1976, Juan Ajuriaguerra presented the Basque cause, addressing issues arising from violence and emphasizing the need for a solution.[749] Ajuriaguerra highlighted the distinctiveness of the Basque cause within the broader Spanish democratic context, articulating grievances faced by Basque nationalists, such as the release of prisoners, the reintegration of exiles, assistance for the disabled, and the replacement and compensation of civil servants.[750]

The party's reorganization demanded experience, and although Irujo actively participated in changes and decisions while advising the young Basque nationalists, the pressure for his return increased. Alberto Elósegui, preparing to move from London to Bilbao with his family, candidly shared the situation in Gipuzkoa, stating that the PNV leadership there was heavily influenced by left-wing patterns and engaged in a somewhat sterile focus on the unification of the Basque language. However, the situation in Bizkaia appeared more promising. Despite this, Irujo's charisma was deemed essential for other parts of Euzkadi, with some suggesting his potential assignment to Southern Euskadi, although opinions on this were not unanimous among the burukides.[751]

Manuel Irujo has not yet made a decision regarding his return to the Basque Country. He has been actively collaborating with Anasagasti and Ajuriaguerra while continuing his involvement with the European Federal Movement. Additionally, he has dedicated his efforts to the preparation of Lehendakari Leizaola's 80th-anniversary celebration and has marked the 100th anniversary of the Abolitionist law of 1876[752] as a pivotal moment for the recovery of Basque laws. In emphasizing the significance of the date, he stated, "July 21 is the anniversary of the abolitionist law. I believe that the PNV should make an effort to mark the date. And I say this, not because I believe too much in it, but because it is in our interest to take advantage of it, we can and should do so, associating it with the 1839, to the Statute of Autonomy."[753]

Irujo's proposed strategy, outlined in an article published in the PNV's journal Euskadi in the second half of May 1976, was presented as a defense of the importance of the 1876 law that repealed the remains of the Basque code of laws. In the article titled "La Ley 21 de Julio de 1876," Irujo, blending his roles as a historian and lawyer, explained, "This law, whose centenary we are living, was the one that repealed the foral remains of Araba, Guipúzcoa and Vizcaya, putting an end, in fact, to their foral regime in the three Basque regions. We can only consider it under this point of view, reasoning against it and symbolizing our protest as Basques, democrats, and men of rights."[754]

Through his historical vindication, Irujo sought to highlight the opportunity for the Basques to reestablish their own code of laws, providing Basque nationalism with a more enduring foundation beyond the ethnic trait. This perspective was not new, as Irujo had promoted the idea since his early days in London. He aimed to draw parallels between Basque and British Whig historical narratives, advocating for a change within permanent frameworks of tradition rather than revolutionary change. In Irujo's view, Basque constitutional law shared similarities with common law, both evolving from oral customs to written legislation.[755]

Despite the changes in Euzkadi, Manuel Irujo does not currently feel the need to return from exile. He finds comfort in collaborating remotely and maintains ties with his daughter Miren and grandchildren in the UK, as the family's properties in the Basque Country are no longer in their possession. Nevertheless, there was a strong desire within the PNV to bring Irujo back to Pamplona for the 1976 Aberri Eguna. Alberto Elósegui, collaborating with Anasagasti in the edition of Euzkadi, was tasked with conveying the request for Irujo's participation: "The Aberri Eguna will be in Iruñea. And I am going to pass on a request from those in the interior: they want you to be in Iruñea on Easter Day and they have begged me to be the one to ask you."[756]

In early 1976, the PNV was gearing up for the Aberri Eguna,[757] an appeal for unity among all Basque forces. The call emphasized the day as one for the Fatherland, transcending political, ideological, regional, and linguistic differences. The announcement from the "Asamblea patriótica de Nabarra" outlined the challenges faced by traditional Basque nationalists, including political disputes among various nationalist parties, differing concepts of Euzkadi's geography, the conflict over the Basque language, and the Euskara batua (Unification of the Basque language). The Basque Country was undergoing a process of nation-building after the death of the dictator, and the 1976 Aberri Eguna marked the first one without him, albeit not without the lingering impact of the regime's violence.

On March 3, amid protests during a general strike, the police killed three young strikers inside the church of San Francisco de Asís in Pamplona. Described as a massacre, the police broke into the church, firing at the gathered people inside.[758] The Aberri Eguna of 1976 became a call for unity, protest, and vindication. Despite efforts to celebrate it in Iruñea, the violent situation in the Basque Country, including ETA's kidnapping and killing of Ángel Berazadi, a Basque industrialist close to the PNV, led to the cancellation of the event. Traditional

Basque nationalists condemned the action, but the EBB canceled its participation in the Aberri Eguna, despite protests from representatives in Bilbao.[759]

On April 13, 1976, the Basque Government issued a statement explaining its decision not to attend the Aberri Eguna in Pamplona due to escalating tension and incidents resulting in loss of human lives. Although a subsequent announcement in Euzkadi[760] aimed to clarify the reasons for the cancellation, not all PNV members received the decision positively. The Basque government's headquarters in Paris proceeded with some planned events, leading to discord when Manuel Irujo learned that Lehendakari Leizaola had canceled almost everything despite prior agreements. Irujo expressed his frustration, stating, "The agreement was that there would be, first Mass, then a lecture given by you, and then lunch. You have suppressed your lecture in the announcement. And you have done so because that is the way it came out of your head."

Known for his respectfulness and loyalty to the Basque Government, Manuel Irujo could not tolerate any breach of agreement, especially when it came to matters of patriotism. On this occasion, he found himself aligned with those advocating for the celebration of the Aberri Eguna, expressing his dissatisfaction with the cancellation of the agreed conference by the Basque collective of Paris. In a pointed critique, he stated, "That the Aberri Eguna is suppressed in the face of the monstrosity of the crime committed with Berazadi is one thing. But that you, by your personal decision, suppress the conference agreed in the joint meeting with the Basque collective of Paris held under your presidency, is quite another. The truth is that I do not know in which Gospel you have learned this rule of governance."[761]

Despite being physically distant, Manuel Irujo actively contributed to the rebuilding of the Basque Country. His focus included the incorporation of Navarre into the future political Basque Country within Spain. He collaborated with Amaiur, the information bulletin of the NBB (Napar Buru Batzar) from its inception,[762] demonstrating his commitment to reconstructing a political space for Basque nationalism from within. However, he was not willing to return unconditionally, stating, "They want me to go to Iruñea. I understand their desire. It seems childish to me. I think that going to Iruñea today does not expose me to jail. That is why it has less merit."[763]

While maintaining constant contacts with the inside, particularly with Anasagasti, the Bizkaia group, and Ramon de la Sota, Manuel Irujo stayed informed about the progress within the Basque Country. Irujo's collaboration with Anasagasti and his brother Jon involved assisting in publishing their articles. Anasagasti regularly reported news, challenges, and achievements, revealing the influence of old Basque traditionalist values. Anasagasti pointed out the inefficacy of the EBB (Euzko Buru Batzar)[764] in the inside, referencing Juan Ajuriaguerra, who led the PNV internally. The relationship between Irujo and Anasagasti was characterized by cordiality, productivity, and loyalty, as evidenced by Anasagasti's acknowledgment of Irujo's valuable opinions and ideas.[765]

Manuel Irujo got married in 1916, but tragically, two short years later, his spouse, Aurelia Pozueta, succumbed to the devastating "Spanish flu." Bereft of a second marriage, his unwavering dedication centered on Basque nationalism and the Basque Country, with the only exceptions being his offspring. Irujo, an untiring advocate for the Basque cause, remained committed to it even at the advanced age of 85.

Anasagasti, in correspondence with Irujo, conveyed the surging popularity of Xabier Arzallus.[766] Arzallus, a former Jesuit who aligned with the nationalist Basque party following the execution of Melitón Manzanas, gained prominence through his compelling oratory skills. Anasagasti reported, "The party continues its rapid reorganization, with a meeting in Iruñea today, gathering about forty individuals from various regions… In Forua the other day, Arzallus held a small rally attended by approximately 400 people from Marquina, Ondárroa, Lekeitio, Bermeo, etc., all conversing about the party entirely in the Basque language."[767]

Despite his advancing age, Arzallus emerged as a significant figure internally, acknowledging, "The current Navarre, influenced by social currents, neither recognizes nor is interested in me. I am nothing more than history and old age to them." Conversely, Irujo, as explained to Alberto Elósegui, became a symbol for the new generation in exile.[768]

Anasagasti's letter in June 1976 closed with the words, "Take care; in Navarre, you are the Arzallus of Biscay, in spite of your slight fever."[769] Irujo saw his return as synonymous with the return of democracy, considering the exiles emblematic of it. However, he deemed the situation in October 1976 unfit for his return due to persistent violence, political imprisonments, and violations of basic human rights. Pertur was presumed dead amid rumors implicating parallel police involvement; the Civil Guard suppressed demonstrations, firing upon students and workers; and in Montejurra (Navarre), an ex-commander, Italian fascists, and members of Guerrilleros de Cristo Rey and Falange killed two Carlists during the annual pilgrimage.

Spain, not yet a democracy, maintained the legality of the TOP, prisons overflowed with democrats, and the exiles were branded as criminals by the Minister of Information, Manuel Fraga Iribarne.[770] Irujo, however, resisted, stating, "I will resist as much as I can to cross over, holding a position, not to see it compensated. Exile is a stance against a regime imposed by violence that denies Basque freedom and human rights; someone must maintain that stance until tangible and real changes occur."[771]

Irujo's stance towards the regime remained unwavering, a constant throughout his entire exile. Countless times, he and his compatriots had envisioned a return to their homeland, only to be repeatedly disappointed by the seemingly interminable regime. Irujo persisted in maintaining his faith, engaging in intense work across Europe, and advocating for a federal union that could acknowledge peoples rather than states, all the way until his final days in exile. His dedication was primarily focused on securing international recognition for the Basque cause within the European context.

While the efforts of the Basque government and nationalism aimed at rebuilding political strength were concentrated internally, the ideology and strategies continued to predominantly emanate from the exile, as evidenced in Irujo's contacts, a trend that would persist.

In the early months of 1977, Irujo, at the age of 85, displayed signs of fatigue, offering excuses for not actively participating in the Party's reconstruction. Acknowledging the necessity for the youth to take charge, he remarked, "They want me to go, taking advantage of one of those dates, to the PNV National Assembly or Aberri-Eguna. We will see what happens. I have told them that I do not forget that I count 85 autumns (...). We need new values, young people who go out to fight. We have to help them, not overshadow them. We are living in a historical moment in which the youth take precedence, believing they have the right to everything, knowing everything, without recognizing experience as a right or an advantage of any kind."[772]

The importance of involving the youth in the political landscape became evident, especially considering that many young Basque nationalists had aligned with ETA. The PNV faced the risk of evolving into a political party dominated by older exiles with no connections to the emerging society. Anasagasti emphasized the presence of youth in meetings, stating, "In Zalla, at a Board meeting of 33 people, 13 were women and under 30 years of age."[773]

Despite the approaching end of exile, Irujo recognized the need to return. In late February 1977, he expressed his willingness to go back to Navarre, to the Basque Country, despite his advanced age: "They ask me to go there. I am infinitely lazy... But I don't have that, nor youth, nor courage, nor anything, but the pressing need to go, to push, to do, to try to lift that."[774]

"40 Años de exilio os saludan" (40 years of exile greet you).

More than 2000 individuals eagerly awaited the arrival of two small planes at the Hondarribia airport, situated on the border of France and Spain, where the Bidasoa river meets the sea. On the chilly afternoon of March 24th, 1977, Manuel Irujo's exile was poised to conclude.

Expressing his reluctance to Iñaki Anasagasti, the organizer of the welcome, Irujo remarked, "I don't like to make a fool of myself. We organized a reception for him much to his regret; he didn't want to, but we insisted. 'We want you to come from the air, and we want to organize a big reception for you,' we told him."[775]

Opting to travel by train to Donibane alongside Lehendakari Leizaola and his brother, Pello, also concluding his exile, Irujo visited Lehendakari Aguirre's tomb and attended a mass before deciding it was time to return home.[776] He had flown from Biarritz in a small plane piloted by Pedro Sota, leaving Lehendakari Leizaola and other Basque Government members with whom he had fled into exile. Leizaola would remain in exile until 1979, returning only after the approval of the Statute of Gernika and the reestablishment of the Basque Government.[777]

Descending from the small plane with tears in his eyes, Irujo was welcomed by a massive sign reading "Irujo jauna: ongi etorri" and a large ikurrina adorned with a lauburu, overseeing a crowd waving ikurrinas.[778] His initial words succinctly encapsulated his identity and dedication: "At 85 years of age, I am only here as an affiliate. I am sure that the Basque people will have the appropriate instruments to achieve a democracy that will lead us to freedom. The great sadness when I set foot on my land is to see that there are still prisoners in jail."[779]

Irujo, a devoted "soldier" of the PNV, unwaveringly followed its orders and staunchly defended democracy. The plight of the Basques in the Basque Country had been a significant reason for his initial refusal to return.

The meticulously prepared welcome featured a display of symbols of Basque nationalism long concealed during the dictatorship. A young girl greeted Irujo in Basque, and patriotic songs such as "Emon, emon," "Batasuna," and "Eusko Gudariak gara" echoed through the crowd.

In the same small plane that had brought him to Hondarribia, Irujo flew to Pamplona, arriving at Noain's airport to yet another jubilant reception, this time in his beloved Navarre. The mayor of Estella, Pedro Arbizu, and other city hall members presented him with the golden insignia of the city.

At the airport, members of the PNV and his brother, Pello Mari, who had just returned from exile in Argentina, welcomed Irujo. Amidst chants of "Askatasuna" and "Gora Euskadi Askatuta," Irujo left the airport, seemingly akin to a Head of State, and was driven to the Hotel Tres Reyes, where he delivered a speech accompanied by Pedro Basaldúa, Estanis Aranzadi, and Iñaki Anasagasti.

In a poignant moment, Manuel Irujo, after once again highlighting the plight of political prisoners in the Basque Country and advocating for their freedom and amnesty, fervently asserted the importance of a legal framework for political parties and autonomy for the Basque Country, aligning it directly with the Republic. Despite acknowledging the social challenges faced by the people, Irujo, consistent with his stance over four decades in exile, vehemently rejected violence, declaring, "I am not in favor of dialogue with guns or violence. I am against the institutionalized violence that has been in power for 40 years. Let there be no winners and losers. We are going to build a country with the effort of all. We are going to start from zero."[780]

In a relentless schedule, Irujo was honored with a tribute dinner at the sports citadel of Pamplona, presided over by Carlos Garaikoetxea, who would later become the Lehendakari during the reinstated autonomy (1980-1985).[781] Standing on the platform for speeches, Irujo, displaying no signs of weariness, delivered one of his most memorable addresses to the audience: "40 years of exile greet you. 40 years since the military fined me, stripped me of my property and forced me into exile. We are in a constituent moment. The Basque cause for another 40 years can be at stake in these moments."[782]

Continuing his speech, Irujo reflected on the 40 years of the Basque Government-in-exile, recalling significant figures he had collaborated with, such as Aguirre, Landaburu, and Leizaola, and the collective efforts undertaken to uphold the historical rights of the Basque Country. The exile, he emphasized, had served as a vault safeguarding Basque rights.

The welcoming ceremonies persisted at the city hall of Pamplona and subsequently in Estella over the ensuing days. Irujo, during his visit to the cemetery and church, fielded questions and expressed gratitude for the warm receptions, underscoring his own humility: "I have been in exile because it was a protest against the regime imposed by the War. I have returned because the PNV has told me that my position is now here. I am neither a myth nor am I anything that could mean prominence, or to give lessons or to set a chair. I know very well the limitations that age imposes. One of the things that would bother me the most would be to overshadow the authentic values that Navarre needs."[783]

Iruñea, 1977. The Assembly of the PNV

"Batzar Nagusia Iruñean. Batasuna ta Indarra."[784]

The Basque streets awoke adorned with PNV posters calling for the General Assembly in Pamplona. A vibrant, full-color poster featured the Ikurrina's colors cutting through a black chain symbolizing the prolonged Franco dictatorship. It called for the unity of traditional Basque nationalists and urged strength for the challenging task of rebuilding the political party that had endured nearly forty years in exile.

The Iruñea assembly convened on March 24, marking the modernization of the PNV and its nationalism, becoming a catalyst for the party's significance in the Basque Country. Despite divergences among representatives, especially between those from Bizkaia and the rest, differences in political and socio-economic communications, and variations in the use of the Basque language,[785] the assembly, directed by Juan Ajuriaguerra, aimed to renew the party's statutes, unchanged since 1933, and update Basque nationalist ideology.

Ajuriaguerra instructed that each region should have a representative, and the President should be from Navarre. The elected officials included Garaikoetxea (President), Pello Irujo (Navarra), Pedro Arrizabalaga (Alaba), Txomin Saratxaga (Bizkaia), and Jesús Mari Alkain (Gipuzkoa).

Discussions centered on four key areas to establish new policies and political principles: organization, politics, socioeconomics, and culture and identity. Xabier Arzallus defended political communication, Iñigo Agirre explained the cultural and identity section, Kepa Sodupe tackled socioeconomics, and Josu Bergara addressed the party's structure.

From March 24th to March 27th, party members, legalized in February, engaged in debates, discussions, and presentations on the exile and the Basque government's work during those years. New topics, like the role of Basque women in exile, were introduced, with Garbiñe Urresti detailing the importance of Emakume Abertzale Batza[786] and the work of Basque women.

The assembly's closure at Anaitasuna pavilion featured a speech by Manuel Irujo, who captivated the audience with his vitality, appealing to both old and young Basque nationalists. However, the assembly's fruition was the result of intense debates, meetings, and discussions carried out in exile to present communications in Iruñea. Similar to the World Basque Congress in 1956, the research's focus lies in the debates, impressions, and the exile's impact on decisions about the future of traditional Basque nationalism.

The Iruñea assembly issued a declaration of principles extracted from the four main communications. Yet, how did they reach this point? How did the weight of 40 years in exile shape these principles? These questions will be explored in the following sections, examining how the exile's significance influenced these foundational principles.

Structure and essence of the party

The structure of the political party, although not directly within the study's scope, reveals the exile's significant influence in reorganizing administrative bodies—a testament to the exile's importance in shaping new structures.

In pre-assembly documents outlining the organization, the assembly was divided into four regions, each with its own voice and vote: Araba, Gipuzkoa, Bizkaia, and Navarra, along with two Extraterritories.[787] This underscores the weight given to the voice of the exile, considered the "8th province," completing the system of imaginary geographic regions of Basque nationalism.

The presence of the exile was evident from the beginning at the General Assembly in Pamplona. It marked the first time post-dictatorship that the Party could convene an assembly from outside its clandestine marginality. The symbolism of Irujo's return from exile coinciding with the assembly in Pamplona was carefully studied and planned.

Many speakers were PNV members arriving from exile, establishing connections with influential young members, including Xabier Arzallus, who played a significant role. The assembly bridged the past with the future, connecting exile with the internal resistance. In the words of Basaldua, it acknowledged those in exile as having "more merit than all of us who have spent 40 years finally breathing a bit of freedom."[788]

For 40 years, exiles had staunchly defended Basque rights, experiencing the bitterness of exile but also relishing the blessing of freedom, as articulated by Antoon de Baets.[789] The exile's weight in defining the four main topics debated at the Assembly and the declaration of principles itself is evident.

The opening line of the declaration of principles—"Euzko alderdi jeltzalea. Basque Nationalist Party, founded by Sabino Arana, is named after the motto: 'Jaungoikoa eta Lege Zarra' (God and Old Law)" —was not without its challenges.

In a concerned letter from Alberto Onaindia to Manuel Irujo on November 3, 1976, the priest expressed worry about the evolving features of the Basque party. He highlighted a strong tendency to omit "God," potentially causing a split within the party. These concerns would spark debates on the old motto and the social aspect of the party during the assembly's preparation.[790]

The changing social circumstances from the party's creation in 1895 to the transition from dictatorship to democracy in 1976 prompted discussions on updating the PNV's tenets to align with contemporary political and social demands. Debates revolved around the old motto and the party's social features, aiming to broaden its appeal to potential voters.[791]

During those times, discussions on self-management socialism and whether the party should define itself as confessional or not were prevalent. Young Basque nationalists within the PNV sought to modernize the party, redirecting its focus to address the needs of the youth while preserving the traditional values of Basque nationalism. This effort aimed to counter the loss of supporters to new and diverse political parties emerging in the Basque Country.

In parallel, in exile, Alberto Onaindia engaged in a lengthy letter exchange with Doctor Dunixi de Oñatibia, a Basque nationalist seeking Onaindia's opinion on these crucial subjects.

Alberto Onaindia, a Basque nationalist clergyman, staunchly defended the preservation of the motto "Jaungoikoa eta lege zarra" as an integral part of the PNV's history and its affiliation with the Catholic faith. Onaindia argued that, following the Second Vatican Council, the Church advocated for alternative names to "Catholic" for Catholic parties. Thus, although the PNV's name does not explicitly reflect its Catholicism, the motto created by Sabino Arana holds great importance. Onaindia likened the motto to a background that gathers initial inspiration and a historical past, without constituting a definitive definition. Drawing a parallel with the British Monarchy's use of a motto in French, Onaindia emphasized tradition.[792]

Addressing the second question regarding the social aspect, Onaindia contended that the PNV's politics had always been inherently social. He connected the party's social work for Basque workers with its Christian inspiration and the principles laid down by its founder. In a defense of Christian Democracy, Onaindia advocated for social justice and politics within the PNV but rejected the idea of incorporating the term "socialist" into the party's identity. He questioned the necessity of adopting the label "socialist,"[793] emphasizing the PNV's commitment to social justice and the promotion of workers without needing such terminology.

Onaindia's opinion, sent to Dr. Dunixi, was published in the January issue of the journal "Goiz Argi," where an entire section was dedicated to the debated questions. The opinions of Onaindia and José Miguel Barandiaran,[794] another nationalist Basque priest, were also distributed among Basque society in leaflet form, contributing to a heated debate.

In December of that year, Onaindia reached out to Manuel Irujo once again, updating him on activities related to the party's rebuilding and expressing ongoing concerns about the "Jaungoikoa eta lege zarra" motto. Onaindia, attributing these changes to the influence of the youth, specifically mentioned Xabier Arzallus and referred to a meeting in Bergara where socialist-leaning sentiments were reportedly expressed. Onaindia conveyed a sense of urgency, asserting a strong reaction against these perceived socialist elements within the party.[795]

While it remains unclear whether Manuel Irujo shared Onaindia's level of concern about the socialist features emerging within the party, we do know from a text he authored titled "Jaungoikoa eta lege-zarra" that he was committed to preserving Sabino's motto. Irujo, invoking history and tradition, defended the slogan as a symbolic link between the past and the present: "Like the emblem of a coat of arms, a political motto entails patriotic and human emotions, historical continuity, and virtual reality."[796]

In this regard, Manuel Irujo aligns with Onaindia, emphasizing that defending tradition does not imply a fear of change but rather a plea for continuity. He understands and shares the opinion that the PNV is not inherently confessional, in line with the Church's stance against confessional parties. However, he questions the desire of some to abandon Sabino's motto, asking why the party should cease being "Eusko Alderdi Jeltzalea."

The extraterritorial assembly convened in Paris a few days later, on January 30, to deliberate, amend, and ratify the proposals sent by the PNV.[797] During the discussion on political communication, attendees unanimously approved the proposal. However, at the explicit request of some members, they also agreed to introduce an amendment recognizing the "Jaungoikoa eta Lege Zarra" motto as a historical legacy.[798]

Ultimately, the declaration of principles outlined the PNV as follows:

a) A Basque Party in its territorial scope of action and obedience, without organic ties to non-Basque political forces.

b) A democratic party with an internal confederal structure that respects the peculiarities of each region of Euzkadi and formulates internal regulations democratically.

c) A popular party defending the cause of an entire people rather than the interests of a specific group or social class.

d) A party of the masses seeking to unite the energies of a people in an emergency situation to recover its integral personality.

e) A non-confessional party open to individuals of any creed or humanist philosophy who share the fundamental principles of Basque cultural heritage, including equality in human dignity, autonomy of will, democratic governance, respect for others, family cohesion, and social solidarity.

f) A party open to all Basques, defining belonging to the people not by blood or birth but by the will to integrate, cultural influence, and contribution to its development in any aspect of life.

These definitions signify a notable departure from the PNV that went into exile. Despite retaining the "Jaungoikoa eta lege zarra" motto, the abandonment of the confessional character, coupled with a definition of Basque identity not tied to blood or birthplace, positions the traditional Basque nationalism of the PNV as more civic than ethnic. It recognizes nationality as a dynamic characteristic acquired through language, culture, or free will, rather than static features such as ethnicity or blood ties.

We can assume that Irujo's viewpoint was duly considered, and while we cannot definitively state that Irujo's opinion compelled the initial statements in the Party's declaration of principles, it is significant to highlight a question directed at him during an interview published in the Journal of the Assembly. When asked about his thoughts on the opening paragraph of the "statement of principles," Irujo responded with a succinct "Very good."[799]

In terms of political principles, the first point explicitly outlines the political objectives of the traditional Basque nationalism of the PNV. It states that the Party will strive for "a) An autonomous Basque State that is a progressive political entity, within the scope of its political democratization, with the constant deepening of the levels of civic freedom to be achieved, and in a position of solidarity with the freedom of the other peoples of the State." This mirrors the political strategy employed by the PNV during the exile, but the updated principles leave no room for interpretation. The key lies in the second point, confirming the autonomy project: "b) Strongly supporting the action of the Basque political forces of continental Euzkadi for the achievement of an autonomous political framework of the continental Basque regions and reinforcing the cultural, economic, and road links between Basque areas."

A potential future change in the Statutes regarding the political autonomy of the Basque Country, directly influenced by the exile, is the European aspect of the principles. Despite the incidental presence of Basque nationalism in Europe during the 60s and 70s, the European Federal Movement remained Irujo's cherished cause, persisting even upon his return from exile.[800]

In the 1970s, the shaping of Europe emphasized nation-states, leaving little room for nations without a State. While Basque nationalism, particularly the PNV, differed significantly from ethnic and collectivistic nationalism associated with the Nazis or Italian Fascio, the demands of nations without a State were deemed too precarious for a Europe still grappling with the aftermath of two world wars and the lingering influence of totalitarian Russian nationalism. During this period, the PNV embraced the term "Europe of Peoples" to describe the emerging Europe, rejecting concepts like "Europe of Regions" and "Europe of Ethnic Groups."[801] Manuel Irujo, a recognized Europeanist, supported the idea of "Euzkadi Region of Europe" in 1961, suggesting that, akin to the Flemish and the Walloon being regions of Europe within Belgium, Catalonia and Euzkadi could be European regions while still belonging to the Spanish State.[802]

In their 1966 Statement, the PNV articulated an international political strategy characterized by a firm commitment to democracy, European integration, and nationalism, while intertwining nationalism with elements of culture, history, and language. Concerning Europe, they advocated for the establishment of a Federation of peoples, eschewing the term "nation" and aligning their terminology with mainstream analyses of nationalism and European integration of that era, as seen in the works of Denis Rougemount and Guy Héraud. These analysts, featured in Alderdi, explored the concept of Europe and its formation, focusing on "regions" or "ethnic groups" while deliberately sidestepping the term "nation."

The vision of "Europe of the peoples" or "Europe of the regions" promoted by the PNV diverged significantly from the stance of left-wing Basque nationalism during the period of 1974-1976, as exemplified by the Brest Charter. However, it marked the integration of Revolutionary Basque nationalism into the European Movement.[803] The PNV's advocacy for the Europe of peoples also entailed a preference for a Federation of the European Union over a Confederation of State-nations. Embracing federalism, they championed the idea of "natural communities" and stressed the importance of respecting minority rights, nationalities, and regional autonomy within member states, advocating for internal structural modifications as a precondition for any federation.[804]

Manuel Irujo held contrasting views; he advocated for the Federal Movement, aligning more closely with the idea of a Europe of States. This perspective put him at odds with the official stance of the PNV, leading to criticism from the EBB for his dissent. Irujo's pragmatic approach, emphasizing negotiation with Spanish political parties, directly challenged the PNV's declaration, albeit without formal declarations of intent. His vision of Europe and Federalism envisioned a superstructure that rendered nation-states, like Spain, obsolete, as articulated in his articles, including one published in Ibérica from New York in 1972. Irujo expressed a longing for a Federal Europe characterized by unified governance across various domains.[805]

The PNV also witnessed internal divergence, notably represented by the EGI section, which, through their publication Gudari, advocated for a "Europe of the peoples" aligned with left-wing nationalist movements of the 1970s. They emphasized the rights of nations over those of states, infusing their stance with Christian ideals.[806] Despite the party's internal restructuring focusing on domestic matters, Manuel Irujo remained committed to his European strategy aimed at garnering recognition for the Basque cause throughout his exile.

Drawing from his experiences in exile, Manuel Irujo developed the theory of the superstructure, which he illustrated through his travels and encounters. In 1974, amidst the rising tide of Basque nationalisms advocating for independence, Irujo penned an article titled "Independencia, Autonomia, Federación," wherein he sought to elucidate the evolution of these three concepts. Central to his argument was the notion of "interdependence," which he envisioned as the cornerstone of a future federal union in Europe, emphasizing the union of regions. He asserted that for the Basques, becoming a region of Europe represented a political equivalent to national independence.

Irujo envisioned a future of interdependence within a unified Europe, transcending borders, with Europe serving as the guarantor of Euskadi's national independence. Addressing the youth directly, he urged them to embrace the European ideal, highlighting that a "United Europe" translated to "Free Euzkadi"[807] for them. In an effort to instill the same fervor for the European movement in young Basque nationalists as he possessed, Irujo advocated for their participation in various meetings convened by PNV-affiliated bodies. Ramon Sota recounted his experiences at several European gatherings, mentioning encounters with notable figures such as Jesús Insausti and Gonzalo Nárdiz.[808]

Despite his efforts, there was reluctance within the PNV to align too closely with European Christian Democracy, fearing it might dilute their national identity. Spanish representatives[809] often failed to comprehend the Basque interest in international affairs, dismissing it as mere anthropology.[810] Despite the crisis facing European bodies traditionally engaged by Basque nationalists during the exile, figures like Irujo and Ajuriaguerra persisted in advocating for the European Federal Movement as a means to pressure Spain towards democratization.[811]

Irujo's commitment to this cause was underscored by his presidency of the CFEME from 1973 to 1976, a strategy he had formulated during the Congress of Europe in February 1976—a role that would mark the culmination of his European endeavors.

According to a report authored by Irujo on December 5, 1976, the congress aimed to emulate the significance of the 1948 Hague Congress and sought to establish the European Union. With this objective in mind, the CFEME developed a project proposal envisioning the potential democratization of Spain. The Congress convened in Brussels from February 5 to 7, 1976, during which Manuel Irujo articulated his strategy of advocating for a European federation supportive of Spain's democratization: "The Congress of Europe asserts that only a fully democratic Spain can join the group of nations comprising the European Community."[812]

This strategy mirrored the approach of the Spanish European Movement, particularly since the Munich Congress, yet Irujo maintained confidence in European institutions. Despite Europe's burgeoning engagement with the Spanish dictatorship, Irujo insisted that EU membership should be reserved for democracies alone. In his address, he highlighted the Spanish desire to join the European Union while simultaneously demanding the immediate release of political prisoners, the free return of exiles, restoration of freedom of expression and assembly, recognition of all political parties without discrimination, and respect for the rights of different nationalities and communities within Spain.[813] The proposal was met with acclaim and a prolonged ovation.

However, despite Irujo's success on the European stage, where he enjoyed recognition, the PNV[814] appeared disinterested in the European movement, a sentiment underscored by Irujo's resignation from the CFEME presidency on November 19, 1976. The Secretary General of the European Movement, Mr. Van Schendel, had proposed a gradual incorporation of CFEME into Spain, as it was the only member with a presidency in exile. A dual presidency model was accepted in February, and by May, it was decided that the headquarters would relocate to Madrid.

Faced with the party's lack of enthusiasm for these changes, and despite his efforts to communicate the proposed shifts to the EBB in June 1976, Irujo resigned from the presidency. Miquel Coll i Alentorn, a Catalan politician from the Christian democrat party Unió Democràtica de Catalunya and recommended by Irujo, assumed his position. However, the CFEME essentially became defunct following its transfer to Spain.

In a letter penned to Iñaki Ansagasti in January 1977, Irujo expressed his lamentation regarding the situation, privately hoping that the young man could effect change: "The federal council has relocated to the Spanish State, as you know (...) The council has already convened two plenary sessions. All members have designated their representatives, except for the Basques. (...) We Basques are one of the founding 'families' of the Council, and we must maintain our representation. That, at least, is my understanding. Let's get to work."[815]

Despite the prolonged ordeal of the European Federal Movement, it was likely the PNV's longstanding tradition of Europeanism that led to the inclusion of a special reference to Europe in the declaration of political principles, reaffirming its commitment to European ideals:

> -Acknowledging its responsibility to contribute to the construction and advancement of Europe, which it envisions: Not only as a federation of existing state structures but as a union of free peoples, each maintaining their political and cultural distinctiveness, united under a common political and economic framework capable of fostering community development."
>
> -Furthermore, the declaration directly addressed the international division into blocs arising from World War II and the subsequent Cold War: "Freeing itself from the constraints and dependencies of bloc politics resulting from the aftermath of World War II and the ensuing Cold War.
>
> -Embracing progressiveness, striving for new forms of coexistence and collaboration through the convergence of political and social systems and the exchange of valuable experiences gained within diverse contexts.
>
> -Embracing a global outlook, towards the Third World, technological underdevelopment, and the fight against oppression."

-Finally, the declaration circled back to the notion of "Europe of the peoples": "It is within the framework of this Europe of Peoples that the political unity and freedom of the Basques will find their place, in equality and solidarity with other European peoples and within their own political structure, arising from the collective will of all Basques."[816]

Regarding culture, if anything changed during the years of exile, it was the heightened significance of culture in defining Basque nationalism. As evidenced by the creation of Ikastolas and the revitalization of Euskaltzaindia following the Basque Studies congress in Aranzazu in 1968, where linguists and literary figures convened to establish a standardized Basque language, led by Koldo Mitxelena, a linguistics professor at the University of Salamanca, and affiliated with the PNV.[817] Culture and the Basque language played pivotal roles in the declaration of principles at the Iruñea Assembly, linking Basque culture to the nation's existence and definitively shaping Basque nationalism into a civic ideology: "Culture is an expression of a people's existence, a force of unity, and an instrument of identification."[818]

The discussion surrounding communication on culture was among the most contentious at the assembly, particularly concerning the use of the Basque language and which dialect should be adopted by Basque nationalists affiliated with the PNV. The necessity for a standardized Basque language had been an ongoing debate, but it gained renewed emphasis in the 1960s, with a surge in studies and promotion efforts.

Starting from 1963, primarily from Bayonne, a group led by Txillardegi advocated for the creation of a standardized Basque language, outlined in the document Baiona'ko Biltzarreren Erabakiak, sparking significant interest and debate within the Basque cultural sphere. In 1968, another report emerged from the same group, this time convened in Ermua, and was published in the journal Jakin (nos. 31-32). Subsequently, Euskaltzaindia commissioned linguist Koldo Mitxelena to undertake a project, which was later published in full in Euskera (1968).[819]

The push for a "national language" signaled a commitment to nation-building and the aspiration to establish a State, centering around cultural and educational ideals and projects. At the extraterritorial assembly in Paris, there was a consensus that the communication on Culture should distinguish between culture and education, emphasizing that the proper development of culture was essential for building a robust educational framework. The use of the Basque language was deemed indispensable: "All Basque nationalists agree on the goal: Basque language should be the medium of instruction at all levels and across the Basque territory."[820]

Regarding the use of the Basque language and stemming from the need for a standardized variant, a contentious issue arose concerning the selection of the dialectal variant to be adopted by the PNV. Euskara batua, emerging from various studies, notably Koldo Mitxelena's project, was based on central dialectal variants, primarily those from Gipuzkoa, Navarre, and Lapurdi. However, this sparked reservations, particularly among Biscayans, who felt that the language of a minority was being imposed on the majority. They launched a campaign against the use of the Gipuzkoan Basque, alleging an overuse of the letter "H."

These accusations were reflected in a letter from Alberto Onaindia to Manuel Irujo at the end of 1976, detailing the situation internally and the divisions caused by language use: "All this with registration sheets and official texts full of H and H and H. Many have returned the sheets. This 'aitchist' work is mainly attributed to the nephew of the Lehendakari, a son of Ricardo who must be from the GUI.B.B. There is a current against him."[821]

Although the declaration of principles did not explicitly specify the chosen dialectal variant, historical records indicate that the Party decided to adopt the Gipuzkoan variant and promoted its use as the national language:

"The Basque nationalist party commits itself to promoting the collective task of cultural freedom in Euzkadi through continuous study, preservation, development, and creation in all cultural aspects. It advocates:

- The promotion of the Basque language as the national language of Euzkadi, a cultural vehicle with immediate social value for public functions.
- Basque control over our culture, preventing foreign interference in regulating the promotion and management of cultural expressions, media, and channels."[822]

In the realm of education, the PNV advocated for a socially oriented solution, defending "Free education, free of charge, adapted, permanent, decentralized, and practical, in accordance with laws enacted by bodies delegated power by Basque society." Furthermore, as a marker of modernity and differentiation, the party promoted bilingualism, as highlighted by Joseba Azkarraga: "The Basque language is one of the most distinguishing elements of the Basque nation. We must strive for progressive and effective bilingualism."[823]

In fact, the Iruñea Assembly endorsed the immediate promotion of bilingualism from kindergarten to university, advocating for the creation of "national ikastolas" to integrate all Basques and a Basque University organized around a single university district.[824] Culture and language became integral components of nationalism, shaping a unified nation not only under the same political organization but also under shared cultural structures and language.

Socio-economic Basque nationalism

Moving to socio-economic Basque nationalism, the communication slated for presentation at the General Assembly in Pamplona was deemed crucial by the Extraterritorial Assembly in Paris. This recognition stemmed from the consciousness developed during the long exile, crafting an imagined community with a positive perception of Basque society:

"Paris affiliates, who have spent most of our lives abroad, have developed an idealized image of Euzkadi[825]... this situation, proving Plutarch's theory right, could be seen as an advantage, since it has been contrasted with the daily events of the most advanced countries. It is therefore a modest contribution, but not without interest, in trying to find the future of the Basque people."[826]

The eighth province acknowledged its importance and the significant contribution the exile community could make to renew traditional Basque nationalism. Despite the challenges of exile, lives distanced from the Basque Country, and the autarchic situation under the dictatorship, the community in exile had constructed an alternative system through analysis and experience, ready to be implemented in a new Basque Country.

"Reflecting on the behavior of Basque communities in Europe and the Americas, with their failures and contradictions, it can be said that they have been driven by three main notions: the spirit of work, the love of freedom, and the feeling of solidarity."[827] These qualities, inherent in the Basques despite the autarchic situation of the dictatorship, were deemed essential for introduction into the Basque Country by the extraterritorial assembly in Paris.

As Alberto Onaindia had anticipated, the discussion on the social politics from an economic perspective within the PNV sparked heated debates. While this didn't imply a consideration of adopting socialism, there was indeed pressure from certain groups within the PNV to align the economic program with the social needs of the Basques.

Analyzing the section titled "Hacia un sistema socializado" (Towards a socialized system), members of the extraterritorial assembly in Paris emphasized that the economic and social tradition of the PNV had always been rooted in populism:

"The people were the dynamic element that made the decisions and put them into practice... the party rejected the approaches of minority groups when they tried to set themselves up as protagonists of processes of immobilism or protection of vested interests."[828]

Despite significant economic changes in the Basque Country since their exile, the PNV advocated for the economic tradition developed alongside the people. However, other political parties viewed matters differently. The conservative economic feature of traditional Basque nationalism had drawn criticism from emerging leftist and abertzale (Basque nationalist) groups like ETA. Hence, there was a strong necessity to clarify its stance on "social economy."

Criticism from the parallel assembly in Paris centered on the socio-economic communication for neglecting not only the socio-economic activities undertaken by the PNV during the short period of the Republican Government but also its work in local councils and provincial governments. The members felt that the communication failed to acknowledge the accomplishments and took the accusations of political opponents at face value:

"In reviewing the antecedents, with the alterations of time, it would be appropriate to consider the work of the PNV in city councils and provincial councils... The public services of city councils and provincial councils in general, in 1936, could have been favorably compared with those in other countries at the beginning of our exile."[829]

Once again, the exile and the experiences it afforded were deemed invaluable for the construction of a new nationalism. It wasn't merely about vindicating tradition but also about valuing the experience—with no intention of stagnation but rather advocating for the good work that had been done. The differences stemmed not only from generational divides but also from the distinctions between the exile and the local party members.

Maite Garmendia, present in Paris, believed that such an important communication as the socio-economic proposal should involve an economic program based on data and statistical information, rather than just a simple exposition of problems found in socialist and capitalist systems:

"It proposes an attempt to overcome the deficiencies but does not provide any solutions to solve the problems. It is a very theoretical account..."[830]

For the nationalist members in Paris, the socio-economic communication represented an exercise in challenging political and economic prejudices, particularly against capitalism, which they, drawing from their experiences in exile, could refute:

"The Paper is concerned with condemning, and justly so, the errors and excesses of Basque capitalism. A first qualification of the author's affirmations could consist in paying proper homage to the working people. Has it not fulfilled its duty to a great extent?"[831]

Despite intense criticism of capitalism, based on their experiences in exile, industrialization was seen as the future and a sign of progress. However, similar to France, there was a social tendency to critique capitalism while simultaneously demanding more industries to balance regional disparities.

Drawing from their experiences in exile and the work carried out by the Basque Government, Basque nationalists in Paris recommended establishing a group within the PNV responsible for studying and overseeing the situation.

A sharp reprimand was directed towards the communication for its lack of references to workers' rights. The extraterritorial assembly in Paris suggested including references to the defense of workers' rights, in line with the Basque nationalist trade unionist tradition, as proposed by Ramon Agesta, representative of the ELA-STV.

The declaration of principles of the Assembly in Iruñea incorporated some of these proposals, but the debate was long and heated, particularly regarding the perception of "socialism" within the PNV.

The most significant agreements in the declaration pertained to the economic and social aspects, encapsulated under the title "Económico Social." This indicated the PNV's desire to reclaim the social aspect inherent in Basque nationalism and win over the portion of the populace shared with other Basque nationalist organizations that emerged in the late 1970s.[832]

The development of the "social economy" was envisaged in all economic principles, where egalitarianism was emphasized in both social and economic terms to transform society and ensure every citizen's participation in decision-making. Power was to be vested in the people as agents of transformation.[833]

The principles directly incorporated suggestions from exile, such as emphasizing workers' rights in the social economy, valuing private property, and implementing control over certain community services.

Furthermore, there was a constant appeal to the connection between social economy and democracy, emphasizing that the PNV's nationalism aimed to defend social democracy, not socialism. This was reflected in statements highlighting the inseparable concepts of political and economic democracy and the importance of democratic planning in economic decision-making.[834]

Abbreviations

In the writing of this book, it is used the acronyms in the original language.

ANV – Acción Nacionalista Vasca (Basque nationalist action) BA CBE – Basque Archive Center for Basque Studies
CFEME – Consejo Federal Español del Movimiento Europeo. (Spanish Federal Council of the European Movement)
CISC – Confédération internationale des syndicats chrétiens (International Confederation of Christian Unions)
CVFE – Consejo Vasco por la Federación Europea (Basque council for the European Federation)
CNT – Confederación Nacional del Trabajo (National Confederation Labour)
EBB – Euskadi Buru Batzar (Basque country central Office)
EGI – Euzko Gaztedi Indarra (Basque Youth Force) EI – Eusko-Ikaskuntza
EEC – Economic European Community
ELA-STV – Eusko Langileen Alkartasuna-Solidaridad de los Trabajadores Vascos (Basque solidarity workers)
ERC – Esquerra Republicana de Catalunya (Catalan Republican Left) ETA – Euskadi ta Askatasuna (Basque Homeland and Freedom)
FEVA-EABA – Federación de Entidades Vasco Argentinas – Eusko Argentinar Bazkun Alkartasuna (Federation of Basque-Argentine Associations)
FET y de las JONS – Falange Española Tradicionalista y de las Juventudes orgánicas nacional socialistas.
IR – Izquierda Republicana (Republican Left)
LIAB – Ligue Internationales des Amis des Basques (International League of Basque's friends)
NARA – National archives and Records Administration
PCE – Partido Comunista de España (Spanish Communist Party)
PSOE – Partido Socialista Obrero Español (Spanish socialist workers' party)
EAJ-PNV – Partido Nacionalista Vasco (Basque nationalist party)
UFD – Unión de Fuerzas Democráticas (Union of democratic forces) UGT – Unión General de Trabajadores (General Union of workers) UR – Unión Republicana (Republican Unity)
UE – Unión Española (Spanish Unity)

Bibliography

ACOSTA RUBIO, Raoul. 1977. *Cuba, todos culpables: relato de un testigo: lo que no se sabe del dictador Batista y su época*. Miami: Universal Ed.
AGUILA, Juan José del. 2001. *El TOP. La represión de la libertad (1963-1977)*. Barcelona: Ed. Planeta.
AGUIRRE, José Antonio. 1944. *Cinco conferencias pronunciadas en un viaje por América*. Buenos Aires: Editorial Vasca Ekin
AGUIRRE, José Antonio. 1981. *Obras completas*. Donostia: Sendoa. 3 Vols.
AGUIRRE, José Antonio; GOIOGANA, Iñaki (Ed.). 2010. *Diario, 1941-1942*. Bilbao: Sabino Arana Fundazioa
AGIRREAZKUENAGA, Joseba. 2016. "Reinterpreting the Basque Past in exile; Scholars, Narratives and Agendas (1936-1977)." In *Storia della Storiografia*. Pisa-Roma: Fabrizio Serra Editore. 1: 65-82.
———. 2011. *The Making of the Basque Question Experiencing Self-Goverments, 1793-1877*. Reno: Centre for Basque Studies.
AGIRREAZKUENAGA, Joseba (Ed.) [Et.Alt.]. 2007. *Diccionario biográfico de los parlamentarios de Vasconia. 1876-1939*. 3 vols. Vitoria-Gasteiz: Eusko Legebiltzarra.
AGIRREAZKUENAGA, Joseba; SOBREQUÉS, Jaume. 2007. *Eusko Jaurlaritza eta Catalunyako Generalitatea: Erbestetik Parlamentuen eraketara arte (1939-1980)*. Bilbao: Herri-Ardularitzaren Euskal Erakundea.
AJURIA, Peru, and SAN SEBASTIÁN. 1992. *El exilio vasco en Venezuela*. Gasteiz : Eusko Jaurlaritzaren argitalpen zerbitzu nagusia.
ALMEIDA, Linda Dowling. 2001. *Irish immigrants in New York City 1945-1995*. Bloomington: Indiana University Press
ÁLVAREZ GILA, Óscar. 2005. "De «América y los vascos» a la «octava província»: 20 años de historiografía sobre la emigración y presencia vasca en las Américas (Siglos XIX-XX). In *Vasconia*, 34, pp. 275-300.
AMAT, Jordi. 2016. *La primavera de Múnich. Esperanza y fracaso de una transición democrática*. Barcelona: Tusquets Editores.
———. 2016. *La semilla del liberalismo: Política y literatura en torno a la actividad española del Congreso por la libertad de la cultura. (1958-1969)*. Barcelona: Universitat de Barcelona. Recurs en línia: http://hdl.handle.net/10803/392675
AMEZAGA IRIBARREN, Arantzazu. 1999. *Manuel Irujo. Un hombre vasco*. Bilbao: Sabino Arana Fundazioa.
AMIGO, Ángel. 1978. *Pertur: ETA 71-76*. Donostia: Hórdago.

ANASAGASTI, Iñaki and ERKOREKA, Josu. 2013. *A basque patriot in New*

York : Jose Luis de la Lombana y Foncea and the Euskadi delegation in the United States . Reno: Center for Basque Studies.

ANASAGASTI, Iñaki, and SAN SEBASTIÁN, Koldo. 1985. *Los años oscuros : El Gobierno vasco. El exilio 1937-1941*. San Sebastián : Txertoa.

ANASAGASTI, Iñaki. 2006. *Llámame Telesforo*. Tafalla: Txalaparta

ANDERSON, Benedict. 2006 (1983 1st Ed.) *Imagined communities*. New York: Verso.

ARREGI, Natxo . 1981. *Memorias del KAS. 1975-78*. San Sebastián : Hórdago

ARRIETA ALBERDI, Leyre. 2009. "Landáburu, el alavés europeísta" in *Sancho el Sabio*, 31, pp.199-220.

———.2008. "Red de relaciones europeas del PNV (1945-1977)" in *Cuadernos de historia contemporánea*. Vol. 30, pp.313-331. Also in : https://revistas.ucm.es/index.php/CHCO/article/viewFile/CHCO0808110313A/6738

———.2007. *Estación Europa. La política europeista del PNV en el exilio (1945-1977)*. Madrid: Editorial Tecnos.

ARTEGA, Federico de. 1971. *ETA y el proceso de Burgos*. Madrid: Editorial E.Aguado.

ARZALLUS, Xabier. 2005. *Así fue*. Madrid: Foca.

ARZALLUS, Xabier [Et.Alt.]. 1989. *Vascos en la construcción de Europa*. Bilbao EAJ-PNV.

AUGÉ, Marc. 1995. *Non-places. Introduction to an anthropology of supermodernity*. London-New York: Verso.

AZCONA PASTOR, José Manuel (Ed.) 2015. *Identidad y estructura de la emigración vasca y navarra hacia Iberoamérica (siglos XVI-XXI). Redes sociales y desarrollo socioeconómico*. Pamplona: Thomson Reuters Aranzadi.

———.2011. *El ámbito historiográfico y metodológico de la emigración vasca y navarra hacia América*. Vitoria-Gasteiz: Servicio central de publicaciones del gobierno vasco.

———.2004. *Basque emigration to Latin America (s. XVI-XX)*. Reno: University of Nevada;

———.1992. *Los paraísos posibles, historia de la emigración vasca a Argentina y Uruguay en el siglo XIX*. Bilbao: Universidad de Deusto.

AZURMENDI, José Félix. 2013. *Vascos en la Guerra Fría. ¿Víctimas o cómplices? Gudaris en el juego de los espías*. Donostia: Editorial Ttarttalo

AZURMENDI, José Félix. 2012. *PNV-ETA. Crónica oculta (1960-1979)*. Donostia: Editorial Ttarttalo

BAETS, Antoon de. 2011 "Plutarch's Thesis: The contribution of refugee historians to historical writing, 1945-2010" a *In defense of learning* . British Academy. pp.211-224

BASALDÚA, Pedro. 1956. *Jesús de Galíndez: Víctima de las tiranías en América*. Buenos Aires: Mac-Co

BATISTA, Antoni. 2010. *La Carta. Historia de un comisario franquista*. Madrid: Debate.

———. 2007. *Madariaga. De las armas a la palabra*. Barcelona: RBA Libros.

———. 1995. *La brigada social*. Barcelona: Empúries.

BERNARDO URQUIJO, Iñaki. 1993. *Galíndez: La tumba abierta. Los vascos y los Estados Unidos*. Vitoria-Gasteiz: Eusko Jaurlaritzaren Argitalpen Zerbitzu Nagusia.

BOTTI, Alfonso. 2012. *Luigi Sturzo e gli amici Spagnoli. Carteggi (1924, 1951)*. Modena: Soveria Mannelli, Rubbettino Editore

BULLAIN, Iñigo. 2011. *Revolucionarismo patriótico. El Movimiento de liberación nacional vasco. (MLNV)*. Madrid: Editorial Tecnos.

BULTZAGILLEAK. 1979. ¿Qué pasa en el País Vasco? Zaratuz: Itxaropena.

CANAL, Jordi. (Ed.). 2007. *Exilios. Los éxodos políticos en la historia de España. Siglos XV-XX*. Madrid. Sílex.

CASANELLAS, Pau. 2014. *Morir matando. El Franquismo ante la práctica armada. 1968-1977*. Madrid: Los Libros de la catarata.

CASANOVA, Iker. 2007. *ETA 1958-2008. Medio siglo de historia*. Tafalla: Editorial Txalaparta.

CASTRO RUANO, José Luis de; UGALDE ZUBIRI, Alexander. 2004. *La acción exterior del País Vasco (1980-2003)*. Oñati: Instituto Vasco de Administración Pública.

CHIROT, Daniel; GREENFELD, Liah. 1994. "Nationalism and Aggression" in *Theory and Society*, 23: 79-130.

CLARK, Robert P. 2009. "Patterns in the live of ETA members", in *Terrorism*, Vol. 6, Issue 3. Pp. 423-454 Taylor & Francis Online.

———. 1987. "The legitimacy of ethno-nationalist insurgency", in *The legitimacy of political violence?: The case of western Europe*. Amherst: University of Massachusetts.

———. 1984. *The basque insurgents. ETA, 1952-1980*. Madison: The university of Wisconsin Press.

COLOMINES, Joan. 2003. *Crònica de l'antifranquisme a Catalunya*. Barcelona: Angle Editorial

CONGRESO POR LA LIBERTAD DE LA CULTURA. 1961. *El Congreso por la libertad de la cultura*. Paris.

CONVERSI, Daniele. "Dommino effect or internal developments? The Influente of International Events and Political Ideologies on Catalan and Basque Nationalism". *West European Politics*, 3, 1993, 245-70.

CRESPO MACLENNAN, Julio. *Spain and the process of European integration, 1957-85*. Houndmills: Palgrave in association with St. Anthony's College.

DE LA GRANJA, José Luis; DE PABLO, Santiago (Eds.). 2002. *Historia del País Vasco y de Navarra en el siglo XX*. Madrid : Editorial Biblioteca Nueva

DE LA SOTA, Ramon. 2016. *Euskadi. Siete años. 1969-1976.* Unpublished.
DELGADO, Lorenzo. 2003. "¿El "amigo americano" ?: España y Estados Unidos durante el Franquismo" in *Studia Historica. Historia Contemporánea.* Salamanca: Ediciones universidad de Salamanca. 21: 231-276. Online Access: http://gredos.usal.es/jspui/bitstream/10366/80166/1/El_amigo_americano_Espana_y_Estados.pdf
DÍAZ ESCULIES, David. 1996. *L'oposició catalana al franquisme: El Republicanisme liberal i la nova oposició (1939-1960).* Barcelona: Publicacions de l'Abadia de Montserrat. pp.114 and ff.
DOUGLASS, William A.; ZULAIKA, Joseba. 1990. "On the interpretation of terrorist violence: ETA and the Basque political process". In *Comparative studies in Society and history.* Vol. 32, No. 2. April 1990. pp.238-257.
ELORZA, Antonio. (Coord.). 2000. *La historia de ETA.* Madrid: Ediciones Temas de Hoy.
———. 1992. "Euzkadi-Europa. La cultura política del nacionalismo vasco y los referentes europeos". In *XI Congreso de Estudios Vascos.* Donostia: Eusko Ikaskuntza. Also in: http://www.euskomedia.org/PDFAnlt/congresos/11/11215223.pdf
———.1978. *Ideologías del nacionalismo vasco, 1876-1937: de los euskáricos a Jagi jagi.* Donostia: Haranburu.
ESTÉVEZ, Xosé. 2009. *Galeuzca, la rebelión de la periferia. (1923-1998).* Madrid: Cyan Ed.
ESTORNÉS, Idoia. 2013. *Cómo pudo pasarnos esto. Crónica de una chica de los 60.* Donotia: Erein.
ESTRUCH TOBELLA, Joan. 2000. *Historia oculta del PCE.* Madrid: Temas de Hoy;
———. 1982. *El PCE en la clandestinidad.* Madrid: Siglo XXI.
EUSKO JAURLARITZAREN ARGITALPEN SERBITZUAK- SERVICIO CENTRAL DE PUBLICACIONES DEL GOBIERNO VASCO. 1983. *Euskal Batzar Orokorra. Congreso Mundial Vasco. 25 aniversario.* Bilbao.
ETXEBARRIETA ORTIZ, José Antonio. 1999. *Los vientos favorable. Euskal Herria 1839-1959.* Tafalla: Txalaparta.
FERNÁNDEZ SOLDEVILLA, Gaizka. 2016. *La voluntad del "gudari" : Génesis y metástasis de la violencia de ETA.* Madrid : Tecnos.
———. 2015. "De Aberri a ETA, pasando por Venezuela. Rupturas y continuidades en el nacionalismo vasco radical (1921-1977). In *Bulletin d'historie contemporaine de l'Espagne.* No. 51, pp. 259-264.
———. 2009. "Ellos y nosotros. La cumbre de Chiberta y otros intentos de crear un frente abertzale en la transición". *Historia del presente*, 13, 2009/1 II epoca, pp. 97-114
———. 2007. "El nacionalismo vasco radical ante la transición española". *Historia Contemporánea* 35, 817-844.

FLYNN, Barry. 2009. *Soldiers of folly: The IRA Border campaign*. Cork: The Collins Press.
FURIÓ Antoni; ROMERO, Juan. 2015. *Historia de las Españas. Una aproximación crítica*. València: Tirant Humanidades.
GARDE-ETAYO Mª Luisa. 2012. "ELA en 1947: de la esperanza a la represión", in *Memoria y civilización* , 15: 211-227.
GARMENDIA, José Mari. 1979. *Historia de ETA*. Donosti: L.Haramburu Editor. Vol.I . p. 167
GARRIDO YEROBI, Iñaki; LEKOUNA ILUNDAIN, Aitziber. 2006. *Las raíces del árbol en el exilio. Las biografías de los consejeros del primer gobierno de Esukadi*. Oñati: Instituto Vasco de Administración pública.
GELMAN, Irwin. 1973. *Roosevelt and Batista: good neighbor diplomacy in Cuba, 1933-1945*. Alburquerque: University of New Mexico Press
GENOVESE, Eugene D. 1979. *From Rebellion to Revolution: Afro-American slave revolts in the making of the modern world.* Baton Rouge: Louisiana State University Press
GHOSH, Devleena. 2008. "Coda. Eleven stars over the last moments of Andalusia." pp.277-289. In ALLATSON, Paul; Mc. CORMACK, Jo. (Eds.) *Exile cultures, misplaced identities*.(Critical Studies. Vol. 30). Amsterdam- New York: Rodopi Editions.
GIACOPUZZI, Giovanni. 1997. *ETApm. El otro camino*. Tafalla: Txalaparta.
GLONDYS, Olga. 2012. *La guerra fría cultural y el exilio republicano español*. Madrid: Consejo Superior de Investigaciones Científicas.
GOIGOGANA, Iñaki; IRUJO, Xabier; LEGARRETA, Josu. 2007. *Un nuevo 31. Ideología y estrategia del gobierno de Euzkadi durante la Segunda Guerra Mundial a través de la correspondencia de José Antonio Aguirre y Manuel Irujo*. Bilbao: Sabino Arana Fundazioa.
GOIOGANA, Iñaki. 2009. "Antón Irala y la primera delegación del Gobierno vasco en los Estados Unidos" in *Hermes* 31.
GONZÁLEZ MADRID, Damián-Alberto. (Ed.). 2008. *El franquismo y la transición en España: desmitificación y reconstrucción de la memoria de una época*. Madrid: Libros de la Catarata.
GORKIN, Julián. 2001. *Contra el Stalinismo*. Barcelona: Laertes.
———. 1975. *El Revolucionario Profesional: Testimonio de un hombre de acción*. Barcelona: Aymà.
———. 1974. *El proceso de Moscú en Barcelona: El sacrificio de Andrés Nin*. Barcelona: Aymà.
GREENFELD, Liah. 2016. *Advanced introduction of Nationalism*. Northampton: Edward Elgar.
———. 2005. "Nationalism and the mind" in *Nations and Nationalism*, 11 (3). pp. 325-342.

———. 1993. *Nationalism. Five roads to modernity*. Cambridge: Harvard university Press.
Gudaris y rehenes de Franco. (1936-1943). Diarios de José Antonio Mendizábal, José Luís Lasa y Fernando Aguirre. Irún: Alberdania
GÜELL AMPUERO, Casilda. 2006. *The Failure of Catalanist opposition to Franco: 1939-1950*. Madrid: Consejo Superior de Investigaciones científicas.
GURRUCHAGA, Ander. 1985. *El código nacionalista vasco durante el franquismo*. Barcelona: Anthropos Editorial
———. 1985. "La persistencia del nacionalismo periférico". *Revista Internacional De Sociología, 43* (4), 551. Retrieved from https://search-proquest-com.sire.ub.edu/docview/1299276530?accountid=15293 .
GÜELL AMPUERO, Casilda. 2006. *The Failure of Catalanist opposition to Franco: 1939-1950*. Madrid: Consejo Superior de Investigaciones científicas.
GUIBERNAU, Montserrat. 1999. *Nacions sense estat*. Barcelona: Columna edicions.
———. 1998. *Los nacionalismos*. Barcelona : Ariel.
HALIMI, Gisèle. 1971. *Le procès de Burgos*. París: Gallimard.
HÓRDAGO (Ed.). 1979. *Documentos Y (18 volums)*. Donostia: Lur Ed. Vols 1-12.
———. 1978. Burgos: *Juicio a un pueblo*. Donostia: Lur. Ed.
IBARRA, Pedro. 1987. *La Evolución estratégica de ETA. (1963-1987)*. Donostia: Kriselu
IBARZÁBAL, Eugenio. 1980. "José Antonio Ayestarán y la historia de ELA-STV" in *Muga*, no.3, 1980.
———. 1978. *50 años de nacionalismo vasco (1928-1978) a través de sus protagonistas*. San Sebastián: Ediciones Vascas.
INTXAUSTI, Joseba. *Euskera. La lengua de los vascos*. Donostia: Elkar, 1992.
IRUJO, Manuel. 1984. *Desde el partido nacionalista vasco*. Bilbao: Idatz Ekintza.
———. 1981. *Escritos en Alderdi* (vols. I-II). Bilbao: Partido Nacionalista Vasco.
———. 1958. *La comunidad occidental europea y los vascos*. VII Congreso de Estudios Vascos. Biarritz. Also in : http://www.euskomedia.org/PDFAnlt/congresos/07/07259281.pdf
IRUJO, Xabier. 2012. *Expelled from motherland. The government of President José Antonio Aguirre on exile, 1937-1960*. Reno: Center for Basque studies. University of Nevada.
———. 2008. "Euskal erebestea eta erbesteak" in *Gurengandik: Revista del Centro de estudios Arturo Campion*, 4, May 2008: 66-100.
JARDÍ, Enric. 1983. *El pensament de Prat de la Riba*. Barcelona: Alpha Ed.
JÁUREGUI BERECIARTU, Gurutz. 1981. *Ideología y estrategia política de ETA. Análisis de su evolución entre 1959 y 1968*. Madrid: Siglo XXI.

JIMÉNEZ ABERASTURI, Juan Carlos. 2009. *Al servicio del extranjero: historia del servicio vasco de información. De la Guerra Civil al exilio. (1936-1943)*. Boadilla del Monte: Antonio Machado Libros.

———. 1999. *De la derrota a la esperanza : políticas vascas durante la segunda Guerra mundial. (1937-1947)*. Oñati: Instituto vasco de administración pública.

———. 1994. *Catálogo del Archivo de Irujo: Guerra y exilio. 1936-1981*. San Sebastián : Eusko Ikaskuntza.

———. 1991. *Los Vascos en la Segunda Guerra Mundial. El Consejo Nacional vasco (1940-1944). Recopilación documental*. San Sebastián: Cuadernos del Centro de Documentación de Historia contemporánea del País Vasco.

JIMÉNEZ ABERASTURI, Juan Carlos; SAN SEBASTIÁN, Koldo. (Ed.) 1991. *La huelga general del 1º de Mayo de 1947*. (artículos y documentos). Donostia: Eusko Ikaskuntza

JUDT, Tony. 2006. *Postguerra. Una historia de Europa desde 1945*. Madrid: Taurus.

KAISER, Wolfram. 2007. *Christian Democracy and the origins of European Union*. Cambridge: Cambridge University press.

KENNEDY, Robert F. 1968. *Thirteen days. A Memoir of the Cuban Missile Crisis*. New York: W.W. Norton & Company.

KRAUZE, Enrique. 2011. *Redentores. Ideas y poder en América latina*. Barcelona: Debate.

KRUTWIG, Federico. 2014. *Años de peregrinación y lucha*. Tafalla: Txalaparta.

LA PORTE, María Teresa. 1992. *La política europea del régimen de Franco : 1957-1962*. Pamplona : EUNSA.

LARRONDE, Jean-Claude. 1997. *Exil et solidarité: La ligue Internationale des amis des basques*. Villefranche: Bidasoa.

LISBONA, José Antonio. 2002. *España – Israel. Historia de unas relaciones secretas*. Madrid: Temas de Hoy.

LÓPEZ ADÁN, Emilio "Beltza." 1977. *El nacionalismo vasco en el exilio, 1937-1960*. Editorial Txertoa: San Sebastián.

LORENZO ESPINOSA, José María. 1994. *Txabi Etxebarrieta: Armado de palabra y obra*. Tafalla: Txalaparta.

MADARIETA, Asier. 2007. "El último grito de unidad en el exilio. El Congreso Mundial Vasco de 1956". pp.123-157 in AGUIRREAZKUENAGA, Joseba; SOBREQUÉS, Jaume. (Eds.). *Eusko Jaurlaritza eta Catalunyako Generalitatea: Erbestetik Parlamentuen eraketara arte (1939-1980)*. Oñati: Instituto Vasco de Administración Pública.

MARTÍNEZ RUEDA, Fernando. 2016. "Telefosro Monzón, del nacionalismo aranista a Herri Batasuna: Las claves de una evolución". *Revista de estudios políticos*, 174, 267-297.

MCKINLEY, MICHAEL. 1991. "Of «Alien influences»: Accounting and discounting for the international contacts of the Provisional Irish Republican army". *Conflict Quarterly*, Vol 11, No 3.

MEES, Ludger. 2007. *El profeta pragmático. Aguirre, el primer lehendakari. (1939-1960)*. Irún: Alberdania

MIRALLES, Jaime. 1996. "La acción política de Unión Española". pp.133-140. In FONTÁN, Antonio (Dir.). *Los monárquicos y el régimen de Franco*. Madrid: Universidad Complutense

MORALES, Mercè, and SOBREQUÉS I CALLICÓ, Jaume. 2008. *La Generalitat a l'exili*. Barcelona : Ara Llibres.

MORALES, Mercè, and SOBREQUÉS I CALLICÓ, Jaume. 2008. *La Generalitat de Josep Irla i l'exili Polític Català*. Barcelona : Base.

MORÁN, Gregorio. 2003. *Los españoles que dejaron de serlo*. Barcelona: Editorial Planeta.

———. 1986. *Miseria y grandeza del partido comunista de España. 1939-1985*. Barcelona: Editorial Planeta.

MORENTE VALERO, Francisco. 2006. *Dionisio Ridruejo: del fascismo al antifranquismo*. Madrid: Síntesis.

MOTA ZURDO, David. 2015. "A Orillas Del Potomac. Pedro Beitia y las labores de lobbying de la Delegación del Gobierno vasco en Washington DC (1958-1963)." *Intus-Legere Historia* 9 (1): 89–113.

———. 2016. *Un Sueño Americano. El Gobierno vasco en el exilio y Estados Unidos (1937-1979)*. Vitoria-Gasteiz-Gasteiz : Instituto vasco de administración pública.

MOVIMIENTO POR LA AUTODETERMINACIÓN Y LA INDEPENDENCIA DEL ARCHIPIÉLAGO CANARIO. 1970. *El Nacionalismo revolucionario de Canarias: La "crisis" colonial de Madrid ; Fase actual de nuestra lucha nacional y revolucionaria*. Alger.

NÚÑEZ SEIXAS, Xose M. 2007. "Los nacionalistas vascos durante la Guerra civil (1936-1939): Una cultura de guerra diferente" in *Historia contemporánea*. Vol. 35. pp.559-599

———. 1995. "Relaciones exteriores del nacionalismo vasco. (1895-1960)" in DE PABLO, Santiago (Ed.) *Los nacionalistas. Historia del nacionalismo vasco. 1876-1960*. Gasteiz: Fundación Sancho el Sabio. pp.381-417.

———. 1995. "¿Protodiplomacia exterior o ilusiones ópticas? El nacionalismo vasco en el contexto internacional y el congreso de nacionalidades europeas (1914-1937)" in *Cuadernos de sección*. Historia-Geografía 23. Donostia: Eusko-Ikaskuntza. pp.243-275

———. 1992. "El mito de Irlanda: la influencia del nacionalismo irlandés en los nacionalismos gallego y vasco (1880-1936)" in *Historia 16*. No.199. pp.32-44.

NYE, Joseph. 2004. *Soft power.* New York: Public Affairs.

———. 1990. *Bound to lead. The Changing Nature of American Power.* New York: Basic books.

ODRIOZOLA IRIZAR, Onintza. 2016. *Erakunde bat baino gehiago: ETA herri mugimendu gisa (1958-1968).* UPV-EHU.

ORDAZ ROMAY, Mª Ángeles. 1995. "La delegación vasca en Nueva York, una década bajo el punto de mira del FBI (1938-1947)" in *Estudios de historia social y económica de América.* Num.12. pp.179-198;

PABLO CONTRERAS, Santiago de. 2015. *La patria soñada. Historia del nacionalismo vasco desde su origen hasta la actualidad.* Madrid : Editorial Biblioteca nueva.

———.2002. "Manuel Irujo: Un nacionalista vasco en la Transición democrática. (1975-1981). *Vasconia*, 32, pp. 169-184.

PABLO CONTRERAS, Santiago de (Ed.) 1995. *Los nacionalistas. Historia del nacionalismo vasco. 1876-1960.* Vitoria-Gasteiz: Fundación Sancho el Sabio.

PABLO CONTRERAS, Santiago de; MEES, Ludger and RODRÍGUEZ RANZ, José Antonio. 2001. *El Péndulo Patriótico : Historia del Partido nacionalista vasco.* Barcelona : Crítica

PARTIDO COMUNISTA DE ESPAÑA. 1958. *La lucha de clases y la política de reconciliación nacional.* Madrid: PCE.

———.1956. *Declaración del Partido Comunista de España: por la reconciliación nacional por una solución democrática y pacífica del problema español.* Publishing place unkown: PCE.

PÉREZ-AGOTE, Alfonso. 2006. *The social roots of Basque nationalism.* Reno: University of Nevada Press.

PLUTARCH. 1968 (2nd ed) *Plutarch's Moralia / with an English translation by Frank Cole Babbitt, [W.C. Helmbold, Phillip H. de Lacy ... [et al.]].* Cambridge: Harvard University Press. Vol. 7

PUIG, Lluís Maria de. 1999. *Gironella, la izquierda europeísta.* Madrid: Fundación Españoles en el mundo.

RENOBALES, Eduardo. 2010. *Jagi-Jagi: historia del independentismo vasco.* Bilbao: Ahaztuak 1936-1977.

ROMERO SAMPER, Milagrosa. 2005. *La oposición durante el franquismo. El exilio republicano.* Madrid: Ediciones Encuentro.

RODRÍGUEZ RANZ, José Antonio. 2002 "Manuel de Irujo. Lealtad crítica. (1960-1975)". *Vasconia*, 32, pp. 155-168.

RUBIRALTA CASAS, Fermí. 2003. "Els intel·lectuals en la conformació del nou nacionalisme radical gallec, català i basc durant la dècada de 1960". *Revista del Centre de Lectura de Reus.* No. 8.

SAGARRA, Pablo et Alt. 2015. *Gudaris: Euzko Gudarostea (Ejército Vasco) durante la Guerra Civil. (1936-1937).* Madrid: Esfera de los libros.

SALABERRI, Kepa. 1971. *Sumarísimo 31-69. El proceso de Euskadi en Burgos*. Paris: Ruedo Ibérico.

SÁNCHEZ CERVELLÓ, Josep. 2011. *La Segunda República en el exilio (1939-1977)*. Barcelona: Editorial Planeta

SÁNCHEZ SOLER, Mariano. 2010. *La transición sangrienta. Una historia violenta del proceso democrático en España (1975-1983)*. Barcelona: Península

SAN SEBASTIÁN, Koldo. 2015. *Basques in the United States : A biographical encyclopedia of first-generation immigrants*. Reno: Center for Basque studies- University of Nevada.

———. 2014. *El exilio vasco en América*. 1st ed. Vitoria-Gasteiz-Gasteiz : Servicio Central de publicaciones del Gobierno vasco.

———. 1991. *The Basque archives: Vascos en Estados Unidos (1938-1947)*. San Sebastián : Txertoa

———. 1989. "Prensa vasca en América (I). Los medios de comunicación en Venezuela ". In *Muga*, 70.

———. 1988. *El exilio vasco en América, 1936-1946 : La acción del Gobierno : Política, organización, propaganda, economía, cultura, diplomacia*. San Sebastián : Txertoa.

———.1981. "En torno a dos obras de F.J. Landáburu" in *Muga*, 12, 108-112.

SARRIONANDIA, Joseba. *Hilda dago poesía? ¿La poesía está muerta?* Iruña: Pamiela.

SARTRE, Jean Paul. 1973. *El procès de Burgos*. Perpinyà: Edicions E.C.T.

SATRÚSTEGUI, Joaquín [Et.Alt.]. 1993. *Cuando la transición se hizo possible: El Contubernio de Munich*. Madrid: Tecnos.

SEBASTIÁN GARCÍA, Lorenzo. 1995. "«Euzkadi Mendigoxale batza» durante la guerra civil española (1936-1939)" in *Cuadernos de sección. Historia-Geografía* 23. pp.335-357. Donostia: Eusko Ikaskuntza

SERVICIO CENTRAL DE PUBLICACIONES DEL GOBIERNO VASCO. 2010. *Delegaciones de Euzkadi (1936-1975)*. Vitoria-Gasteiz-Gasteiz;

SORULAZE, Andoni de. 1980. "Delegacions vascas en América y quiénes han sido los delegados del Gobierno Vasco en 40 años" a *Euzkadi*, nº 206.

———.1980. "Delegaciones de Euzkadi en una de sus épocas y sus delegados", *Euzkadi*, nº 209.

STONOR SAUNDERS, Frances. 2001. *La CIA y la Guerra fría cultural*. Madrid: Debate.

SULLIVAN, John. 1988. *ETA and Basque nationalism. The fight for Euskadi. 1890-1986*. New York: Routledge.

TAUBMAN, William. 2004. *Khrushchev: The Man and his Era*. New York: W.W. Norton & Company.

TORRE, Joseba de la; SANZ LAFUENTE, Gloria. (Eds.) 2008. *Migraciones y coyuntura económica del franquismo a la democracia*. Zaragoza: Prensas

universitarias de Zaragoza.
TOTORICAGÜENA EGURROLA, Gloria. 2005. *Basque migration and diaspora. Transnational Identity*. Reno: Center for the Basque studies.

———.2003. *The Basques of New York*. Vitoria-Gasteiz-Gasteiz: Servicio central de publicacions del gobierno vasco.

TXALAPARTA. (Eds.). 1994. *Euskadi eta Askatasuna = Euskal Herria y la libertad*. Tafalla: Txalaparta. 9 Vols.

UGALDE ZUBIRI, Alexander. 2008. *Xabier de Landaburu : bizitza osoa Euskal Herriaren kausarentzat : 1907-1963 =Xabier de Landaburu : una vida dedicada a la causa del pueblo vasco : 1907-1963*. Bilbao: Sabino Arana Fundazioa

———.2007. "Presencia histórica pública y privada vasca en Europa" in *Eurobask* no.12, July 2007, pp.94-95

———.2004. "Nacionalismo vasco y relaciones internacionales", in *Hermes*, Bilbao, Fundación Sabino Arana, no11, 2004, pp.34-39

———.2001. *El Consejo Vasco del Movimiento Europeo (1951-2001). La aportación vasca al federalismo Europeo/ Europako Mugimenduaren Euskal Kontselua (1951-2001)*. Vitoria-Gasteiz: Consejo Vasco del Movimiento Europeo/ Europako Mugimenduaren Euskal Kontseilua.

———.1996. *La acción exterior del nacionalismo vasco (1890-1939) : Historia, pensamiento y relaciones internacionales,* Bilbao, Instituto Vasco de Administración pública, 1996

UNANUE, Manuel de Dios. 1999
El Caso Galíndez: los vascos en los Servicios de Inteligencia de EEUU. Tafalla: Txalaparta.

URLA, Jaqueline. 1993. "Cultural Politics in an Age of Statistics: Numbers, Nations, and the Making of Basque Identity." In *American ethnologist*. Vol. 20, No. 4. pp. 818-843.

WARNER, Michael. "Origins of the Congress for Cultural Freedom, 1949-50", in *Studies in Intelligence*, 38, 1995.

ZANCA, José. 2013. *Cristianos antifascistas, conflictos en la cultura católica Argentina*. Buenos Aires: Siglo Veintiuno editors

ZULAIKA, Joseba. 2014. *That Bilbao old moon. The passion and resurrection of a city.* Reno: Center for Basque studies.

———. 1982. *Basque violence. Metaphor and Sacrament*. Reno: University of Nevada Press.

Archives

Biblioteca de Catalunya. Barcelona.
Center for Basque Studies. Reno, NV. USA.
CRAI Pavelló de la República. Barcelona.
Euskadiko Artxibo Historikoa Bilbao, Bizkaia.
Lazkaoko Beneditarren Fundazioa. Lazkao, Gipuzkoa.
National Archives and Records Administration. Washington & College Park, MD. USA.
New York Public Library. New York, NY. USA.
Sabino Arana Fundazioa. Bilbao, Bizkaia.

Internet Sources

http://www.euskomedia.org/ Contains more than 20.000 digitalized documents from the Manuel Irujo's archive. Besides, it contains the useful Basque encyclopedia, *Auñamendi*.
http://urazandi.euskaletxeak.net/default.html Digital archive of Basque publications in exile.
http://www.lehendakariagirre.eu/ Website on Lehendakari Aguirre. Contains speeches, communications, articles, books, etc. by Lehendakari Aguirre.
http://ope.euskaletxeak.net/ Website with the bulletins of the *Oficina de Prensa de Euzkadi*.
https://www.boe.es/diario_boe/ Website of the *Boletín Oficial del Esta*do.

Newspapers and Magazines

Alderdi (1947-1974)
Cuadernos
Euzko Deya
Gudari
La Vanguardia
Tximistak
Hautsi
Kemen
Zutik

End Notes

1. AGUIRRE, José Antonio. 1981. Obras completas. Donostia: Sendoa. Vol.II., pp. 575.
2. KOLAKOWSKI, Leszek. 1990. Modernity on Endless Trial. Chicago: University of Chicago Press. p. 55.
3. GREENFELD, Liah. 1993. Nationalism. Five roads to modernity. Cambridge: Harvard University Press. p. 31
4. MOTA ZURDO, David. 2016. Un Sueño Americano. El Gobierno vasco en el exilio y Estados Unidos (1937- 1979). Vitoria-Gasteiz : Instituto vasco de administración pública., p. 193.
5. AGUIRRE, José Antonio, op. cit., pp. 565-575
6. The "Bayonne's pact" was an agreement by the Basque political and union forces (formed before the Spanish Civil War) signed in Bayonne on March 31st 1945 ratifying the legitimacy of the Basque government, following the 1936 Basque Statute of Autonomy. MORÁN, Gregorio, 2003, Los españoles que dejaron de serlo.Barcelona: Editorial Planeta., pp. 256-257; MOTA ZURDO, David, 2016, op. cit., p. 193.
7. DE PABLO CONTRERAS, Santiago. 2015. La patria soñada. Historia del nacionalismo vasco desde su origen hasta la actualidad. Madrid : Editorial Biblioteca nueva., p. 314. LÓPEZ ADÁN, Emilio. 1977. El gobierno vasco en el exilio. 1937- 1960. Donostia: Txertoa Ed., pp. 21-22. MOTA ZURDO, David, 2016, op. cit., pp. 201-202.
8. Letter from Manuel Irujo to Jesús María Leizaola, December 28th, 1944, London. GOIGOGANA, Iñaki; IRUJO, Xabier; LEGARRETA, Josu. 2007. Un nuevo 31. Ideología y estrategia del gobierno de Euzkadi durante la Segunda Guerra Mundial a través de la correspondencia de José Antonio Aguirre y Manuel Irujo. Bilbao: Sabino Arana Fundazioa., p. 781
9. Letter from José Antonio Aguirre to Manuel Irujo. September 17th, 1945. New York, ibid., p. 826.
10. "Galeuzca" was the name given to the several nationalist agreements and the nationalist movement between Galicia, Euskadi and Catalonia beginning from 1923. ESTÉVEZ, Xosé. 2009. Galeuzca, la rebelión de la periferia. (1923-1998). Madrid: Cyan Ed. See the Declaration of Galeuzca principles, statutes and drafts on the Galeuzca project in GOIGOGANA, Iñaki; IRUJO, Xabier; LEGARRETA, Josu, op. cit., pp. 740-759.
11. GOIGOGANA, Iñaki; IRUJO, Xabier; LEGARRETA, Josu, op. cit., pp. 817-837.
12. Anton Irala was the founder and first delegate of the New York delegation of the Basque government from 1938 to 1949, when Jesús Galíndez replaced him. GOIOGANA, Iñaki. 2009. "Antón Irala y la primera delegación del Gobierno vasco en los Estados Unidos," in Hermes, 31, pp. 85-86.
13. AZURMENDI, José Félix. 2013. Vascos en la Guerra Fría. ¿Víctimas o cómplices? Gudaris en el juego de los espías. Donostia: Editorial Ttarttalo., pp. 43-45. MOTA ZURDO, David, 2016, op. cit., pp. 202-204.
14. Ibidem, p. 50.
15. GÜELL AMPUERO, Casilda. 2006. The Failure of Catalanist opposition to Franco: 1939-1950. Madrid: Consejo Superior de Investigaciones científicas., p. 164-165
16. United Nations' resolutions on Spain in 1946: http://www.un.org/en/ga/search/view_doc.asp?symbol=S/RES/10(1946); http://www.un.org/en/ga/search/view_doc.asp?symbol=S/RES/7(1946); http://www.un.org/en/ga/search/view_doc.asp?symbol=S/RES/4(1946).
17. Manifiesto a los españoles, Paris, February 23,1946. LÓPEZ ADÁN, Emilio, 1977, op. cit., pp. 54-55.
18. There are many different causes that might explain the decision of non-intervention, but authors consider the geostrategic situation of Spain, along with the "red scare,"

the fear of the advent of a new communist State, to have been the main cause. Despite the mistrust of the Truman administration regarding the Franco government, the danger of creating a new Soviet satellite on the western side of the newly-established "iron curtain" was decisive. AZURMENDI, José Félix, 2013, op. cit., pp. 51-53; DE PABLO CONTRERAS, Santiago, 2015, op. cit., pp. 314-316; MOTA ZURDO, David, 2016, op. cit., pp. 202-207. ROMERO SAMPER, Milagrosa. 2005. La oposición durante el franquismo. El exilio republicano. Madrid: Ediciones Encuentro, pp. 272-283.

19 Manuel Irujo was a member of the Spanish Republican government in exile twice: during José Giral's Government (August, 1945- February, 1947) and then in Rodolfo Llopis' Government (February-August 1947). During the first government, Irujo was a Minister without portfolio, and in the second, he occupied the post of Minister of Justice. During the Republican Government (1931-1936), Manuel Irujo was also a Minister without portfolio from September 1936 to May 1937, when he was appointed Minister of Justice until December 1937, at which date he resigns, yet continues again as Minister without portfolio until August 1938, when he abandons the government.

20 Rodolfo Llopis Ferrandiz was president of the Spanish Republican government in exile from February to August, 1947. SÁNCHEZ CERVELLÓ, Josep. 2011. La Segunda República en el exilio (1939-1977). Barcelona: Editorial Planeta, pp. 99-117 / 456.

21 DE PABLO CONTRERAS, Santiago, 2015, op. cit., p. 316; MEES, Ludger. 2006. El profeta pragmático. Aguirre, el primer lehendakari. (1939-1960). Irún: Alberdania, p. 139.

22 This great feat was all the more considerable given the Spanish nationalism of Martínez Barrio and his clear support to Lerroux's doctrines. MEES, Ludger, 2007, op. cit., pp. 135 and ff.

23 Lehendakari Aguirre's speech on the 11th anniversary of the Basque Government. October 1947. AGUIRRE, José Antonio, 1981, op. cit., Vol.II, p. 733.

24 MEES, Ludger, 2007, op. cit., p. 137.

25 It was probably due to that pragmatism, which Ludger Mees considers one of the main features of Aguirre's policies, that the Lehendakari probed the Monarchist option in order to assess the possibilities of success. With the objective of creating an alternative to the Franco regime, Aguirre contacted the monarchists several times in 1945 and 1946, although the members in the Basque Nationalist Party, especially Manuel Irujo, did not agree with and did not trust the Monarchist option. Ibidem, pp. 161-168.

26 Aguirre to Doroteo Ziaurritz, president of the Euskadi Buru Batzar (EBB), 1946, ibidem, p. 136.

27 Letter from Lizaso to Irujo, London, February 21st, 1947. Euskomedia, Irujo Fund, Signature J, Box, 34, File 3 http://www.euskomedia.org/PDFFondo/irujo/12422.pdf (Consulted on December 4th, 2016.)

28 Indalecio Prieto was a politician, member of the Spanish Socialist Party (PSOE), Minister in the governments of 1931 and 1936, and Minister of Defense during the Spanish Civil War. In 1946, Prieto became leader of the monarchist option when he struck conversations with Don Juan de Borbón in order to reach a provisional government, the nature of which was to be decided through a plebiscite. LÓPEZ ADÁN, Emilio, 1977, op. cit., p. 52.

29 CEDA: Confederación Española de Derechas Autónomas.

30 DE PABLO CONTRERAS, Santiago, 2015, op. cit., p. 316.

31 Telesforo Monzón was Minister of Governance and Security of the Basque government during the Spanish Civil War, and Minister of Culture during the exile. In the 1950's he decided to abandon the PNV, due to disagreements with the executive, but never filed the petition. Jesús Maria Leizaola was Minister of Justice and Culture of the Basque government, Vice-President during the Aguirre administration, and President of the Basque government since the death of President Aguirre and until the end of the exile in 1979. José María Lasarte organized the Basque secret services,

established relations with America and some European states, and was Minister of Governance (1946-1952) of the Basque government. More biographical information on the members of the Basque government can be found in: GARRIDO YEROBI, Iñaki; LEKOUNA ILUNDAIN, Aitziber, 2006, Las raíces del árbol en el exilio. Las biografías de los consejeros del primer gobierno de Esukadi. Oñati: Instituto Vasco de Administración pública. A comprehensive dictionary of the Basque Members of Parliament, in this case until 1939, is: AGIRREAZKUENAGA, Joseba (Ed.) [Et. Alt.], 2007, Diccionario biográfico de los parlamentarios de Vasconia. 1876-1939. 3 vols. Vitoria: Eusko Legebiltzarra

32 Words of Telesforo Monzón recorded in the document "Reunión entre Dionisio, Axpe, Víctor, Ángel, Barazar, Jon y Teles," 1948, DE PABLO CONTRERAS, Santiago, MEES, Ludger and RODRÍGUEZ RANZ, José Antonio, 1999, El Péndulo Patriótico: Historia del Partido nacionalista vasco. Barcelona: Crítica. Vol.2., p. 162.
33 Declarations of Manuel Irujo. Ibidem, p. 161.
34 MEES, Ludger, 2007, op. cit., p. 181.
35 Christmas and New Year's Eve speech by José Antonio Aguirre in 1947. AGUIRRE, José Antonio, 1981,
op. cit., p. 742. (Vol.II)
36 Ibidem.
37 The collaboration with the American Department of State regarding South America was done through Mr. Laurence Duggan, adviser on political relations at the Department of State. In his diary, President Aguirre wrote about the progress of the meetings starting in January 1942; and in Iñaki Goiogana's edition, we can read an extract of a memorandum by the Department of State where the collaboration is defined as: "proposal of help by Basques in other American republics to create an attitude more sympathetic to the democracies." The collaboration included economic funds to increase the distribution of Euzko Deya and for the establishment of a Basque information service that would control politics, economy, Church, consulates, embassies, Falangist centers or other centers, aristocratic circles, and the merchant navy, according to Aguirre's letter. The details of the project and Aguirre's impressions on it can be found, as aforementioned, in: AGUIRRE, José Antonio; GOIOGANA, Iñaki (Ed.), 2010, Diario, 1941-1942. Bilbao: Sabino Arana Fundazioa. Part of the speeches given during the tour were published in: AGUIRRE, José Antonio, 1944, Cinco conferencias pronunciadas en un viaje por América. Buenos Aires: Editorial Vasca Ekin. An analysis of the South American tour can be found in MOTA, David, 2016, op. cit., pp. 143-154.
38 AGUIRRE, José Antonio, 1981, op. cit., p. 747. (Vol.II)
39 MESS, Ludger, 2007, op. cit., p. 205.
40 Ley de Sucesión en la Jefatura del Estado: http://www.boe.es/datos/pdfs/BOE/1947/160/A03272-03273.pdf BOE.
41 http://www.boe.es/datos/pdfs/BOE/1947/160/A03272-03273.pdf
42 http://www.boe.es/datos/pdfs/BOE/1947/160/A03272-03273.pdf
43 DE PABLO CONTRERAS, Santiago, MEES, Ludger and RODRÍGUEZ RANZ, José Antonio, 1999, op. cit., pp. 165-168.
44 Joseba Rezola was Vice-President during the first Basque government and Head of the Basque resistance movement during the exile. Ramón de la Sota was a Basque industrialist and well-known Basque nationalist who supported the PNV and the Basque government in exile.
45 LÓPEZ ADÁN, Emilio, 1977, op. cit., pp. 129-132.
46 SAN SEBASTIÁN, Koldo, 1995, "El PNV durante el primer franquismo (1937-1953)," pp. 145-167, in DE PABLO, Santiago (Ed.). Los nacionalistas. Historia del nacionalismo vasco. 1876-1960. Vitoria-Gasteiz: Fundación Sancho el Sabio, p. 163.
47 Declaración política del Partido Nacionalista Vasco, EBB, 1949, AN, IRUJO-0071-C2.
48 DE PABLO CONTRERAS, Santiago, MEES, Ludger and RODRÍGUEZ RANZ, José Antonio, 1999, op. cit., p. 170.

49 DE BAETS, Antoon, 2011, "Plutarch's Thesis: The contribution of refugee historians to historical writing, 1945-2010," in In Defense of Learning, British Academy, p. 211.
50 "Muga," as well as being the Basque word for "border," is also an important concept in the symbolical universe of Basque nationalism.
51 LÓPEZ ADÁN, Emilio, 1977, op. cit., pp. 73-74.
52 "Ikurrina" is the oficial name of the Basque flag.
53 Section IV of the "Declaración Política del Partido Nacionalista Vasco," 1949, ibidem, pp. 131-132.
54 Although the pro-European Movement had begun to be organized some years before, as we will see in the next chapters, The Hague Conference held between 7th and 10th May, 1948, is seen as the boosting of the European Union process. ARRIETA ALBERDI, Leyre, 2007, Estación Europa. La política europeísta del PNV en el exilio (1945-1977). Madrid: Editorial Tecnos, pp. 66-70.
55 Section IV-c of the "Declaración Política del Partido Nacionalista Vasco," 1949, ibidem, pp. 132.
56 President Aguirre' speech in the 12th Anniversary of the Gernika bombing.
57 "Manifiesto de Trucios" published in Euzko Deya, Paris, July 4th, 1937.
58 "Bases para una situación transitoria vasca," July 22nd, 1949 in AN, EBB, 79-16.
59 DE PABLO CONTRERAS, Santiago, MEES, Ludger and RODRÍGUEZ RANZ, José Antonio, 1999, op. cit.,
pp. 171-177; MEES, Ludger, 2007, p. 207.
60 MEES, Ludger, 2007, op. cit., pp. 206-207; SAN SEBASTIÁN, Koldo. 1995, p. 164.
61 DE PABLO CONTRERAS, Santiago, MEES, Ludger and RODRÍGUEZ RANZ, José Antonio, 1999, op. cit., p. 172.
62 Declaración política del Partido Nacionalista Vasco, EBB, 1949, op. cit.
63 Letter from Manuel Irujo to Juan Ajuriaguerra, Paris, 11/10/1949, EI, IRUJO-38-Sig.J-228.
64 "El Estatuto vasco" by Manuel Irujo, in Euskomedia, Irujo Fund, Signature J, Box 52, File 2, 1953. http://www.euskomedia.org/PDFFondo/irujo/4350.pdf (consulted on December 10th, 2016).
65 "El signo de nuestra hora" by Manuel Irujo, published in Alderdi, n.24, March 1949, in IRUJO, Manuel, 1981, Escritos en Alderdi. Vol.I. Bilbao: Partido Nacionalista Vasco., p. 11-14.
66 Ibid.
67 "Las elecciones de Cerdeña y el Caballo de Troya (Mensaje de Sturzo)," Alderdi, n. 27, June 1949. Published in IRUJO, Manuel, 1981, op. cit., pp. 25-27.
68 Luigi Sturzo was an Italian Catholic priest and politician, considered one of the founders of Christian Democracy. He was forced into exile in 1924 due to the rise of fascism in Italy, first to London and ultimately to the USA, where he met President Aguirre at some meetings held by the "Catholic Association for International Peace" to promote an American Christian Democracy. Some of the meetings are described in Aguirre's diary: AGUIRRE, José Antonio; GOIOGANA, Iñaki (Ed.) 2010, op. cit. President Aguirre, José Ignacio de Lizaso and Alberto Onaindía exchanged letters on Christian Democracy and the Basque situation, published in: BOTTI, Alfonso, 2012, Luigi Sturzo e gli amici Spagnoli. Carteggi (1924, 1951). Modena: Soveria Mannelli, Rubbettino Editore. More on Luigi Sturzo and Christian Democracy: KAISER, Wolfram, 2007, Christian Democracy and the Origins of European Union. Cambridge: Cambridge University press; ZANCA, José, 2013, Cristianos antifascistas, conflictos en la cultura católica Argentina. Buenos Aires: Siglo Veintiuno Editores.
69 "Lo que vale una autonomía" (on the autonomous system of North Ireland), in Euskomedia, Irujo Fund, Signature J, Box 52, File 13.1952. http://www.euskomedia.org/fondo/225?idi=en (consulted on December 10th, 2016); "Gran Bretaña, Egipto y el Sudán," in Euskomedia, Irujo Fund, Signature J, Box 52, File 3. 1952. http://

www.euskomedia.org/PDFFondo/irujo/3175.pdf (consulted on December 10th, 2016); "El Estatuto de Autonomía de Túnez," in Alderdi, n. 99, June 1955. Published in IRUJO, Manuel, 1981, op. cit., pp. 237-240. Later on, Irujo will continue with his analysis of the Statutes and his comparisons with the Basque case with the examples of Kurdistan: "Los kurdos y nosotros," in Euskomedia, Irujo Fund, Signature J, Box 53, File 4B, 1966, http://www.euskomedia.org/PDFFondo/irujo/14756.pdf (consulted on December 10th, 2016), the Swiss and the Mizo: "Los jura y los mizo," in Euskomedia, Irujo Fund, Signature J, Box 53, File 4B, 1966, http://www.euskomedia.org/PDFFondo/irujo/14790.pdf (consulted on December 10th, 2016), or the case of Gibraltar: "El Estatuto de autonomía de Gibraltar," in Euskomedia, Irujo Fund, Signature J, Box 53, File 5B, 1969, http://www.euskomedia.org/PDFFondo/irujo/14637.pdf (consulted on December 10th, 2016).

70   MORAN, Gregorio, 2003, Los españoles que dejaron de serlo. Barcelona: Editorial Planeta, p. 255.
71   "Estatutos de autonomía en Italia" by Manuel Irujo, in Alderdi n.26, May 1949. Published in IRUJO, Manuel, 1981, op. cit., pp. 19-23.
72   "Gran Bretaña, Egipto y el Sudán," 1952, op. cit.
73   Irujo used to take part in some radio transmissions on Radio Euzkadi, and some of the aforementioned analyses are drafts for preparing the broadcasts.
74   Manuel Irujo was always a declared republican, he only defended the pacts with the monarchists when the situation forced him to do so for the sake of the Basques, although he understood that monarchies were incompatible with a democracy. Nevertheless, Irujo distinguished between the northern European and the British monarchies, as well as some others, such as the Eastern monarchies. In that regard, he considered the situation of the Kurdish and the Basques as similar: "The difference between monarchists and republicans for the Kurds, as for us, is the same: monarchists cannot be democrats, even if they proclaim it loudly and with music, because monarchists are interested in the royal crown and the people, today, are no longer interested in the royal crown or anything like it". Again, Irujo talked about the possibilities of full sovereignty made available by the Statutes of Autonomy: "The Kurds, like us, when faced with the current reality, opposed to the creation of new borders and new customs, and new armies and new homes and state struggles, instead of proclaiming independence, they proclaimed autonomy, which gives them the right to dispose of their country, to govern it, to teach their language, to maintain their customs, to keep alive their civil genius, to take care of public order, to apply social laws, to build their roads, to have their building construction policy, and, in a word, to have all the rights of government of a national character, leaving the rights of a purely state character to the rulers of Iraq: international representation, foreign trade and military defence." In "Los kurdos y nosotros," 1966, op. cit.
75   "Las elecciones de Cerdeña y el Caballo de Troya (Mensaje de Sturzo)," Alderdi, n.27, June 1949. Published in IRUJO, Manuel, 1981, op. cit., p. 27.
76   95 On Basque migrations, there are several books written by Navarre historian José Manuel Azcona Pastor: 2011, El ámbito historiográfico y metodológico de la emigración vasca y navarra hacia América. Vitoria: Servicio central de publicaciones del gobierno vasco; 2004, Basque Emigration to Latin America (s. XVI-XX), Reno: University of Nevada; 1992, Los paraísos posibles, historia de la emigración vasca a Argentina y Uruguay en el siglo XIX, Bilbao: Universidad de Deusto. A broader analysis can be found in AZCONA PASTOR, José Manuel (Ed.) 2015, Identidad y estructura de la emigración vasca y navarra hacia Iberoamérica (siglos XVI-XXI). Redes sociales y desarrollo socioeconómico. Pamplona: Thomson Reuters Aranzadi. A complete analysis of the Basque diaspora and identity is found in a work by Gloria Totoricagüena: 2005, The Basque Diaspora: Migration and Transnational Identity. Reno: Center for Basque Studies. University of Nevada.
77   On LIAB, see: IRUJO, Xabier. 2012. Expelled from motherland. The government of President José Antonio Aguirre on exile, 1937-1960. Reno: Center for Basque studies. University of Nevada., pp. 70 and ff.; LARRONDE, Jean-Claude, 1997, Exil et

solidarité: La ligue Internationale des amis des basques. Villefranche: Bidasoa.
78 In fact, according to some references, we can talk about "Basque delegations" even before the constitution of the Basque government, for example the offices that were opened in Mexico in 1936, mainly for commercial purposes, but which later on, and under the supervision of the Basque government, would become an important base for the Basques in America. On the Basque delegations, see: SERVICIO CENTRAL DE PUBLICACIONES DEL GOBIERNO VASCO, 2010, Delegaciones de Euskadi (1936-1975). Vitoria-Gasteiz; SAN SEBASTIÁN, Koldo, 2014, El exilio vasco en América. 1st ed. Vitoria-Gasteiz: Servicio Central de publicaciones del Gobierno vasco., pp. 97-123; SORULAZE, Andoni de, 1980. "Delegaciones vascas en América y quiénes han sido los delegados del Gobierno Vasco en 40 años," in Euzkadi, no. 206; 1980, "Delegaciones de Euzkadi en una de sus épocas y sus delegados," Euzkadi, no. 209.
79 CASTRO RUANO, José Luis de; UGALDE ZUBIRI, Alexander, 2004, La acción exterior del País Vasco (1980-2003). Oñati: Instituto Vasco de Administración Pública., p. 50.
80 SAN SEBASTIÁN, Koldo, 2014, op. cit., pp. 125-150.
81 According to Ramon Sota, whose father was one of the Basque nationalists who used to work for the USA through the Basque services, the funds received from the American government were used by the Basque government to spread Basque nationalism among the Basque communities in America, who were not particularly nationalist. Statements made in an interview carried out in November 2016. On the "Basque services" and the activities developed in America, see: UNANUE, Manuel de Dios, 1999, El Caso Galíndez: los vascos en los Servicios de Inteligencia de EEUU. Tafalla: Txalaparta; AZURMENDI, José Felix, 2013, op. cit., pp. 61 and ff.; JIMÉNEZ DE ABERASTURI, Juan Carlos, 1999, De la derrota a la esperanza. Políticas vascas durante la II Guerra Mundial (1937-1947), Bilbao: Instituto Vasco de Administración Pública. pp. 423-500; JIMÉNEZ DE ABERASTURI, Juan Carlos, 2009, "Al servicio del extranjero: historia del servicio secreto vasco de información de la Guerra Civil al exilio. (1936-1943)." Boadilla del Monte: Antonio Machado Libros; CASTRO RUANO, José Luis de; UGALDE ZUBIRI, Alexander, 2004, op. cit., pp. 56 and ff.; IRUJO, Xabier, 2014, op. cit., pp. 123-126; SAN SEBASTIÁN, Koldo, 2014, op. cit., pp. 319-349.
82 According to the information revealed at an EBB meeting in 1937, the Basque diaspora was divided between "carlistas y nacionalistas." MOTA, David, 2016, op. cit., p. 48.
83 Jon Bilbao fought with the Basque army during the Spanish Civil War and was named sub delegate of the Basque government in Boise, Idaho, after being one of the first members of the Basque delegation in New York. In 1944 he returned to New York and collaborated with several Basque publications. For more on Jon Bilbao, see: http://www.euskomedia.org/aunamendi/14146 (consulted on December 15th, 2016).
84 Jon Bilbao to José Antonio Aguirre, La Habana, February 23rd, 1954, BA CBS, Jon Bilbao Archive, BSQAP 0177 1939-1958.
85 Ibid.
86 SAN SEBASTIÁN, Koldo. 1991. The Basque archives: Vascos en Estados Unidos (1938-1947). San Sebastián: Txertoa, p. 55; IRUJO, Xabier, 2012, op. cit., p. 122
87 IRUJO, Xabier, op. cit., pp. 123-126.
88 AGUIRRE, José Antonio; GOIOGANA, Iñaki (Ed.), 2010, op. cit., p.106
89 MOTA, David, op. cit., p. 56.
90 SAN SEBASTIÁN, Koldo, 1988, op. cit., pp. 392-395; IRUJO, Xabier, 2014, op. cit., pp. 123-126. Five of the conferences held by Aguirre during his trips in 1942 were published in: AGUIRRE, José Antonio, 1944, Cinco conferencias pronunciadas en un viaje por América. Buenos Aires: Ekin.
91 David Mota also refers to the need of finding funds as one of the objectives of the presence of Basque nationalists in America, and, again, the dichotomy between the

exiles and the emigrants with regard to the Basque national sentiment posed an issue in achieving their goals. MOTA, David, 2016, op. cit., p. 50.
92 Manuel Ynchausti had been responsible for getting contacts for the Basque government in different countries and was in charge of obtaining the passport and visa to the USA for President Aguirre. Ynchausti was not only one of the most loyal friends of the Lehendakari, but also his financial supporter, sometimes through personal loans transferred either to Aguirre or to the PNV, or through the payment of Aguirre's stipend at Columbia University—a detail that Aguirre never found out. TOTORICAGÜENA, Gloria, 2003, The Basques of New York. Vitoria-Gasteiz-Gasteiz: Servicio central de publicacions del gobierno vasco.
93 On the Basque delegation in New York: MOTA, David, 2016, op. cit., pp. 47-65 and 87-100; ORDAZ ROMAY, Mª Ángeles. 1995. "La delegación vasca en Nueva York, una década bajo el punto de mira del FBI (1938-1947)," in Estudios de historia social y económica de América, No. 12., pp. 179-198; SAN SEBASTIÁN, Koldo, 2014, op. cit., pp. 212-215; ANASAGASTI, Iñaki and ERKOREKA, Josu, 2013, A basque patriot in New York : Jose Luis de la Lombana y Foncea and the Euskadi delegation in the United States . Reno: Center for Basque Studies.
94 "Hegoalde" is a word in Basque meaning "South of the country" and is used by Basque nationalists to refer to the Basque Country which belongs politically to Spain.
95 Meeting of EBB with President Aguirre, October 2nd, 1950. In MEES, Ludger, op. cit., pp. 309-310.
96 Jesús Galíndez was one of the most well-known members of the Basque government in America, notoriously because of his ultimate disappearance under unclear circumstances. We will look at his case later on in this chapter.
97 SAN SEBASTIÁN, Koldo, op. cit., pp. 213-219.
98 MEES, Ludger, 2006, op. cit., pp. 264-283.
99 Ibid., p. 275.
100 In a 1950 UN session the 1946 Tripartite Note was formally revoked and some western ambassadors (included the American) were resent to Spain. Ibid., p. 272.
101 Jesús Galíndez warned President Aguirre in 1951 about the possibility of future economic agreements between Spain and the USA, and his suspicions turned out real when the American administration promoted two Franco supporters: John Foster Dulles, appointed new Secretary of State, who had worked as attorney of the Banco de España during the Spanish Civil War; and the new American Ambassador in Madrid, James Clement Dunn, who was one of the supporters of American non-intervention policies. Ibid., p. 290 and p. 293.
102 The Basque government signed a joint manifest entitled "A los vascos de América," published in Euzkadi, 49, Caracas, July 1947. Also in http://www.lehendakariagirre.eu/pdf/Mensajes/11_01.pdf (Consulted on December 25th, 2016.)
103 President Aguirre's declaration, in JIMÉNEZ ABERASTURI, Juan Carlos; SAN SEBASTIÁN, Koldo (Ed.), 1991. La huelga general del 1º de mayo de 1947 (articles and documents). Donostia: Eusko Ikaskuntza. He also showed his support in a declaration published in OPE, 12-5-1947, p. 1 under the title "Un mensaje del Presidente Aguirre al pueblo vasco."
104 The causes and effects of the 1947 strike have been widely studied; a good example of this is the aforementioned collection of documents compiled in La huelga general del 1º de Mayo, or the interesting article by Maria Luisa Garde-Etayo, "ELA en 1947: de la esperanza a la represión," published in Memoria y civilización, 15 (2012): 211-227, in http:/hdl.handle.net/10171/34935 (consulted on December 25th, 2016).
105 DE PABLO CONTRERAS, Santiago, MEES, Ludger and RODRÍGUEZ RANZ, José Antonio, 1999, op. cit., p. 196.
106 Ibid., p. 194.
107 GARDE-ETAYO, Mª Luisa, 2012, op. cit., pp. 219-221.
108 SAN SEBASTIÁN, Koldo, op. cit., 2014., p. 395.
109 Aguirre was probably influenced by the reports sent by Anton Irala after the 1947 strike in which he alerted about its consequences, since international politics were

plunging into a profound anti-communist stance, and the Spanish protest could be identified with socialism. DE PABLO CONTRERAS, Santiago, MEES, Ludger and RODRÍGUEZ RANZ, José Antonio, 1999, op. cit., p. 201.
110 In Irujo Fund, Signature J, Box 32, File 2. http://www.euskomedia.org/PDFFondo/irujo/13128.pdf (consulted on December 25th 2016.)
111 The 1951 strike, unlike that of 1947, had as its basis the social protests and discontent due to life conditions. However, the 1951 strike was organized in the interior by the Resistance council, although neither the results nor the development of all the resulting riots were linked to political resistance, but to social unrest. DE PABLO CONTRERAS, Santiago, MEES, Ludger and RODRÍGUEZ RANZ, José Antonio, 1999, op. cit., pp. 199-201.
112 IRUJO, Xabier, 2012, op. cit., pp. 145-146.
113 MEES, Ludger, 2006, op. cit., p. 292.
114 IRUJO, Xabier, 2012, op. cit., pp. 147-148.
115 Letter from the President of the Spanish Republican Government to Dag Hjalmar Agne Carl Hammarskjöld, Secretary General of the UN, February 8th, 1955. EAH-AHE, Archivo gobierno vasco, Fondo especial Beyris, C-134/1-7.
116 AZURMENDI, José Félix, 2013, op. cit., pp. 111-118; IRUJO, Xabier, 2012, op. cit., p. 147.
117 The articles signed as Javier de Iranzu can be found at the Eusko Ikaskuntza's archive within the Manuel Irujo fund, signature J, Box 52, Files 1-3. They can be consulted in their digital version at: http://www.euskomedia.org/bilatu?q=Javier+de+Iranzu
118 Resolution S/RES/109(1955) accepted the admission of several countries, such as Albania, Jordan, Portugal, Ireland, Bulgaria, Cambodia, Hungary, or Laos regardless of whether the governments of these states were dictatorships or democracies. The strategy of faith in the UN as a guardian of democracy had been overridden by the great divide of the Cold War which, more than dividing the world politically, had at its base economic reasons for the division between capitalism and communism. http://hdl.handle.net/11176/184644 (consulted on December 27th, 2016.)
119 MEES, Ludger, 2006, op. cit., pp. 295-296.
120 "Lo que importa es el futuro," in Alderdi, 70, January 1953, p. 15.
121 MOTA, David, 2016, op. cit., pp. 275-277.
122 Ceferino Jemein, a member of the "old guard" nationalists, was president of the Federation of Mendigozales (Basque nationalist mountaineers) when the Civil War broke out. Jemein was famous for his defense of the orthodoxy of Sabino Arana's ideas, which caused him to engage in heated debates with Aguirre, Irujo, and Eli Gallastegi, among others. More on Jemein, at: http://www.euskomedia.org/aunamendi/63966 (Consulted on December 27th 2016.)
123 "Rojos-separatistas" was published in Alderdi, 71, February 1953, pp. 13-14; and "Pasado, presente y futuro de Euzkadi," in Alderdi, 72, March 1953, pp. 8-9.
124 "Pasado, presente y futuro de Euzkadi," ibid., p. 8.
125 Jesús de Galíndez in "Parece que estamos solos," published in Alderdi, no.73, April 1953.
126 Francisco Javier Landáburu was appointed political representative of the LIAB by the end of the Spanish Civil War, and Basque delegate in Paris after the Second World War. As President Aguirre's loyal collaborator, he helped create several international and European organizations. He was appointed Vice-President of the Basque government after Lehendakari Aguirre's death, although he himself passed away three years later, in 1963, while he was writing a biography of President Aguirre, "José Antonio Aguirre, forjador de la nación vasca," which would be published posthumously. He is considered as one of the ideologists of the PNV, focused primarily on Christianity and Europeanism. More on Francisco Javier de Landáburu in ARRIETA, Leyre, 2009, "Landáburu, el alavés europeísta," in Sancho el Sabio, 31, 199-220; UGALDE, Alexander, 2008, Xabier de Landaburu: bizitza osoa Euskal Herriaren kausarentzat: 1907-1963 =Xabier de Landaburu: una vida dedicada a la causa del pueblo vasco: 1907-1963. Bilbao: Sabino Arana Fundazioa; SAN SEBASTIÁN, Koldo, 1981, "En

torno a dos obras de F.J. Landáburu," in Muga, 12, pp. 108-112.
127 MEES, Ludger, 2012, op. cit., p. 321.
128 Ibid., pp. 321-324. We will see more about the Federal movement in greater detail in the chapter about the IV Conference of the European Federal Movement in Munich, 1962.
129 Ibid., pp. 325-326.
130 EAH-AHE, Archivo Histórico del Gobierno Vasco, Fondo del departamento de presidencia, File 91. Also, at: http://dokuklik.snae.org/badator_zoom.php?cdc=001&cdd=00548#
131 The income received as a result of the agreement with the US government had been one of the main financial sources of the Basque government, and the end of the collaboration with the Americans forced the Basques to create a new financing system. The Basque Diaspora would lend money to the Basque government, and the earnings made from the interests of that money would create a source of income. Even if the new way of financing was pretty new, it is worthwhile remembering that the fundraising campaign had begun in 1947 with the aforementioned declaration "A los vascos de América." IRUJO, Xabier, op. cit., pp. 155-163. AZURMENDI, José Félix, 2013, op. cit., pp. 79 and ff.
132 Aguirre to Jon Bilbao, Paris, January 26th, 1954. BA CBS, Jon Bilbao Archive, BSQAP 0177 1939-1958.
133 Ibid.
134 Fulgencio Batista ruled Cuba during different periods after the 1933 Revolt of the Sergeants that overthrew the authoritarian government of Gerardo Machado. From 1952 to 1959, he made Cuba into a dictatorship with the aid of the USA, until the Cuban Revolution led by Fidel Castro and Ernesto Che Guevara took over power. More on Fulgencio Batista in: GELMAN, Irwin, 1973, Roosevelt and Batista: Good Neighbor Diplomacy in Cuba, 1933-1945. Alburquerque: University of New Mexico Press; ACOSTA RUBIO, Raoul, 1977, Cuba, todos culpables: relato de un testigo: lo que no se sabe del dictador Batista y su época. Miami: Universal Ed.
135 Jon Bilbao to Aguirre, Cuba, February 23rd, 1954. BA CBS, Jon Bilbao Archive, BSQAP 0177 1939-1958.
136 Gordejuela was a weekly publication until 1950, when it went on to be monthly. It was published from Cárdenas, in Cuba. The issues can be consulted in the Hemeroteca de la diáspora vasca: http://urazandi.euskaletxeak.net/vol1/dvd06/CUBA/Gordejuela/htm/index.htm (consulted on January 3rd, 2017).
137 Some issues of these publication are also found in Hemeroteca de la diáspora vasca, http://urazandi.euskaletxeak.net/vol1/dvd06/default.html (consulted on January 3rd, 2017).
138 Alderdi, Euzko Alderdi-Jeltzalia'ren deya- Boletín del Partido Nacionalista vasco, Bayonne, n.90, September 1954.
139 Alderdi, Euzko Alderdi-Jeltzalia'ren deya- Boletín del Partido Nacionalista vasco, Bayonne, n.90, September 1954.
140 Alderdi, Euzko Alderdi-Jeltzalia'ren deya- Boletín del Partido Nacionalista vasco, Bayonne, n.90, September 1954.
141 These statements referring to the 1954 American trip are taken from a speech given at the Ateneo Español de México on May 10th 1954. In http://www.lehendakariagirre.eu/pdf/Discursos/478_01.pdf (consulted on January 3rd, 2017).
142 IRUJO, Xabier, 2012, op. cit., pp. 141-150; MOTA, David, 2016, op. cit., pp. 253 and ff.
143 Alderdi, Euzko Alderdi-Jeltzalia'ren deya- Boletín del Partido Nacionalista vasco, Bayonne, n.90, September 1954.
144 GREENFELD, Liah, 2005, "Nationalism and the mind" in Nations and Nationalism, V, 11:4, pp. 325-342.
145 Ibid.
146 MEES, Ludger, 2006, op. cit., p. 327.
147 DE PABLO CONTRERAS, Santiago, MEES, Ludger, and RODRÍGUEZ RANZ,

José Antonio, 1999, op. cit., pp. 213 and ff.
148 MEES, Ludger, 2006, op. cit., p. 327.
149 Gabon means Christmas in Basque language. Christmas message by President Aguirre. January 1955. AGUIRRE, José Antonio, 1981, op. cit. Vol.II, pp. 881-887 and also in http://www.lehendakariagirre.eu/pdf/Mensajes/34_01.pdf (consulted on January 3rd, 2017).
150 GHOSH, Devleena, 2008, "Coda. Eleven stars over the last moments of Andalusia," pp. 277-289. In ALLATSON, Paul; Mc. CORMACK, Jo (Eds.), Exile cultures, misplaced identities (Critical Studies. Vol. 30). Amsterdam – New York: Rodopi Editions.
151 MADARIETA, Asier, 2007, "El último grito de unidad en el exilio. El Congreso Mundial Vasco de 1956," in AGUIRREAZKUENAGA, Joseba; SOBREQUÉS, Jaume (Eds.), Eusko Jaurlaritza eta Catalunyako Generalitatea: Erbestetik Parlamentuen eraketara arte (1939-1980). Oñati: Instituto Vasco de Administración Pública.
152 More on José María Lasarte at http://www.euskomedia.org/aunamendi/87008 (consulted on January 4th, 2017).
153 Instrucción General, Paris, January 1955. Published in Alderdi, n. 96, March 1955
154 Ibid.
155 Ibid.
156 BAETS, Antoon de, 2011, op. cit., p. 211.
157 Instrucción General, Paris, January 1955. Published in Alderdi, n.96, March 1955.
158 The section "Vascos en el Mundo", as we have already commented, was a vindication of the Basque communities in the world, with a preminence of the South American communities, where diferent Basque delegations exposed their situation. It is interesting to point out the aim of these communitites to contribute in the Basque developement in the exile, like Pedro Basaldúa, Basque delegate in Argentina highlighted: "Con este espíritu comprenderéis señores congresistas las posibilidades que se ofrecen a que las Entidades vascas sean algo más que un club social o un departamento que está fomentando y viviendo de un simple folklore artístico pero frío. No, en estos centros vascos se está elaborando cultura vasca. Y se está desarrollando y vigorizando el espíritu patriótico profundamente y son centenares las conferencias que se dan en estos Centros (…). EUSKO JAURLARITZAREN ARGITALPEN SERBITZUAK- SERVICIO CENTRAL DE PUBLICACIONES DEL GOBIERNO VASCO, 1983. op. cit., p. 443.
159 Ibid.
160 Reglamento Interior, Euskomedia, Irujo Fund, Signature J, Box 48, File 4 (consulted on January 12th).
161 Ibid.
162 IRUJO, Xabier, 2012, op. cit., p. 202; Documentación referente al Congreso Mundial Vasco. Incluye: programas, instrucción general, cuestionario y reglamento interior. Euskomedia, Irujo Fund, Signature J, Box 48, File 4. Also, in: http://www.euskomedia.org/PDFFondo/irujo/10224.pdf (consulted on January 12th).
163 MADARIETA, Asier, 2007, op. cit., p. 133.
164 Euzko Deya, Buenos Aires, May 31st, 1956. Fundación Indalecio Prieto. 2. Concha Prieto. General. PNV. AFIP/2.1/ Folder 189/ Subfolder 4. Also in: http://dokuklik.snae.org/badator_zoom.php?cdc=283&cdd=0108 (consulted on January 12th, 2017).
165 The questions listed here are only those that are most representative and of interest for this study, and those that are related to the fields that were developed in the communications sent to the political section (the object of our study here). The complete questionnaire can be found in the following reference: Congreso Mundial Vasco. Cuestionario. Euskomedia, Irujo Fund, Signature J, Box 48, File 4. Also, in: http://www.euskomedia.org/PDFFondo/irujo/10224.pdf (consulted on January 12th), and also in the minute's book: EUSKO JAURLARITZAREN ARGITALPEN SERBITZUAK- SERVICIO CENTRAL DE PUBLICACIONES DEL GOBIERNO VASCO, 1983, Euskal Batzar Orokorra. Congreso Mundial Vasco. 25 aniversario.

Bilbao, pp. 21-32.
166 Congreso Mundial Vasco. Cuestionario. Euskomedia, Irujo Fund, Signature J, Box 48, File 4. Also in: http://www.euskomedia.org/PDFFondo/irujo/10224.pdf (consulted on January 12th, 2017).
167 IRUJO, Xabier, 2012, op. cit., pp. 201-202; MENDIETA, Asier. 2007. "El último grito de unidad del exilio. El Congreso Mundial Vasco de 1956," pp. 129-130. In AGIRREAZKUENAGA, Joseba; SOBREQUÉS, Jaume, 2007, Eusko Jaurlaritza eta Catalunyako Generalitatea: Erbestetik Parlamentuen eraketara arte (1939-1980). Bilbao: Herri-Ardularitzaren Euskal Erakundea. The full letter sent by Indalecio Prieto on August 4th, 1946 from Mexico as well as some other documents are found in EAH-AHE, Archivo gobierno vasco, Fondo del Departamento de Presidencia, Congreso Mundial Vasco, Correspondencia-Aguirre. File 360, Bundle 02. Also, in: http://dokuklik.snae.org/badator_zoom.php?cdc=001&cdd=01313 (consulted on January 20th, 2017).
168 Congreso Mundial Vasco. Cuestionario. Euskomedia, Irujo Fund, Signature J, Box 48, File 4. Also in: http://www.euskomedia.org/PDFFondo/irujo/10224.pdf (consulted on January 12th, 2017) .
169 Ethnic nationalism—using the origin of the Basques to include them or not within the Basque nationalist imagery—will be a part of our analysis that we will see in later chapters.
170 The Reconciliación Nacional was a very famous strategy deployed by the Spanish Communist Party, who had not recognized the Franco Regime until that time and still maintained armed militias (the Maquis) mainly in the Pyrenees. The declaration was published in PARTIDO COMUNISTA DE ESPAÑA. COMITÉ CENTRAL, 1956, Declaración del Partido Comunista de España: por la reconciliación nacional por una solución democrática y pacífica del problema español. Publishing place unknown: PCE. There is an important amount of bibliography and resources on this topic, since it generated controversy among the communists and the Spanish resistance. The following are some of the most representative studies. For an internal view of the issue: PARTIDO COMUNISTA DE ESPAÑA, 1958, La lucha de clases y la política de reconciliación nacional. Madrid: PCE. And for an external view, where the change of strategy can be seen: MORÁN, Gregorio, 1986, Miseria y grandeza del partido comunista de España. 1939-1985. Barcelona: Editorial Planeta; ESTRUCH TOBELLA, Joan, 2000, Historia oculta del PCE. Madrid: Temas de Hoy; ESTRUCH TOBELLA, Joan, 1982, El PCE en la clandestinidad. Madrid: Siglo XXI.
171 Confidential Report No. 29, October 2nd, 1956. NARA, General Records of the Department of State. Records of the Office of Western European Affairs. Records of the Spanish and the Portuguese desk officers. 1942-1958. NND887210 RG59 Box.8
172 LANDABÚRU, Javier, 1956, La causa del Pueblo Vasco. Paris: Cuadernos Alderdi, p. 2.
173 Letters between Manuel Irujo and Josu Hickman, 1954-1956. Euskomedia, Irujo Fund, Signature J, Box 35, File 1. Also, in http://www.euskomedia.org/PDFFondo/irujo/4123.pdf (consulted on January 14th, 2017).
174 Stuart W. Rockwell, who was fluent in different languages, including French, Arabic, German, and Spanish, worked for the American Foreign Office in several positions between 1946 and 1979. He was second secretary- consul in Ankara, 1946-48; officer-in-charge for Palestine-Israel-Jordan Affairs, 1948-50; political advisor to the Secretary of Air Force, 1950-52; first secretary-consul in Madrid, 1952-55; principal adviser to U.S. members of the U.N., present at the Palestine Conciliation Commission, 1949; political adviser for the U.S. Delegation to the U.N. General Assembly, 1949, 1950, and 1951. In 1988, when the Library of Congress interviewed him, he talked about his career. https://cdn.loc.gov/service/mss/mfdip/2004/2004roc01/2004roc01.pdf (consulted on January 14th, 2017).
175 Memorandum. From Mr. Rockwell to Mr. Byngton. March 16th, 1955. NARA, General Records of the Department of State. Records of the Office of Western Eu-

ropean Affairs. Records of the Spanish and the Portuguese desk officers. 1942-1958. NND887210 RG59 Box.6
176 Ibid.
177 MIRALLES, Jaime, 1996, "La acción política de Unión Española," pp. 133-140. In FONTÁN, Antonio (Dir.), Los monárquicos y el régimen de Franco. Madrid: Universidad Complutense de Madrid.
178 Memorandum. From Mr. Rockwell to Mr. Byngton. March 16th, 1955. NARA, General Records of the Department of State. Records of the Office of Western European Affairs. Records of the Spanish and the Portuguese desk officers. 1942-1958. NND887210 RG59 Box.6
179 ABC, March 18th, 1955, p. 5. http://hemeroteca.abc.es/nav/Navigate.exe/hemeroteca/madrid/abc/1955/03/18/005.html (consulted on January 15th, 2017).
180 "Lecture of Italian Monarchist at Ateneo Last night." From R.D. Mc. Clelland to Mr. Rockwell. April 19th, 1955. NARA, General Records of the Department of State. Records of the Office of Western European Affairs. Records of the Spanish and the Portuguese desk officers. 1942-1958. NND887210 RG59 Box.6
181 Confidential Memorandum. From Mr.Rockwell to Mr. Byngton. June 20th, 1955. NARA, General Records of the Department of State. Records of the Office of Western European Affairs. Records of the Spanish and the Portuguese desk officers. 1942-1958. NND887210 RG59 Box.6
182 Ibid.
183 Report No. 36. American Consulate. Bilbao. June 23rd,1955. NARA, General Records of the Department of State. Records of the Office of Western European Affairs. Records of the Spanish and the Portuguese desk officers. 1942-1958. NND887210 RG59 Box.6
184 Irujo to Hickman. Paris, September 14th, 1955. Letters between Manuel Irujo and Josu Hickman, 1954-1956. Euskomedia, Irujo Fund, Signature J, Box 35, File 1. Also, in http://www.euskomedia.org/PDFFondo/irujo/4123.pdf (consulted on January 14th, 2017).
185 Memorandum. From Mr. Rockwell to Mr. Byngton. March 16th, 1955. NARA, General Records of the Department of State. Records of the Office of Western European Affairs. Records of the Spanish and the Portuguese desk officers. 1942-1958. NND887210 RG59 Box.6
186 LANDÁBURU, Javier, 1956, op. cit., p. 9.
187 Ibid., p.14
188 Javier de Landaburu to Manuel Irujo, Paris, September 25th, 1951. Euskomedia, Irujo Fund, Signature J, Box 38, File 3. Also, in: http://www.euskomedia.org/PDFFondo/irujo/1648.pdf (consulted on January 17th).
189 LANDABURU, Javier, 1956, op. cit., p. 10 (part III).
190 Ibid., p. 14 (part III).
191 Ibid., p. 15 (part III).
192 Ibid., p. 18 (part III).
193 JARDÍ, Enric, 1983, El pensament de Prat de la Riba. Barcelona: Alpha Ed., pp. 93 and ff.
194 LANDABURU, Javier, 1956, op. cit., p. 25 (part III).
195 Ibid., pp. 24-25.
196 "Interview of Spanish Pretender with Mr. Pinay." From Mr. Jones to Mr. Elbrick. November 8th, 1955. NARA, General Records of the Department of State. Records of the Office of Western European Affairs. Records of the Spanish and the Portuguese desk officers. 1942-1958. NND887210 RG59 Box 6.
197 The Basque government and President Aguirre himself asked for the documents justifying the activity of the Basque government during those 20 years. In the archives of the Basque Government we can find, among the correspondence, those documents that were asked for in order to fulfill all the information requirements: documents on the elaboration of the Statute of Autonomy, from the Department of Agriculture, from the Basque delegations, etc. In EAH-AHE. Archivo Histórico del Gobier-

no Vasco. Fondo del Departamento de Presidencia. Also at: http://dokuklik.snae.org/badator_sencilla_result_nivel.php?archivo=01031890010&nomarchivo=Euskadiko%20Artxibo%20Historikoa%20-%20%20Archivo%20Hist%C3%B3rico%20de%20Euskadi&fondo=001&nomfondo=Archivo%20Hist%C3%B 3rico%20del%20Gobierno%20Vasco.%20Fondo%20del%20Departamento%20de%20Presidencia&nivel=11&n omnivel=Unidad%20Documental (consulted on January 21st, 2017).

198 Veinte años de gestión del Gobierno vasco (1936-1956). EUSKO JAURLARITZAREN ARGITALPEN SERBITZUAK- SERVICIO CENTRAL DE PUBLICACIONES DEL GOBIERNO VASCO, 1983, op. cit., pp. 63-98.

199 Aguirre to Santiago Zarranz in Chile, April 25th, 1956. MENDIETA, Asier, 2007, op. cit., p. 134. The full letter and other letters and documents for the preparation of the Congress are found in EAH-AHE, Archivo gobierno Vasco, Fondo del Departamento de Presidencia, Congreso Mundial Vasco, Correspondencia-Aguirre. File 360, Bundle 02. Also, in: http://dokuklik.snae.org/badator_zoom.php?cdc=001&cdd=01313 (consulted on January 20th, 2017).

200 EAH-AHE, Archivo gobierno vasco, Fondo del Departamento de Presidencia, ibid.

201 MENDIETA, Asier, 2007, op. cit., pp. 133-135.

202 EUSKO JAURLARITZAREN ARGITALPEN SERBITZUAK- SERVICIO CENTRAL DE PUBLICACIONES DEL GOBIERNO VASCO. 1983. Euskal Batzar Orokorra. Congreso Mundial Vasco. 25 aniversario. Bilbao, p. 149.

203 Although my research leads me to focus my attention on the nationalist features and nationalist policies of the Basques, the document and the Basque Congress itself were prepared and organized by the Basque Government, and therefore were arranged according to the interests of all the different political parties that were part of the Government.

204 Anteproyecto de la ponencia política dirigida al Congreso Mundial Vasco. Euskomedia, Irujo Fund, Signature J, Box 48, File 4. Also, in: http://www.euskomedia.org/PDFFondo/irujo/10249.pdf (consulted on January 20th, 2017).

205 Ibid., p. 21.

206 In the letter from Indalecio Prieto to Lehendakari Aguirre, Mr. Prieto argues "La circunstancia, según usted apunta, de que en el Congreso Mundial Vasco se llegará a recomendaciones (no acuerdos) y a una posible Declaración, en nada disminuye la responsabilidad de quienes las adopten." EAH-AHE, Archivo Gobierno Vasco, Fondo del Departamento de Presidencia, Congreso Mundial Vasco, Correspondencia-Aguirre. File 360, Bundle 02. Also, in: http://dokuklik.snae.org/badator_zoom.php?cdc=001&cdd=01313 (consulted on January 20th, 2017).

207 Anteproyecto de la ponencia política dirigida al Congreso Mundial Vasco. Euskomedia, Irujo Fund, Signature J, Box 48, File 4.

208 Ibid.

209 Ibid.

210 Ibid.

211 Ibid.

212 Different versions of the draft can be found in Manuel Irujo's personal archive, along with the letters containing the amendments sent by Joseba Rezola and Gonzalo Nárdiz, as well as an unsigned but very detailed document which includes some amendments that were applied in the next versions of the draft. Owing to the hardworking nature and extreme tidiness of Manuel Irujo, today it is possible to see and compare the different versions of the draft and get an idea of which aspects were more controversial. Anteproyecto de la ponencia política dirigida al Congreso Mundial Vasco. Euskomedia, Irujo Fund, Signature J, Box 48, File 4.

213 Ibid.

214 Letter from Manuel Irujo to Lehendakari Aguirre. Donibane Lohitzune, August 28th, 1956. Ibid.

215 Comunicado n°10 "El hecho vasco, el euskera y el territorio de Euzkadi." EUSKO JAURLARITZAREN ARGITALPEN SERBITZUAK- SERVICIO CENTRAL DE

PUBLICACIONES DEL GOBIERNO VASCO, 1983, op. cit., pp. 130-131.
216 Ibid., p. 152
217 Comunicado n°10 "El hecho vasco, el Euskera y el territorio de Euzkadi." EUSKO JAURLARITZAREN ARGITALPEN SERBITZUAK- SERVICIO CENTRAL DE PUBLICACIONES DEL GOBIERNO VASCO, 1983, op. cit., pp. 130-131.
218 The conclusions of the political draft that was ultimately removed said in one of its items: "It calls the attention of the Government and its members to the political-social fact that can be qualified as of maximum national concern for a Basque. The genocidal policy pursued by the current regime is aimed at the rapid extinction of the Basque language as a living language." Anteproyecto de la ponencia política dirigida al Congreso Mundial Vasco. Euskomedia, Irujo Fund, Signature J, Box 48, File 4.
219 EUSKO JAURLARITZAREN ARGITALPEN SERBITZUAK- SERVICIO CENTRAL DE PUBLICACIONES DEL GOBIERNO VASCO, 1983, op. cit., pp. 122-123;128;152.
220 The ANV communication contains parts that are exactly the same as the draft of the political paper written by Irujo. Irujo had already informed Aguirre about this in his letter of August 28th, 1956, because Gonzalo Nárdiz had told him of his intentions of using it, given that he completely agreed with the Navarrese. EUSKO JAURLARITZAREN ARGITALPEN SERBITZUAK- SERVICIO CENTRAL DE PUBLICACIONES DEL GOBIERNO VASCO, 1983, op. cit., pp. 165-177.
221 Ibid., pp. 177-179.
222 In it are described the main factors driving the seven approved items. The full text can be found in: EUSKO JAURLARITZAREN ARGITALPEN SERBITZUAK- SERVICIO CENTRAL DE PUBLICACIONES DEL GOBIERNO VASCO, 1983, op. cit., pp. 179-182.
223 EUSKO JAURLARITZAREN ARGITALPEN SERBITZUAK- SERVICIO CENTRAL DE PUBLICACIONES DEL GOBIERNO VASCO, 1983, op. cit., p. 190.
224 EUSKO JAURLARITZAREN ARGITALPEN SERBITZUAK- SERVICIO CENTRAL DE PUBLICACIONES DEL GOBIERNO VASCO, 1983, op. cit., p. 206.
225 MENDIETA, Asier, 2007, op. cit., p. 148.
226 This is the most accepted version of Galíndez's disappearance, that was followed by the investigation firstly open by the New York Police, although as for today, part of the documentation related with the investigation carried by the American Department of State is still confidential. MOTA, David, 2016, op. cit., p. 284.
227 These are some of the most representative works on Galíndez's case: UNANUE, Manuel de Dios. 1999. El caso Galíndez: los vascos en los Servicios de inteligencia de EEUU. Tafalla: Txalaparta; BERNARDO URQUIJO, Iñaki. 1993. Galíndez: La tumba abierta. Los vascos y los Estados Unidos. Vitoria-Gasteiz: Eusko Jaurlaritzaren Argitalpen Zerbitzu Nagusia; BASALDÚA, Pedro. 1956. Jesús de Galíndez: Víctima de las tiranías en América. Buenos Aires: Mac-Co.;
228 Galíndez. Alderdi, no.112/113, August, 1956.
229 MOTA, David, 2016, op. cit., p. 288.
230 Referring to Trujillo.
231 Jesús Galíndez to Manuel Irujo. New York, November 9th, 1956. Euskomedia. Irujo Fund. Signature J, Box 56, File 2C, p. 21.
232 Manuel Irujo to Jesús Galíndez. February 15th, 1955. Ibid., p. 15.
233 The ups and downs of Galíndez's relationship with the UN is related in several chapters, such as "Galíndez y la ONU" (pp. 163-200), "La Guerra ya no está en las Naciones Unidas" (pp. 225-239), and "De la esperanza a la desilusión" (pp. 285-320), in BERNARDO URQUIJO, Iñaki, 1993, Galíndez: La tumba abierta. Los vascos y los Estados Unidos. Vitoria-Gasteiz: Eusko Jaurlaritzaren Argitalpen Zerbitzu Nagusia.
234 The articles published in Alderdi no.95, February of 1955, "Triunfo de la democracia en Costa Rica" or Alderdi no. 98, May of 1955, "Los vascos somos demócratas" (which was the conference he gave at the 2nd Christian-Democrat Congress held in

New York on April 15th -17th, 1955) are good examples of this.
235 "Puerto Rico y Euzkadi. Fórmulas parecidas de autodeterminación," in Alderdi no. 99, June, 1955, pp. 11-12.
236 Alderdi no. 99, June, 1955, pp. 8-9
237 Manuel Irujo to Pedro Basaldúa (Basque delegate in Argentina), June 12th, 1956. Euskomedia. Irujo Fund. Signature J, Box 56, File 2C. Source Sig. 88-89.
238 "It is necessary that the International Federation, be it only of Basque Centers, be even wider as the International League of the Friends of the Basques was projected in the past." Galíndez in Alderdi no. 107, February 1956, pp. 16.
239 Israel was a great influence for Basque nationalism from the very beginning; for instance, The Revolt: Story of the Irgun, by Menachem Begin, first published in 1952, was one of the reference books of the Basque nationalists in the Paris Delegation, and later on for the young members of EGI. The relations between the Basques and Israel have been documented in several studies and books, such as: BATISTA, Antoni, 2007, Madariaga. De las armas a la palabra. Barcelona: RBA; LISBONA, José Antonio, 2002, España-Israel. Historia de unas relaciones secretas. Madrid: Temas de Hoy; SELLARÉS, Miquel, 2008, Un pas endavant. La història dels Mossos que mai no s'ha explicat. Barcelona: L'Arquer;
240 On this subject the following can be consulted: UGALDE, Alexander, "Nacionalismo vasco y relaciones Internacionales," in Hermes, Bilbao, Fundación Sabino Arana, no. 11, 2004, pp. 34-39; CONVERSI, Daniele, "Dommino effect or internal developments? The Influente of International Events and Political Ideologies on Catalan and Basque Nationalism," in West European Politics, 3, 1993, pp. 245-70; NÚÑEZ SEIXAS, Xosé M., "Relaciones exteriores del nacionalismo vasco. (1895-1960)," in DE PABLO, Santiago (Ed.), Los nacionalistas. Historia del nacionalismo vasco. 1876-1960, Gasteiz, Fundación Sancho el Sabio, 1995, pp. 381-417; NÚÑEZ SEIXAS, Xosé M., "El mito de Irlanda: la influencia del nacionalismo irlandés en los nacionalismos gallego y vasco (1880-1936)," in Historia 16, no.199. 1992. pp. 32-44.
241 In a letter from Hickman to Irujo dated April 6th, 1956, the former declared: "It is possible that the Americans, I mean the police, do not give much news of the case for the reason that the American State is the one that supports Trujillo." In Euskomedia, Irujo Fund, Signature J, Box 35, File 1.
242 EUSKO JAURLARITZAREN ARGITALPEN SERBITZUAK- SERVICIO CENTRAL DE PUBLICACIONES DEL GOBIERNO VASCO, 1983, op. cit., p. 478.
243 Hickman to Irujo, London, April 11th, 1956. In Euskomedia, Irujo Fund, Signature J, Box 35, File 1.
244 On the Doctoral ceremony at Columbia University, see Alderdi, no. 111, June, 1956, p. 4; and for Irujo's article see Alderdi, no. 112, August, 1956, pp. 10-15.
245 "The Galindez case," New York Times, April 28th, 1956. We also find other articles and news on Galíndez in the New York Times of April 5th, May 11th, 14th, 24th, and 30th, July 12th and 18th, and also in 1957 and 1958.
246 The folder can be found in: NARA, General Records of the Department of State. Records of the Office of Western European Affairs. Records of the Spanish and the Portuguese desk officers. 1942-1958. NND887210 RG59 Box.8
247 Basque World Case Resolution on Galíndez case, Letter from Mr. Beam to Mr. Howe, October 19th, 1956, and Basque World Case Resolution on Galíndez case, Memorandum signed by Fisher Howe, October 20th, 1956, in NARA, General Records of the Department of State. Records of the Office of Western European Affairs. Ibid.
248 Washington Visit of Sr. Aguirre, President, Basque Government-in-exile. Confidential report, May 13th, 1957. Ibid.
249 There is a folder containing the activities that the Basque Government carried out between 1956 and 1963 in connection with Galindez's case, especially (but not only) with respect to his will and the difficulties they had in making it effective, as well as the undertakings and the diplomacy carried out; all these are on display in: EAH- AHE, Archivo Histórico del Gobierno Vasco. Fondo del Departamento

de Presidencia. Secretaría General (Paris). Gobierno. Delegaciones del Gobierno de Euzkadi Delegaciones en América. File 79, Bundle 02. Also in: http://dokuklik.snae.org/badator_zoom.php?cdc=001&cdd=00499. Manuel Irujo made all the efforts he could—as was usual in him—in order to clear up the mysterious disappearance and, apart from some letters, already mentioned and quoted, he kept an eye on the investigations and followed up on the news about Galíndez. In 1958, he sent some letters to a newspaper with the intention of clearing Galíndez of the accusations of being a communist. Some letters and articles that he collected in 1958 can be consulted in: Euskomedia. Irujo Fund. Signature J, Box 56, File 2-D; Irujo furthermore acted as a lawyer in the resolution of Galindez's will in 1962: Euskomedia. Irujo Fund. Signature J, Box 56, File 2-B.

250 The Dominican authorities tried to prevent the Basque World Congress from being held in Paris, because they were sure that the Basques would make use of the Congress to demonstrate against Trujillo's regime. BERNARDO, Iñaki, 1993, op. cit., pp. 485-486.
251 The repercussions of the Basque World Congress were published specifically in OPE nos. 2290- 2296, and in Alderdi nos. 115-119.
252 Euzko Deya devoted an entire issue to the World Basque Congress after its closing. Euzko Deya, Paris, no. 400, October, 1956.
253 Aguirre to Irujo. Paris, July 13th, 1957. Euskomedia. Irujo Fund. Signature J, Box 30, File 5.
254 The Gabon messages and the speeches given by Aguirre in 1957 can be consulted at: http://www.lehendakariagirre.eu/ppal.php
255 "Los últimos momentos de José Antonio. El primer presidente de Euzkadi," in Alderdi, no. 157/158, May, 1960.

256 Alderdi, no. 156, March, 1960; Alderdi, nos. 157-158, May, 1960; OPE 3123, March 22nd, 1956; OPE 3124, March 28th, 1956; OPE 3125, March 29th, 1956; OPE 3126, March 30th, 1956.
257 "Emakume abertzale Batza" literally "Basque nationalists women association", was founded as a women's section within the Basque Nationalist Party in 1922. During Franco dictatorship all its activity was moved to exile.
258 The Battalion was named after Major Cándido Sasaeta, who was responsible for organizing the Basque militias of the PNV, and later on became commander of the Euzko Gudarostea (Basque army). More on the Sasaeta battalion in: Gudaris y rehenes de Franco (1936-1943). Diarios de José Antonio Mendizábal, José Luís Lasa y Fernando Aguirre. Irún: Alberdania, pp. 52-53. More on the Basque army: SAGARRA, Pablo et al., 2015, Gudaris: Euzko Gudarostea (Ejército Vasco) durante la Guerra Civil (1936-1937). Madrid: Esfera de los libros.
259 The oath was read in both Spanish and Basque. It can be consulted in: OPE 3126, March 30th, 1956. Also at: http://ope.euskaletxeak.net (consulted on February 4th, 2017).
260 MOTA, David, 2016, op. cit., pp. 314-315; ANASAGASTI, Iñaki, 2007, "El Gobierno vasco presidido por Jesús María de Leizaola. Transición política y disolución. 1960-1979," pp. 162-168. In AGIRREAZKUENAGA, Joseba; SOBREQUÉS, Jaume, 2007, Eusko Jaurlaritza eta Catalunyako Generalitatea: Erbestetik Parlamentuen eraketara arte (1939-1980). Bilbao: Herri-Ardularitzaren Euskal Erakundea; DE PABLO CONTRERAS, Santiago, MEES, Ludger, and RODRÍGUEZ RANZ, José Antonio, 2001, op. cit., pp. 237-238, 250.
261 "Manifiesto del EBB 'Al pueblo vasco'". Alderdi, no. 156-157, May 1960. pp. 2-8.
262 Ibid.
263 Ibid.
264 "Jelkide" is the word used to refer to the members of the PNV.
265 "Baserri" is the Basque voice to refer to the typical Basque farmhouse.
266 For more on Basque immigration and economy between 1950-1970 see: http://www.usc.es/revistas/index.php/rips/article/viewFile/106/87;

267 Ez dok amairu, which means "There is no thirteen" in English, was a cultural movement that sought to renew Basque culture mainly through songs, by including social and political critique against the dictatorship, although it also relied on other disciplines. More on that movement in: http://www.euskomedia.org/aunamendi/43522/31445
268 Several studies differ on the exact date of the foundation of ETA, but this is a subject that will be addressed in the following chapters.
269 DE PABLO CONTRERAS, Santiago, MEES, Ludger, and RODRÍGUEZ RANZ, José Antonio, 2001, op. cit., pp. 231-236.
270 EQUIPO HÓRDAGO (Ed.), 1979, Documentos Y. Vols. 1-16. Donostia: Lur. Vol. 1, pp. 432 and ff.
271 Ibid., p. 436.
272 ETA to Lehendakari Leizaola. Euzkadi, May 15th, 1960. EHA-AHE, Fondo Leizaola, Box. 32, C-32/15.
273 During the years we are analyzing in this chapter, and especially after the disagreement of Monzón in the Basque World Conference, Manuel Irujo received criticism from certain members of the EBB. As has already been explained, the internal conflicts that did not affect the development of Basque nationalism are outside thescope of this research, but the following may serve as proof and example: Jesús de Solaun wrote some letters to Jesús de Leizaola complaining about the handling of the Basque detainees who had been prosecuted by the Franco regime in 1961, and accusing Manuel Irujo of outright incompetence. When Irujo wrote back, he gave all kinds of explanations about the actions that the Basque government had taken in order to help the detainees and, of course, made use of irony to disarm Solaun's accusations. The letters are a good example of the disagreement and tensions between the inside and the exile, and of the somewhat frequent lack of coordination between Paris and Beyris. Letters from Solaun to Leizaola can be found in: EAH-AHE, Archivo Histórico del Gobierno Vasco. Fondo del Lehendakari D. Jesus María de Leizaola. C33/11. Letters from Irujo to Solaun: Euskomedia, Irujo Fund, Signature J, Box, 39, File 1.
274 Letter from Indalecio Prieto to Jesús Mª Leizaola, June 22nd, 1960. EAH-AHE, Archivo histórico del gobierno vasco, Fondo del Lehendakari D. Jesus María de Leizaola. C33/8.
275 Ibid.
276 Letter from Miguel José Garmendia (future president of the Basque extraterritorial council in Mexico) to Manuel Irujo. Mexico, April 1st, 1960. Euskomedia, Irujo Fund, Signature J, Box, 3, File 8.
277 Ibid.
278 DE PABLO CONTRERAS, Santiago, MEES, Ludger, and RODRÍGUEZ RANZ, José Antonio, 2001, op. cit., p. 246.
279 Garmendia to Irujo. Mexico, D.F., April 4th, 1960. Euskomedia, Irujo Fund, Signature J, Box, 3, File 8.
280 Ibid.
281 DE PABLO CONTRERAS, Santiago, MEES, Ludger, and RODRÍGUEZ RANZ, José Antonio, 2001, op. cit., p. 240.
282 Letter from Irujo to Leizaola. Leigh-on-Sea, August 16th, 1960. EAH-AHE, Archivo histórico del gobierno vasco, Fondo del Lehendakari D. Jesus María de Leizaola. C-32/24.
283 MOTA, David, 2016, op. cit., p. 319.
284 These reflections were made in Speculation on form and nature of a Post-Franco Government, Madrid, September 11th, 1961, and Letter from Frederick G. Dutton, Assistant Secretary, to Congressman William Fitts Ryan, Washington DC, February 16th, 1962. NARA, General Records of the Department of State. RG 59. Records of the Office of Western European Affairs. 1960-63 General Decimal File. Box, 1808.
285 Letters from Leizaola to Irujo, Paris, September 19th, 1960, Euskomedia, Irujo Fund, Signature J, Box, 3, File 13.
286 NARA, General Records of the Department of State. RG 59. Bureau of European

Affairs, Records of the Office of Western European Affairs, 1953-1962, Box, 7.
287 Ibid.
288 Ibid.
289 "El presidente Aguirre y el Movimiento Europeo," Alderdi, no.168, March, 1961.
290 IRUJO, Manuel, 1958, La comunidad occidental europea y los vascos. VII Congreso de Estudios Vascos. Biarritz.
291 Euskomedia, Irujo Fund, Signature J, Box, 58, File 1, p. 88. The file is made up of 242 pages comprising letters between Irujo, Saurat, Madariaga, and Pi i Sunyer, invitations to the Meetings, foundation documents, and some other important documents on the Cultural Union.
292 Ibid.
293 "In the first session he attended, he (Madariaga) maintained the opinion that Spanish democracy was not Christian, or was anti-Christian, for which reason it seemed paradoxical that the Spanish democrats were represented in an institution of Christian orientation," Ibid. p. 44.
294 "We do not want to end without repeating that this association is not political, but cultural and spiritual, admitting of no political principles other than Christian ideals and democracy, within the norms of which its activities are to be developed," Ibid. p. 108.
295 ARRIETA, Leyre, 2008, "Red de relaciones europeas del PNV (1945-1977)," in Cuadernos de historia contemporánea, Vol. 30, p. 315. Also in: https://revistas.ucm.es/index.php/CHCO/article/viewFile/CHCO0808110313A/6738.
296 Luis de Eleizalde was a well-known Basque language scholar and promoter. His reflections on nationalism are disclosed in a bilingual (Basque-Spanish) biography: AMÉZAGA, Elías (et. al.), 1999, Koldo Eleizalde: Gizona, euskaltzalea/ Luis de Elizalde: El hombre, el vascólogo. Donostia: Eusko-Ikaskuntza.
297 CASTRO RUANO, José Luis de; UGALDE ZUBIRI, Alexander, 2004, op. cit., p. 88.
298 NÚÑEZ SEIXAS, Xose M., op. cit., p. 387; ELORZA, Antonio, 1992, "Euzkadi-Europa. La cultura política del nacionalismo vasco y los referentes europeos," in XI Congreso de Estudios Vascos. Donostia: Eusko Ikaskuntza, pp. 218-219.
299 The activities—protodiplomatic activities, according to the author—developed and carried out by Basque nationalism in an international context previous to the exile are analysed in NÚÑEZ SEIXAS, Xosé M., 1995, "¿Protodiplomacia exterior o ilusiones ópticas? El nacionalismo vasco en el contexto internacional y el congreso de nacionalidades europeas (1914-1937)," in Cuadernos de sección. Historia-Geografía 23. Donostia: Eusko- Ikaskuntza, pp. 243-275.
300 CASTRO RUANO, José Luis de; UGALDE ZUBIRI, Alexander, 2004, op. cit., p. 89.
301 NÚÑEZ SEIXAS, Xosé M., 1995, "Relaciones exteriores del nacionalismo vasco. (1895-1960)," in DE PABLO, Santiago (Ed.), Los nacionalistas. Historia del nacionalismo vasco. 1876-1960, Gasteiz, Fundación Sancho el Sabio, p. 405.
302 Ibid.
303 Leyre Arrieta thoroughly analyzes the NEI and its relations with the Christian Democrats' parties in (2007)Estación Europa. La política Europeísta del PNV en el exilio (1945-1977), pp. 85-90; 110-116; 126-143; 210-219; 285-298.
304 Within the Honor Committee, Aguirre was accompanied by important personalities of the Christian Democrat movement, such as Luigi Sturzo (Founder of the Italian Popular Party, that we have already mentioned), Marc Sagnier (Member of Parliament and Honor President of the Mouvement Républicaine Populaire), P.J.S. Serrarens (Secretary General of the International Confederations of Christian Trade Unions), Joseph Escher (President of the Swiss Conservative Party), Emile Reuter (President of the Luxemburg Chamber of Deputies). Ibid., pp. 135-137.
305 There are three tables complete with dates, places, and Basque attendees in Arrieta's book. Ibid., pp. 348- 350.
306 "Les NEI dans le Congrés de Luxembourg," Euzko Deya, February 15th, 1948, p. 5.

307 ARRIETA, Leyre, 2007, op. cit., pp. 139-140.
308 ARRIETA, Leyre, 2008, "Red de relaciones europeas del PNV (1945-1977)," in Cuadernos de historia contemporánea, Vol. 30, pp. 313-331. Also in: https://revistas.ucm.es/index.php/CHCO/article/viewFile/CHCO0808110313A/6738 , pp. 319-320.
309 Ibid., p. 320.
310 Ibid.
311 Euskomedia. Irujo Fund. Signature J, Box 55, File 5. Also, in http://www.euskomedia.org/fondo/11174
312 ARRIETA, Leyre. ARRIETA ALBERDI, Leyre, 2009, "Landáburu, el alavés europeísta," in Sancho el Sabio, 31, p. 215-216.
313 "Federación Occidental Europea," Alderdi, no.25, April, 1949. Published in IRUJO, Manuel, 1981, op. cit., pp. 13-15.
314 UGALDE ZUBIRI, Alexander, 2007, Eurobask, no.12, July, 2007, p. 94.
315 Although the European movement was not fully developed and lacked organizations due to the dictatorship, there was a considerable and growing European sentiment, especially in Catalonia, where the pro-European activities and tendencies of certain personalities were well known. There is a confidential report, called "Situación del Movimiento Europeo en España," which details the European activities carried out within Spain. Some of the personalities that are referred to in that report as "interested persons" are: Lluís Duran i Ventosa, Juan Estelrich, Josep Maria Ainaud de Lasarte, and Joan Triadú. (Undated, probably 1952). In a radio intervention, probably on Radio Euzkadi in 1955, Manuel Irujo talks about the Federal Movement and its success among Catalans, both in the exile and in the inside, quoting musician Pau Casals as one of the highest representatives of the European Federal Movement among the Catalans, and criticizes the absence of Federal Movement activities among the Basques in the inside. In this intervention, Irujo refers to certain federal organizations within Spain, in Madrid and Seville. Eusko-Ikaskuntza. Irujo Fund. Signature J, Box 53, File 1ª.
316 UGALDE ZUBIRI, Alexander, 2001, "El Consejo Vasco del Movimiento Europeo (1951-2001). La aportación vasca al federalismo Europeo/ Europako Mugimenduaren Euskal Kontselua (1951-2001)." Vitoria- Gasteiz: Consejo Vasco del Movimiento Europeo/ Europako Mugimenduaren Euskal Kontseilua, p. 77-78. Also of interest is the answer, probably written by Manuel Irujo, to a questionnaire sent by the NEI in 1950 about the PNV. This answer, 19 pages long, explains the federal European sentiment of the Basque Nationalist Party, the history of Basque nationalism, and the participation in Federal and European movements. In Eusko-Ikaskuntza, Irujo Fund, PNV Section, Signature J, Box, 38, File 2. pp. 37-54.
317 Aguirre was the Honor president (as President of the Basque Government), and Irujo was the Chairing president (acting on behalf the PNV); Juan Carlos Basterra (ANV), Laureano Lasa (PSOE), and Ramon María Aldasoro (IR) (until his death in 1952) were vice-presidents; Landáburu was the Secretary and José María de Lasarte, José Ignació Lizaso, Ángel Gondra, and Jesús Galíndez were members and delegates, representing the broad Basque community.
318 Among others, Winston Churchill, Léon Blum, or Paul-Henry Spaak were some of the international politicians who attended the Congress. From Spain, it is important to highlight the presence of Salvador de Madariaga, who chaired the cultural committee, and Josep Trueta; and on behalf of the Basques, the representation was trusted to Aguirre, Landaburu, and Basterra, as well as Indalecio Prieto. A complete list of the bureau of the Congress can be found in the official program in: Eusko-Ikaskuntza, Irujo Fund, Signature J, Box, 45, File 1. pp. 77-78.
319 "The Hague. Congress of Europe. Resolutions," ibid., pp. 7-16.
320 The report can be found in the aforementioned Irujo Fund file, pp. 55-65; and a detailed analysis of the obstacles that the Basques encountered can be read in: UGALDE ZUBIRI, Alexander, 2001, op. cit., pp. 83-89.
321 "El presidente Aguirre y el Movimiento Europeo," op. cit.

322 ARRIETA, Leyre, 2007, op. cit., pp. 117-118; UGALDE ZUBIRI, Alexander, 2001, op. cit., pp. 93-94.
323 ARRIETA, Leyre, 2007, op. cit., pp. 118-119 ; UGALDE ZUBIRI, Alexander, 2001, op. cit., pp. 95-96.
324 Al Pueblo patriota Vasco. Unsigned, 1950, Euskomedia, Irujo Fund, Section PNV, Signature J, Box, 38, File 1.
325 OPE 756 (03/05/1950), OPE 757 (04/05/1950), OPE 758 (05/05/1950).
326 ARRIETA, Leyre, 2007, op. cit., pp. 119-120.
327 Based on the different documents that refer to a Basque council or a Basque group, Alexander Ugalde argues that the Basque Council already existed before its official foundation. UGALDE ZUBIRI, Alexander, 2001, op. cit., p. 107. The CVFE has been widely studied and its activity analyzed in the aforementioned book, which describes the activities carried out and the changes suffered in the CVFE since 1951 and until 2001.
328 ARRIETA, Leyre, 2008, op. cit., p. 328.
329 Khrushchev served as First Secretary of the Communist Party of the Soviet Union from 1953 to 1964, after the death of Josef Stalin. In February of 1956, at the XX PCUS Congress, Nikita Khrushchev gave a speech, entitled "Secret Speech," denouncing Stalin's purges and repression. Despite his intentions of ushering in a less repressive and conflictive policy into the Soviet Union, his administration was forced to deal with the "Cuban Missile Crisis," one of the tensest episodes of the Cold War. One of the latest and most interesting biographies of Khurschev is: TAUBMAN, William, 2004, Khrushchev: The Man and his Era. New York: W.W. Norton & Company. The full Secret Speech can be read at: https://sourcebooks.fordham.edu/mod/1956khrushchev-secret1.asp. Among all the books on the Cuban Missile crisis, I would like to recommend the memories written by Robert F. Kennedy, (1969) Thirteen days. A Memoir of the Cuban Missile Crisis. New York: W.W. Norton & Company.
330 IRUJO, Manuel, 1956, "El fondo religioso de la vida y el comunismo," Alderdi, no.116, November, 1956.
331 Manuel Irujo wrote some articles on the Hungarian Revolt and human and national rights, having watched closely the movements of the Cold War and the situation of nationalities without a State in "the free World." Examples of this can be found in the articles: "Los húngaros y nosotros," Alderdi, no. 118, January, 1957; "Los crímenes contra la humanidad," Alderdi, no. 119, February, 1957; "La agresión de Hungría," Alderdi, no. 120, March, 1957.
332 "Los Crímines contra la Humanidad," op. Cit.
333 LANDÁBURU, Javier, "…Comunismo tampoco," Alderdi, no.156, March, 1960.
334 Ibid.
335 The repression against Basque priests and Basque nationalism by the Franco Regime and its international repercussion will be studied in next chapter.
336 IRUJO, Manuel. "En España empieza a amanecer," Alderdi , August,-September, 1962, nos. 84-185. The title also was an ironic reference to the lyrics of Cara al Sol, the anthem of the Spanish Falange party.
337 The leading articles in Alderdi grew more and more aggressive before the situation of the Basques living in the "Peninsular Basque Country." "Regímenes terroristas" was the editorial written in Alderdi, no. 163, 1960, denouncing the use of war decrees by the Franco regime, including death sentences and increasing numbers of prisoners suffering tortures since May 1960.
338 Mr. Enric Adroher i Pascual was a well-known anti-Franco activist who was a member of the CNT, the UGT, and the POUM. He lived in exile until 1976 and participated in the European Movement. More on "Gironella" in: http://www.fcampalans.cat/arxiu/uploads/publicacions/pdf/separata30web.pdf , and PUIG, Lluís Maria de, 1999, Gironella, la izquierda europeísta. Madrid: Fundación Españoles en el mundo.
339 Entrevista del Sr. Gironella con el Lendakari (Sic.), Irujo y Landáburu, Paris, June 20th, 1960. Eusko-Ikaskuntza, Irujo Fund, Section CFE, Signature J, Box 28, File 6.

340 DELGADO, Lorenzo, 2003, "¿El "amigo americano" ?: España y Estados Unidos durante el Franquismo,"Studia Historica. Historia Contemporánea. Salamanca: Ediciones Universidad de Salamanca, 21, pp. 231-276.
341 AMAT, Jordi, 2016, La primavera de Múnich. Esperanza y fracaso de una transición democrática. Barcelona: Tusquets Editores.
342 Julián Gorkin was the alias of Julián Gómez García, a communist member of the PCE who had worked for the Kommintern in Paris before the Spanish Civil War. After his return from the USSR, Gorkin abandoned orthodox communism and denounced Stalinism, joining the POUM during the Spanish Civil War. He wrote several books on Marxism and communism and against Stalin. In a later section, we will see more on Gorkin and his activities against Stalinism.
343 Dionisio Ridruejo was a poet and writer who initially followed the dictates of Falange, and even participated in the creation of its anthem, "Cara al Sol," but who left the Franco postulates in 1942, and ever since then developed a critical attitude against the Franco regime that would bring him to prison and, finally, to exile. More on Dionisio Ridruejo in: MORENTE VALERO, Francisco, 2006, Dionisio Ridruejo: del fascismo al antifranquismo. Madrid: Síntesis.
344 AMAT, Jordi, 2016, op. cit., p. 153.
345 Ibid.
346 Nárdiz to Landáburu, Bayonne, October 1st, 1959. Euskomedia, Irujo Fund, UFD Section, Signature J, Box 46, File 2. Source 165
347 Ibid., Source 176.
348 Meeting between Martínez Vera and Manuel Irujo. Paris, July 7th, Eusko-Ikaskuntza, Irujo Fund, Signature J, Box 28, Exp. 9A. The previous meeting with Gil Robles can be found in: Eusko-Ikaskuntza, Irujo Fund, Signature J, Box 47, Expedient 1. (The translation of Irujo's notes is especially difficult due to the high level of irony they contain).
349 LA PORTE, María Teresa, 1992, La política europea del régimen de Franco: 1957-1962. Pamplona: EUNSA.
350 ARRIETA, Leyre, 2007, op. cit., p. 306.
351 Entrevista del Sr. Gironella con el Lendakari (Sic.), Irujo y Landáburu. Paris, June 20th, 1960. Eusko-Ikaskuntza, Irujo Fund, Section CFE, Signature J, Box 28, File 6.
352 The Congress of Cultural freedom is analyzed in the next section of this chapter, given to its relation to Manuel Irujo.
353 AMAT, Jordi, 2016, op. cit., pp. 172-173. Amat analyses the interests and objectives of the Congress for Cultural Freedom, as well as the "Centro de Estudios y documentación" and its publications, especially in relation with Julián Gorkín, in the chapters "Operación Congreso" (166-185) and "Desactivar la máquina" (186- 231). Some of this information given by Amat will be used in the following section to describe the Basque interaction with the Congress for Cultural Freedom.
354 Gorkin at a CFEME meeting, Paris, April 18th, 1961. AMAT, Jordi, 2016, op. cit., p. 220.
355 Confidential Report "An evaluation of the Munich meeting of the Spanish opposition." Madrid, June 19th, 1962. NARA, General Records of the Department of State. RG 59. Records of the Office of Western European Affairs. 1960-63 General Decimal File. Box, 1808.
356 Letter to Manuel Irujo from Julián Gorkin, writing as representative and on the letterhead of Congreso por la Libertad de la cultura. Paris, June 21st, 1962. Eusko-Ikaskuntza, Irujo Fund, Signature J, Box 43, File 6, p. 25
357 GLONDYS, Olga, 2012, La guerra fría cultural y el exilio republicano español. Madrid: Consejo Superior de Investigaciones Científicas, pp. 215-216.
358 Invitation to the Congress and participation form sent by Maurice Faure, president of the European Movement. EAH-AHE, Fondo PNV-0076-09.
359 CRESPO MACLENNAN, Julio, Spain and the process of European integration, 1957-85. Houndmills: Palgrave in association with St. Anthony's College, pp. 53-54.
360 Invitation to the Congress sent by Robert van Schendel, Secretary General of the

European Movement. EAH- AHE, Fondo PNV-0076-09.
361 Letters between Gorkin and Irujo talking about the lists of invited members (30/05/1962), and minutes of the CFEME meetings written by Irujo (25/05/1962). Eusko-Ikaskuntza, Irujo Fund, Signature J, Box 43, File 6, p. 25.
362 Among others, there were representatives of the most important Spanish political parties, with the exception of the PCE, which was not invited: Fernando Álvarez de Miranda (Democracia Social Cristiana), Jesús Barros de Lis (Izquierda Demócrata Cristiana), José María Gil Robles (Democracia Social Cristiana), Jaime Miralles (Unión Española), Dionisio Ridruejo (Partido Democrático Acción Social), José María Satrústegui (Unión Española), Fernando Valera (Futuro del Gobierno Español de la República en el Exilio, Acción Republicana Democrática Española), Rodolfo Llopis (PSOE), etc.
363 Madariaga went so far as to state that "We are all here except the totalitarians on both sides," in reference to the communists and the fascists; apparently, some members of the PCE, like Tomás García, and of the PSUC, such as Francesc Vicens, had been seen at the Hotel Regine in Munich, accompanying some of the Spanish participants who were staying for the Munich meeting. http://www.lavanguardia.com/hemeroteca/20120605/54303390132/contubernio-munich-politica-oposicion- antifranquista-movimiento-europeo.html
364 Minutes CFEME, 15/05/1962. Eusko-Ikaskuntza, Irujo Fund, Signature J, Box 43, File 6, p. 33.
365 ARRIETA, Leyre, 2007, op. cit., p. 307; AMAT, Jordi, 2016, op. cit., p. 261.
366 When it refers to Cedist, it is referring to the CEDA party (Confederación de derechas autónomas), founded by Gil Robles (among others) in 1933.Minutes CFEME, 03/05/1962. Euskomedia, Irujo Fund, Signature J, Box 43, File 6, p. 34.
367 Confidential Report "An evaluation of the Munich meeting of the Spanish opposition," Madrid, June 19th, 1962. NARA, General Records of the Department of State. RG 59. Records of the Office of Western European Affairs. 1960-63 General Decimal File. Box, 1808.
368 Confidential Report "An evaluation of the Munich meeting of the Spanish opposition," ibid., p. 6.
369 ARRIETA, Leyre, 2007, op. cit., p. 308.
370 The different works on the Munich meeting that we have consulted (UGALDE, ARRIETA, SATRÚSTEGI, AMAT) agree on the figure of 34 Basque representatives, based on the information given by the list found in the Irujo Fund in Eusko Ikaskuntza. Eusko-Ikaskuntza, Irujo Fund, Signature J, Box 43, File 6, p. 163.
371 There are some lists and letters with the names proposed, in the already mentioned Irujo fund. Ibid., pp. 58- 69.
372 Ibid., p. 87.
373 Gil Robles' letter to the Minister Under-Secretary of the government, Luis Carrero Blanco, Madrid, June 2nd, 1962, p. 2. In the Confidential Report "An evaluation of the Munich meeting of the Spanish opposition." NARA, General Records of the Department of State. RG 59. Records of the Office of Western European Affairs. 1960- 63 General Decimal File. Box. 1808.
374 Eusko-Ikaskuntza, Irujo Fund, Signature J, Box 43, File 6, p. 163.
375 ARRIETA, Leyre. op. cit., p. 310.
376 The Marqués de Valdeiglesias, the Spanish Francoist representative, had been hovering around on the fringes of the Congress, trying to stop the Spanish democrats' resolution, with the help of Von Merkatz, a member of Adenauer's cabinet. Confidential Report "An evaluation of the Munich meeting of the Spanish opposition." NARA, General Records of the Department of State. RG 59. Records of the Office of Western European Affairs. 1960-63 General Decimal File. Box, 1808, p. 8; SAN SEBASTIÁN, Koldo, "1962: El llamado contubernio de Munich," p. 34. In ARZALLUS, Xabier [et.al.], 1989, Vascos en la construcción de Europa. Bilbao EAJ-PNV.
377 Projet de resolution. Eusko-Ikaskuntza, Irujo Fund, Signature J, Box 43, File 6, p.

163.
378 Confidential Report "An evaluation of the Munich meeting of the Spanish opposition." NARA, General Records of the Department of State. RG 59. Records of the Office of Western European Affairs. 1960-63 General Decimal File. Box, 1808, p. 8.
379 On the Munich meeting, see OPE nos.: 3637 (15/06/1962); 3670 (20/06/1962); 3642 (22/06/1962); 3645 (27/06/1962); 3656 (12/07/1962). And Alderdi nos.:183 (July 1962); 184-185 (August-Septemebr 1962).
380 Larrea's letter can be found in: Eukso-Ikaskunta, Irujo Fund, Signature J, Box 3, File 13. Gudari's report on Munich is found in issue no. 12, August 1962.
381 Eusko-Ikaskuntza, Irujo Fund, Signature J, Box 43, File 6, p. 163
382 José Antonio Ayestarán, Iñaki Aguinaga, and Kepa Anabitarte were three of the members of EGI and ELA-STV who were critical with the resolution in Munich.
383 Ayestarán was not able to attend the Munich meeting because he did not have a passport; but he was very actively critical against the position taken by the Basques in Munich. Ayestarán had been a member of EKIN, was member of EGI since 1960, and in 1964 would join ELA-STV. Interview by IBARZÁBAL, Eugenio, "José Antonio Ayestarán y la historia de ELA-STV," in Muga, no.3, 1980, pp. 57-72.
384 ESTÓRNES, Idoia, 2013, Cómo pudo pasarnos esto. Crónica de una chica de los 60. Donostia: Erein, p. 302. Although Idoia Estornés follows the explanation given by Anabitarte or Ayestarán about the creation of ELA-Berri, Koldo San Sebastián (in "1962: El llamado contubernio de Munich," op. cit., p. 37) relates a second version where the real cause of the secession would be the demand inside the group of ELA-STV of having greater presence in the Consultative Council and other bodies.
385 Ibid., p. 305.
386 SAN SEBASTIÁN, Koldo "Vascos en el contubernio de Munich," in Muga, Bilbao, 1983, no. 26, pp. 56-69.
387 ARRIETA, Leyre. op. cit., p. 248.
388 The UFD was an agreement signed on June 4th, 1961 initially by Izquierda Democrática Cristiana, Partido Socialista Obrero Español, Acción Republicana Democrática, Unión General de Trabajadores, Partido Nacionalista Vasco, Acción Nacionalista Vasca, and Solidaridad de Trabajadores Vascos. The UFD was created as a way to organize collectively the opposition to Franco. The Foundation acts and some of the first meetings' minutes can be found in: Eusko-Ikaskuntza, Irujo Fund, Signature J, Box 47, File 4
389 SAN SEBASTIÁN, Koldo.1989, op. cit., p. 32.
390 Salvador de Madariaga finished his speech with the sentence: "The Spanish Civil war is over today." OPE. No. 3637, June 15th, 1962.
391 SATRÚSTEGUI, Joaquín [Et.Alt.], 1993, Cuando la transición se hizo posible: El Contubernio de Munich. Madrid: Tecnos. pp. 74-77.
392 OPE. No. 3637. June 15th, 1962.
393 ABC published it openly on its front page on June 10th, 1962, with the headline "Marcel Niedergang has attended the top-secret meeting in Munich. The treasonous conspiracy."
394 OPE. No. 3642 (22/06/1962); OPE 3656 (12/07/1062)
395 Speculation of the form and nature of the Post-Franco Spanish Government. Madrid, September 11th, 1961. NARA, General Records of the Department of State. RG 59. Records of the Office of Western European Affairs. 1960-63 General Decimal File. Box, 1808.
396 The Statement is a free translation done by the author of the American report, found in the telegram sent from Brussels to the Secretary of State on June 20th, 1962. NARA, ibid.
397 "Exilio es papel en que escribimos" is a verse of Sarrionandia's poem "Propuestas para una definición de exilio." SARRIONANDIA, Joseba, 2017, Hilda dago poesia?/¿La poesía está muerta? Iruña: Pamiela.
398 A very interesting account of Julián Gorkin's life can be read in an autobiography that was censored during many years in Spain: (1975) El Revolucionario Profesional:

Testimonio de un hombre de acción, Barcelona: Aymà; and although there is not a biography on him available, we can also follow part of his life in the works of Jordi Amat (2016) La primavera de Múnich…, op. cit., and (2016) La semilla del liberalismo: Política y literatura en torno a la actividad española del Congreso por la libertad de la cultura. (1958-1969). Barcelona: Universitat de Barcelona, pp. 26-53; 74-79.

399 Michael Warner, the CIA former historian who studied the Congress based on the CIA's confidential documents, suggests that there was some CIA connection between that fact and the creation of the Congress, although due to the lack of information the question is not studied. "Origins of the Congress for Cultural Freedom, 1949-50," in Studies in Intelligence, 38, 1995. Among all the publications dealing with the Congress for Cultural Freedom, it is important to highlight the following, which I made use of to write this section: GLONDYS, Olga, 2012, op. cit.; STONOR SAUNDERS, Frances, 2001, La CIA y la Guerra fría cultural. Madrid: Debate; CONGRESO POR LA LIBERTAD DE LA CULTURA, 1961, El Congreso por la libertad de la cultura. Paris; as well as the works already mentioned by Jordi Amat: (2016) La primavera de Múnich…, op. cit., and (2016) La semilla del liberalismo, op. cit.

400 CONGRESO POR LA LIBERTAD DE LA CULTURA, 1961, op. cit., pp. 1-2

401 WARNER, Michael, 1995, op. cit., p. 1.

402 The Ford Foundation was the same private American foundation that paid for the "Centro de Estudios y documentación," as already mentioned, and their participation in the organization of the Munich Congress is what arouses the suspicions on the American funding. After having read all the sources that talk about the Munich meeting, especially those from the American State Department, I cannot confirm whether the USA was behind the funding of the Munich meeting, mainly in view of the report where they deny it, but also because of the financing troubles some attendees experienced to be at Munich. Nevertheless, since some of the NARA documents related to the Munich Congress are still classified, I cannot totally dismiss the possibility.

403 CONGRESO POR LA LIBERTAD DE LA CULTURA, 1961, op. cit.; SAUNDERS, Frances, 2001, op. cit., pp. 300-304.

404 AMAT, Jordi. 2016. La semilla del liberalismo, op. cit., p. 69.

405 Joseph Nye first coined the concept in his 1990 book Bound to Lead: The Changing Nature of American Power. New York: Basic books. He describes soft power as: "when one country gets other countries to want what it wants-might be called co-optive or soft power in contrast with the hard or command power of ordering others to do what it wants." Later, Nye developed the concept in his 2004 book Soft Power. New York: Public affairs. I believe that what the Congress for Cultural Freedom was doing can be considered as a kind of Soft Power, especially if we contrast the activities developed through that strategy with the selective targets, or military invasions, or cooperation that are related to "hard power."

406 CONGRESO POR LA LIBERTAD DE LA CULTURA, 1961, op. cit., pp. 2-3.

407 Hugh Wildford "The Permanent Revolution?," quoted in GLONDYS, Olga, op. cit., p. 56.

408 CONGRESO POR LA LIBERTAD DE LA CULTURA, 1961, op. cit., pp. 5.

409 Manuel Irujo to Jesús Mª de Leizaola, Paris, June 23rd, 1950. Eusko-Ikaskuntza, Irujo Fund, Signature J, Box 30, File 9. There is also information on the Berlin meeting in a letter from Hickman to Irujo, June 23rd, 1950, in Eusko-Ikaskuntza, Irujo Fund, Signature J, Box 34, File 4.

410 GLONDYS, Olga, op. cit., p. 60.

411 AMAT, Jordi, 2016, La Primavera de Múnich…, op. cit., p. 187.

412 AMAT, Jordi, 2016, La semilla del liberalismo…, op. cit., pp. 80-81.

413 "Libertad y universalidad de la cultura," in Cuadernos del Congreso por la Libertad de la Cultura, Paris, Num. 1, March, 1953, p. 4.

414 "Marx y Rusia," article unpublished, 1957(?). AN, Irujo-0068-C3.

415 GLONDYS, Gloria, 2012, op. cit., p. 76.

416 Manuel Irujo to Alberto Onaindia, Paris, 25th June, 1953. Eusko-Ikaskuntza, Irujo Fund, Signature J, Box 2, File 9.
417 Manuel Irujo to Julián Gorkin. Paris, October 1953. Eusko-Ikaskuntza, Irujo Fund, Signature J, Box.50, File 4A. It is also interesting to comment that the letter by Irujo begins with "We said yesterday...," probably quoting his professor Miguel de Unamuno, who after Primo de Rivera's dictatorship, in 1930, retook his classes after having being forced into exile, with these words. Unamuno was in turn quoting what Fray Luis de León had said four centuries before. Beginning the letter with that sentence was probably because Manuel Irujo wanted to emphasize the cultural nature of it.
418 Ibid., p. 10.
419 GLONDYS, Olga, 2012, op. cit., pp. 192-193.
420 There is a fact sheet in the journal Cuadernos that details all of the data as well as the full list of participants, sections, and special issues. See: GLONDYS, Olga, 2012, op. cit., pp. 351-353.
421 STONOR SAUNDERS, Frances, 2001, op. cit., p. 300.
422 Science and Freedom, Num. 6, August, 1956.
423 Letters from Gorkin to Irujo, Paris, December 17th, 1953. Eusko-Ikaskuntza, Irujo Fund, Signature J, Box.50, File 4A, and letters from Gorkin to Irujo, Paris, February and April, 1962. Eusko-Ikaskuntza, Irujo Fund, Signature J, Box.4, File 2c, 2d.
424 The letters sent by Gorkin to Irujo where he says "This week we will send you some copies of Issue I of the Bulletin of the Center for Documentation and Spanish Studies that I told President Aguirre about," "Thank you for the letter you sent me," or "I received your letter and immediately wrote and telephoned Quintanilla to recommend that he sends (sic.) your manuscript on my behalf to our representative in Argentina, Carlos P. Carranza," show the relationship and the interest of both parts in the participation in and reception of Cuadernos and other publications of the Congress for Cultural freedom, and they also show that other Basque nationalists, apart from Irujo, were knowledgeable of the participation of the Navarrese in it. Letters sent by Gorkin between February 1960 and December 1961. Eusko-Ikaskuntza, Irujo Fund, Signature J, Box.3, File 8. Sources: 19,25,76 & 90.
425 «Projet de travaux de la commission pour la vérité sur les crimes de Staline.» Eusko-Ikaskuntza, Irujo Fund, Signature J, Box.4, File 2d.
426 Gorkin to the executive committee of the PSOE, Paris, February 12th, 1962.
427 Gorkin wrote about these disappearances on several occasions in his works, but we recommend consulting El proceso de Moscú en Barcelona: El sacrificio de Andrés Nin. Barcelona: Aymà, 1974, and Contra el Stalinismo. Barcelona: Laertes, 2001.
428 Projet de travaux de la commission pour la vérité sur les crimes de Staline, Eusko-Ikaskuntza, Irujo Fund, Signature J, Box.4, File 2d.
429 Gorkin to Irujo. Paris, February 12th, 1962, Eusko-Ikaskuntza, ibid.
430 The whole list of the participants to the Commissions, as well as the letters between Gorkin and Irujo, are found in: Eusko-Ikaskuntza, Irujo Fund, Signature J, Box.4, File 2d. Source signature: 3-5.
431 AMAT, Jordi, 2016, La primavera...., op. cit., pp. 186 and ff.
432 Some issues of the Boletin Informativo del Centro de Documentación y estudios can be consulted online at: http://mdc.cbuc.cat/cdm/ref/collection/premsapolc/id/10416
433 The letters between Irujo and Gorkin, as well as the document "Por las libertades culturales, civiles y penales en España y Portugal," are found in: Eusko-Ikaskuntza, Irujo Fund, Signature J, Box 43, File 6, pp. 75-90.
434 IRUJO, Manuel, 1962, "Comunistas anti-stalinianos," in Desde el partido nacionalista vasco.
435 "Patriotas y gamberros," op. cit.
436 "Nuevos Hombres, nuevas ideas," Tximistak, Frente Nacional Vasco. March 1962. Also, in: http://urazandi.euskaletxeak.net/vol1/dvd03/Publicaciones/Tximistak/htm/index.htm

437 http://ianasagasti.blogs.com/mi_blog/2006/05/la_causa_del_pu.html
438 Letter from Xabier Landaburu to Elias Gallastegi, Saint Jean de Luz, November 30th, 1962. Euskomedia, Irujo Fund, Signature J, Box, 5, File 7.
439 "Fueros sí, Estatuto no," Alderdi, November, 1961, no.176.
440 Uzueta is referring to José Antonio Etxebarrieta who, although we don't have the conference he gave, we know he participated in the meetings in Paris. Iñaki de Unzueta to Manuel Irujo, November 8th, 1961 and December 19th, 1961. Eusko-Ikaskuntza, Irujo Fund, Signature J, Box, 39, File 1
441 "Juventud pesimista" in Alderdi January 1962, nº177-178
442 "The bitter Cubalibre of exile".
443 JÁUREGUI BERECIARTU, Gurutz, 1981, Ideología y estrategia política de ETA. Análisis de su evolución entre 1959 y 1968. Madrid: Siglo XXI. p. 89.
444 Letter from Lucio Aretxabaleta to Lehendakari Jesús Leizaola. Caracas, October 3rd, 1961. EAH-AHE, Archivo Histórico del Gobierno Vasco. Fondo del Lehendakari D. Jesus María de Leizaola. C-32/05.
445 Reflections on the life in Venezuela and the Basque exiles living there, by Iñaki Anasagasti in an interview in Bilbao, on November 30th, 2016.
446 Letter from the Euzko Mendigozale Bazta in Argentina to Lehendakari Leizaola, Buenos Aires, November 9th, 1960. EAH-AHE, Archivo Histórico del Gobierno Vasco. Fondo del Lehendakari D. Jesus María de Leizaola. C-32/18.
447 SEBASTIÁN GARCÍA, Lorenzo, 1995, "«Euzkadi Mendigoxale batza» durante la guerra civil española (1936-1939)," in Cuadernos de sección. Historia-Geografía 23, pp. 335-357. Donostia: Eusko Ikaskuntza. More on Euzko Mendigoizale Batza in: NÚÑEZ SEIXAS, Xosé M., 2007, "Los nacionalistas vascos durante la Guerra civil (1936-1939): Una cultura de guerra diferente," in Historia contemporánea, vol. 35. pp. 559-599; ELORZA, Antonio, 1978, Ideologías del nacionalismo vasco, 1876-1937: de los euskáricos a Jagi jagi. Donostia: Haranburu. pp. 441-464.
448 Some issues of these publications and an uncountable number of very valuable Basque publications can be consulted in the vast online archive focused on the Basque publications in the exile: Hemeroteca de la diáspora vasca: http://urazandi.euskaletxeak.net/default.html
449 LÓPEZ ADÁN, Emilio "Beltza," 1977, op. cit. The word "Aberrianos" refers to the followers of the Basque nationalist political party Aberri.
450 Although the letter is undated, its date can be deduced. See further on.
451 Letter from ETA Venezuela to Lehendakari Leizaola. Undated. EAH-AHE, Archivo Histórico del Gobierno Vasco. Fondo del Lehendakari D. Jesus María de Leizaola. C-32/15.
452 The funding issue can be followed in several letters sent to Lehendakari Aguirre by Lucio de Aretxabaleta, Basque delegate in Venezuela, and in the letters containing the information about the contacts made in Bayonne by Gonzalo Nárdiz, including important information provided by Juan Carlos Basterra, member of ANV in Caracas. EAH-AHE, Archivo Histórico del Gobierno Vasco. Fondo del Lehendakari D. Jesus María de Leizaola. C-32/5 and C-33/1.
453 Lucio Aretxabaleta had been President of the Euzko Gaztedi in Bilbao and fled into exile in 1941. Established in Venezuela, he presided the Basque Center in Caracas and the CEVA, and was Delegate of the Basque Government in Venezuela. He and his wife died in the Caracas earthquake of July 29th, 1967. Fernando Carranza was appointed his successor as Delegate.
454 Letter from Lucio de Aretxabaleta to Lehendakari Leizaola. Caracas, November 9, 1961. EAH-AHE, Archivo gobierno vasco, Fondo del presidente Leizaola. Box 32/5.
455 Letter from Lucio de Aretxabaleta to Lehendakari Leizaola. Caracas, October 3rd, 1961. Ibid.
456 http://ianasagasti.blogs.com/mi_blog/2015/09/la-prensa-nacionalista-en-venezuela.html)
457 Iñaki Anasagasti, http://ianasagasti.blogs.com/mi_blog/2015/09/la-prensa-nacionalista-en-venezuela.html More on the Basque press in Venezuela: AJURIA, Peru,

and SAN SEBASTIÁN, Koldo, 1992, El exilio vasco en Venezuela. Gasteiz: Eusko Jaurlaritzaren argitalpen zerbitzu nagusia; SAN SEBASTIÁN, Koldo, 1989, "Prensa vasca en América (I). Los medios de comunicación en Venezuela," in Muga, no. 70.

458 Manuel Fernández Etxebarria, Matxari, was a committed nationalist Basque journalist who fled to Venezuela after being imprisoned in El Dueso prison during the Spanish Civil War. He was expelled from the PNV due to his repeated attacks against the Basque Government and the PNV. He published Irrintzi (1957-1962), Frente Nacional Vasco (1960/1964-1968), and Sabindarra (1970-1974) from Venezuela, from where he also wrote in 1965 the controversial book Euzkadi, patria de los Vascos.

459 Manuel Fernández Etxebarria "Matxari," to Manuel Irujo. Caracas, June 29th, 1961. Eusko-Ikaskuntza, Irujo Fund, Signature J, Box 3, Exp. 14.

460 Eustaquio de Echave-Susaeta was a journalist and writer who directed, among others, the Carlist weekly "Chapel Zuri" and "Pensamiento Navarro." More at: http://www.euskomedia.org/aunamendi/36474

461 "A un gazte de Euzko Gaztedi de Caracas," by Eibar'ko Betikua, Irintzi, no. 11, p. 196.

462 Although Gurutz Jáuregui and Gaizka Soldevilla have dated this document to 1960, the first line runs: "Considerando que después de 23 años de acabada la guerra civil que España impuso a los vascos…," therefore it seems to me that the real date should be 1962. Besides, in Documentos Y, where the document is reproduced, it has been placed in the 1962 section.

463 2015. "De Aberri a ETA, pasando por Venezuela. Rupturas y continuidades en el nacionalismo vasco radical (1921-1977)," in Bulletin d'historie contemporaine de l'Espagne. No. 51, p. 237.

464 "Manifiesto de Caracas," Documentos Y, vol. 1, p.511.

465 Since there are countless examples of Basque nationalist publications to support the view that the presence of the Basque language was more frequent in these editions, we will only mention the most relevant and the most interesting to consult, just as an example: "Euskara eta Euskal Kulturaren alde"in Alderdi no.182; "En defensa de las lenguas amenazadas en el mundo (UNESCO)", "Euskararen eguna"; in Alderdi no.183; "Gure umeak eta Euzkara" in Gudari no. 13, 1962.

466 Declarations and statements of the PNV, 1945-1976. AN, Manuel Irujo, 0071, C-2.

467 Eusko Aberri Alkartasuna, Caracas, 1960; Tximistak, May 1961. Tximistak, May 1962.

468 "Carta de Condición Vasca," in Eusko Gaztedi, Caracas. June, 1962. Also, at: http://urazandi.euskaletxeak.net/vol1/dvd10/Euzko%20Gaztedi/htm/port2.htm

469 "Día de la condición vasca," in Eusko Gaztedi, Caracas, October 1962. Also, at: http://urazandi.euskaletxeak.net/vol1/dvd10/Euzko%20Gaztedi/htm/port2.htm

470 "Patriotas y gamberros," in Alderdi, May 1962, no. 182.

471 RODRÍGUEZ RANZ, José Antonio, 2002, "Manuel de Irujo. Lealtad crítica. (1960-1975)," Vasconia, 32, p. 165.

472 Although the conference is not signed and is said to have been given by a "member of ETA," according to the information received by Irujo on the organization of the conferences the first speech should correspond to Txillardegi's, on his own petition. Eusko-Ikaskuntza, Irujo Fund, Signature J, Box 3, Exp. 1.

473 "Ha pasado un cuarto de siglo," Zutik no. 15. Also in: http://urazandi.euskaletxeak.net/vol1/dvd10/Zutik/htm/port2.htm

474 José Luis Álvarez Enparantza (1929-2012), best known as "Txillardegi," was a committed, self-taught linguist who worked for and promoted the Basque language from the Euskaltzaindia (the Basque Academy of Language), wrote books, and helped to update the language and promote its use in the Basque country. In his political activity, he was member of ETA, ESB, Herri Batasuna, and Aralar, always combining the vindication of the Basque national cause with the use of the Basque language, and denouncing those Basque nationalists who had abandoned it. More on Txillardegi in: http://www.euskomedia.org/aunamendi/9273

475 "La juventud vasca ante el 7 de octubre de 1961," in Zutik, En tierras americanas. April, 1961, no.15, pp. 3 and ff. Also, in: http://urazandi.euskaletxeak.net/vol1/dvd10/Zutik/htm/port2.htm
476 "Patriotas y Gamberros," op. cit.; Letter from Eli Gallastegui to Manuel Irujo, op. cit.
477 The conference given by Iker Gallastegi, "El sentimiento de nacionalidad," can be found in Documentos Y, vol. 1, pp. 504 and ff. All the extracts presented here have the same source.
478 CASANOVA, Iker, 2007, ETA 1958-2008. Medio siglo de historia. Tafalla: Editorial Txalaparta, pp. 30-31.
479 More on Jagi-Jagi in: RENOBALES, Eduardo, 2010, Jagi-Jagi: historia del independentismo vasco. Bilbao: Ahaztuak 1936-1977; ELORZA, Antonio, 1978, op. cit.
480 Not only the Basque government did not consider ETA as a threat, but ETA felt likewise towards them. The information that the Basque government had about ETA was first-hand information: the youth Basque organization sent its publications to the Basque Government and offered their collaboration, as can be confirmed if one reads the letters sent on June 9th, 1960 directly addressed to the Lehendakari: "Please find enclosed for your information several copies of the first two issues of the newsletter "ZUTIK" published in Caracas by the EUZKADI TA AZKATASUN (E.T.A.) subsidiary." Or another letter sent from Bayonne on June 15th, 1960: "We will soon be publishing a book on Basque training, and we are faced with the difficulty of not knowing exactly what the Basque Government is doing. We would be very grateful for a three-page statement, for example, on this point." In EAH-AHE, Archivo Histórico del Gobierno Vasco. Fondo del Lehendakari D. Jesus María de Leizaola. C33/15.
481 Francisco Belausteguigoitia Landaluce had fled into exile in the 1920's. Established in Mexico, and in a wealthy situation, he collected funds for the Basque Government during the Spanish Civil War, helping the government purchase the Basque headquarters in Paris. He was the Basque delegate in Mexico until 1942. More on Belausteguigoitia in: http://www.euskomedia.org/aunamendi/23678
482 Francisco Belausteguigoitia to Manuel Irujo. Mexico, November 23rd, 1961. Euskomedia, Irujo Fund, Signature J, Box, 3, File 5
483 He is referring to an incident involving the director of La Vanguardia, Luis de Galinsoga, who, during a Mass at the Catalan church of Sant Ildefons in 1959 stated "All the Catalans are bullshit." The statement had been motivated by the fact that the Mass had been offered in Catalan. These declarations provoked a Catalanist campaign against the newspaper that ended with the dismissal of Galinsoga. DÍAZ ESCULIES, David, 1996, L'oposició catalana al franquisme: El Republicanisme liberal i la nova oposició (1939-1960). Barcelona: Publicacions de l'Abadia de Montserrat, pp. 114 and ff.
484 Confidential Report no.17. Bilbao, August 28th, 1961. NARA General Records of Department of State. Records of the Office of Western European Affairs. Bureau of European affairs. 1953-1962. NND959219 RG59 Box.7.
485 Ibid.
486 Letter from Manuel Irujo to Jesus de Solaun and Xabier de Landaburu. London, 1961. EAH-AHE, Archivo Histórico del Gobierno Vasco. Fondo del Lehendakari D. Jesus María de Leizaola. C-32/24.
487 Letter from Jesús Solaun to Lehendakari Leizaola. 1961 Undated. EAH-AHE, Archivo gobierno Vasco, Fondo del Presidente Leizaola. Box 33/14.
488 The full list of the detainees after the police raid is the following: Rafael Albisu, Imanol Laspiur, Iñaki Larramendi, Evaristo Urrestarazu, Iñaki Balerdi, Eduardo Ferrán, Julen adariaga, Andoni Iriondo, Angel Aranzabal, José Urbieta, José Antonio Eizaguirre, Eustakio Narbaiza, Serafín Basauri, Javier Aguirre, Agustín Olaskoaga, Robén López de la Calle, Javier Elosegi, José Mari Quesada, Ildefonso Iriarte, Sabin Uribe, Guillermo Mariñelarena, José Ramón Luzarraga, Patxi Amezaga, José Muñoa, Santiago Iturrioz, Juan José Etxabe, and José Antonio Lizarribar. Thanks to the license plate on the motorbike that was used for burning some flags on the same day

as the attack on the train, the police were able to track all the names and successfully carry out an operation against the ETA members, getting close to dismantling the organization. David López Dorronsoro, Paco Iturrioz, and Eneko Irigaray were able to escape and cross the border into exile, joining the fate of the traditional Basque nationalists.

489 Ibid.
490 Ibid.
491 PÉREZ-AGOTE, Alfonso, 2006, The social roots of Basque nationalism. Reno: University of Nevada Press, p. 74.
492 "La Violencia inútil," in Alderdi, March-April, 1962, nos. 180 -181.
493 The Border Campaign is explained in full in: FLYNN, Barry, 2009, Soldiers of folly: The IRA Border campaign. Cork: The Collins Press. Flynn explains how the campaign turned to guerrilla warfare and tactics that had been useful in the independence war, to attack Northern Ireland. It is interesting how a romantic uprising was constructed by taking advantage of southern voluntaries who knew barely anything about the north. Another reference on the Border Campaign, especially interesting for its focus on the Irish community in New York is: ALMEIDA, Linda Dowling, 2001, Irish immigrants in New York City 1945-1995. Bloomington: Indiana University Press. Relevant to this is the section on politics and nationalism, pp.130 and ff.
494 Ibid.
495 Ibid.
496 Ibid.
497 Although the letter was written in July, according to the information given by Irujo he probably received it later, perhaps in September.
498 Irujo to Jon Bilbao. November 5th, 1953. Euskomedia, Irujo Fund, Signature J, Box, 2, File 9.
499 Elias Gallastegi to Manuel Irujo. May 29th, 1962. Irujo Fund, Signature J, Box, 3, File 8.
500 This concept is developed in: CLARK, Robert P., 1984, The basque insurgents. ETA, 1952-1980. Madison: The University of Wisconsin Press.
501 Letters between Antonio Ruiz de Azua Zabalbeaskoa and Manuel Irujo. October, 1962. Irujo Fund, Signature J, Box, 3, File 16
502 Letters between Gallastegi's brothers and Manuel Irujo. January-February, 1974. Irujo Fund, Signature J, Box, 16, File G.
503 All references from Irujo's article "Patriotas y Gamberros" can be found in: IRUJO, Manuel, 1981, Escritos en Alderdi, vol II, pp. 41-46.
504 Although in the article "Patriotas y Gamberros" Irujo does not refer to the youth as a product of the Franco regime, it is in some previous articles like "Juventud pesimista" (Alderdi nos. 177-178, January, 1962) that he suggests it when talking about the youth: "They are patriotic. They are driven by high ideals. They will be the ones who will occupy our posts or other equivalent ones the day we have to leave office. But first they will have to be cured of their pessimism and of that conception of select, behind which, as behind the arms of the cross of the inquisitor, the horns of the totalitarian devil project themselves."
505 Iñaki de Unzueta to Manuel Irujo. November 8th, 1961 and December 19th, 1961. Eusko-Ikaskuntza, Irujo Fund, Signature J, Box, 39, File 1.
506 JÁUREGUI, Gurutz, "Los orígenes ideológicos de ETA," pp. 171-232. In ELORZA, Antonio (coord.), 2000, op. cit.
507 "Cuadernos ETA. Iglesia y Estado," in HÓRDAGO (ed.), 1979, op. cit., vol. 2, pp. 146.
508 "Principios Ideológicos Primera Asamblea," May, 1962. In HÓRDAGO (ed.), 1979, op. cit., vol. 1, pp. 532- 533.
509 JÁUREGUI BERECIARTU, Gurutz, 1981, op. cit., pp. 133-135.
510 "Nationalism is the most important social and political phenomenon of our time. It is the cultural framework of modernity and, as such, it defines all of the specifically

modern experience, be it social, political, economic, personal, that is, it defines the ways we, modern men and women, live our lives." GREENFELD, Liah, 2016, Advanced introduction of Nationalism. Northampton: Edward Elgar.
511 RUBIRALTA CASAS, Fermí, 2003, "Els intel·lectuals en la conformació del nou nacionalisme radical gallec, català i basc durant la dècada de 1960." Revista del Centre de Lectura de Reus, no. 8; URLA, Jaqueline, 1993, "Cultural Politics in an Age of Statistics: Numbers, Nations, and the Making of Basque Identity," in American ethnologist, vol. 20, no. 4, pp. 818-843.
512 "Euskera y patriotismo vasco." In HÓRDAGO (Ed.), 1979, op. cit. Vol.1, pp. 104-109.
513 It is usual to alternate popular words in Basque when speaking in Spanish in the Basque Country, as well as the opposite when speaking in Basque. In this case aundiki, jauntxos and aiton semes are words used to describe rich kids and siblings coming from wealthy families.
514 "Euskera y patriotismo vasco." In HÓRDAGO (Ed.), 1979, op. cit. Vol.1, pp. 104-109.
515 GUIBERNAU, Montserrat, 1999, Nacions sense estat. Barcelona: Columna edicions, pp. 61-62.
516 DE LA GRANJA, José Luis; DE PABLO, Santiago (eds.), 2002, Historia del País Vasco y de Navarra en el siglo XX . Madrid : Editorial Biblioteca Nueva, pp. 333-339.
517 Interview to Xabier Kintana, member of Euskaltzaindia, the Academy of Basque Language. Bilbao, November, 2011.
518 INTXAUSTI, Joseba. 1992. Euskera. La lengua de los vascos. Donostia: Elkar. pp. 184-185.
519 The Congresses on Basque studies were celebrated between 1918 and 1930 in the Basque Country. During the exile, the Congress was celebrated in three different occasions in Bayonne. In 1978 was reestablished in the Basque Country. More on the Basque Studies congresses at: http://www.euskomedia.org/aunamendi/32088/123009 . Regarding the creation and promotion of ikastolas, even they were private schools, we cannot ignore that the founders of the ikastolas movements, like Resurrección Maria de Azkue, were linked to the Basque nationalism. The expansion of the ikastolas, as well as the culturalist movement aforementioned, was developed during the 1960's. More on Ikastolas at: http://www.euskomedia.org/aunamendi/73307/76032
520 "Principios Ideológicos Primera Asamblea." Op.Cit.
521 GHOSH, Devleena. 2008. Op.Cit. p. 285.
522 Xabier Kintana. Cited interview.
523 "Principios Ideológicos Primera Asamblea," op. cit.
524 "Los coreanos," by Manuel Irujo. In Alderdi, no. 123, June, 1957.
525 Both words, Maketo and coreano are pejorative nouns used to refer to immigrants settled in the Basque Country.
526 More on Ceferino Jemein at: http://www.euskomedia.org/aunamendi/63966
527 This idea was quite extended in some parts of Spain, including the Basque Country and Catalonia, but if it was true, nobody has ever found a document proving that the Franco regime had such a strategy. Moreover, the fact that the Basque Country, as well as Catalonia, were two of the most industrialized areas in Spain means that no immigration plan was needed in that respect. On the other hand, what is easily verifiable is that immigrants were being confined in camps in Barcelona, for instance, and forced to return to their places of origin. On the immigration process during the Franco regime, consult: GONZÁLEZ MADRID, Damián-Alberto (ed.), 2008, El franquismo y la transición en España: desmitificación y reconstrucción de la memoria de una época. Madrid: Libros de la Catarata; as well as another analysis, focused on the economy and the repercussions of the immigration: TORRE, Joseba de la, SANZ LAFUENTE, Gloria (eds.), 2008, Migraciones y coyuntura económica del franquismo a la democracia. Zaragoza: Prensas universitarias de Zaragoza

528 Letter from Ceferino Jemein to Manuel Irujo. Pau, December 21st, 1950. Eusko-Ikaskuntza, Irujo Fund, Signature J, Box, 2, File 5.
529 "Maquetos y Coreanos," Tierra Vasca, Buenos Aires, August 15th, 1957.
530 GHOSH, Devleena, 2008, op. cit., p. 284. In fact, Ghosh is quoting Richard Eder's commentaries in a book review published in The New York Times on a book by Dubravka Ugresic, The Museum of unconditional surrender. The review can be consulted at: http://www.nytimes.com/1999/11/09/books/books-of-the-times- treating-exile-as-a-separate-country.html
531 As an outsider, although a good ideologist and member of the Basque Government, Manuel Irujo normally made someone else speak to or put pressure on the Lehendakari. He confronted his ideas with the Basque president, but, as we can see in his letters, he also generated a group of pressure on several occasions in order to get the Basque Government involved. In that specific case, we can follow the controversial debate on immigration through the letters he exchanged in November 1957 with Francisco Belausteguigoitia, former Basque delegate in Mexico. AN, PNV, 0097, C-5.
532 Christmas message, December, 1957. AGUIRRE, José Antonio, 1981, op. cit., pp. 985-991.
533 Letter from Elias Gallastegi to Manuel Irujo, July 19th, 1962. Euskomedia, Irujo Fund, Signature J, Box, 5, File 7. p.27.
534 CASANOVA, Iker. 2007. Op.Cit. pp. 33-36; JÁUREGUI BERECIARTU, Gurutz. 1981. Op.Cit. pp. 170-173.
535 Irujo wrote in his article "Patriotas y Gamberros": "It is demagogic and poorly serves the country to blame the industrialists and traders who live in our country and turn to Madrid to solve their problems."
536 When ETA began to be identified with the working-class movement and attracted to the worker's protests, they published some articles related to that question in Zutik, like: "Los trabajadores guipuzcoanos enseñan el camino," Zutik, unnumbered, Dec-January 1961 1963; "Los obreros hemos comenzado la lucha," Zutik, no.4, August 1962; "Perspectivas de la lucha obrera en Euzkadi," Zutik, no.5, October 1962; "Euskadi Libre con obreros libres," Zutik en tierras americanas, no. 20, 1962.
537 Letter from Elias Gallastegi to Manuel Irujo, July 19th, 1962. Op.Cit. p. 34.
538 Ibid.
539 JÁUREGUI BERECIARTU, Gurutz, 1981, op. cit., pp. 174-176.
540 "Marxismo" and "Comunismo." HÓRDAGO (ed.), 1979, op. cit., pp. 199-215.
541 Francisco Belausteguigoitia to Manuel Irujo, August 8th, 1962. Eusko-Ikaskuntza, Irujo Fund, Signature J, Box, 5, File 5.
542 Manuel Irujo to Francisco Belausteguigoitia. September 12th, 1962. Eusko-Ikaskuntza, Ibid.
543 EHA-AHE, Fondo Leizaola. C-33-1.
544 CASANOVA, Iker, op. cit., p. 17.
545 "El Español" was a Falangist-ideology weekly magazine published in Madrid during the Franco dictatorship. It was founded in 1942 by Juan Aparicio and was dependent on the National Delegation of Press and Propaganda. A good proportion of the fascist intellectuals, such as Ernesto Giménez Caballero, wrote or collaborated in that weekly during the 1940's. The magazine had several phases, and in the sixties, it was dominated by Manuel Fraga Iribarne, Minister of Information and Tourism, who made use of it for his regime-opening operation, linking it to the School of Journalism of Madrid. That drift meant that some well-known anti-Francoist activists and writers, such as Manuel Vázquez Montalbán, would write articles for the magazine, since it formed part of the compulsory course for future journalists in Madrid.
546 "Activities of ETA," from the Embassy in Madrid to the Department of State. October 26th, 1962. NARA, RG 59 General Records of the Department of State. Bureau of European Affairs. Office of Western European Affairs. Records Relating to Spain, 1963-1976. NND959000 Box.5.
547 "Patriotas y Gamberros," op. cit.

548 Letter from Elias Gallastegi to Manuel Irujo, July 19th, 1962, op. cit., p. 40.
549 "Principios políticos constitucionales." HÓRDAGO (ed.), op. cit., vol. 2, pp. 75-83.
550 "El sentimiento de nacionalidad," in HÓRDAGO (ed.), vol. 1, pp. 504 and ff.
551 "Patriotas y Gamberros," op. cit.
552 Letter from Elias Gallastegi to Manuel Irujo, July 19th, 1962, op. cit., p. 16.
553 "La Federación Europea," in Cuadernos. HÓRDAGO (ed.), op. cit., vol. 1, pp. 84-85
554 "Principios Ideológicos Primera Asamblea," op. cit.
555 "Neo-Carlismo," in Zutik (third series), no. 5, 1962; Zutik en Tierras Americanas, no. 23, 1962. Also, at: http://urazandi.euskaletxeak.net/vol1/dvd10/Zutik/htm/port2.htm
556 "Patriotas y Gamberros." Op.Cit.
557 Letter from Elias Gallastegi to Manuel Irujo, July 19th, 1962. Op.Cit. p. 10.
558 IBARRA, Pedro, 1987, La evolución estratégica de ETA (1963-1987). Donostia: Kriselu. p. 63.
559 Analysis of Tunis' conflict, pp. 57-73; Analysis of Ireland's conflict: pp. 75-85, in Libro Blanco, op. cit.
560 SARRAILH DE IHARTZA, Fernando, 1963, Vasconia. Buenos Aires: Ediciones Norbait.
561 More on the important life and vast work of Resurrección María de Azkue at: http://www.euskomedia.org/aunamendi/1368
562 KRUTWIG, Federico, 2014, Años de peregrinación y lucha. Tafalla: Txalaparta, p. 26.
563 For this research I used the second edition of Vasconia, since copies of the first edition of the book are very difficult to come by. The second edition was published in April 1973, with no changes regarding the contents, but with the documentary part missing. Krutwig explains in the prologue why it is important to read it that way and appreciate the changes that Basque society has undergone since the original text was written—but I wanted to illustrate here something I discovered about this second edition when I interviewed Sabin Atxalandabaso, member of ETA-PM, who was in charge of the international area of the organization until 1977: "There are two editions of Vasconia (...) Pertur and I went to the Aosta Valley, where Krutwig used to live, to ask permission to republish it. Once there, we thought about the problems, which were that it had to weigh little to pass it to the other side, and so on. It was the same as the first edition, but full of documents, so, at the time of printing it, I think it was me, who decided to have them removed. So, when you read that edition, it refers to documents that are not there. We edited it in Baiona, it says Buenos Aires, but it is Baiona. Krutwig reacted by climbing up the walls, telling us that we had no idea of anything..." Interview with Eneko Irigaray and Sabin Atxalandabaso. Donostia, April 20, 2012.
564 Ibid., pp. 15-39.
565 KRUTWIG, Federico, 2014, op. cit., p. 69.
566 Roger Trinquier was a Colonel of the French army during the Algerian Independence war (1954-1962). He wrote La Guerre Moderne. Paris: La Table Ronde, 1961
567 KRUTWIG, Federico, 2014, op. cit., p. 42.
568 GENOVESE, Eugene D., 1979, From Rebellion to Revolution: Afro-American slave revolts in the making of the modern world. Baton Rouge: Louisiana State University Press.
569 SARRAILH DE IHARTZA, Fernando, op. cit., p. 330.
570 "Guerra Revolucionaria / Insurrección en Euskadi," Cuadernos de ETA nº20, 1964, in: HÓRDAGO (ed.), op. cit. (vol. III), pp. 21-70.
571 Antoni Batista, in his book Madariaga de las armas a la palabra (Barcelona: RBA, 2008), defends that Julen Madariaga was the ideologist behind the armed struggle and the identification of the Basque Country as a colony, but, as we have already seen, the anti-colonialist idea and the armed struggle were concepts that had been developed beforehand in documents that were previous to Guerra Revolucionaria/

Insurrección en Euskadi. Nevertheless, it is true that Madariaga was the leader of an ETA faction that supported political violence, against an opposing faction that defended a non-violent resistance inspired by Gandhi; "En torno a la no violencia," Zutik, no.7, pp. 9-10; MADARIAGA, Julen, "Quién es el culpable de la violencia," Zutik, no. 8, p. 5.
572 Letters by Sven Johanssen informing Enbata and the Basque Government about the petition sent to the court of Bayonne. Eusko-Ikaskuntza, Irujo Fund, Signature J, Box, 7, File 1.
573 Txillardegi finally abandoned ETA (together with Benito del Valle and Xabier Imaz), due to the Marxist tendency of the organization: "ETA has ceased to be a movement of diverse tendencies, and has progressively become a party with a clearly Marxist-Leninist tendency," affirmed in their letter of permanent withdrawal of the organization of April 1967. (In Eusko-Ikaskuntza, Irujo Fund, Signature J, Box, 10, File 5). Years later, in 1971, Txillardegi confessed in a long letter to Manuel Irujo that a part of the organization (ETA VI), as Irujo had expressed, got ran out of control: "There is an ETA, (...) ETA VI, which is an obvious transmission belt of the PCE." Txillardegi was worried about the veer of a part of Basque nationalism which was turning into a Spanish Marxism: "The transition from a Basque nationalist idea to a Spanish Marxism-Leninism is taking place with regularity (...)." In Eusko-Ikaskuntza, Irujo Fund, Signature J, Box, 13, File A.
574 Letters between Txillardegi and Irujo. November 1964. Eusko-Ikaskuntza, Irujo Fund, Signature J, Box, 7, File 1.
575 Irujo to Solaun. November 30th, 1964. Eusko-Ikaskuntza, Irujo Fund, Signature J, Box, 7, File 1.
576 Guerra Revolucionaria/Insurrección en Euskadi, op. cit., p. 8.
577 In fact, the concept had previously been fully developed in Vasconia, where Krutwig explains that the high density of industrial population is a problem in the Basque Country, and he goes on to imagine a group of warriors in formations of three, named "hirurkos," wholly inspired on the Israeli experience. Vasconia, op. cit., pp. 332-335.
578 Guerra Revolucionaria/Insurrección en Euskadi, op. cit., p. 25.
579 Interview with Julen Madariaga. Saint-Pée-Sur-Nivelle, November 22nd, 2011.
580 Menachem Begin was a leading member of the Irgun who, after the creation of the State of Israel, joined the political party Herut and became its leader. Years later he would become Prime Minister of the State of Israel.
581 Interview with Julen Madariaga. Saint-Pée-Sur-Nivelle, November 22nd, 2011.
582 LISBONA, José Antonio, 2002, España – Israel. Historia de unas relaciones secretas. Madrid: Temas de Hoy, p. 377.
583 Ibid., p. 379.
584 Interview with Julen Madariaga. Saint-Pée-Sur-Nivelle, November 22nd, 2011.
585 Interview with Eneko Irigaray and Sabin Ataxalandabaso. Donostia, February 20th, 2012.
586 The "Movimiento para autodeterminación e independència del archipélago Canario" (MPAIAC) developed its activities between 1964 and 1979, resisting the Spanish control of the Canary Islands and vindicating the full independence of the archipelago. There is no bibliography on the organization, save for the work of a self- publishing organization: MOVIMIENTO POR LA AUTODETERMINACIÓN Y LA INDEPENDENCIA DEL ARCHIPIÉLAGO CANARIO, 1970, El Nacionalismo revolucionario de Canarias:La "crisis" colonial de Madrid ; Fase actual de nuestra lucha nacional y revolucionaria. Alger.
587 BATISTA, Antoni, 2007, Madariaga, de las armas a la palabra. Barcelona: RBA Editores, p. 114.
588 SARRAILH DE IHARTZA, Fernando, op. cit., Appendices I, II, and III.
589 IBARRA, Pedro, op. cit., p. 66.
590 Zutik, no. 31, July, 1965. In HÓRDAGO (ed.), 1979, op. cit., vol. III, p. 521.
591 HÓRDAGO (ed.), 1979, op. cit., vol. III, pp. 514-518.

592 Ibid., p. 517.
593 "Carta a los intelectuales," Zutik, no. 30, June, 1965.
594 JÁUREGUI BERECIARTU, Gurutz, 1981, op. cit., p. 254.
595 Ibid., p. 256.
596 "It is unthinkable that while accusing, for example, the PNV of being bourgeois and affirming the need to link national liberation with social liberation, at the same time the confusion between the Algerian FLN, the Israeli Irgun, or Eoka is maintained, considering them all national liberation movements without further nuances." GARMENDIA, José Mari, 1979, Historia de ETA. Donosti: L.Haramburu Editor, vol. I, p. 167.
597 The influence that the labor front had within ETA will be shown clearly from the moment that Zalbide is imprisoned and Patxi Iturrioz is left to manage ETA's executive on his own. This stage is recognizable in the analysis that Zutik made from October 1965 to December 1966, explaining the history of the Basque Country no longer from a nationalist perspective, which it had discarded, but instead from a Marxist perspective that considered a union of all working-class groups fighting together as a better alternative to the national front.
598 Back then this group was formed by the founding members, Txillardegui, Benito del Valle and Julen Madariaga.
599 Zutik, no. 31, p. 6. In HÓRDAGO (ed.), op. cit., vol. III, p. 521.
600 Zutik, from November 1965 to July 1966.
601 BATISTA, Antoni, 2007, op. cit., p.119.
602 Otello Saraiva de Carvalho was a Portuguese military officer who was chief of strategy during the 1974 Carnation Revolution in Portugal that put an end to the authoritarian regime. Patricie Lumumba was the first president of Independent Congo, but since he was assassinated in 1961, and the Che's tour in Africa was in 1963, he was probably invited by Cyrille Adoula, who formed part of the Mouvement National Congolais (MNC) that was responsible for the Independence movement. Ernesto Che Guevara was a Marxist revolutionary warrior who participated in the Cuban Revolution; he served as Minister of Industry for Castro's first government and gave up his government duties in order to travel and spread the revolution. He gave a speech in Alger in 1965 and visited some African countries. He was assassinated in 1967 in Bolivia.
603 KRAUZE, Enrique, 2011, Redentores. Ideas y poder en América latina. Barcelona: Debate, p. 328.
604 According to some ETA members, in those days José Antonio, like Patxo Unzueta, was not an official member of the organization. He had to wait until 1966, just before the Vth Assembly, although due to his disease he was never able to attend any of the assemblies. His brother Txabi, became his voice in the presentation and defense of his works. LORENZO ESPINOSA, José María, 1994, Txabi Etxebarrieta: Armado de palabra y obra. Tafalla: Txalaparta, p. 58.
605 ZULAIKA, Joseba, 2014, That Bilbao old moon. The passion and resurrection of a city. Reno: Center for Basque studies, p. 55.
606 IBARRA, Pedro, 1987, op. cit., p. 69.
607 ZULAIKA, Joseba, 2014, op. cit., p. 48
608 Declarations of Iker Gallastegi in: ETXEBARRIETA ORTIZ, José Antonio, 1999, Los vientos favorables. Euskal Herria 1839-1959. Tafalla: Txalaparta, pp. 31-32. In the same book, but in the chapter signed by Txomin Ziluaga, it is stated that José Antonio would receive a scholarship from the Basque Government for studying political science in Paris. Ibid., p. 41.
609 Irujo to Elías Gallastgui. May 4th, 1962. Eusko-Ikaskuntza, Irujo Fund, Signature J, Box, 3, File 8.
610 Irujo to Belausteguigoitia. September 12th, 1962. Eusko-Ikaskuntza, Irujo Fund, Signature J, Box, 5, File 5.
611 ETXEBARRIETA ORTIZ, José Antonio. 1999, op. cit., p. 74
612 Ibid., p. 100.

613 Ibid., pp. 120-122.
614 Ibid., p. 145.
615 ZULAIKA, Joseba, 2014, op. cit., p. 49.
616 BULLAIN, Iñigo, 2011, Revolucionarismo patriótico. El Movimiento de liberación nacional vasco. (MLNV). Madrid: Editorial Tecnos, p. 100.
617 KRUTWIG, Federico, 2014, op. cit., pp. 73-89.
618 "Abi Gezund!" was the way among the members of the Irgum to say goodbye to a comrade who was departing on a mission to carry out a patriotic action. Ibid., p. 82.
619 LORENZO ESPINOSA, José María, 1994, op. cit., p. 62.
620 The report was lost and no copy is left. We know about its contents from the testimonies of the members who attended the assembly, especially the recollections of Patxo Unzueta in Documentos Y, vol. 5, pp. 127-128. Its original title was "Análisis y crítica del españolismo social-chauvinista," leaving no doubt as to its intentions.
621 The first issue of Branka saw the light in April 1966, with the aim, according to Txillardegi, of stopping the social-imperials thesis, what meant the Spanish communists' tendency that Txillardegi had denounced in several occasions. Branka was published until 1972 and was the official publication of those who abandoned ETA after the Vth, mainly being a Basque nationalist cultural journal of the Basque nationalists in the exile, as Txillardegi, the founder and principal promoter, liked to define it. More in: 1979. Branka. Donostia: Ediciones Vascas. 2 vols.
622 ELORZA, Antonio. (Coord.). 2000. Op.Cit. p. 240.
623 HÓRDAGO (Ed.). 1979. Op.Cit. Vol. 5, pp. 127-128.
624 There are several books and sources on the Vth Assembly. The ideological basis can be found in HÓRDAGO (Ed.). 1979. Op.Cit. Vol. 5, pp. 174-177; Different historical analysis can be read in: ELORZA, Antonio. (Coord.). 2000. Op.Cit. pp. 233-251 and CASANOVA, Iker. 2007. Op.Cit. pp. 77-84. Besides, the testimony of Krutwig is essential to understand the elaboration of the thesis and the ideology from the exile, as well as it shows us a different version of the events: KRUTWIG, Federico. 2014. Op.Cit. pp.103-132.
625 His poems and some of his personal and political writings are published in: LORENZO ESPINOSA, José María, 1994, op. cit.
626 ZULAIKA, Joseba, 2014, op. cit., p. 57.
627 CASANOVA, Iker, 2007, op. cit., pp.91-92.
628 A detailed explanation on the repression is developed in the next chapter.
629 LORENZO ESPINOSA, José María, 1994, op. cit., pp. 262-269.
630 GURRUCHAGA, Ander. 1985. El código nacionalista vasco durante el franquismo. Barcelona: Anthropos
631 A complete analysis of the Decree is found in SALABERRI, Kepa, 1971, Sumarísimo 31-69. El proceso de Euskadi en Burgos. Paris: Ruedo Ibérico, pp. 49-73. The law can be consulted in: Decreto-Ley sobre rebelión militar, bandidaje y terrorismo. https://www.boe.es/publicaciones/anuarios_derecho/abrir_pdf.php?id=ANU-P- 1960-30045500459_ANUARIO_DE_DERECHO_PENAL_Y_CIENCIAS_PENALES_Decreto_de_21_de_septiemb re_de_1960,_revisando_y_unificando_la_Ley_de_2_de_marzo_de_1943_y_el_Decreto- Ley_de_18_de_abril_de_1947
632 Ley 154/1963, de 2 de diciembre, sobre creación del Juzgado y Tribunales de Orden Público. https://www.boe.es/diario_boe/txt.php?id=BOE-A-1963-22622
633 More on the Brigada político social and on TOP in: AGUILA, Juan José del, 2001, El TOP. La represión de la libertad (1963-1977). Barcelona: Ed. Planeta. BATISTA, Antoni, 1995, La brigada social. Barcelona: Empúries
634 The Francoist regime declared 11 different states of emergency within the period 1956-1975; four of them affected the whole of Spain (1956, 1962, 1969, and 1970), one was declared in Asturias (1958), and the rest, six, were exclusively declared in Basque provinces, which means that at least on ten occasions one of the Basque provinces was affected by a state of emergency. The exact lengths, dates, causes, and number of detainees of the states of exceptions during Francoism are detailed in GURRUCHAGA, Ander, 1985, El código nacionalista vasco durante el franquismo.

Barcelona: Anthropos Editorial, pp. 291-309.
635 Ibidem, p. 293.
636 The defense and development of this concept of ETA is analyzed in: ODRIOZOLA IRIZAR, Onintza, 2016, Erakunde bat baino gehiago: ETA herri mugimendu gisa (1958-1968). UPV-EHU.
637 "Guerra revolucionaria- Insurrección en Euskadi," 1963, in "Cuadernos de ETA," num. 20. HÓRDAGO (Ed.), 1979, Documentos Y (18 volums). Donostia: Lur Ed. (vol.III), pp. 21-70. "Bases teóricas de la guerra revolucionaria" can be found in: HÓRDAGO (Ed.), 1979, Documentos Y (18 volums). Donostia: Lur Ed. (vol.IV), pp. 514-518.
638 Mutil is a Basque word meaning "boy," and was used to refer to the members of ETA, denoting their youth. The popular Basque singer Mikel Laboa composed a song titled "Haika Mutil" (Rise, boy) that encouraged the young Basque boys to rise.
639 "Guerra revolucionaria- Insurrección en Euskadi," 1963, op. cit., p. 8.
640 IBARRA, Pedro. 1987. La Evolución estratégica de ETA. (1963-1987). Donostia: Kriselu, p. 25
641 "Guerra Revolucionaria- Insurrección en Euskadi," 1963, op. cit., p. 15.
642 BATISTA, Antoni. 2008. Madariaga. De las armas a la palabra. Barcelona: RBA, p. 110.
643 SULLIVAN, John, 1988, "ETA and Basque nationalism. The fight for Euskadi. 1890-1986." New York: Routledge, p. 68.
644 Ibid. p. 70.
645 "Manifiesto," Euskadi Ta Askatasuna, March, 1968, in CASANOVA, Iker, 2007, ETA 1958-2008. Medio siglo de historia. Tafalla: Editorial Txalaparta, p. 94.
646 If Txabi Etxebarrieta happened to be the first martyr of ETA, it was because, in spite of his youth, he was a recognized intellectual and ideologist, a political member, and a natural leader. More on Txabi Etxebarrieta in: LORENZO ESPINOSA, José María, 1994, Txabi Etxebarrieta: Armado de palabra y obra. Tafalla: Txalaparta.
647 An account of the killing of Txabi Etxebarrieta was published by ETA, in: Zutik, num.49, July, 1968.
648 "Manifiesto de ETA. Melitón Manzanas ejecutado." In HÓRDAGO (Ed.), 1978. Burgos: Juicio a un pueblo. Donostia: Lur Ed., p. 16.
649 Article 14 refers to the right to fix one's residency anywhere within the Spanish territory; Article 15 establishes the inviolability of one's home; and Article 18 limits detentions without a trial to up to 72 hours. http://www.boe.es/datos/pdfs/BOE/1945/199/A00358-00360.pdf
650 On May 30th, 1960, the Bishops of Vitoria, San Sebastian, Bilbao, and Pamplona, together with 339 priests, presented a writing denouncing the Franco Regime. The document denounced not only the situation of the Basque Church, something that could have been deemed acceptable by the regime, but also referred to society's lack of freedom, the repression suffered, the tortures, and the attacks on the Basque language and culture. A copy of that writing (translated into English) was sent to the President of the United States by reverend J. Arana, of the Incarnation Rectory in New York. In a letter that was attached to the document, the reverend tells of the attacks suffered by the priest who had signed the denouncing document, and asks the American President to sever relations with Spain, appealing to the fight against communists that the USA had been carrying out. The Basque priest compares communism with the Franco regime, using the same strategy many times employed by the Basque nationalists of the PNV in their attempt to equate totalitarianisms. NARA, General Records of Department of State, Bureau of European affairs. Office of Western European Affairs 1953-1962. RG 59, NND 959219. Box 7. An original copy of the letter can also be found in: AN, Irujo, 0098,03.
651 Manuel Irujo to Jesús Leizaola. Leigh-on-See, August 16th, 1960. EAH-AHE, Archivo gobierno Vasco, Fondo del Presidente Leizaola. Box 32/1.
652 HÓRDAGO (Ed.), 1978, op. cit., p. 20.
653 Vicente Carranza detailed his horrible ordeal in La hora tercia, published posthu-

mously, and can be read in the work by Antoni Batista on Antonio Juan Creix: (2010) La Carta. Historia de un comisario franquista. Madrid: Debate, p. 140. In the book, Batista also points out that Carranza was not right about Creix's use of drugs; it seems to be a rumor about his person that only gives an even more negative impression of the Commissioner. He didn't need to be on drugs to beat, torture, and even kill a detainee.

654 EGI, num.48, 1968, p. 1.
655 TXALAPARTA (Ed.), 1994, Euskadi eta Askatasuna = Euskal Herria y la libertad. Tafalla: Txalaparta, p. 123, Vol. 2.
656 CASANELLAS, Pau, 2014, Morir matando. El Franquismo ante la práctica armada. 1968-1977. Madrid: Los Libros de la catarata, p. 38.
657 Ibid., p. 36.
658 In April, 1969, there was a spectacular detention and chase in Artecalle Street in Bilbao, where Mikel Etxebarrieta managed to get away, Victor Arana was seriously injured, and a taxi driver was shot dead by the police. In the town of Urabain, in Araba, Segundo Urteaga was killed by the police because they thought he was trying to help ETA members by ringing the church's bells; and, in Irun, a young man called Roberto Pérez Jáuregi was killed by police shots while he was at a demonstration against the Burgos Trial on December, 1970. Lehendakari Leizaola sent a letter of condolence to his family, which can be consulted in: EHA-AHE, Fondo Archivo Histórico Gobierno Vasco, Fondo Especial Beyris, P-61/1-6. These are just some examples of the fatal victims of the Franco repression. More in: HÓRDAGO, 1978, op. cit., pp. 21-24; SALABERRI, Kepa, 1971, op. cit., pp. 93-102.
659 More on Basque protest songs in: https://www.etxepare.eus/en/basque-songwriting
660 "La persecución al pueblo vasco," Alderdi, nos. 244-245, 1968.
661 Since 1968 and until 1971, Alderdi and OPE tried to inform the Basques in the exile, but also those in the inside, making known the lists of those who had been detained, prosecuted, or tortured. There is extensive information on the OPE of 1968, especially from August 1969 and 1970. Alderdi presented a series of reports on the repression since nos. 246-247, at the beginning of 1969, and articles in the following numbers. In the first issue of 1970 (nos. 256-257), there is again a special report on repressive activities in 1969 entitled "La persecución contra el pueblo Vasco en 1969."
662 Gabon Message, December 24th, 1968. Alderdi, nos. 246-247, 1969.
663 "Gudariak," January 17th, 1968. IRUJO, Manuel, 1984, Desde el partido nacionalista vasco. Bilbao: Idatz Ekintza, pp. 480-481.
664 "El discurso de Irujo en Caracas," May – June, 1969. Ibid., pp. 464-466. "Agur, Jaunak!", meaning "Greetings, Sirs!" is a way to welcome or to say goodbye, displaying honor. It is also a popular Basque song. More in: https://aunamendi.eusko-ikaskuntza.eus/artikuluak/artikulua.php?id=eu&ar=7269
665 Indictment written by the prosecutor, "Sumarísimo nº31/69." SALABERRI, Kepa, 1971, op. cit., p. 91.
666 La Vanguardia Española, December 13th, 1968. http://hemeroteca.lavanguardia.com/preview/1970/12/29/pagina- 10/34342891/pdf.html?search=Dorronsoro%20 1968
667 SALABERRI, Kepa, 1971, op. cit., p. 92; "La actitud de los obispos Aryaga y Ciriarda," Alderdi, no. 260, Feb., 1971.
668 Ibid., pp. 102-110.
669 GURRUCHAGA, Ander, 1985, op. cit., p. 273.
670 Leaflet distributed in Barcelona in November, 1970. Unknown author. CRAI. Biblioteca del Pavelló de la República. Universitat de Barcelona. FV.1970/1
671 Ibid.
672 COLOMINES, Joan, 2003, Crònica de l'antifranquisme a Catalunya. Barcelona: Angle Editorial, p. 150.
673 Sumarísimo Militar. VI Región. Nº 31/69. CRAI. Biblioteca del Pavelló de la República. Universitat de Barcelona. FV.1970/2.
674 JUDT, Tony, 2006, Postguerra. Una historia de Europa desde 1945. Madrid: Taurus,

pp.
675 ARRIETA ALBERDI, Leyre, 2007, op. cit., p. 250.
676 http://www.lemonde.fr/archives/article/1970/11/04/la-police-disperse-un-millier-d-etudiants-qui-tenaient- une-reunion-en-faveur-de-l-amnistie_2658550_1819218.html?xtmc=burgos&xtcr=23 ; http://www.lemonde.fr/archives/article/1970/11/05/greves-et-manifestations-ont-marque-la-journee-nationale- pour-l-amnistie_2657993_1819218.html?xtmc=burgos&xtcr=22 Le Monde followed with interest the Burgos trial and sent its journalists to cover the news. Both before and after the process, the French newspaper was able to interview ETA members, make reports on Basque violence, and publish more than 50 articles and editorials on the Basque conflict. Among all the articles and interviews published in those days by the international media, the following can be highlighted: Politique Hebdo, a left-wing French journal, also showed interest in the process and ETA, and published an interview with ETA members in January 1971, "Aprés Burgos l'ETA nous parle;"; Le monde Diplomatique left the reports on the Basque country in the hands of the biographer (he would write a biography of Charles De Gaulle) and well-known anti-colonialist journalist Jean La Couture, who wrote the article "Des deux Côtes de la frontière" , where he interviews Julen Madariaga; L'Express dedicated to the Trial some articles written by Edouard Bailby, including "Décembre 1970 : Le procès de Burgos"
677 DE LA SOTA, Ramon, 2016, Euskadi. Siete años. 1969-1976. Unpublished.
678 Manifestación de protesta en Londres con motivo del próximo consejo de Guerra de Burgos. In OPE, October 20th, 1970.
679 Hoja Informativa. Consejo de Guerra de Burgos. Proceso al régimen. Unknown author. CRAI. Biblioteca del Pavelló de la República. Universitat de Barcelona FV.1970/2
680 TXALAPARTA. (Ed.), 1994, op. cit., pp. 66-67.
681 Manuel Irujo to Mr. Danie Mayer, President of the Ligue des Droites de l'Homme. Paris, November 7th, 1969. Eusko-Ikaskuntza, Irujo Fund, Signature J, Box, 12, File M-N
682 Lucio Aretxabaleta had been President of the Euzko Gaztedi in Bilbao and fled into exile in 1941. Established in Venezuela, he presided the Basque Center in Caracas and the CEVA, and was Delegate of the Basque Government in Venezuela. He and his wife died in the Caracas earthquake of July 29th, 1967. Fernando Carranza was appointed his successor as Delegate
683 Letter from Lucio de Aretxabaleta to Lehendakari Leizaola. Caracas, November 9th, 1961. EAH-AHE, Archivo gobierno vasco, Fondo del presidente Leizaola. Box 32/5.
684 Letter from Lucio de Aretxabaleta to Lehendakari Leizaola. Caracas, October 3rd, 1961. Ibid.
685 Confidential Report no.17. Bilbao, August 28th, 1961. NARA General Records of Department of State. Records of the Office of Western European Affairs. Bureau of European affairs. 1953-1962. NND959219 RG59 Box.7
686 ibid.
687 Letter from Jesús Solaun to Lehendakari Leizaola. 1961 Undated. EAH-AHE, Archivo gobierno Vasco, Fondo del Presidente Leizaola. Box 33/14.
688 The full list of the detainees after the police raid is the following: Rafael Albisu, Imanol Laspiur, Iñaki Larramendi, Evaristo Urrestarazu, Iñaki Balerdi, Eduardo Ferrán, Julen adariaga, Andoni Iriondo, Angel Aranzabal, José Urbieta, José Antonio Eizaguirre, Eustakio Narbaiza, Serafín Basauri, Javier Aguirre, Agustín Olaskoaga, Robén López de la Calle, Javier Elosegi, José Mari Quesada, Ildefonso Iriarte, Sabin Uribe, Guillermo Mariñelarena, José Ramón Luzarraga, Patxi Amezaga, José Muñoa, Santiago Iturrioz, Juan José Etxabe, and José Antonio Lizarribar. Thanks to the license plate on the motorbike that was used for burning some flags on the same day as the attack on the train, the police were able to track all the names and successfully carry out an operation against the ETA members, getting close to dismantling the organization. David López Dorronsoro, Paco Iturrioz, and Eneko Irigaray were able to escape and

cross the border into exile, joining the fate of the traditional Basque nationalists.
689 Manuel Irujo to Jesús Solaun. October 23rd, 1961. EAH-AHE, Archivo gobierno Vasco, Fondo del Presidente Leizaola. Box 33/14.
690 "El año Internacional de los Derechos Humanos," Alderdi, no. 242-243. 1968.
691 TXALAPARTA (Ed.), 1994, op. cit., p. 127.
692 MOTA, David, 2016, op. cit., pp. 391-396; "El Gobernador del Estado de Idaho en favor de los vascos," Alderdi, nos. 252-253, July- September, 1969.
693 "Mensaje del Presidente del Gobierno de Euzkadi," Alderdi, ibid., pp. 6-7.
694 "El proceso de Burgos en la Prensa Italiana," Alderdi, no. 260, February, 1971.
695 Letter to Amintore Fanfani. Paris, September 20th, 1969; Letter to Pietro Nenni. Paris, Ocotber 14th, 1969, EHA-AHE, Fondo Archivo Histórico Gobierno Vasco, Fondo Especial Beyris, Box 54, P-93/2-3; P-94/2-3.
696 "Mensaje del Presidente del Gobierno de Euzkadi," Alderdi, nos. 252-253, July- September, 1969.
697 The following were prosecuted in absentia: Pedro Aquizu, Juan José Echave, Juan Manuel Echevarria, Miguel Echeverria, José María Eskubi, María Asunción Goenaga, José Ángel Iturbe, Pablo Iztueta, Emilio López Adán, Julen Madariaga, and Francisco Montero Hormaechea.
698 Drafts on the Burgos trial. December, 1970. Eusko-Ikaskuntza, Irujo Fund, Signature J, Box, 36, File 2.
699 HÓRDAGO (Ed.), 1979, op. cit., vol. 10, pp. 85-89.
700 HÓRDAGO (Ed.), 1978, op. cit., pp. 51-53.
701 "Spain Puts Curbs on a Basque area," The New York Times, December 5th, 1970. Also in: https://timesmachine.nytimes.com/timesmachine/1970/12/05/355164802.html?action=click&contentCollection= Archives&module=LedeAsset&region=ArchiveBody&pgtype=article&pageNumber=1
702 "Comunicado de la dirección nacional de ETA." HÓRDAGO (ed.), 1979, op. cit., vol. 10, p. 117.
703 Anai Artea, meaning "between brothers," was an organization to help the Basque Refugees, established in Donibane Lohitzune. In 1970 Telesforo Monzón was its President and the Abbot Pierre Larzabal its Secretary. More information on Anai Artea at: http://anai-artea.com/-Nuestra-historia-.html
704 Manuel Irujo to Victoria Kent. Paris, December 11th, 1970. Eusko-Ikaskuntza, Irujo Fund, Signature J, Box 12, File H-I-J-K
705 Julián de Illarramendi to Manuel Irujo. Berferec, December 20th, 1970. Eusko-Ikaskuntza, Irujo Fund, Signature J, Box 13, File U-Z. Note that December 28 is April Fools' Day in Spain.
706 KRUTWIG, Federico, 2014, Años de peregrinación y lucha. Tafalla: Txalaparta, p. 30.
707 MARTÍNEZ RUEDA, Fernando, 2016, "Telesforo Monzón, del nacionalismo aranista a Herri Batasuna: Las claves de una evolución," Revista de estudios políticos, 174, p. 289.
708 TXALAPARTA (ed.), 1994, op. cit., vol. 3, p. 59.
709 Drafts on the Burgos trial. December, 1970. Eusko-Ikaskuntza, Irujo Fund, Signature J, Box, 36, File 2
710 Letter from Krutwig to Irujo. Undated. Eusko-Ikaskuntza, Irujo Fund, Signature J, Box 13, Exp. HIJK
711 We Will see more on the National Front in the following sections.
712 "Comunicado de ETA al Pueblo Vasco y a la opinión pública mundial," ETA, Euskadi, December 24th, 1970. Documentos Y, Vol. XII, pp. 237-238.
713 TXALAPARTA (ed.), 1994, op. cit., vol.3, p. 60.
714 "Memoria escrita de J.A. Echebarrieta Ortiz, abogado de Francisco Javier Izko de la Iglesia." In HÓRDAGO (ed.), 1978, op. cit., pp. 327-362.
715 Drafts on the Burgos trial. December, 1970. Eusko-Ikaskuntza, Irujo Fund, Signature J, Box, 36, File 2.
716 TXALAPARTA (Ed.), 1994, op. cit., vol. 3, p. 60, pp. 307-308.

717 The recording can be consulted at the CRAI Archive in Pavelló de la República: PCD Dis-8.
718 Drafts on the Burgos trial. December, 1970. Eusko-Ikaskuntza, Irujo Fund, Signature J, Box, 36, File 2.
719 CASANOVA, Iker, 2007, ETA 1958-2008. Medio siglo de historia. Tafalla: Editorial Txalaparta, pp. 99-100.
720 ELORZA, Antonio (coord.), 2000, La historia de ETA. Madrid: Ediciones Temas de Hoy, p. 147.
721 Ibid., pp. 148-149; SULLIVAN, John, 1988, op. cit., pp. 99-100.
722 CASANOVAS, Iker, 2008, op. cit., pp. 110-115; ELORZA, Antonio (coord.), 2000, op. cit., pp. 150-153.
723 Krutwig to Irujo, Rome, December 22nd, 1970. Eusko-Ikaskuntza, Irujo Fund, Signature J, Box, 13, File HIJK.
724 Documento de los presos de Burgos dirigido al Biltzar Ttipia de su Organización Euskadi ta Askatasuna," ETA, Burgos, January 1st, 1971. Documentos Y, Vol.X, pp. 199-218.
725 CLARK, Robert, p. 1984. The basque insurgents. ETA, 1952-1980. Madison: The University of Wisconsin Press, pp. 58-59.
726 Ibid., p. 62.
727 The governments of Austria, Venezuela, Chile, Ireland, Denmark, Germany (FRG), Italy, Sweden, Norway, Belgium, and the Vatican asked Franco to make use of the right of clemency.
728 TXALAPARTA (ed.), 1994, op. cit., vol. 3, pp. 68-71; SULLIVAN, John, 1988, op. cit., pp. 108-109.
729 OPE, no. 5589, January 4th, 1971.
730 Fermín Monasterio was a taxi driver who was found dead after having presumably transported Mikel Etxeberria, an ETA member who was running from the police in Bilbao in 1969. ETA never recognized that murder, and the case was closed by the police without any evidence of ETA's authorship.
731 OPE, no. 5611, February 3rd, 1971.
732 Letter sent to the UN's Human Rights commission, Basque Government, March, 1971. EAH-AHE, Archivo gobierno vasco, Fondo Especial Beyris. Box 54 P-2/2-2.
733 Brief note of protest from different bodies of the region against the refugees' expulsion. Eusko-Ikaskuntza, Irujo Fund, Box 7, Exp.1.
734 Letter from Alberto Onaindia to Manuel Irujo, Saint Jean de Luz, February 8th, 1971. Eusko-Ikaskuntza, Irujo Fund, Sig. J, Box 13, File 0.
735 ANASAGASTI, Iñaki, op. cit., p. 29.
736 Kepa Ordoki Vázquez was Major of the Gernika Battallion during the Spanish Civil War, and after that he enrolled in the French army. Letters from Ramon Agesta and Kepa Ordoki in: EAH-AHE, Archivo Gobierno Vasco, Fondo Especial Beyris. Box 53 P-63.
737 Letters exchanged between Irujo and Monzón. From April to July, 1971. Eusko-Ikaskuntza, Irujo Fund, Signature J, Box 13, Exp. M-N.
738 Iñaki Anasagasti is a Basque nationalist who was born in Venezuela, son of a Basque nationalist family that fled into exile after the Spanish Civil War. He was educated in the Basque Country by his grandparents, but he returned to Venezuela in 1965 after his father's death and got involved in the Basque nationalist movement, first in EGI, with the promotion of Radio Euzkadi or by editing Gudari. On his return to the Basque Country in 1975, he published the journal of the PNV Euskadi and during the democracy was elected Member of Parliament from 1980 to 2004. He was recently retired from his position at the Spanish Senate.
739 Journal on the 1977 Iruña Assembly. AN, DP-0506-05; Interview with Iñaki Anasagasti. Bilbao, November 29th, 2016.
740 The UK underwent a financial crisis in 1976 (just after coming out of the oil crisis of 1973) that forced the Government to apply to the International Monetary Fund (IMF) for a loan. The result was that the IMF negotiators obliged the Government to

make deep cuts in public expenditure that would affect the economy and the social situation. More at: http://www.nationalarchives.gov.uk/cabinetpapers/themes/imf-crisis.htm#Harold%20Wilson's%201974%20government
741 Correspondence between Alberto Elósegui and Manuel Irujo. London, March 18th, 1976. Eusko-Ikaskuntza, Irujo Fund, Signature J, Box, 18, File E-F.
742 "Al Pueblo Vasco," Euzkadi, November 20th, 1975. OPE no. 6702, December 1st, 1975.
743 Interview with Iñaki Anasagasti. Bilbao, November 29th, 2016.
744 Manuel Irujo to Martín García Urtiaga, May 28th, 1971. Eusko-Ikaskuntza, Irujo Fund, Signature J, Box, 13, File G.
745 In the ideological positions approved by ETA in its Vth Assembly one of the items asserted with regard to the PNV: "It is, today, an outdated party in both aspects: national and social. (...) To survive either it claims Basque national sovereignty and for that abandon the economic interests that link it to Spain, or it dedicates itself to those economic interests betraying its Basque content, or it disappears by extinction." in HÓRDAGO (Ed.). 1979. op.cit. Vol.5. pp. 176-177.
746 Manuel Irujo to Martín García Urtiaga. May 28th, 1971, op. cit.
747 Ibid.
748 "Euskadi. Boletín informativo del Partido Nacionalista Vasco," February 15th-21th, 1976. AN, Irujo Fund, 0071, C-2.
749 Eduardo Moreno Bergaretxe "Pertur" was a member of ETA-PM, the political-military branch of ETA, who was presumably kidnapped and killed on July 23rd, 1976. His body has never been found. His disappearance caused controversy among the two branches of ETA, because ETA-PM was suspicious of ETA-M. The latest research on the case has revealed a possible involvement of the Italian fascist paramilitary group "Triple A" in the disappearance. The Italian fascists would have handed Pertur over to the Francoist police, according to research made by Ángel Amigo and presented in a documentary in 2007, "El año de todos los demonios." More on Pertur in: AMIGO, Ángel, 1978, Pertur: ETA 71-76. Donostia: Hórdago; GIACOPUZZI, Giovanni, 1997. ETApm. El otro camino. Tafalla: Txalaparta.
750 Correspondence between Alberto Elósegui and Manuel Irujo. London, September 9th, 1976, op. cit.
751 Ibid.
752 AGIRREAZKUENAGA Joseba. 2011. The Making of the Basque Question Experiencing Self-Goverments, 1793-1877. Reno, CBS. More on the "Ley Abolitoria de fueros de 21 de Julio de 1876" in: https://dialnet.unirioja.es/descarga/articulo/4966551.pdf .More on the "Ley Abolitoria de fueros de 21 de Julio de 1876" in: https://dialnet.unirioja.es/descarga/articulo/4966551.pdf
753 Irujo to Ajuriaguerra. May 7th, 1976. AN, Irujo Fund, 0071, C-2.
754 "La Ley de Julio de 1876," Euzkadi, 2nd half of May, 1976.
755 AGIRREAZKUENAGA, Joseba. 2016. "Reinterpreting the Basque Past in exile; Scholars, Narratives and Agendas (1936-1977)." In Storia della Storiografia. Pisa-Roma: Fabrizio Serra Editore. 1: p. 71.
756 Alberto Elosegui to Manuel Irujo. London, January 14th, 1976. Eusko-Ikaskuntza, Irujo Fund, Signature J, Box, 18, File E-F.
757 "Aberri Eguna 1976." AN, Fondo Irujo, 0071, C-2.
758 "Última hora. 3 de marzo. Masacre en Gasteiz." Hautsi no. 10, March, 1976.
759 PABLO CONTRERAS, Santiago de; MEES, Ludger, and RODRÍGUEZ RANZ, José Antonio, 2001, op. cit., p. 331.
760 Euzkadi, first half of May, 1976.
761 Irujo to Leizaola. April, 8th, 1976. Eusko-Ikaskuntza, Irujo Fund, Signature J, Box, 18, File L-LL.
762 Amaiur, first published in March 1976, vindicated the Basque Code of Laws, the inclusion of Navarre in the political Basque Country, and the European Federation—a clear signature of Irujo's.
763 Irujo to Elósegui. January 16th, 1976. Eusko-Ikaskuntza, Irujo Fund, Signature J,

Box, 18, File E-F.
764 Correspondence between Manuel Irujo and Iñaki Anasagasti. May-December 1976. Eusko-Ikaskuntza, Irujo Fund, Signature J, Box, 18, File A
765 Ibid.
766 Xabier Arzallus ended up becoming president of the Euzkadi buru Batzar (1980-2004). For more on Xabier Arzallus, consult "Así fue," by Xabier Arzallus (Madrid: Foca, 2005).
767 Letters from Iñaki Anasagasti to Manuel Irujo. May, 1976. Eusko-Ikaskuntza, Irujo Fund, Signature J, Box, 18, File A.
768 The Spanish Amnesty law was approved on October 15th, 1977— https://www.boe.es/boe/dias/1977/10/17/pdfs/A22765-22766.pdf - but there had been a partial amnesty decreed on July 20th, 1976 for political prisoners: http://www.boe.es/boe/dias/1976/08/04/pdfs/A15097-15098.pdf
769 Correspondence between Manuel Irujo and Iñaki Anasagasti. May-December 1976. Eusko-Ikaskuntza, Irujo Fund, Signature J, Box, 18, File A.
770 SÁNCHEZ SOLER, Mariano, 2010, La transición sangrienta. Una historia violenta del proceso democrático en España (1975-1983). Barcelona: Península. pp. 21-43.
771 PABLO CONTRERAS, Santiago de, 2002, "Manuel Irujo: Un nacionalista vasco en la Transición democrática. (1975-1981)." Vasconia, 32, p. 178.
772 Ibid.
773 Letters from Iñaki Anasagasti to Manuel Irujo. May, 1976. Eusko-Ikaskuntza, Irujo Fund, Signature J, Box, 18, File A.
774 Ibid.
775 Interview with Iñaki Anasagasti. Bilbao, November 29th, 2016.
776 AMEZAGA IRIBARREN, Arantzazu. 1999. op.cit., pp. 388-389.
777 Lehendakari Leizaola had crossed the border once, travelling incognito, to celebrate the Aberri Eguna in Gernika in 1974, but he did not officially return until December 15th, 1979
778 "Irujo Jauna: ongi etorri," means "Welcome Mr. Irujo." Ikurrina is the name given to the Basque flag, and lauburu is the name of the Basque cross, carrying important meanings within Basque nationalist symbolism.
779 "El retorno de don Manuel de Irujo," Journal on the 1977 Iruña Assembly. AN, DP-0506-05. In fact, some days before, coinciding with the anniversary of Lehendakari Aguirre's death, on March 20th, some Basque prisoners had been released from prison. The OPE no. 6972 of March 25th would inform about it: "Amnistiados: Declaraciones del señor Jáuregui," "La amnistia tiene aspectos positivos pero los vascos no cederan mientras no salgan todos," or "Los Vascos con la Ikurrina saludan a los primeros hermanos liberados" are articles dealing with the news.
780 Ibid.
781 Garaikoetxea left the presidency of the Basque Country despite being reelected due to discrepancies with the PNV. He would be the founder of a new political party, Euskal Alkartasuna (1986), a split from the PNV.
782 "El retorno de don Manuel de Irujo," Journal on the 1977 Iruña Assembly. AN, DP-0506-05.
783 Ibid.
784 "General Assembly in Pamplona. Union and force."
785 PABLO CONTRERAS, Santiago de; MEES, Ludger, and RODRÍGUEZ RANZ, José Antonio, 2001, op. cit., p. 333.
786 Basque nationalist women's board.
787 "Proyecto de reglamento de la asamblea nacional del Partido Nacionalista Vasco." Eusko-Ikaskuntza, Irujo Fund, Signature J, Box, 40, File 3, p. 52.
788 "Vosotros habéis sido desterrados," Journal on the 1977 Iruña Assembly. AN, DP-0506-05.
789 BAETS, Antoon de, 2011, op. cit.
790 Alberto Onaindia to Manuel Irujo. November 3rd, 1976. Eusko-Ikaskuntza, Irujo Fund, Signature J, Box 18, File O-Q.

791 Interview with Iñaki Anasagasti. Bilbao, November 29th, 2016.
792 Alberto Onaindia to Dunixi de Oñatibia. November 11th, 1976. Eusko-Ikaskuntza, Irujo Fund, Signature J, Box 19, File O-Q.
793 Ibid. "Solidaridad de Trabajadores Vascos" (ELA-STV) is the historically Basque workers union. More at: https://www.ela.eus/en/about-ela/history
794 José Miguel de Barandiaran Ayerbe was a nationalist Basque priest who was very interested in ethnographic and language studies, as well as in prehistory and anthropology. More on Barandiaran at: http://www.Eusko-Ikaskuntza.org/aunamendi/11007
795 Alberto Onaindia to Manuel Irujo. St. Jean de Luz, December 27th, 1976. Eusko-Ikaskuntza, Irujo Fund, Signature J, Box 18, File E-F.
796 "Jaungoikoa eta Lege-zarra." Eusko-Ikaskuntza, Irujo Fund, Signature J, Box 53, File 6.
797 The extraterritorial meeting in Paris took place on January 30th, 1977 under the presidency of Juan Ajuria, who read the regulations of the assembly. The attendees to the meeting and the debate were the following: Manuel Irujo, Josu Arrieta, Faustino Pastor, Julián Garmendia, Patxi Iturrioz, Garbiñe de Arrieta, Pelikene Arrese, Rosario Domínguez, Mari Carmen de Arrarte, Antonio Gamarra, Iñaki Múgica, Satur Gárate, Ramón Agesta, Peru Ajuria, Maria Luisa Axtainza de Ajuria, Gregorio Urrejola, Enrique Sánchez, Maite Garmendia, Pepita Arrieta, José Luis Echebarrieta, and Felipe Malda. The members who took part in the deliberation were: Garmendia, Iturrioz, Arrieta, Gamarra, Mugika, Garate, Agesta, Ajuria, and Maite Garmendia. "Asamblea extraterritorial. 30 enero 1977." AN, PNV-0359-07.
798 "Asamblea extraterritorial. 30 enero 1977." AN, PNV-0359-07, p. 12.
799 "Las impresiones de Irujo. Entrevista," Journal on the 1977 Iruña Assembly. AN, DP-0506-05
800 ARRIETA, Leyre, 2007, op. cit., p. 248.
801 Ibid., p. 273.
802 Ibid., p. 274.
803 The Brest Charter was an agreement signed by different European nationalist organizations in 1974, ratified in 1976 with the participation of the Basque nationalists of EHAS (Euskal Herriko Alderdi Sozialista), the Sinn Fein, the PSANP (Partit Socialista d'Alliberament Nacional Provisional), UDB (Union Démocratique Bretonne), UPG (Union do pobo galego), Cymru Goch, CG (Pays de Galles Rouge), ECT (Esquerra Catalana dels Treballadors), and Su populu Sardu – MCC. This charter was a declaration against colonialism and a defense of a Socialist Europe of peoples.
804 Ibid., p. 272.
805 "Nuestro clamor a 1972," in Ibérica, January 15th, 1972. Published in: IRUJO, Manuel, 1984, op. cit., pp. 296-297.
806 Ibid., pp. 278-279.
807 "Independencia, Autonomía, Federación," in OPE, no. 7. Caracas, September, 1974. Published in: IRUJO, Manuel, 1984, op. cit., pp. 309-310.
808 DE LA SOTA, Ramon, 2016, op. cit., p. 5.
809 Enrique Tierno Galván was a socialist member of the PSOE. Tierno Galván was elected mayor of Madrid within the first democratic elections, and was mayor until his death on January 19th 1986, enjoying a vast popularity.
810 DE LA SOTA, Ramon, 2016, p. 6
811 PABLO CONTRERAS, Santiago de, 2002, op. cit., p. 175.
812 AN, PNV-0128-05.
813 Ibid.
814 Letter to EBB. June 25th, 1976. AN, PNV-0128-05
815 Letter from Manuel Irujo to Iñaki Anasagasti. January 28th, 1977. Eusko-Ikaskuntza, Irujo Fund, Signature J, Box 19, File A
816 "En lo politico," Journal on the 1977 Iruña Assembly. AN, DP-0506-05
817 More on Aranzazu and the agreements approved there at: http://www.Eusko-Ikaskuntza.org/aunamendi/102736/98002
818 "En lo cultural," Journal on the 1977 Iruña Assembly. AN, DP-0506-05

819 More info on the evolution of the unification of the Basque language can be found at: http://www.Eusko-Ikaskuntza.org/aunamendi/137948/92969, as well as a detailed linguistic analysis of the changes in the article "La unificación del Euskera," by Kamarka. AN, Irujo Fund- 0071-02
820 "Asamblea extraterritorial. 30 enero 1977." AN, PNV-0021-11.
821 Alberto Onaindia to Manuel Irujo. St. Jean de Luz, December 27th, 1976. Eusko-Ikaskuntza, Irujo Fund, Signature J, Box 18, File E-F.
822 "En lo cultural," Journal on the 1977 Iruña Assembly. AN, DP-0506-05
823 "Frases Felices," Journal on the 1977 Iruña Assembly. AN, DP-0506-05
824 "En lo cultural," Journal on the 1977 Iruña Assembly. AN, DP-0506-05
825 "Asamblea extraterritorial. 30 enero 1977." AN, PNV-0359-07, p. 2.
826 Ibid.
827 Ibid.
828 Ibid. p.3.
829 Ibid. p.4.
830 Ibid., p. 16.
831 Ibid., p. 17
832 "En lo económico social," Journal on the 1977 Iruña Assembly. AN, DP-0506-05.
833 Ibid.
834 Ibid.

Index

Note: Tables are indicated by *t* following the page number. End note information is indicated by n and note number following the page number.

Aberri Eguna (1976), 199–200
Aberri Eguna Manifesto (Etxebarrieta), 162
Abrisketa Korta, Josu, 180*t*
active political resistance. *See* political activism
Adroher, Enric ("Gironella"), 86, 250n338
Aguinaga, Iñaki ("El Bonzo"), 95, 253n382
Aguirre, Iñaki, 79
Aguirre, Jesús, 91
Aguirre, José Antonio
   Basque diaspora and, 25, 36–38
   Basque World Congress and, 28, 40–43, 54–55, 58–59, 61, 67–68 (*see also* Basque World Congress)
   challenges to, 28–29, 36–38
   character and traits of, 14, 25
   Christian Democracy promotion by, 26–27, 29, 35, 79
   death and funeral of, 68–70, 74
   democracy advocacy by, 20–21, 26, 29–30, 34, 38
   ETA and, 114, 150
   European Federalist Movement and, 35, 39–40, 52–53, 78, 80–82, 249nn317–18
   European strategy of, 34, 35–40, 52–53
   exiled Spanish Republican government alliance and, 12–18, 25, 26, 39
   internal Basque exiles and, 41–43
   legitimacy of exiled Basque government under, 21, 61, 74
   Monarchists and, 15–18, 20–21, 55, 232n25
   reality of exile for, 21
   on return to Basque Country, 11
   strikes and, 21, 30–32, 237–38n109
   successor to, 70 (*see also* Leizaola, Jesús María)
   US relations and, 23, 25–32, 34–39, 52–53, 233n37
   Ynchausti and, 237n92
Aguirre, Txato, 189
Aizpurua Egaña, Itziar, 180*t*
Ajuriaguerra, Juan
   Basque Nationalist Party and, 18, 21–22, 197–98, 204, 273n797
   Christian Democracy and, 80
   ETA and, 152, 167
   European Federalist Movement and, 83, 210
   external exiles opposed by, 28, 31
   post-Pact of Madrid, 33
   US relations and, 75
Albornoz, Claudio Sánchez, 29
Alderdi
   Basque World Congress and, 67
   Burgos trial reporting in, 178, 194, 267n661
   "La Causa del pueblo Vasco" edited by, 52
   European strategy editorialized in, 38
   Irujo's articles in, 33–34, 63, 66, 68, 76–77, 81, 95–96, 110–12, 128, 178
   Jemein's articles in, 35
   "Patriotas y Gamberros" in, 110–12, 128
   repression reports by, 267n661
   totalitarian opposition editorial in, 103, 250n337
Algeria, 149, 151, 152–56
Alkain, Jesús Mari, 204
alliances, networks of, 7, 9–18
Álvarez de Miranda, Fernando, 98
Álvarez Enparantza, José Luis ("Txillardegi")
   background of, 257n474
   Basque language support by, 132–35, 212
   "Branka" by, 160, 193, 265n621
   ETA and, 115, 150, 156, 160, 164, 193, 263n573
   exile of, 150, 164, 196
   "Neo-Carlismo" by, 145
   non-Basque origins of, 132
   at Paris October 1961 conferences, 121–22
Anabitarte, Kepa ("Eladio"), 95, 253n382
Anai Artea, 183–85, 196, 269n703
Anasagasti, Iñaki, 111, 112–13, 116, 200–203, 270n738

ANV (Basque Nationalist Action), 91
Arana, Sabino
    article in *Cuadernos* on, 105
    Basque nationalism generally and, 34–35
    economic ideology of, 140
    ETA and, 114, 117, 132, 158
    Irujo family and, 10
    race theories of, 136–37, 139
Arana, Victor, 267n658
Arana Bilbao, Bittor, 180*t*
Aransaez, 45
Aresti, Gabriel, 134
Aretxabala, Pedro, 45
Aretxabaleta, Lucio de, 112, 115–16, 175–76, 256n453, 268n682
Argentina
    Argentinian Federation (FEVA) in, 65
    Asociación Argentina por la Libertad de la Cultura in, 103
    Basque diaspora in, 24, 31, 60, 240n158
    Burgos trial reactions in, 175
    Christian Democracy promotion in, 27
    ETA in, 113, 117
    exiled Basque government in, 75
Arrizabalaga, Andoni, 168–69
Arrizabalaga, Pedro, 204
Arruti Odriozola, Aranzazu, 171, 173, 180*t*, 189
Arzallus, Xabier, 201, 204, 205, 207, 272n766
Assistance Committee for Basques, 24
Ayestarán, José Antonio ("Baroja"), 95, 253nn382–83
Azkue, Resurrección María, 148, 260n519
Azurmendi, Mikel, 189–90

Baeza, Fernando, 87
Bagués, Jesús María, 180*t*
Bandrés, Juan María, 181*t*
Barrios Lis, Jesús, 98
Basaldúa, Pedro, 27, 45, 203
"Bases for a Basque Transitional Situation," 21
"Bases Teóricas de la Guerra Revolucionaria" (Zalbide), 154, 164
Basque Code of Laws, 56–57, 62, 71, 111, 143, 199
Basque diaspora
    1960s resurgence of, 86, 112
    Basque World Congress for, 41–42, 47, 60, 240n158 (*see also* Basque World Congress)
    Burgos trial response by exiles of, 173–86, 187, 189–91, 194–96
    eighth province and, 28, 31, 114, 205, 214
    exile viewed as blessing in disguise for, 19, 44
    funding of exiled Basque government by, 36, 120, 239n131
    fundraising for strikers in, 31
    history of, 23–24, 236n78
    internal Basque exiles vs., 41–43
    political stances and, 25, 28, 36–38, 236–37nn81,91
    US relations and, 24–25, 42, 236–37nn81,91
Basque government in exile. *See* exiled Basque government
Basque International Organization, 65–66
Basque language
    Basque nationalism and, 59–60, 118–19, 132–35, 212–13
    Basque World Congress on, 59–60, 244n218
    bilingualism with, 213
    Congress for Cultural Freedom and, 109
    Declaration of 1960 on, 71
    education and, 134, 212
    ETA on, 131–36
    European Federalist Movement and, 81
    standardized or unified, 135–36, 212–13
Basque National Front, 110, 113, 115–17, 119, 122, 130, 186
Basque nationalism
    Basque diaspora and stance on, 25, 28, 36–37, 236–37nn81,91
    Basque language and, 59–60, 118–19, 132–35, 212–13
    Basque World Congress for (*see* Basque World Congress)
    Christian Democracy influence on, 8–9, 10, 19, 26–27, 34, 79–80, 206 (*see also* Christian Democracy)
    Congress for Cultural Freedom and, 104–9
    critiques of, generally, 34–35
    democracy advocacy and, 8–9, 17–18, 19–21, 26–27, 29–30, 34, 82, 84–85, 103, 142
    eighth province and, 28, 31, 114, 205, 214
    ethnic nationalism and, 71, 118, 120, 132–33, 136–39, 208, 241n169

of exiled Basque government, 11–12
(*see also* Basque Nationalist Party)
government distinction from, 96
Irujo as ideologue of (*see* Irujo,
Manuel)
national reconciliation and, 49,
51–54, 80–81, 96–97
new/younger participants in
(*see* EGI; ETA; younger Basque
nationalists)
radicalization and violence in, 8, 22,
113, 123–28, 143, 145–47 (*see also*
ETA)
socioeconomic, 213–16 (*see also*
socioeconomics)
US relations and, 26, 29, 34
Basque Nationalist Action (ANV), 91
Basque Nationalist Party (EAJ-PNV)
Basque World Congress stance
of, 60, 63 (*see also* Basque World
Congress)
Burgos trial response by, 173–86
Christian Democracy influence on,
19, 26–27, 79–80, 206 (*see also*
Christian Democracy)
communism conflicts in, 29–30,
139–43
cultural focus of, 212–13 (*see also*
Basque language; culture, Basque)
Declaration of 1960 by, 70–71
Declaration of 1966 by, 118–19, 209
Declaration of Principles of 1977 by,
207–8, 211–12, 213
end of exile and position of, 197–204
ETA and, 72–73 (*see also* ETA)
Etxebarrieta on, 157–62
European Federalist Movement and,
19–20, 39–40, 52–54, 66, 76–93,
96, 179, 208–12 (*see also* Munich
Conference)
exiled Spanish Republican
government and, 12, 14–18, 21
exile influence on, 205–16
internal rift in, 93–100, 110–12,
121–25
internal vs. external exile influencing
views of, 19, 28, 57–58, 71–72,
124–25
Iruñea 1977 assembly of, 204–5
Monarchists and, 15–18, 20–21
motto of, 205–8
Munich Conference and, 86–100
new/younger participants in (*see*
younger Basque nationalists)
Paris October 1961 conferences of,
120–25, 143, 158

Political Declaration of 1949 of,
18–23
socioeconomic nationalism and,
213–16 (*see also* socioeconomics)
strikes and, 21, 30–32
structure and essence evolution in,
205–13
women's section within, 205,
246n257
Basque People's Cause, The ("La Causa
del pueblo Vasco") (Landáburu), 49,
51–54, 110–11
Basque Statute of Autonomy
Basque World Congress addressing,
44, 48, 56–57, 61–62
Declaration of 1960 on, 71
Declaration of Principles of 1977 on,
208
defense of, 21–23
ETA on, 73, 117, 143, 161–62, 186
exiled Basque government on, 11, 12
Galíndez on, 65
Irujo on, 22–23, 57, 87–88, 111–12,
143, 235n74
Navarre inclusion in Basque Country
and, 21–22, 60
new/young Basque nationalists on,
111–12, 113–14, 117, 143
transition to democracy and
recognition of, 87–88
Basque University, 134, 213
Basque Workers' Solidarity (ELA-STV),
91, 94
Basque World Congress
on Basque Code of Laws, 56–57, 62
Basque diaspora and, 41–42, 47, 60,
240n158
on Basque language, 59–60,
244n218
on Basque Statute of Autonomy, 44,
48, 56–57, 61–62
exiled Basque government reports
at, 24, 43–44, 54–63, 67–68,
243nn203,212
on exiled Spanish Republican
government relations, 47–48, 57–58
Galíndez's disappearance and
proposals influencing, 63–67,
246n249
internal Basque exiles and, 41–43,
46, 52, 57–58
Irujo and, 42, 48, 56–59, 63, 67,
243n212
members and attendees of, 45–46, 55
Monzón and, 62–63
on national reconciliation, 48–49, 58,

61–62
  nation imagined from exile at, 54–63
  new/young generation of Basques targeted by, 44, 46, 52, 62
  organization and objectives of, 8, 28, 40–48
  outcomes of, 67–68
  questionnaire to inform, 45–48, 55–56
  Spanish immigrants to Basque Country and, 47
  on unity, 57–60, 62
  White Book at, 43–44, 54
Batarrita, Javier, 124
Batista, Fulgencio, 37, 239n134
Bayonne, France, 24, 260n519
Bayonne's pact, 12, 20, 21, 61, 231n6
Begin, Menachem, 151–52, 245n239, 263n580
Beihl Schaafer, Eugene, 183–86
Beitia, Pedro, 178
Belandia, Bachiller (pen name of Jemein), 35
Belausteguigoitia, Francisco de ("Patxo"), 125, 140, 258n481
Belgium, 60, 92
Ben Cherif, Ahmed, 155–56
Benito del Valle, Luis, 115, 164, 196
Berazadi, Ángel, 199–200
Bilbao, Jon, 25, 37–38, 236n83
Borbón, Juan de, 17–18, 50–51, 93, 232n28
Bordeaux, France, 24
"Branka," 160, 193, 265n621
Brest Charter, 209, 273n803
Brussels, Belgium, 24
Buenos Aires, Argentina, 24, 175
Buj, Alberto, 45
Burgos trial
  context for, 163–66
  defense strategy in, 170, 180, 187–89
  ETA kidnapping to highlight, 183–86, 190, 196
  ETA's fronts/factions and, 189–94
  Franco regime's strategy for, 170–73, 194–95
  international and exile reactions to, 173–86, 187, 189–91, 194–96
  protests and demonstrations against, 172–73, 174–75, 182–83, 194, 267n658
  as trial against Basque people, 166–70, 182, 187

Camiña, Ramón, 181*t*
Campos, José, 45

Cantalupo, Roberto, 51
Caracas, Venezuela, 24, 75, 117–18, 175
"Carta a los intelectuales," 155
Carta de Condición Vasca, 120
Castells, Miguel, 181*t*
Castro, José Luis, 181*t*
Catalan nationalism, 54, 77, 95, 172–73, 249n315, 258n483
Catholicism
  1960s stance against Franco in, 85–86
  Basque Nationalist Party and, 206
  Christian Democracy and, 27, 79
  Franco's relations with, 33, 34, 132, 166, 172, 266n650
"Causa del pueblo Vasco, La" (The Basque People's Cause) (Landáburu), 49, 51–54, 110–11
Cazcarra, Vicente, 167, 266–67n653
Central Intelligence Agency. *See* CIA
Centro de Documentación y Estudios, 108
CFE/CFEME (Consejo Federal Español del Movimiento Europeo)
  admission to European meetings via, 39–40
  Basque Nationalists and, 82–84, 210–11, 249n317
  Cultural Union and, 77
  Irujo and, 31, 35, 83, 210–11
  Munich Conference and, 89–91, 94
Che Guevara, Ernesto, 156–57, 264n602
Chile, 60, 75
Christian Democracy
  Basque nationalism grounded in, 8–9, 10, 19, 26–27, 34, 79–80, 206
  Burgos trial response under, 177, 179
  European Federalist Movement and, 34, 35, 78, 79–80, 85, 210
  Galíndez support for, 64–65
  Irujo and, 10, 23, 27, 80
  NEI for, 34, 35, 78, 79–80
  prisoner treatment opposition under, 127
  reorganization of, 80
  tenets of, 8–9, 10
  US relations and, 26–27
CIA (Central Intelligence Agency), 25, 26, 89, 101–2, 254n399. *See also* OSS
Cold War, communism as central to. *See* communism
Comité pro Comunidad Ibérica de Naciones, 81
Commission for the Truth of Stalin's Crimes, 107–8

Committee of General Interests of the Basque Country, 24
communism
  anti-capitalist evolution to, 139–43
  Basque nationalism conflicts over, 29–30, 139–43
  Basque World Congress on, 62
  Congress for Cultural Freedom opposing, 105–8
  democracy vs. totalitarianism or, 103
  ETA stance on, 139–43, 144, 150
  European Federalist Movement vs., 84–86
  Franco regime tolerated to avoid, 17, 29, 32, 35, 80–81, 231–32n18
  national reconciliation and, 48–49, 50, 51, 241n170
  UN admissions reflecting fears of, 238n118
  US opposition to, 32, 35, 50–51, 84–85, 232n18
Communist Party of Spain (PCE)
  Basque World Congress on, 62
  ETA influenced by, 192–94
  national reconciliation by, 48–49, 50, 51, 241n170
  Spanish Truth Commission on Stalin's Crimes and, 107–8
community
  Christian Democratic focus on, 9, 10
  exiled Basque (*see* Basque diaspora; internal Basque exiles)
  natural, Iberian Resolution on, 94, 95
Concordat (Vatican-Franco), 33, 34, 172
Congresses on Basque studies, 260n519
Congress for Cultural Freedom, 88–89, 100–109, 254nn399,402, 255n424
Congress of European Nationalities, 79
Congress of the Union of Nationalities, 78
Consejo Federal Español del Movimiento Europeo. *See* CFE/CFEME
Consejo Vasco por la Federación Europea (CVFE), 84
Contubernio de Múnich. *See* Munich Conference
"Coreanos, Los" (Irujo), 136–37
Creix, Antonio Juan, 167, 267n653
Cuadernos, 101–2, 103–7, 131–32
Cuba, 10, 25, 37–38, 112–13, 239n134
Cubillo, Antonio, 153
Cultural Union of Occidental Europe, 81, 100
Cultural Union of Western European Countries, 77–78, 81
culture, Basque

  1960s renewal of, 72, 247n267
  Basque Nationalist Party renewed focus on, 212–13
  Basque World Congress on, 41–42, 44, 59–60
  Cultural Union and, 77–78
  exiled Basque government support for, 25, 212
  Irujo's advocacy for, 10
  language as element of (*see* Basque language)
  LIAB focus on spreading, 24
CVFE (Consejo Vasco por la Federación Europea), 84

democracy
  1960s advocacy for, 84–86
  Aguirre's advocacy for, 20–21, 26, 29–30, 34, 38
  Basque nationalist advocacy for, 8–9, 17–18, 19–21, 26–27, 29–30, 34, 82, 84–85, 103, 142
  Basque press on, 38
  Basque World Congress on, 8, 61
  Christian Democracy for (*see* Christian Democracy)
  ETA advocacy for, 144
  European Federalist Movement on, 82, 88, 90–93
  exiled Spanish Republican advocacy for, 14, 17 (*see also* exiled Spanish Republican government)
  Irujo's advocacy for, 9–10, 22, 203
  Munich Conference to promote, 86–93
  transition to, plans for, 86–93
  US-Basque relations and, 26, 76
De Pablo, 45
dignity, 9, 10, 61
Dorronsoro Ceberio, José Maria, 171, 173, 180, 181*t*
Dorronsoro Ceberio, Unai, 181*t*

EAJ-PNV. *See* Basque Nationalist Party
Echabe, Jon, 172
Economic Cooperation Act (1948), 32
economics. *See* socioeconomics
education, 134, 212, 213, 260n519
EGI (Eusko Gaztedi Indarra/Basque Youth), 91, 94, 98, 124, 157–58
eighth province, 28, 31, 114, 205, 214
Eisenhower, Dwight D. and administration, 37, 75, 84, 86
ELA-Berri, 95
ELA-STV (Basque Workers' Solidarity), 91, 94

"El Español," 261n545
Elósegui, Alberto, 198–99, 201
Errenteria, Iñaki, 79
Erroteta, Peru, 189
Eskubi, Jose Mari, 189, 191–92
ETA (Euskadi Ta Askatasuna)
  Arana and, 114, 117, 132, 158
  Basque nationalism withdrawal of, 189–94
  on Basque Statute of Autonomy, 73, 117, 143, 161–62, 186
  Burgos trial against (*see* Burgos trial)
  economic model of, 139–43, 161
  end of exile and position of, 197, 199–200, 202
  Etxebarrieta brothers' influence on, 129, 157–62, 165–66, 264n604, 266n646
  European Federalist Movement and, 97, 145
  evolution to revolution by, 112–20, 148–62, 164–66
  exiled Basque government and, 72–73, 114–18, 258n480
  exile influence on, 148–62, 164, 189, 190–94
  factions of, 183–84, 190–94
  founding and objectives of, 72–73, 124–25, 128, 131–36
  funding issues with, 114–16, 175
  ideology of, 131–36, 139–62, 164–66, 185–86, 188–90, 271n745
  independence advocacy by, 113, 117–18, 123, 144–45, 159, 161–62, 186, 192
  kidnappings by, 183–86, 190, 196, 199
  Paris October 1961 conferences with, 121–25, 143, 158
  on race and ethnicity, 132–33, 136
  radicalization of political activism by, 8, 112–20, 148–62
  on religion, 132, 143
  socialist orientation of, 97, 147, 153–54, 159, 161–62, 188–94, 263n573, 264n597
  third world movement and, 97, 154–56
  US and, 142–43, 193
  violence by, 113, 123–28, 143, 145–47, 149–57, 159–60, 162–66, 176, 183–86, 190–94, 199–200, 258–59n488
  warfare by, 149–56, 159–60, 162, 164–66
  workers' movement and, 139–43,
  155–56, 161, 167, 189–92, 264n597
ethics and morals, 9, 10
ethnic nationalism, 71, 118, 120, 132–33, 136–39, 208, 241n169
Etxabe, Juan José, 189–90
Etxabe Garitazelaia, Jon, 181*t*
Etxebarrieta, José Antonio, 121, 129, 157–62, 181*t*, 187, 256n440, 264n604
Etxebarrieta, Manuel Fernández ("Matxari"), 117, 257n458
Etxebarrieta, Mikel, 267n658, 270n730
Etxebarrieta, Txabi, 157, 159–62, 165–66, 264n604, 266n646
European Federalist Movement
  Aguirre's focus on, 35, 39–40, 52–53, 78, 80–82, 249nn317–18
  Basque nationalism and, 19–20, 39–40, 52–54, 66, 76–93, 96, 179, 208–12 (*see also* Munich Conference)
  Burgos trial intervention requests through, 179
  CFEME and (*see* CFE/CFEME)
  Christian Democracy and, 34, 35, 78, 79–80, 85, 210
  Congress for Cultural Freedom and, 88–89, 102–4
  Cultural Union of Western European Countries before, 77–78
  democracy goals of, 82, 88, 90–93
  ETA and, 97, 145
  Galíndez and, 65–66
  Hague Conference of, 20, 35, 82, 234n54, 249n318
  Irujo's support for, 31, 33–35, 52, 65, 76–77, 78, 81–85, 88, 96, 104, 145, 208, 209–11, 249nn315,317
  Munich Conference of, 86–100, 104
  NEI for, 34, 35, 78, 79–80
European Union of Christian Democrats, 80. *See also* NEI
Euskadi Ta Askatasuna. *See* ETA
Euskaltzaindia (Basque language academy), 148, 212
Eusko Gaztedi Indarra (EGI/Basque Youth), 91, 94, 98, 124, 157–58
Euzko Mendigoizale Batza, 113–14, 129
exiled Basque communities. *See* Basque diaspora; internal Basque exiles
exiled Basque government
  Aguirre's leadership of (*see* Aguirre, José Antonio)
  Basque diaspora and, 24–25, 36–38, 120, 239n131
  Basque nationalism and (*see* Basque

nationalism; Basque Nationalist
Party)
Basque World Congress by (see
Basque World Congress)
Burgos trial response by, 173–86,
187, 189–91, 194–96
defense of, 43
end of exile for, 7, 197–204
ETA and, 72–73, 114–18, 258n480
(see also ETA)
European Federalist Movement and
(see European Federalist Movement)
exiled Spanish Republican
government and, 12–18, 21, 24–26,
39, 232n19 (see also exiled Spanish
Republican government)
funding for, 24–25, 36, 114–16, 120,
236–37nn81,91, 239n131
headquarters of, 7
internal Basque exiles vs., 19, 28, 31,
41–43, 52, 57–58, 71–72, 124–25
Irujo in (see Irujo, Manuel)
legitimacy of, 12, 21, 28, 43, 46–48,
55, 61–62, 67, 73–75, 115, 117
Leizaola's leadership of, 70–76, 127,
169, 177 (see also Leizaola, Jesús
María)
Monarchists and, 15–18, 20–21,
232n25
Munich Conference and, 86–93
nationalism of, 11–12 (see also
Basque nationalism; Basque
Nationalist Party)
national reconciliation by (see
reconciliation, national)
networks built by, 7, 9–18
new/young Basque nationalists vs.,
110–12, 121–25 (see also ETA;
younger Basque nationalists)
overview of role of, 7–10
political activism of (see political
activism)
prisoner support by, 126–28, 169–70,
175–78
reality of exile for, 11–12, 19, 21, 40
return to Basque Country, 7, 197–
204, 205
strikes and, 21, 30–32
UK and, 7, 13, 26, 33–34
UN and, 29–30, 32–34, 55
US and, 7, 13, 17, 23–39, 52–53,
75–76, 233n37, 239n131
White Book detailing actions of,
43–44, 54
exiled Spanish Republican government
Basque World Congress on, 47–48,
57–58
exiled Basque government and,
12–18, 21, 24–26, 39, 232n19
Irujo and, 12–16, 232n19, 235n74
legitimacy of, 33
Monarchists vs., 15–18, 21, 235n74
UN and, 13–15, 32–33

Falange, La, 50–51, 90
Fano, Jon, 189
fascism. See also Nazism/Nazi regime
Basque nationalism opposing, 84–85
exiled Basque government
countering, 25, 26–27
of Franco regime, 7–8, 20, 32–33
journalism reflecting, 261n545
federalism, European. See European
Federalist Movement
Fernández-Cuesta, Raimundo, 51
Fraga Iribarne, Manuel, 149
France
Basque diaspora in, 24, 60, 196
Basque nationalist January 1977
assembly in, 207–16, 273n797
Basque nationalist October 1961
conferences in, 120–25, 143, 158
Basque World Congress in (see
Basque World Congress)
Burgos trial reactions in, 173–75,
268n676
exiled Basque government and, 7,
13, 24
exiled Spanish government and, 16
Franco regime relations with, 13–14
Iberian Resolution approval by, 92
May 1968 social upheavals in, 173
Franco, Francisco and regime
1960s repressive policies of, 85–86,
90, 97–99, 162, 163–64, 166–96,
250n337
Basque nationalist opposition to
(see Basque nationalism; Basque
Nationalist Party)
Burgos trial by (see Burgos trial)
Catholic Church/Vatican relations
with, 33, 34, 85–86, 132, 166, 172,
266n650
communism and tolerance for, 17,
29, 32, 35, 80–81, 231–32n18
death of, 197
ETA and, 123–28, 146, 162, 163,
166–96, 258–59n488 (see also
Burgos trial)
European Federalist Movement
interest by, 86
exile under (see Basque diaspora;

exiled Basque government; exiled Spanish Republican government; internal Basque exiles)
  immigration plan of, 137, 260n527
  Law of Succession under, 18
  legitimization of, 8, 43
  Monarchists and, 49–50, 55
  Munich Conference and, 90, 92, 97–99
  prisoner treatment under, 86, 126–28, 150, 163–64, 166–71, 174–75, 177–78
  State of Emergency declarations by, 163–64, 166–68, 183, 265n634
  Tribunal de Orden Público of, 163–64, 201
  UN relations with, 7–8, 13–14, 17, 32–33
  US relations with, 13–14, 32, 34, 50, 75–76, 237n100
  WW II role of, 7–8
Frente Nacional Vasco, 113, 119, 122. *See also* Basque National Front

Galeuzca, 231n10
Galíndez, Jesús
  abduction and disappearance of, 63–64, 66–67, 106, 237n96, 244n226, 245–46n249
  Basque International Organization proposal by, 65–66
  Basque nationalism and, 34–35, 64–66
  Christian Democratic influence on, 64–65
  Cuban relations and, 37–38
  European Federalist Movement and, 65–66
  US relations and, 29, 64–65, 231n12, 237nn96,101
Galinsoga, Luis de, 258n483
Gallastegi, Elías ("Gudari")
  economic stance of, 139–40
  Euzko Mendigoizale Batza and, 113, 129
  independence vs. autonomy stance of, 143–44
  Irujo and, 110, 122, 128–31, 136, 143–44
  Jagi-Jagi leadership of, 124, 129
  Jemein and, 139
  Landáburu and, 111
  National Front leadership of, 130
  on race, 136, 139
  son Iker and, 111, 123–24, 129–30, 140, 146
  on violence, 146
Gallastegi, Iker
  economic stance of, 140
  Etxebarrieta and, 157, 159–60
  father Elías and, 111, 123–24, 129–30, 140, 146
  Landáburu and, 111
  Paris October 1961 conferences role of, 121–25, 143
  violence stance of, 146, 159–60
Galparsoro, Gurutze, 181*t*
Garaikoetxea, Carlos, 203, 204, 272n781
Garbisu, Ambrosio, 70
Garmendia, Miguel José, 74–75
Germany
  Berlin Wall in, 97
  Burgos trial reactions in, 175
  ETA kidnapping of consul of, 183–86, 190, 196
Gernika, bombing of, 7, 20, 30
Gesalaga Larreta, Enrique, 181*t*
Gil Robles, José Maria, 88, 90–93, 98
Giral, José, 14
Goitia, Gabriel, 45
Gómez Beltrán, Paulino, 46, 70
Gordejuela (journal), 38, 239n136
Gordón Ordás, Félix, 32–33
Gorkin, Julián (aka Julián Gómez García)
  background of, 251n342
  Congress for Cultural Freedom and, 88–89, 100–109, 255n424
  Munich Conference and, 86, 88–90, 104
  Spanish Truth Commission on Stalin's Crimes and, 107–8
Gorostidi Artola, Joaquín, 173, 180, 181*t*
Great Britain. *See* United Kingdom
"Guerra Revolucionaria, La/Insurrección en Euskadi," 149–51, 164
Gurtubay, Carmen de, 103

Herrán, 45
Hickman, Josu, 33, 49, 51, 91
Hitler, Adolf, 7–8, 20, 33. *See also* Nazism/Nazi regime
human rights
  Basque nationalist advocacy for, 8–9, 126–27
  Basque World Congress on, 8, 61
  Burgos trial and abuses of, 174–78, 195
  Christian Democratic focus on, 9
  ETA advocacy for, 144
  European Federalist Movement on, 82, 92
  Irujo defense of, 7, 10, 178

Ibarra Güell, Pedro, 181*t*
Iberian Resolution, 92–100
identification card, Basque, 120
Idoyaga, José Vicente, 189
ikastolas movements, 212, 213, 260n519
Illarramendi, Julián de, 184
immigrants to Basque Country, 47, 72, 133, 136–39, 260n527, 261n531
independence
    Basque nationalist support for, 71, 87, 111
    ETA support for, 113, 117–18, 123, 144–45, 159, 161–62, 186, 192
    exiled Spanish Republican government alliance and, 12
    Irujo's advocacy for, 9, 22–23, 26, 144
Infante, Isidro, 98
"Informe Txatarra" (Etxebarrieta), 157, 160–61
intellectualism, 10, 155, 157–58
internal Basque exiles
    1960s repressive policies affecting, 85–86, 90, 97–99
    external Basque exiles vs., 19, 28, 31, 41–43, 52, 57–58, 71–72, 124–25
    Munich Conference and, 86–93, 97–98
    new/young Basque nationalists as, 110–12, 124–25 (*see also* ETA; younger Basque nationalists)
International Law Commission, 127, 177
International League of Friends of the Basques (LIAB), 24, 65
Intxausti, Philippine Manuel, 24
Irala, Anton, 27, 29, 231n12, 237–38n109
Iranzu, Javier de (pen name of Irujo), 33–34
Ireland, 66, 110, 124, 128, 135, 147, 159–60, 259n493. *See also* North Ireland
Irigaray, Eneko, 150–53, 156, 164, 196
Irintzi, 117
Irizar, Félix, 83
Irla, Josep, 14
Irujo, Daniel, 10
Irujo, Manuel
    Arana and, 10, 105
    on Basque nationalism vs. government, 95–96
    on Basque nationalist motto, 207
    Basque Statute of Autonomy defense by, 22–23, 57, 87–88, 111–12, 143, 235n74
    Basque World Congress and, 42, 48, 56–59, 63, 67, 243n212
    Burgos trial response by, 176–78, 182, 183–84, 186–87, 189–91, 195
    on Catholicism and Franco, 33, 85–86
    Christian Democracy and, 10, 23, 27, 80
    communism and, 49, 51, 140–41, 150
    Congress for Cultural Freedom and, 100–109, 255n424
    "Los Coreanos" by, 136–37
    correspondence of, generally, 9
    criticism of and conflict with, 110–12, 247n273
    on Declaration of Principles, 208
    democracy advocacy by, 9–10, 22, 203
    end of exile and position of, 197–204
    ETA interactions with, 150
    European Federalist Movement and, 31, 33–35, 52, 65, 76–77, 78, 81–85, 88, 96, 104, 145, 208, 209–11, 249nn315,317
    exiled Spanish Republican government and, 12–16, 58, 232n19, 235n74
    Galíndez and, 63–65, 66, 106, 246n249
    Gallastegi and, 110, 122, 128–31, 136, 143–44
    human rights defense by, 7, 10, 178
    independence stance of, 9, 22–23, 26, 144
    as Iruñea 1977 PNV assembly speaker, 205
    Javier de Iranzu as pen name of, 33–34
    legacy of, 7, 9–10
    as Minister of Justice, 7, 14, 232n19
    Monarchists and, 232n25, 235n74
    Monzón and, 196
    Munich Conference and, 86–87, 90, 92, 93, 95–97, 104
    NEI role of, 80
    new/young Basque nationalists and, 110–12, 121, 125–31, 141, 143–46, 158, 202, 259n504
    Paris October 1961 conferences under, 120–24
    "Patriotas y Gamberros" by, 110–12, 121, 122, 128–31
    Prieto and, 74
    prisoner support by, 126–28
    on race, 136–39
    realpolitik of, 22
    return to Basque Country, 7,

197–204, 205
Spanish immigrants and, 136–39, 261n531
Spanish Truth Commission on Stalin's Crimes and, 107–8
strike report by, 31–32
UK relations and, 26, 33–34
US relations and, 26
violence opposition by, 125–28, 145–46, 170, 176, 203
Irujo, Pello, 197, 202–3, 204
Irujo, Xabier, 10, 26
Iruñea 1977 PNV assembly, 204–5
Israel, 66, 132, 135–36, 147, 151–53, 160, 245n239
Italy
   Burgos trial reactions in, 175, 179, 185
   Iberian Resolution approval by, 92
   Mussolini regime in, 7–8, 33
   regional autonomy in, 22–23
Iturrioz, Patxi, 153–54, 156, 160–61
Izko de la Iglesia, Xabier, 171, 173, 180, 181*t*, 187
Izquierda Republicana, 60

Jagi-Jagi, 66, 97, 114, 116–17, 124, 129, 139
Jáuregui, Julio, 18, 60, 80, 84
Jauriaguerra, Juan, 127, 177
Jemein, Ceferino, 35, 83, 137–38, 139, 238n122
Junod, Marcel, 7
Just, Julio, 83

Kalzada, Julen, 172, 181*t*
Karrera Aguirrebarrena, Antton, 181*t*
Kennedy, John F. and administration, 75–76
Khrushchev, Nikita, 84, 107, 250n329
Kintana, Xabier, 134, 135
Krutwig Sagredo, Federico
   background of, 148
   Basque language focus of, 59–60, 134, 148
   Basque World Congress and, 63
   on ETA factions, 191–94
   ETA ideology influenced by, 148–50, 151, 153, 156, 159–61, 164–65, 186
   ETA kidnapping and, 184, 185–86
   exile of, 148, 189, 191
   on Navarre, 60
   non-Basque origins of, 132
   "Vasconia" by, 148–49, 151, 153, 165, 262n563, 263n577
Kurds, 235n74

labor movement. *See* workers' movement
Landáburu, Francisco Javier ("Xabier")
   background of, 238n126
   Basque World Congress and, 67–68
   "La Causa del pueblo Vasco" by, 49, 51–54, 110–11
   European Federalist Movement and, 35, 52–54, 78, 80–82, 88
   exiled Basque government role of, 70
   Munich Conference and, 86–87, 94
   NEI role of, 35, 79–80
   new/young Basque nationalists and, 110–11
   on unity, 85
language, Basque. *See* Basque language
Larena Martínez, Francisco Javier, 173, 180, 181*t*
Lasarte, José María, 16, 18, 24, 42, 79–80, 83, 232–33n31
Lasarte, Juan Bautista, 45–46
Law of Succession to the Head of State (Spain), 18
legitimacy
   of Basque Statute of Autonomy, 57
   ETA challenging, 117–18, 145
   of ETA factions, 192–93
   of ETA ideology, 157
   of exiled Basque government, 12, 21, 28, 43, 46–48, 55, 61–62, 67, 73–75, 115, 117
   of exiled Spanish Republican government, 33
   of Franco regime, 8, 43
Leizaola, Jesús María
   background of, 232n31
   Basque Nationalist Party and, 18
   Basque World Congress and, 42
   Burgos trial response by, 177–79, 184, 195
   end of exile and position of, 200, 202–3
   ETA and, 114, 184
   exiled Basque government leadership by, 70–76, 127, 169, 177
   in exiled Spanish Republican government, 16
   Munich Conference and, 86
   NEI role of, 80
   return to Basque Country, 203, 272n777
   US relations and, 75–76
Leizaola, Ricardo de, 68
Letamendía, Francisco, 180*t*
LIAB (International League of Friends of

the Basques), 24, 65
Libro Blanco. *See* White Book
Llopis Ferrandiz, Rodolfo, 83, 232n20
London, UK, 7, 24, 26, 33, 175
López Angulo, J., 45
López Irasuegi, Goio, 171, 181*t*
Lumumba, Patricie, 264n602

Madariaga, Julen
    ETA and, 115, 126, 140, 150–54, 156, 160, 164, 176, 191, 262–63n571
    exile of, 150, 189, 196
    imprisonment of, 126, 176
Madariaga, Salvador de
    Congress for Cultural Freedom and, 88–89, 101, 103, 106, 108
    Cultural Union and, 77
    European Federalist Movement and, 82–83, 249n318
    Munich Conference and, 86, 88–92, 98, 252n363
"Manifesto a los españoles" (Manifest to the Spaniards), 14
"Manifiesto de Caracas," 117–18
Manzanas, Melitón, 166, 167, 189, 194
Martínez Barrio, Diego, 14–15
Martínez Vera, Romualdo, 87–88
Marxism, 140, 150, 154, 188–94, 263n573, 264n597. *See also* socialism
Mathieu, Clement, 24
Mexico, 24, 31, 37, 60, 75, 236n78
Miangolarra, Francisco, 148
Miralles, Jaume, 50
Miravitlles, Jaume, 29
Mitxelena, Koldo, 212
Monarchists, Spanish, 15–18, 20–21, 47–51, 55, 93, 232n25, 235n74
Monasterio, Fermín, 194, 270n730
Monzón, Telesforo
    Aguirre's death and, 70
    background of, 232n31
    Basque nationalism and, 39–40
    Basque World Congress and, 62–63
    ETA and, 184–85, 196
    on exiled Spanish Republican government, 16
    exile of, 196
    Irujo and, 196
    new/young Basque nationalists and, 110
Moreno, Juan Miguel, 181*t*
Moreno Bergaretxe, Eduardo ("Pertur"), 201, 271n749
Movimiento Federalista Vasco, 81–82
Munich Conference
    Basque nationalist internal differences on outcomes of, 93–100
    Congress for Cultural Freedom and, 88–89, 104
    Iberian Resolution from, 92–100
    organization and objectives of, 86–93
Murphy, Gerald L., 64
Mussolini, Benito and regime, 7–8, 33

Nárdiz, Gonzalo, 58, 70, 87, 115, 141
national reconciliation. *See* reconciliation, national
Navarre (Nafarroa)
    annexation to Basque Country, 21–22, 60
    Basque World Congress on, 48, 60, 61–62
    ETA inclusion of, 73
Navascués, Ibon, 181*t*
Nazism/Nazi regime, 7–8, 25, 26–27. *See also* fascism; Hitler, Adolf
NEI (Nouvelles Équipes Internationalles), 34, 35, 78, 79–80
networks of support/alliance, 7, 9–18
New York, New York, 7, 24–27, 175, 231n12
non-alignment movement, 97
North Ireland, 23

Ojanguren, Ángel, 177, 179
Onaindía, Alberto, 103, 105, 206–7, 213
Onaindía Natxiondo, Mario, 173, 180, 181*t*, 188–89
OPE (Oficina de Prensa Vasca), 42, 67, 194, 267n661
Ordoki Vázquez, Kepa, 270n736
OSS (Office of Strategic Services), 26, 27. *See also* CIA

Pact of Madrid (1953), 32–34
Pact of San Juan de Luz, 18
Pardines, José, 166, 194
Paris, France
    Basque diaspora in, 24
    Basque nationalist January 1977 assembly in, 207–16, 273n797
    Basque nationalist October 1961 conferences in, 120–25, 143, 158
    Basque World Congress in (*see* Basque World Congress)
    Burgos trial reactions in, 175
    exiled Basque government in, 7, 24
    May 1968 social upheavals in, 173
"Patriotas y Gamberros" (Irujo), 110–12, 121, 122, 128–31

PCE. *See* Communist Party of Spain
Peces-Barba, Gregorio, 180*t*
Pérez Jáuregi, Roberto, 267n658
Pezet, Ernest, 79
Pi i Sunyer, Carles, 83
Pinies, Vicente, 50–51
PNV. *See* Basque Nationalist Party
poetry, violence and, 156–57
political activism
    Basque diaspora and, 25, 28, 36–38, 236–37nn81,91
    Basque World Congress on, 41, 44–45, 47–48, 56–63, 67–68
    Christian Democratic (*see* Christian Democracy)
    Irujo's (*see* Irujo, Manuel)
    nationalist (*see* Basque National Front; Basque nationalism; Basque Nationalist Party; younger Basque nationalists)
    networks for (*see* networks of support/alliance)
    radicalization and violence in, 8, 22, 112–20, 123–28, 143, 145–62 (*see also* ETA)
Political Declaration of the Basque Nationalist Party (1949), 18–23
Preuves, 101
Prieto, Indalecio, 15–16, 46, 74, 232n28
Puerto Rico, 65

race, 132–33, 136–39. *See also* ethnic nationalism
realpolitik, 22, 95
reconciliation, national
    Basque nationalist stance on, 49, 51–54, 80–81, 96–97
    Basque World Congress on, 48–49, 58, 61–62
    communist strategy for, 48–49, 50, 51, 241n170
    Landáburu on, 49, 51–54
    Monarchists and, 49–51
    transition to democracy and, 86–93
religion
    Catholic (*see* Catholicism)
    Christian Democratic (*see* Christian Democracy)
    ETA on, 132, 143
"Revolt, The" (Begin), 151–52, 245n239
Rezola, Joseba, 18, 56–59, 62, 80–81, 160, 179, 233n44
Ridruejo, Dionisio, 86, 98, 251n343
Rockwell, Stuart W., 49–51, 241n174
Ruiz Balerdi, Pedro, 181*t*
Ruiz Ceberio, Elías, 181*t*

Rumor, Mariano, 179

Saraiva de Carvalho, Otello, 264n602
Sarasketa, Iñaki, 166, 167
Saratxaga, Txomin, 204
Satrústegui, Joaquín, 50, 98
Shoval, Ariel, 135
socialism. *See also* Marxism
    Basque nationalism and, 105, 206–7, 214–16
    ETA orientation to, 97, 147, 153–54, 159, 161–62, 188–94, 263n573, 264n597
    European Federalist Movement and, 87
    Monarchists tied to, 15–18, 20–21, 50
    strike support under, 30
social justice, 9, 206
socioeconomics
    anti-capitalist to communist evolution in, 139–43
    Basque language and, 133
    Basque Nationalist Party renewed focus on, 213–16
    Basque World Congress on, 41, 44
    ETA stance on, 139–43, 161
    immigration to Basque Country and, 72, 136–39
    industrialization and, 72, 138, 139–40, 215, 263n577
soft power, 102, 107, 254n405
Solaun, Jesús, 45, 81, 95, 127, 176–77, 247n273
Solé Barberà, Josep, 180*t*
Sota, Patrick de la, 150
Sota Aburto, Manuel de la, 27
Sota Aburto, Ramón de la, 18, 91, 174, 233n44
Sota McMahon, Ramon de la, 27
Soviet Union and Soviet bloc
    communism of (*see* communism)
    Congress for Cultural Freedom opposition to, 101–4, 106, 108
    ETA opposition to, 193–94
    Khrushchev administration of, 84, 107, 250n329
Spanish Communists. *See* Communist Party of Spain
Spanish immigrants to Basque Country, 47, 72, 133, 136–39, 260n527, 261n531
Spanish Monarchists, 15–18, 20–21, 47–51, 55, 93, 232n25, 235n74
Spanish Republican Government in exile. *See* exiled Spanish Republican

government
Spanish Truth Commission on Stalin's Crimes, 107–8
State of Emergency, 163–64, 166–68, 183, 265n634
Stevenson, Ralph, 7
strikes
  1947, 21, 30–32, 52, 57, 62, 237–38n109
  1951, 31–32, 52, 57, 62, 238n111
  1956, 57, 62
  1961-1962, 139, 141–42
  1976, 199
  Burgos trial triggering, 172–73, 182–83
Sturzo, Luigi, 9, 22–23, 26, 79, 234n68
Sudan, 23
support networks, 7, 9–18

Tierno Galván, Enrique, 272n809
train derailment, 126–28, 176, 177, 258–59n488
Tribunal de Orden Público (TOP), 163–64, 201
Trinquier, Roger, 149, 262n566
Tripartite Note, 13, 16, 17–18, 237n100
Trujillo, Leónidas, 63–64, 85
Truman, Harry S. and administration, 32, 232n18
Tunisia, 23, 147, 151
Txillardegi. *See* Álvarez Enparantza, José Luis
Tximistak, 110, 113, 119

Unión de Fuerzas Democráticas (UFD), 96, 253n388
Unión Española, 50
United Kingdom (UK)
  Basque diaspora in, 24, 60
  Burgos trial reactions in, 174–75
  exiled Basque government and, 7, 13, 26, 33–34
  exiled Spanish government and, 13–16, 32–33
  financial crisis in, 270–71n740
  Franco regime relations with, 13–14
  Iberian Resolution approval by, 92
United Nations (UN)
  Basque International Organization and, 65
  Burgos trial intervention requests to, 174, 176, 178, 195
  communism and admission to, 238n118
  exiled Basque government and, 29–30, 32–34, 55
  exiled Spanish Republican government and, 13–15, 32–33
  Franco regime relations with, 7–8, 13–14, 17, 32–33
  non-alignment movement under, 97
United States (US)
  Basque diaspora in, 24–25, 42, 236–37nn81,91
  Basque World Congress and, 49
  Burgos trial reactions in, 175, 178
  Christian Democracy in, 26–27
  communism as primary concern of, 32, 35, 50–51, 84–85, 232n18
  Congress for Cultural Freedom and, 89, 101–2, 109, 254nn399,402
  ETA and, 142–43, 193
  exiled Basque government and, 7, 13, 17, 23–39, 52–53, 75–76, 233n37, 239n131
  exiled Spanish government and, 13–16
  Franco regime relations with, 13–14, 32, 34, 50, 75–76, 237n100
  Galíndez's abduction and disappearance from, 63–64, 66–67, 237n96
  Munich Conference and, 89, 99
  Spanish national reconciliation and, 50–51
  strike response of, 30–31, 237–38n109
unity
  Basque Nationalist stance on, 80–81, 85, 129
  Basque World Congress on, 57–60, 62
  Cultural Union on, 78
  Declaration of 1960 on, 71
  ETA challenging, 116 (*see also* ETA)
  linguistic, 135–36
  Munich Conference as opportunity for, 86–93
Unzueta, Iñaki, 111
Unzueta, Patxo, 189–90
Uriarte Romero, Eduardo, 173, 181*t*
Urteaga, Segundo, 267n658
Uruguay, 60, 193
"Useless Violence" ("La Violencia inútil") (Irujo), 128
USSR. *See* Soviet Union and Soviet bloc

"Vasconia" (Krutwig), 148–49, 151, 153, 165, 262n563, 263n577
Vatican. *See also* Catholicism
  Burgos trial intervention request to, 177

Franco's Concordat with, 33, 34, 172
Venezuela
　Aguirre in, 37
　Basque diaspora in, 24, 25, 31, 60, 112
　Burgos trial reactions in, 175
　ETA in, 72, 112–13, 114–17, 119, 175
　exiled Basque government in, 75, 120
Ventura, Vicente, 98
"Violencia inútil, La" ("Useless Violence") (Irujo), 128

White Book, 43–44, 54, 131, 140, 141, 147
Wilson, Woodrow and administration, 78
workers' movement, 139–43, 155–56, 161, 167, 189–92, 264n597. *See also* ELA-STV; strikes
World Basque Congress. *See* Basque World Congress
World War II, 7–8

Ynchausti, Manuel, 27, 237n92
younger Basque nationalists
　alternative parties of (*see* EGI; ETA)
　on Basque Statute of Autonomy, 111–12, 113–14, 117, 143
　Basque World Congress and, 44, 46, 52, 62
　economic model for, 139–43
　end of exile and position of, 197–204
　inclusion in traditional Basque nationalism, 34, 47, 51–52, 71–73
　Irujo and, 110–12, 121, 125–31, 141, 143–46, 158, 202, 259n504
　opposition to traditional Basque nationalism, 94–95, 97, 110–12, 121–25 (*see also* ETA)
　"Patriotas y Gamberros" on, 110–12, 121, 122, 128–31
　structure and essence of PNV challenged by, 206–7
　violence by, 113, 123–28, 143, 145–47, 149–57, 159–60, 162–66 (*see also* ETA)

Zalbide, José Luís, 154
Zarco, Artemio, 181*t*
Zarranz, Santiago, 45
Zumalde, Xabier, 165
Zutik, 112, 121, 160